WINTER WORLD

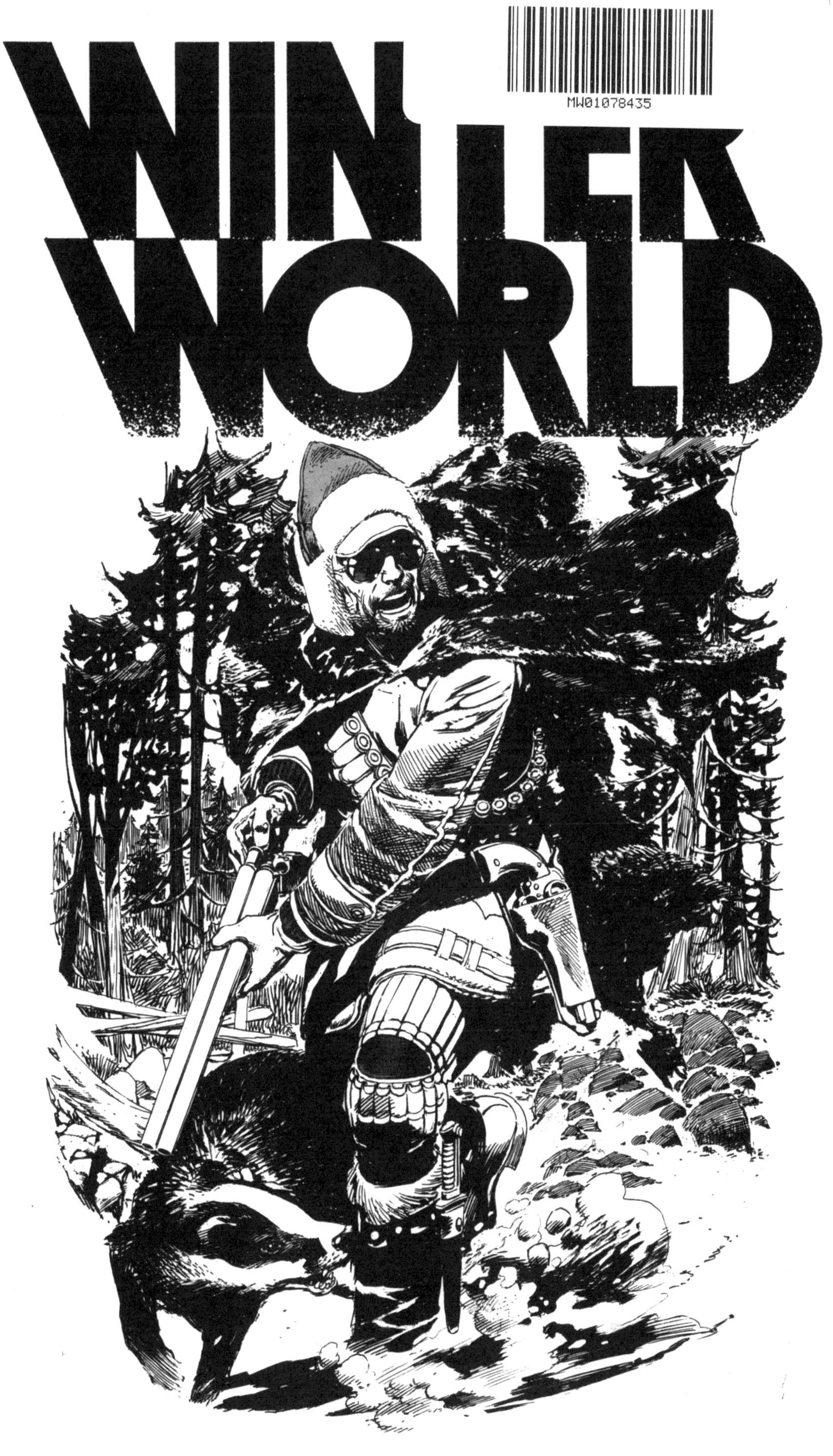

STORY BY CHUCK DIXON
ART BY JORGE ZAFFINO
LETTERING BY TIM HARKINS
WINTERWORLD ORIGINAL EDITS BY TIMOTHY TRUMAN
WINTERSEA ORIGINAL EDITS BY MARCUS MCLAURIN

COLLECTION EDITS BY JUSTIN EISINGER AND MARIAH HUEHNER
COLLECTION DESIGN BY NEIL UYETAKE

IDW®

Special thanks to Beau Smith.

ISBN: 978-1-60010-914-0   17 16 15 14   2 3 4 5
www.IDWPUBLISHING.com

Ted Adams, CEO & Publisher
Greg Goldstein, Chief Operating Officer
Robbie Robbins, EVP/Sr. Graphic Artist
Chris Ryall, Chief Creative Officer
Matthew Ruzicka, CPA, Chief Financial Officer
Alan Payne, VP of Sales

Author's Word
Article originally published in WINTERWORLD #3 (March 1988)

I first saw the work of Jorge Zaffino a little over a year ago. I only saw a couple of portfolio pieces and a handful of pages from an Argentine comic story, but their effect on me was immediate.

I wanted to work with this guy.

I *had* to work with this guy.

My introduction to Jorge's work came through Ricardo Villagran. Ricardo and I had been working together on **Evangeline** for various companies for a while, and I was aware that he had a studio in Argentina that was full of extremely talented artists (including Ricardo's brothers, Enrique and Carlos) who were seeking work in North America and Europe. I looked through samples of all the artists he worked with and was impressed with the level of professionalism and draughtsmanship I saw there. These guys had grown up wanting to emulate the best artists comics has to offer, artists like Raymond, Foster, Salinas, Caniff, and Toth. Their work had a classic look to it that was perfect for adventure comics. As I looked at each artist's sample I cataloged in my mind the type of story he would be best for, the kind of story I would write for him if I were given the opportunity.

Then I saw Jorge's work.

He combined all the strengths of the other Argentines, but brought a *darker* feel to his work. There is a strength and passion and *malevolence* to his work that is rare in comics from any country. Joe Kubert has it. Tim Truman has it. Rich Corben has it.

Zaffino can draw guys you don't want to meet. Ever. His work has an element of *danger* to it. His characters have an animal vitality and ruthlessness about them that makes them live on the printed page.

So what could I write for this guy?

Winterworld came to me a few days after seeing Jorge's drawings. Oh, not all at once, but little by little I thought about a future world that was frozen over and lightly populated with all kinds of desperate characters. The relationship between Scully and Wynn grew out of this bare bones idea and became the core of the story. I wanted to do a story atypical of the average American sci-fi comic. No flashy spaceships and monsters and dudes in tights wielding alien-spawned super powers, just a bunch of gun-toting paranoids fighting it out over ruins of a dead civilization. This wasn't going to be a story about heroes battling to save the universe. This was going to be about folks who weren't sure where, or when, their next meal was going to be and who they'd have to kill to get it.

I felt that the story line was suited for Jorge's talents and, upon receipt of the first issue's script, Jorge agreed. He was very enthusiastic about the story and sent me two drawings of the characters. So, with the sample drawings and a simply worded proposal, I shopped the mini-series around until it found home as part of the 4Winds line for Eclipse.

If you've read the entire **Winterworld** saga, you already know what a tremendous job Zaffino has done. I hope we'll be seeing more work from him in the future. He and I plan a sequel to **Winterworld** so, if you want to see it, let us know.

For now, we reluctantly leave Scully, Wynn, and faithful Rah Rah to their uncertain future in the world of perpetual winter...

Chuck Dixon
March 1988

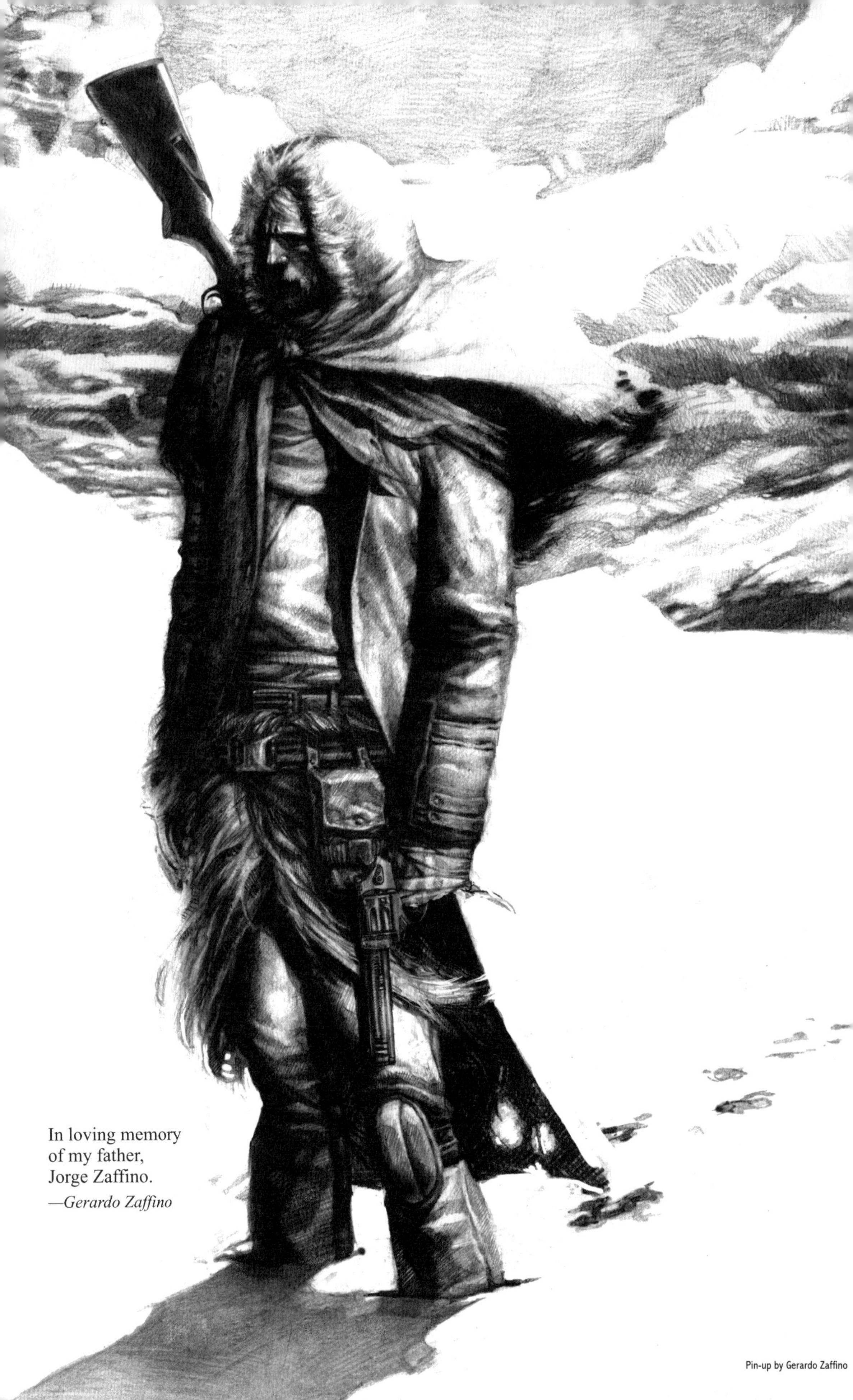

In loving memory
of my father,
Jorge Zaffino.

—Gerardo Zaffino

Pin-up by Gerardo Zaffino

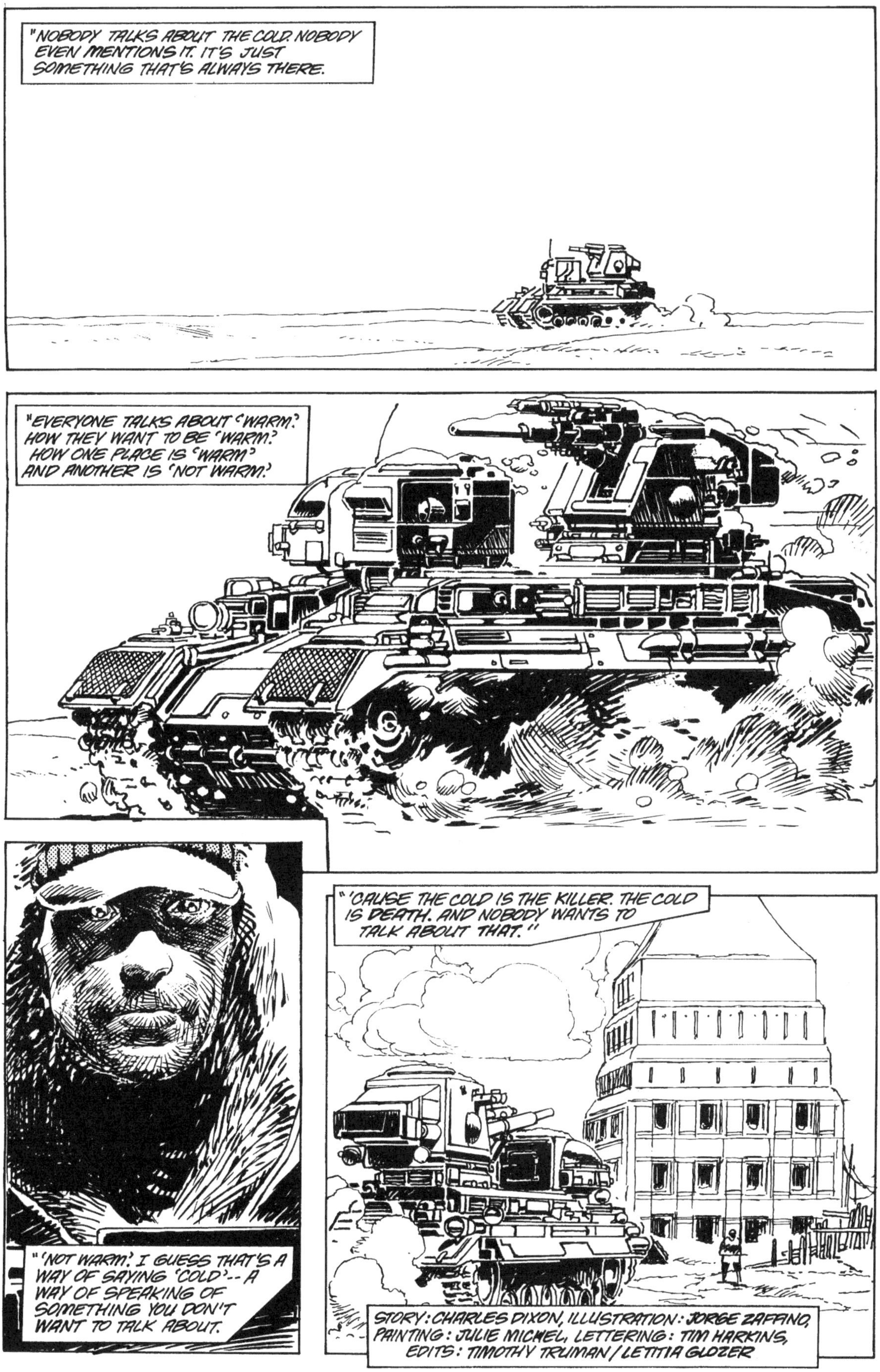
"NOBODY TALKS ABOUT THE COLD. NOBODY EVEN MENTIONS IT. IT'S JUST SOMETHING THAT'S ALWAYS THERE.
"EVERYONE TALKS ABOUT 'WARM.' HOW THEY WANT TO BE 'WARM.' HOW ONE PLACE IS 'WARM' AND ANOTHER IS 'NOT WARM.'
"'NOT WARM.' I GUESS THAT'S A WAY OF SAYING 'COLD'-- A WAY OF SPEAKING OF SOMETHING YOU DON'T WANT TO TALK ABOUT.
"'CAUSE THE COLD IS THE KILLER. THE COLD IS DEATH. AND NOBODY WANTS TO TALK ABOUT THAT."
STORY: CHARLES DIXON, ILLUSTRATION: JORGE ZAFFINO, PAINTING: JULIE MICHEL, LETTERING: TIM HARKINS, EDITS: TIMOTHY TRUMAN / LETITIA GLOZER

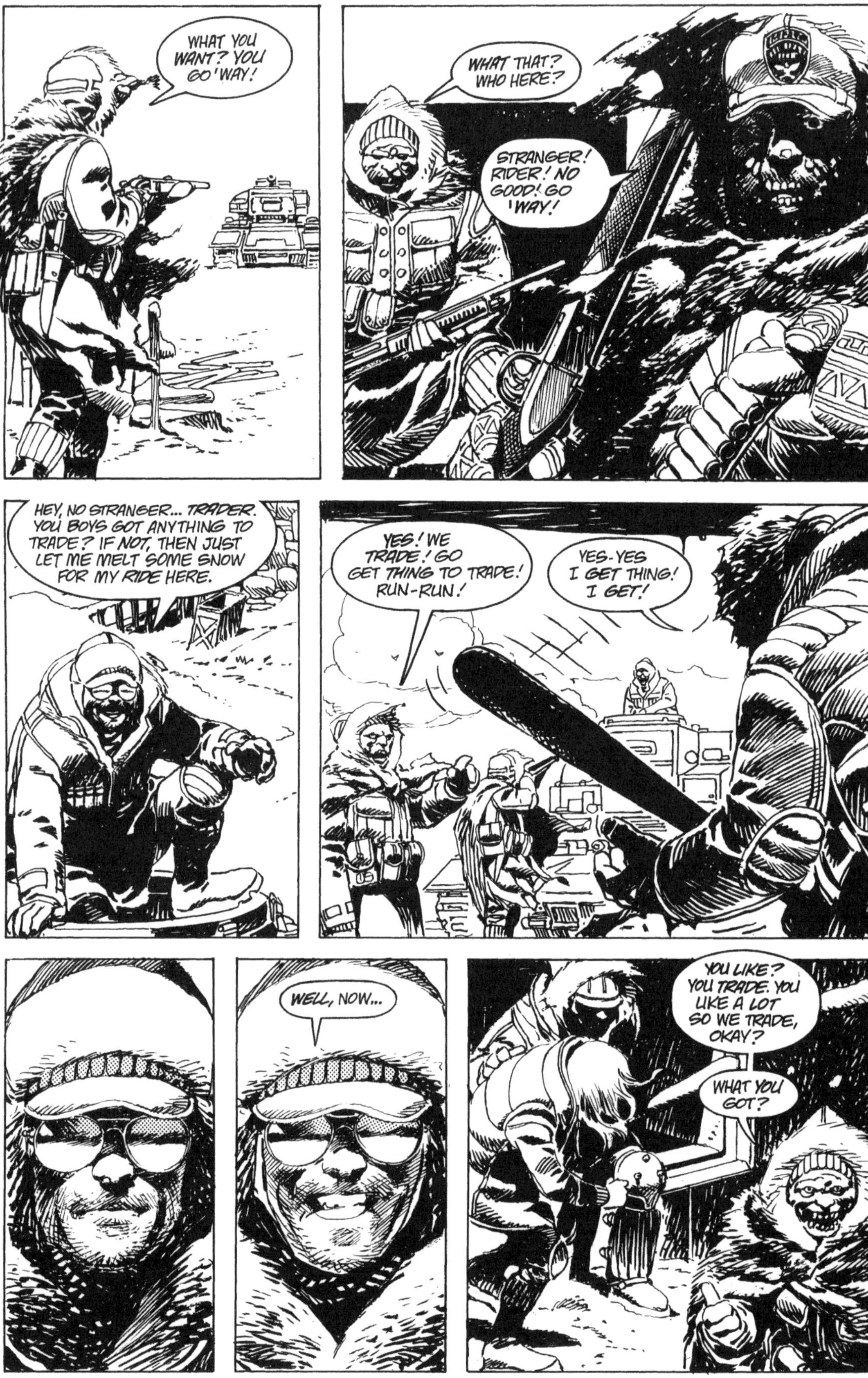

WHAT YOU WANT? YOU GO 'WAY!
WHAT THAT? WHO HERE?
STRANGER! RIDER! NO GOOD! GO 'WAY!
HEY, NO STRANGER... TRADER. YOU BOYS GOT ANYTHING TO TRADE? IF NOT, THEN JUST LET ME MELT SOME SNOW FOR MY RIDE HERE.
YES! WE TRADE! GO GET THING TO TRADE! RUN-RUN!
YES-YES I GET THING! I GET!
WELL, NOW...
YOU LIKE? YOU TRADE. YOU LIKE A LOT SO WE TRADE, OKAY?
WHAT YOU GOT?

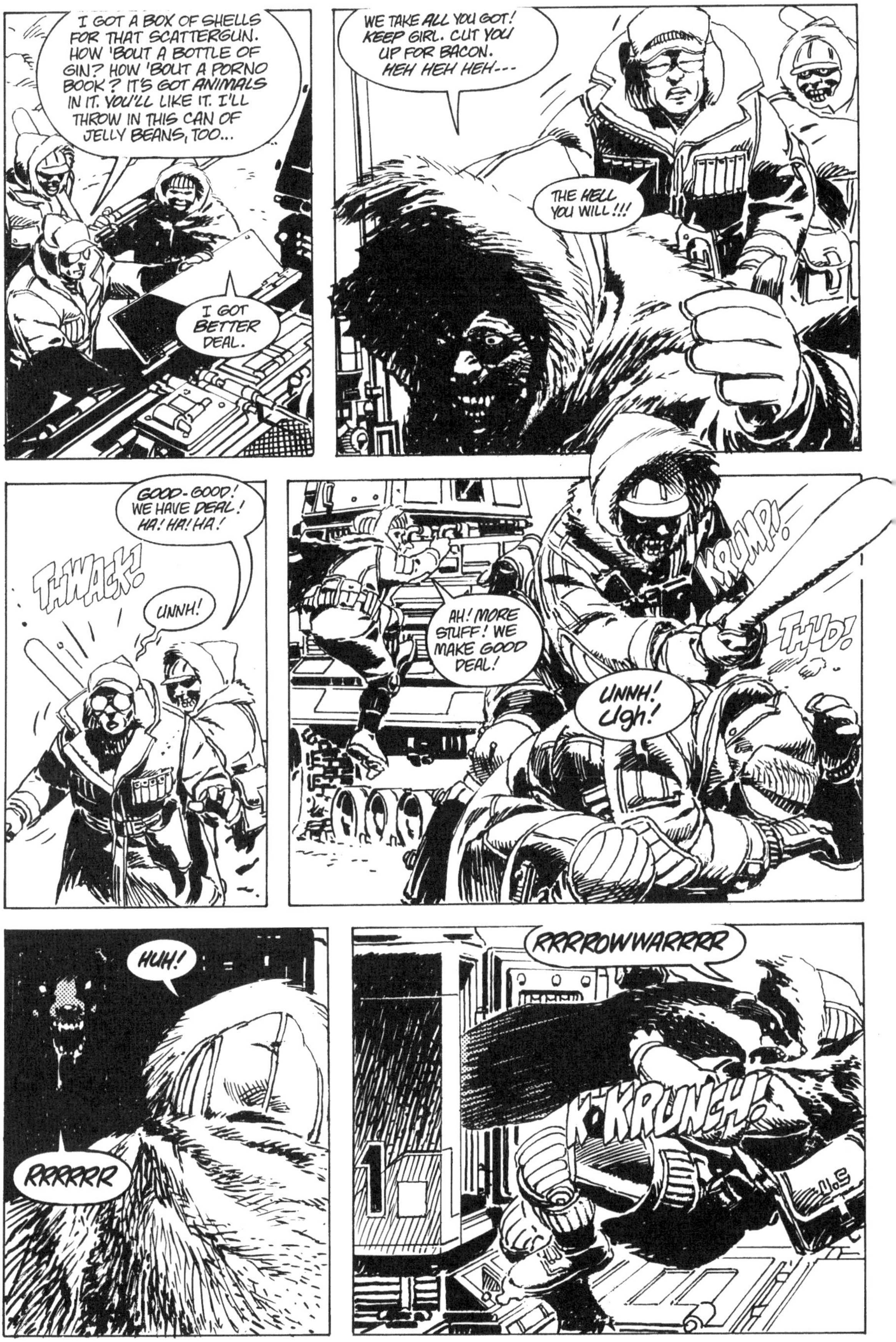
I GOT A BOX OF SHELLS FOR THAT SCATTERGUN. HOW 'BOUT A BOTTLE OF GIN? HOW 'BOUT A PORNO BOOK? IT'S GOT ANIMALS IN IT. YOU'LL LIKE IT. I'LL THROW IN THIS CAN OF JELLY BEANS, TOO...
I GOT BETTER DEAL.
WE TAKE ALL YOU GOT! KEEP GIRL. CUT YOU UP FOR BACON. HEH HEH HEH---
THE HELL YOU WILL!!!
GOOD-GOOD! WE HAVE DEAL! HA! HA! HA!
THWACK!
UNNH!
KRUMP!
AH! MORE STUFF! WE MAKE GOOD DEAL!
THUD!
UNNH! Ugh!
HUH!
RRRRRR
RRRROWWARRRR
K-KRUNCH!
U.S

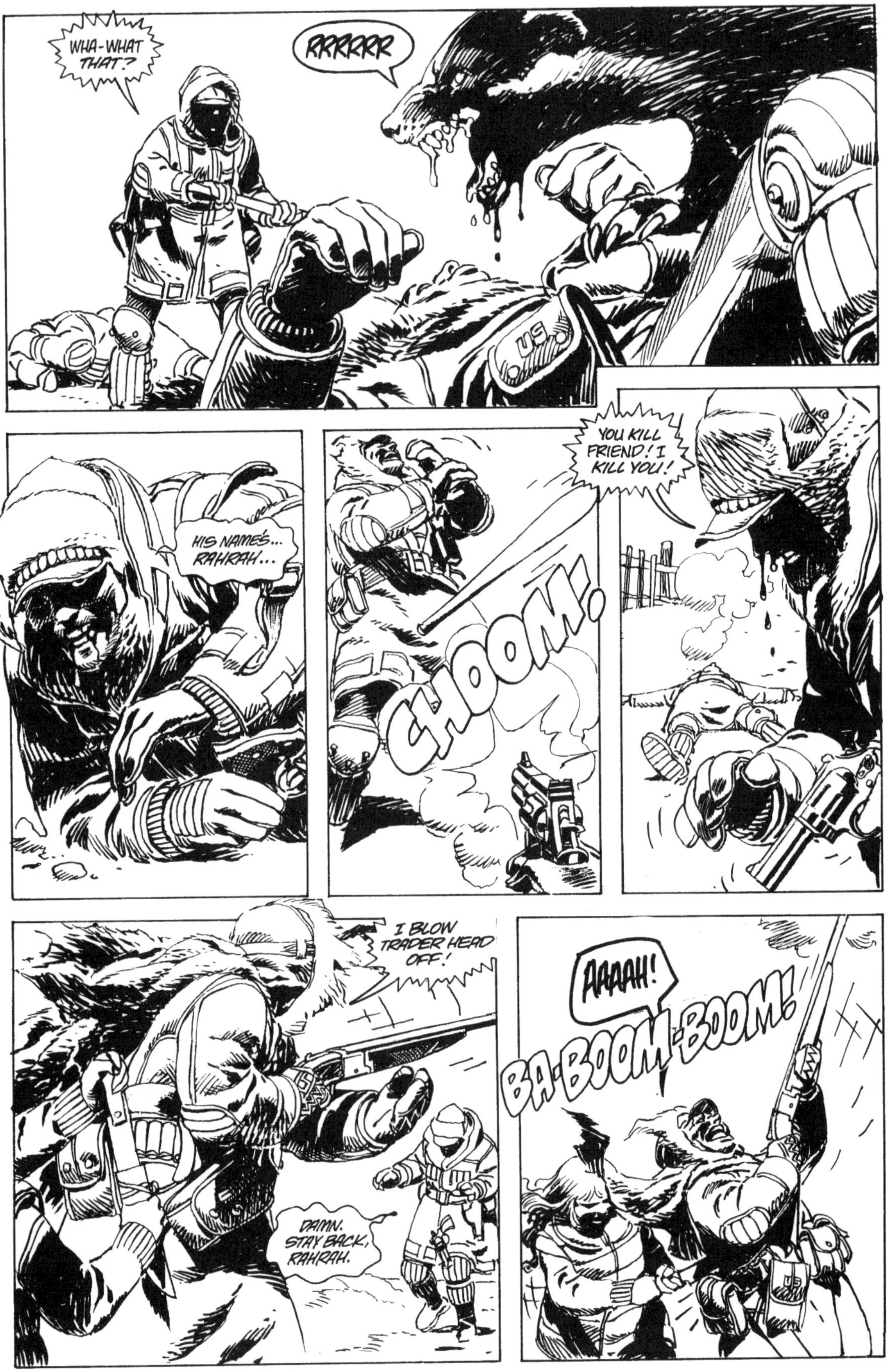
WHA-WHAT THAT?
RRRRRR
U.S.
HIS NAME'S... RAHRAH...
CHOOM!
YOU KILL FRIEND! I KILL YOU!
I BLOW TRADER HEAD OFF!
DAMN. STAY BACK, RAHRAH.
AAAAH!
BA-BOOM-BOOM!

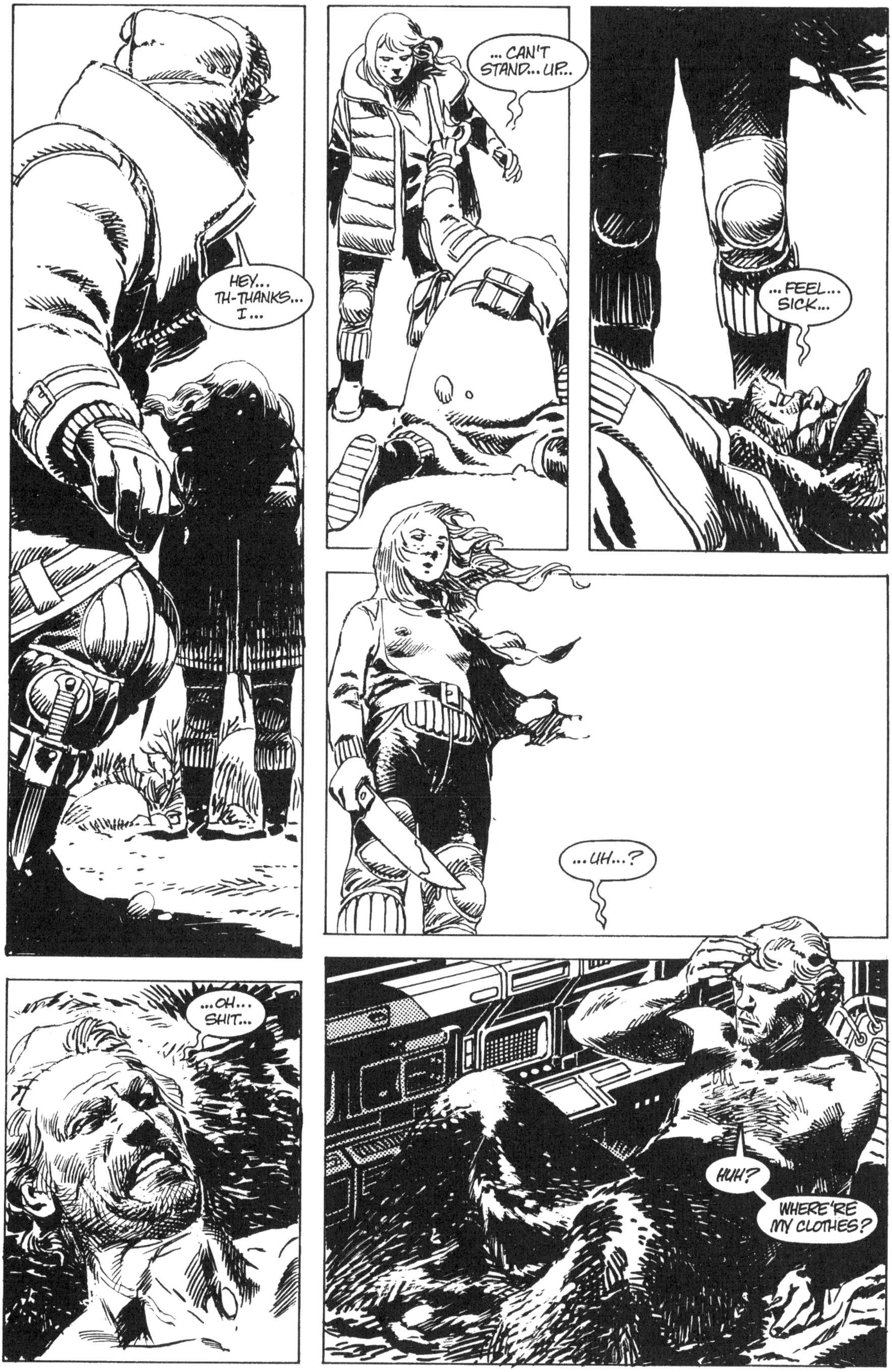
HEY... TH-THANKS... I...
... CAN'T STAND... UP...
... FEEL... SICK...
... UH... ?
... OH... SHIT...
HUH?
WHERE'RE MY CLOTHES?

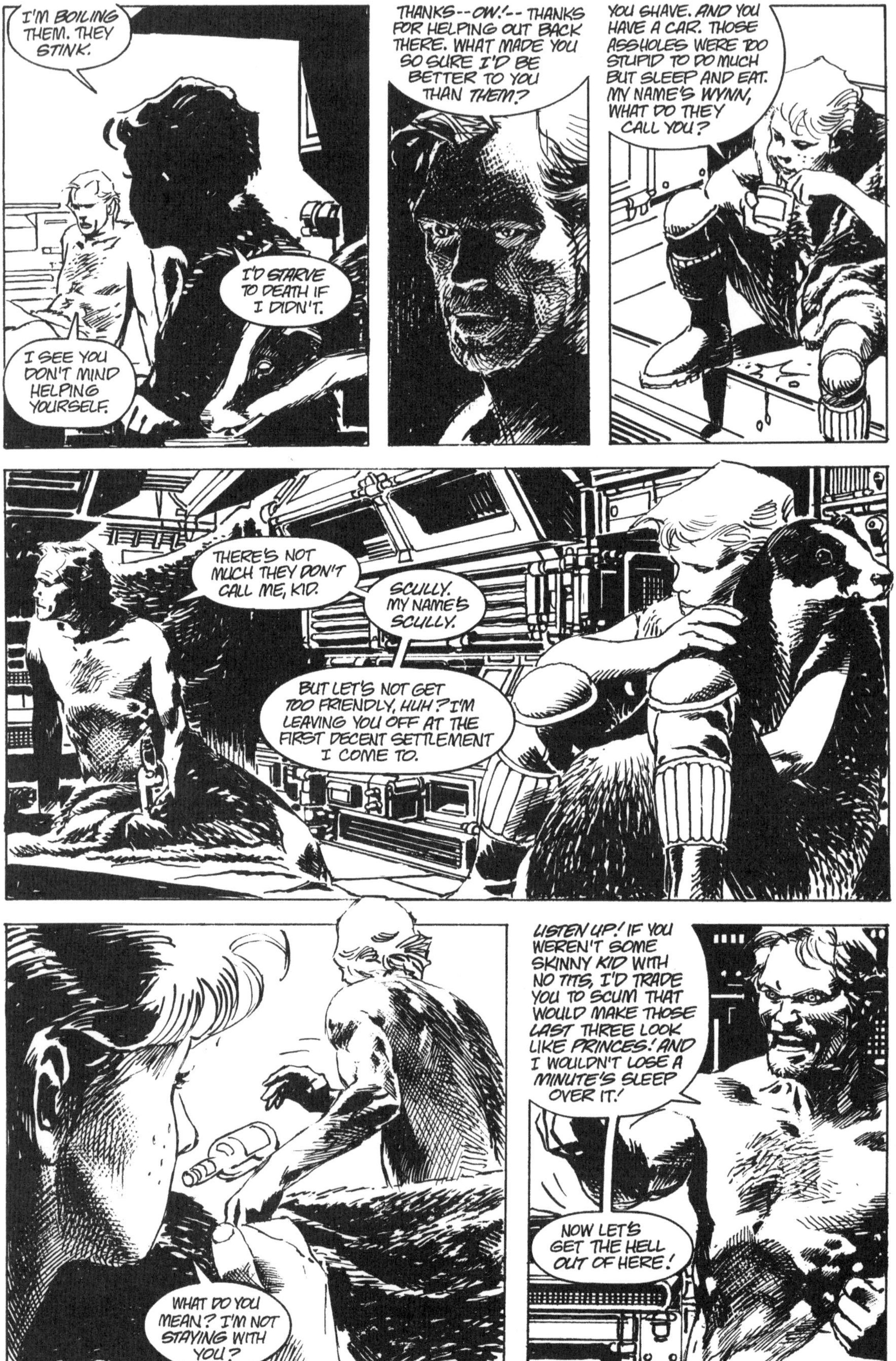
I'M BOILING THEM. THEY STINK.
I'D STARVE TO DEATH IF I DIDN'T.
I SEE YOU DON'T MIND HELPING YOURSELF.
THANKS--OW!--THANKS FOR HELPING OUT BACK THERE. WHAT MADE YOU SO SURE I'D BE BETTER TO YOU THAN THEM?
YOU SHAVE. AND YOU HAVE A CAR. THOSE ASSHOLES WERE TOO STUPID TO DO MUCH BUT SLEEP AND EAT. MY NAME'S WYNN, WHAT DO THEY CALL YOU?
THERE'S NOT MUCH THEY DON'T CALL ME, KID.
SCULLY. MY NAME'S SCULLY.
BUT LET'S NOT GET TOO FRIENDLY, HUH? I'M LEAVING YOU OFF AT THE FIRST DECENT SETTLEMENT I COME TO.
WHAT DO YOU MEAN? I'M NOT STAYING WITH YOU?
LISTEN UP! IF YOU WEREN'T SOME SKINNY KID WITH NO TITS, I'D TRADE YOU TO SCUM THAT WOULD MAKE THOSE LAST THREE LOOK LIKE PRINCES! AND I WOULDN'T LOSE A MINUTE'S SLEEP OVER IT!
NOW LET'S GET THE HELL OUT OF HERE!

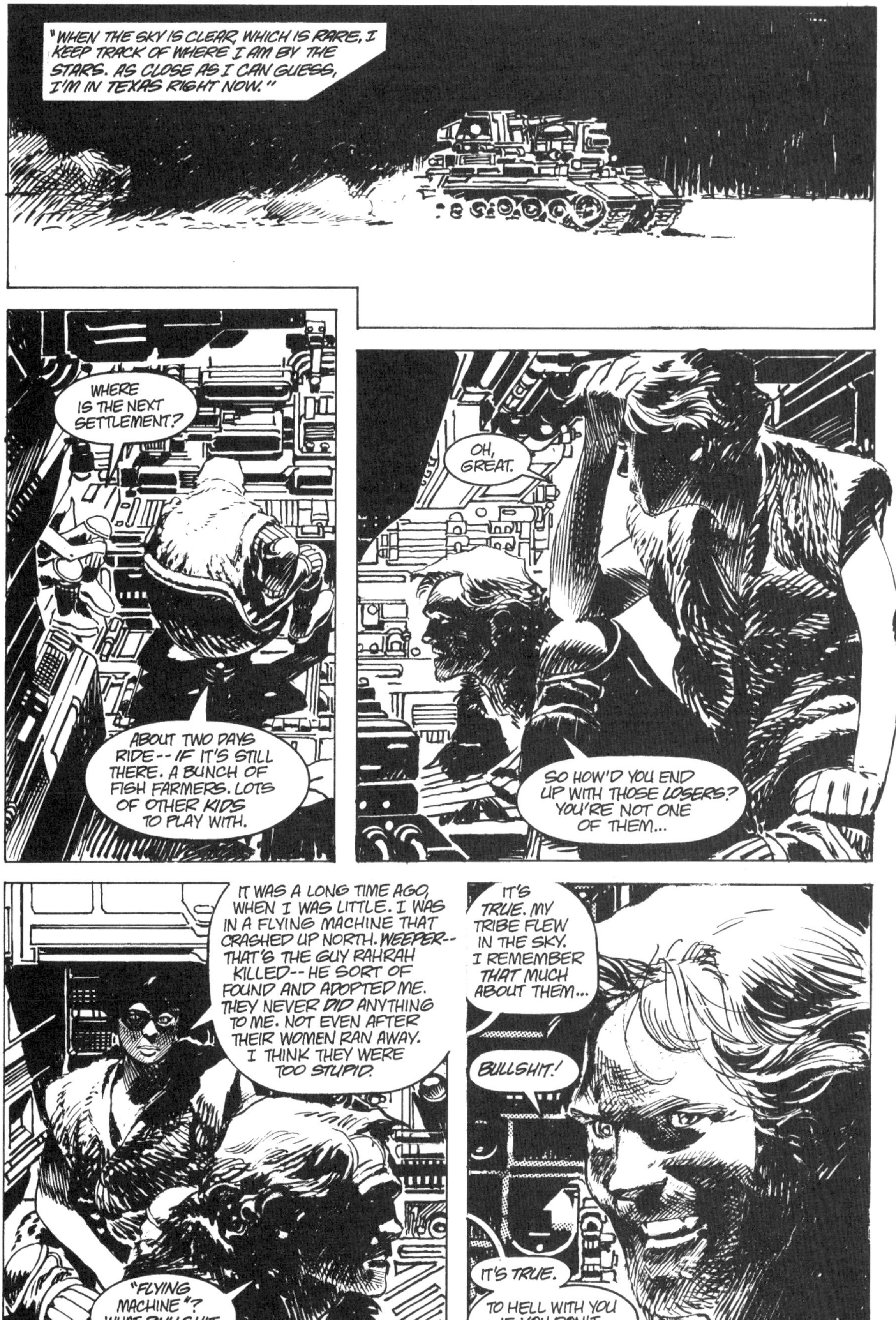
"WHEN THE SKY IS CLEAR, WHICH IS RARE, I KEEP TRACK OF WHERE I AM BY THE STARS. AS CLOSE AS I CAN GUESS, I'M IN TEXAS RIGHT NOW."
WHERE IS THE NEXT SETTLEMENT?
ABOUT TWO DAYS RIDE-- IF IT'S STILL THERE. A BUNCH OF FISH FARMERS. LOTS OF OTHER KIDS TO PLAY WITH.
OH, GREAT.
SO HOW'D YOU END UP WITH THOSE LOSERS? YOU'RE NOT ONE OF THEM...
IT WAS A LONG TIME AGO, WHEN I WAS LITTLE. I WAS IN A FLYING MACHINE THAT CRASHED UP NORTH. WEEPER-- THAT'S THE GUY RAHRAH KILLED-- HE SORT OF FOUND AND ADOPTED ME. THEY NEVER DID ANYTHING TO ME. NOT EVEN AFTER THEIR WOMEN RAN AWAY. I THINK THEY WERE TOO STUPID.
"FLYING MACHINE"? WHAT BULLSHIT IS THAT?
IT'S TRUE. MY TRIBE FLEW IN THE SKY. I REMEMBER THAT MUCH ABOUT THEM...
BULLSHIT!
IT'S TRUE.
TO HELL WITH YOU IF YOU DON'T BELIEVE IT.

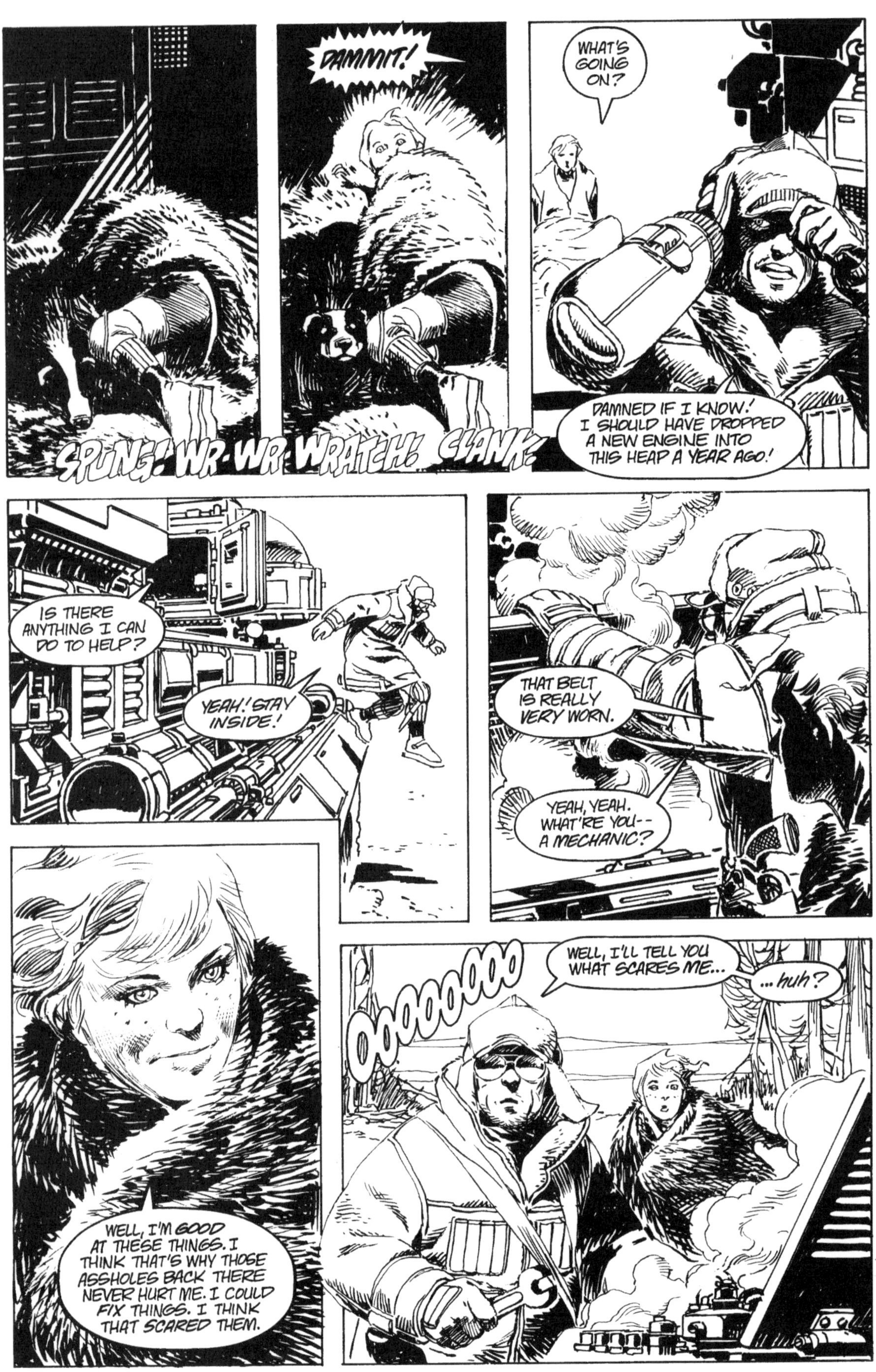

DAMMIT!
SPUNG! WR-WR-WRATCH! CLANK!
WHAT'S GOING ON?
DAMNED IF I KNOW! I SHOULD HAVE DROPPED A NEW ENGINE INTO THIS HEAP A YEAR AGO!
IS THERE ANYTHING I CAN DO TO HELP?
YEAH! STAY INSIDE!
THAT BELT IS REALLY VERY WORN.
YEAH, YEAH. WHAT'RE YOU-- A MECHANIC?
WELL, I'M GOOD AT THESE THINGS. I THINK THAT'S WHY THOSE ASSHOLES BACK THERE NEVER HURT ME. I COULD FIX THINGS. I THINK THAT SCARED THEM.
WELL, I'LL TELL YOU WHAT SCARES ME...
OOOOOOOO
...huh?

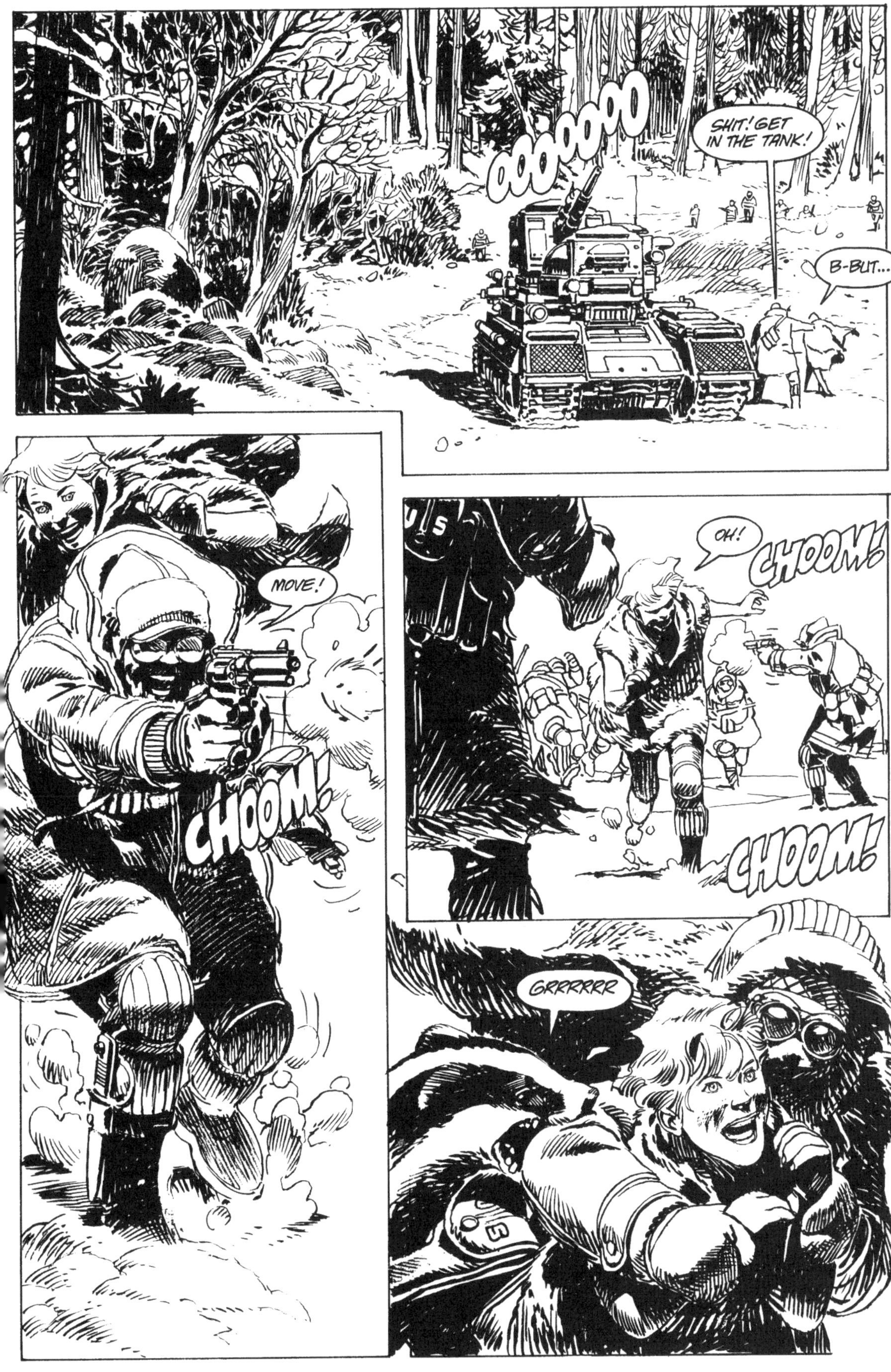
OOOOOOO
SHIT! GET IN THE TANK!
B-BUT...
MOVE!
CHOOM!
OH!
CHOOM!
CHOOM!
GRRRRRR

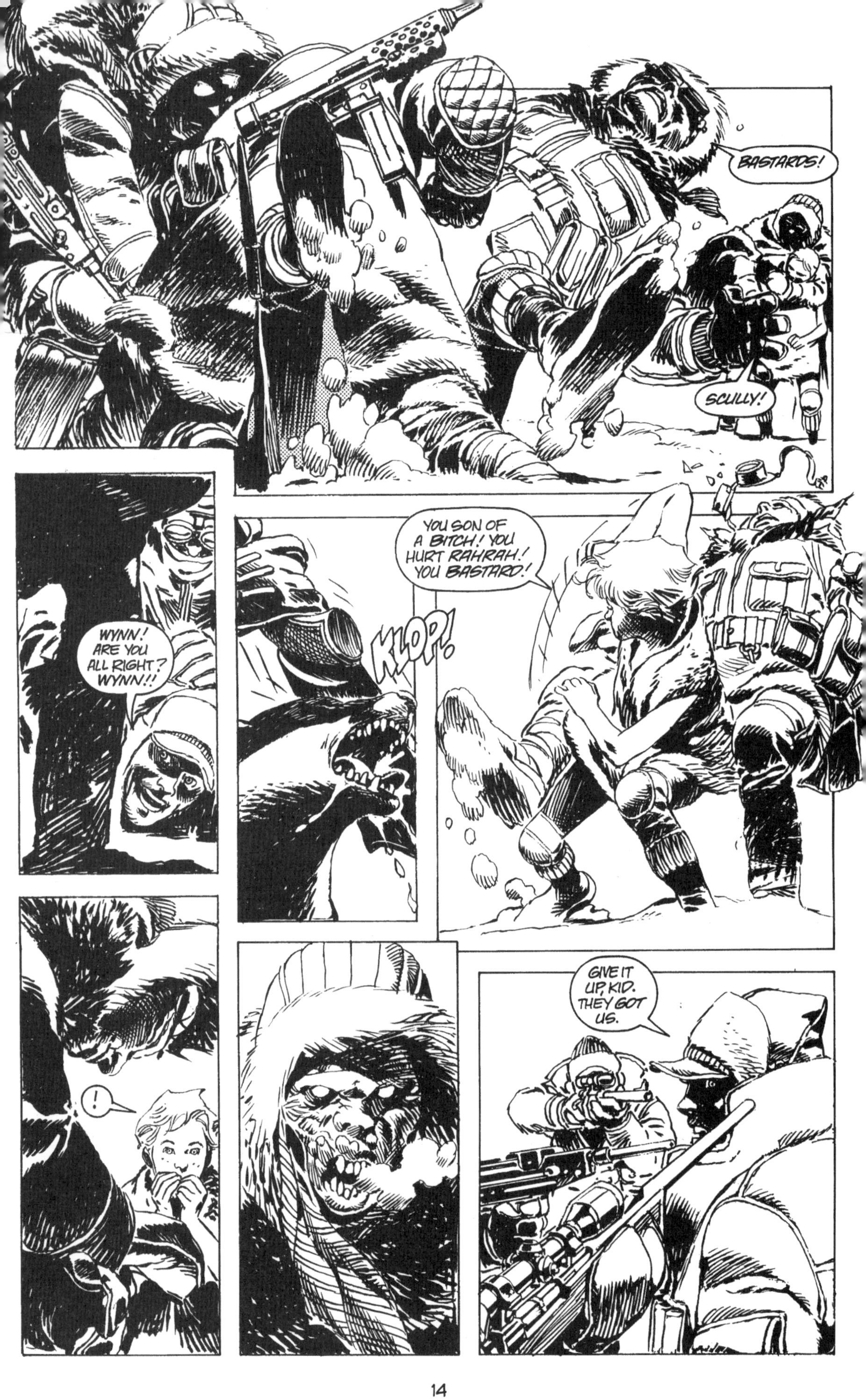
BASTARDS!
SCULLY!
WYNN! ARE YOU ALL RIGHT? WYNN!!
KLOP!
YOU SON OF A BITCH! YOU HURT RAHRAH! YOU BASTARD!
!
GIVE IT UP, KID. THEY GOT US.

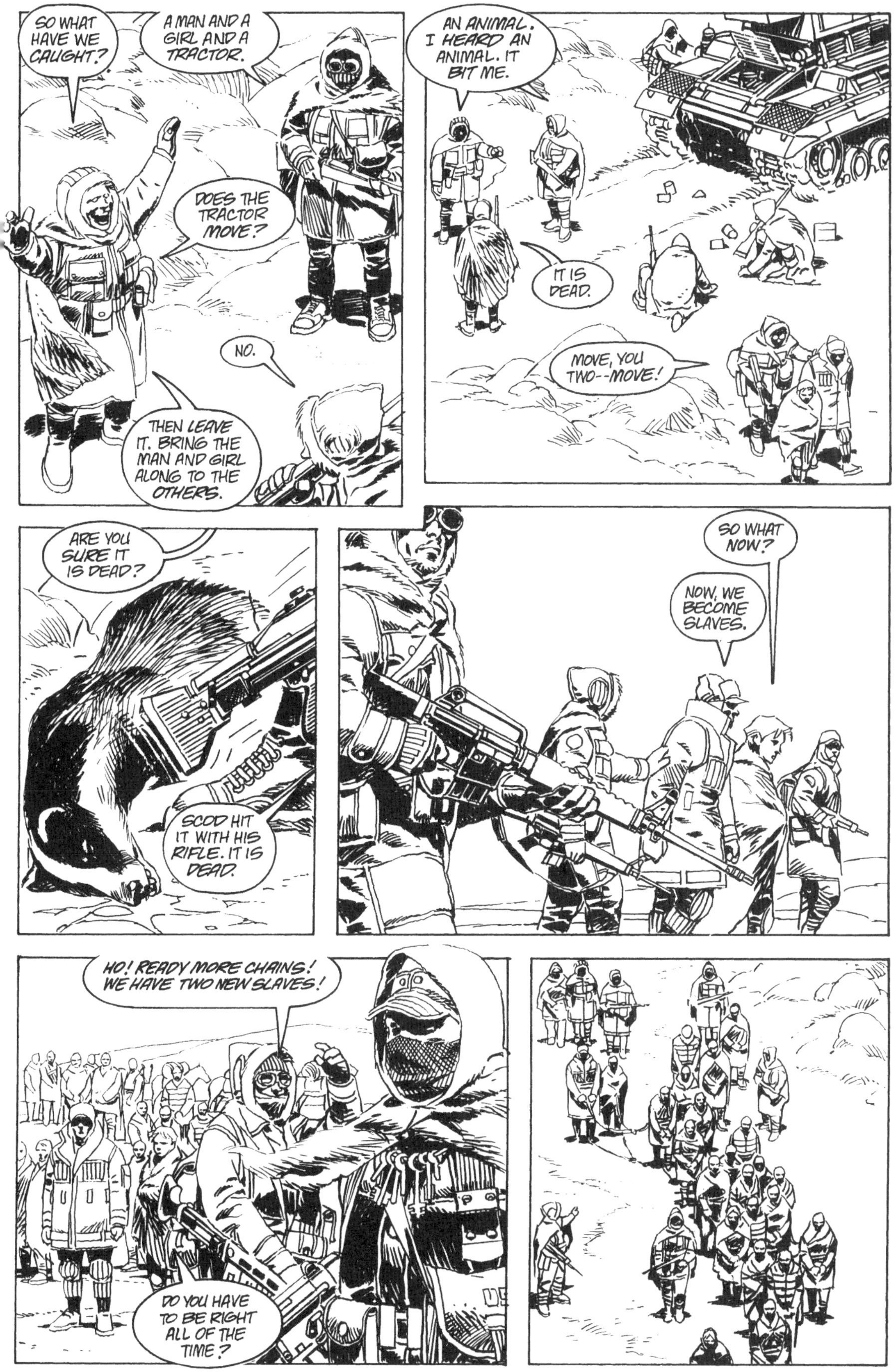
SO WHAT HAVE WE CAUGHT?
A MAN AND A GIRL AND A TRACTOR.
DOES THE TRACTOR MOVE?
NO.
THEN LEAVE IT. BRING THE MAN AND GIRL ALONG TO THE OTHERS.
AN ANIMAL. I HEARD AN ANIMAL. IT BIT ME.
IT IS DEAD.
MOVE, YOU TWO--MOVE!
ARE YOU SURE IT IS DEAD?
SCOD HIT IT WITH HIS RIFLE. IT IS DEAD.
SO WHAT NOW?
NOW, WE BECOME SLAVES.
HO! READY MORE CHAINS! WE HAVE TWO NEW SLAVES!
DO YOU HAVE TO BE RIGHT ALL OF THE TIME?

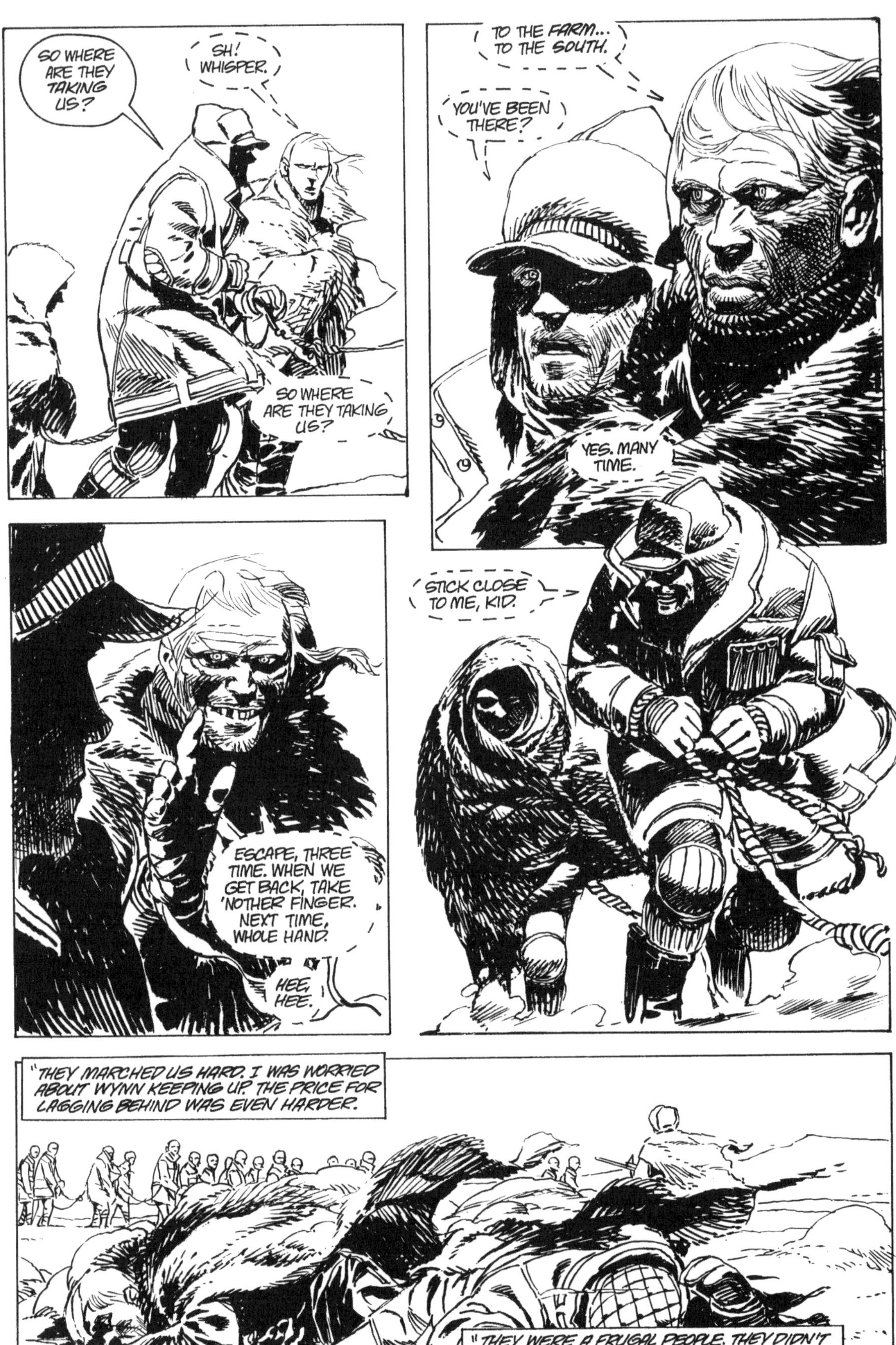
SO WHERE ARE THEY TAKING US?
SH! WHISPER.
SO WHERE ARE THEY TAKING US?
TO THE FARM... TO THE SOUTH.
YOU'VE BEEN THERE?
YES. MANY TIME.
ESCAPE, THREE TIME. WHEN WE GET BACK, TAKE 'NOTHER FINGER. NEXT TIME, WHOLE HAND.
HEE, HEE.
STICK CLOSE TO ME, KID.
"THEY MARCHED US HARD. I WAS WORRIED ABOUT WYNN KEEPING UP. THE PRICE FOR LAGGING BEHIND WAS EVEN HARDER.
"THEY WERE A FRUGAL PEOPLE. THEY DIDN'T WASTE BULLETS ON STRAGGLERS. A KNIFE ACROSS THE THROAT DID FOR THEM."

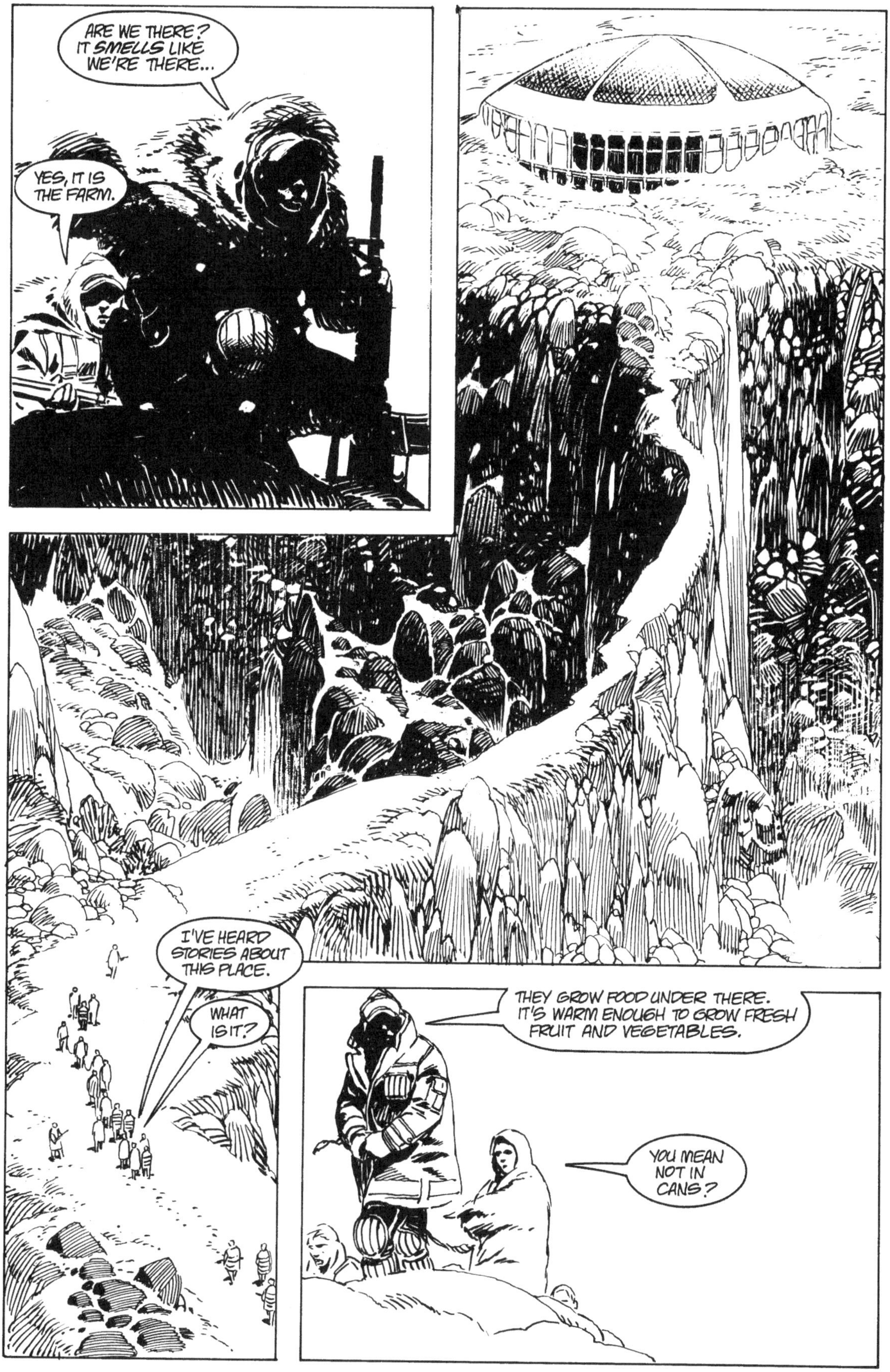
ARE WE THERE? IT SMELLS LIKE WE'RE THERE...
YES, IT IS THE FARM.
I'VE HEARD STORIES ABOUT THIS PLACE.
WHAT IS IT?
THEY GROW FOOD UNDER THERE. IT'S WARM ENOUGH TO GROW FRESH FRUIT AND VEGETABLES.
YOU MEAN NOT IN CANS?

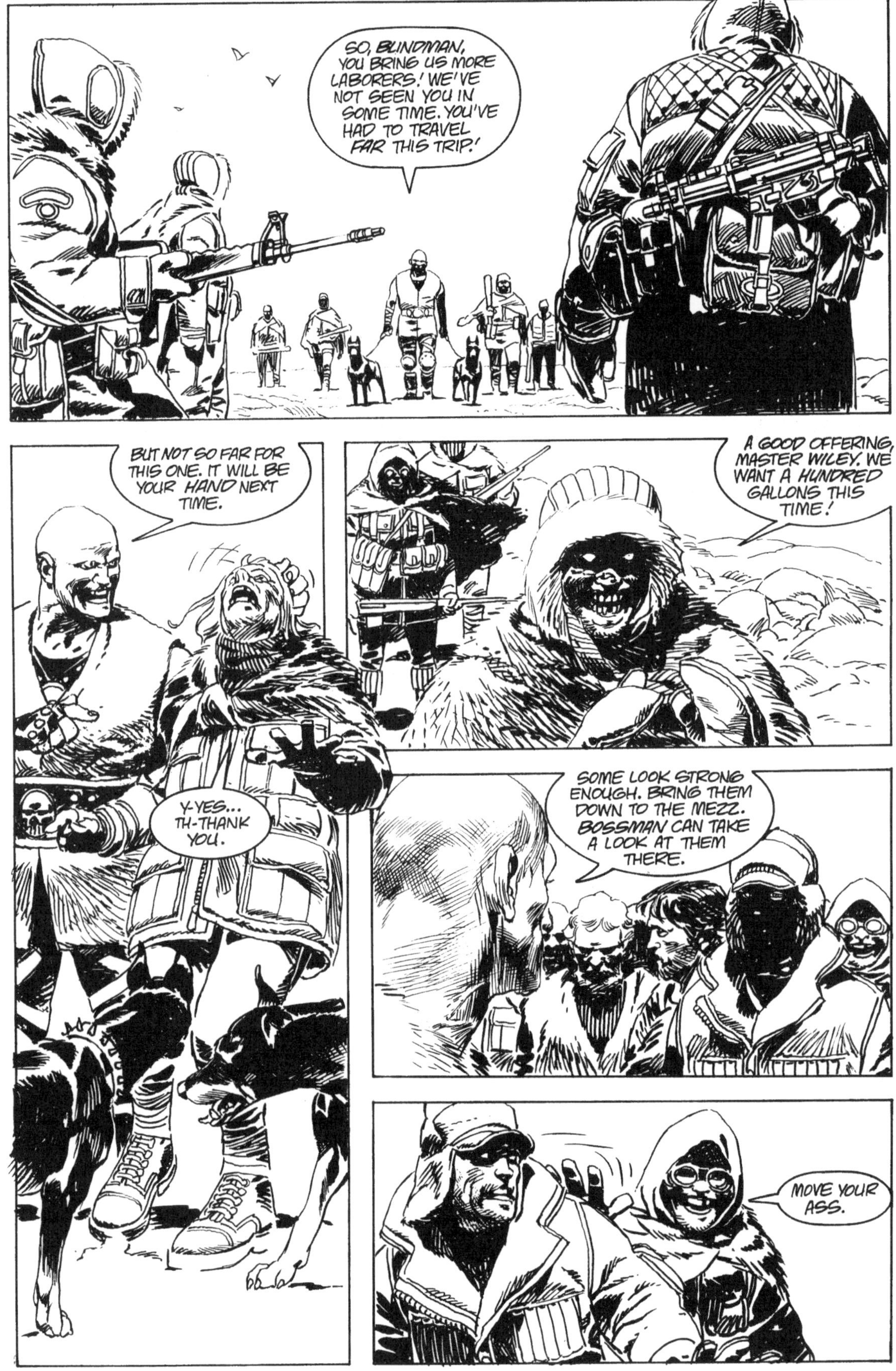
SO, BLINDMAN, YOU BRING US MORE LABORERS! WE'VE NOT SEEN YOU IN SOME TIME. YOU'VE HAD TO TRAVEL FAR THIS TRIP!
BUT NOT SO FAR FOR THIS ONE. IT WILL BE YOUR HAND NEXT TIME.
A GOOD OFFERING, MASTER WILEY. WE WANT A HUNDRED GALLONS THIS TIME!
Y-YES... TH-THANK YOU.
SOME LOOK STRONG ENOUGH. BRING THEM DOWN TO THE MEZZ. BOSSMAN CAN TAKE A LOOK AT THEM THERE.
MOVE YOUR ASS.

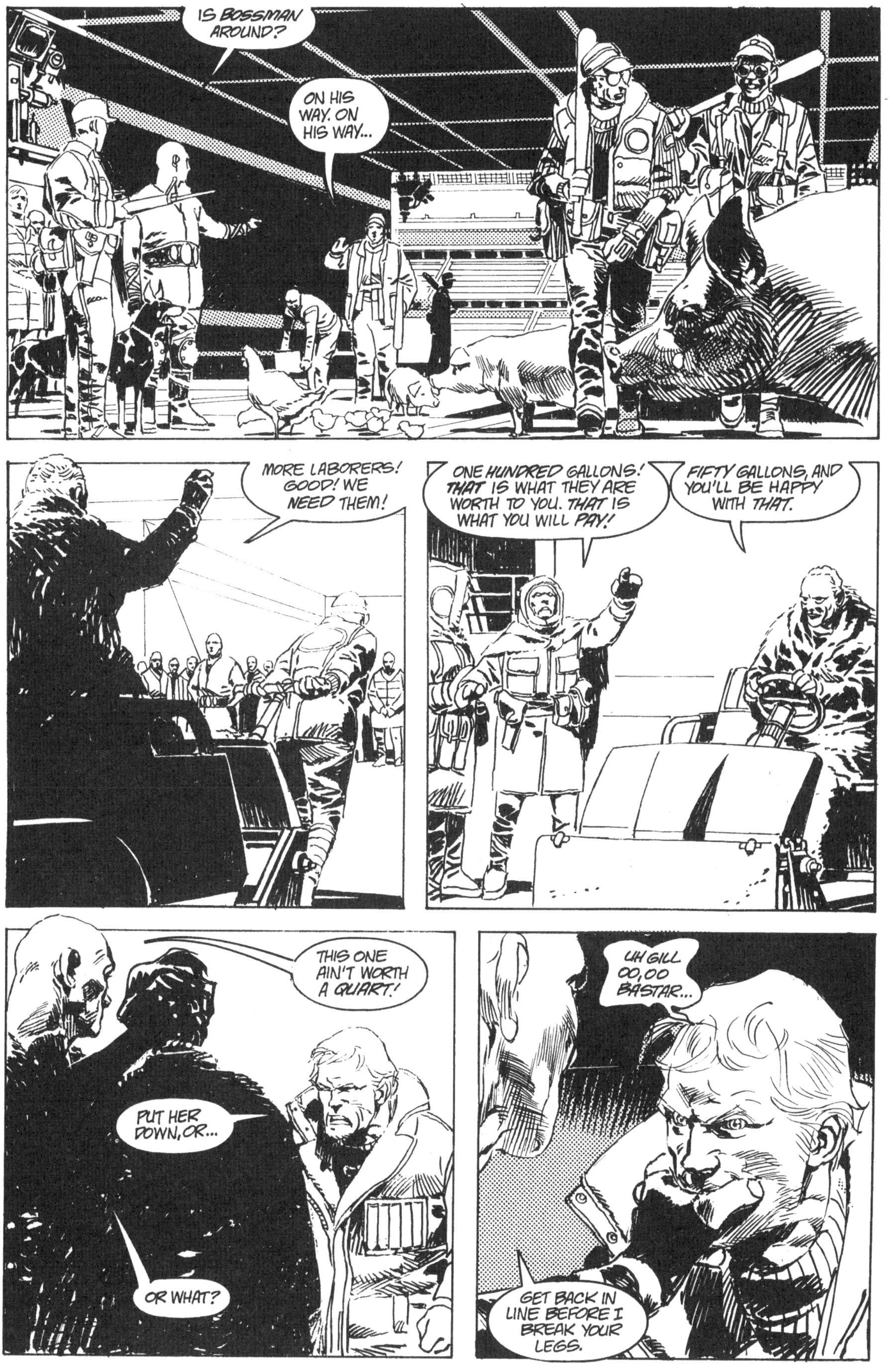
IS BOSSMAN AROUND?
ON HIS WAY. ON HIS WAY...
MORE LABORERS! GOOD! WE NEED THEM!
ONE HUNDRED GALLONS! THAT IS WHAT THEY ARE WORTH TO YOU. THAT IS WHAT YOU WILL PAY!
FIFTY GALLONS, AND YOU'LL BE HAPPY WITH THAT.
THIS ONE AIN'T WORTH A QUART!
PUT HER DOWN, OR...
OR WHAT?
UH GILL 00,00 BASTAR...
GET BACK IN LINE BEFORE I BREAK YOUR LEGS.

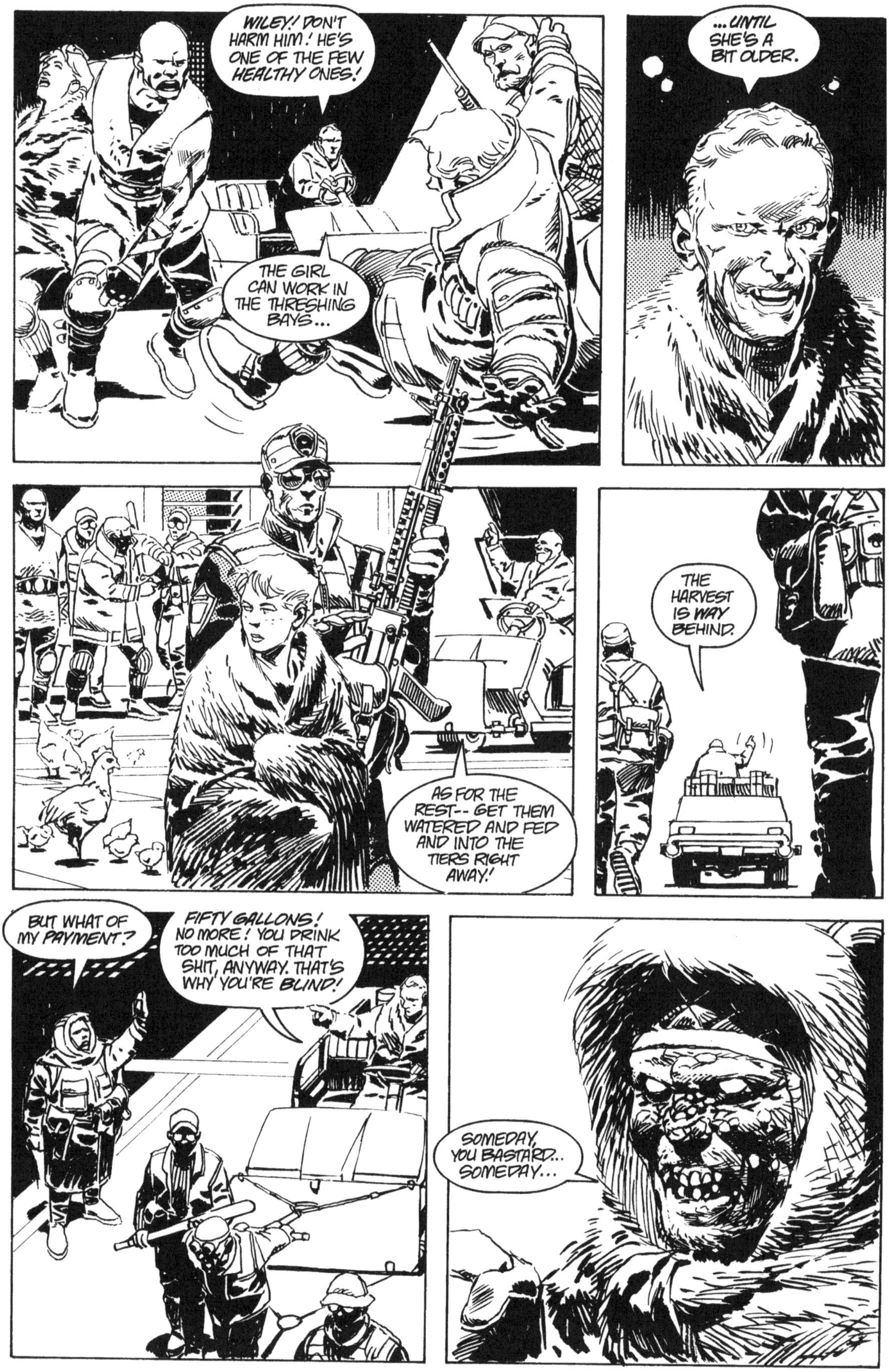
WILEY! DON'T HARM HIM! HE'S ONE OF THE FEW HEALTHY ONES!
THE GIRL CAN WORK IN THE THRESHING BAYS...
...UNTIL SHE'S A BIT OLDER.
AS FOR THE REST-- GET THEM WATERED AND FED AND INTO THE TIERS RIGHT AWAY!
THE HARVEST IS WAY BEHIND.
BUT WHAT OF MY PAYMENT?
FIFTY GALLONS! NO MORE! YOU DRINK TOO MUCH OF THAT SHIT, ANYWAY. THAT'S WHY YOU'RE BLIND!
SOMEDAY, YOU BASTARD... SOMEDAY...

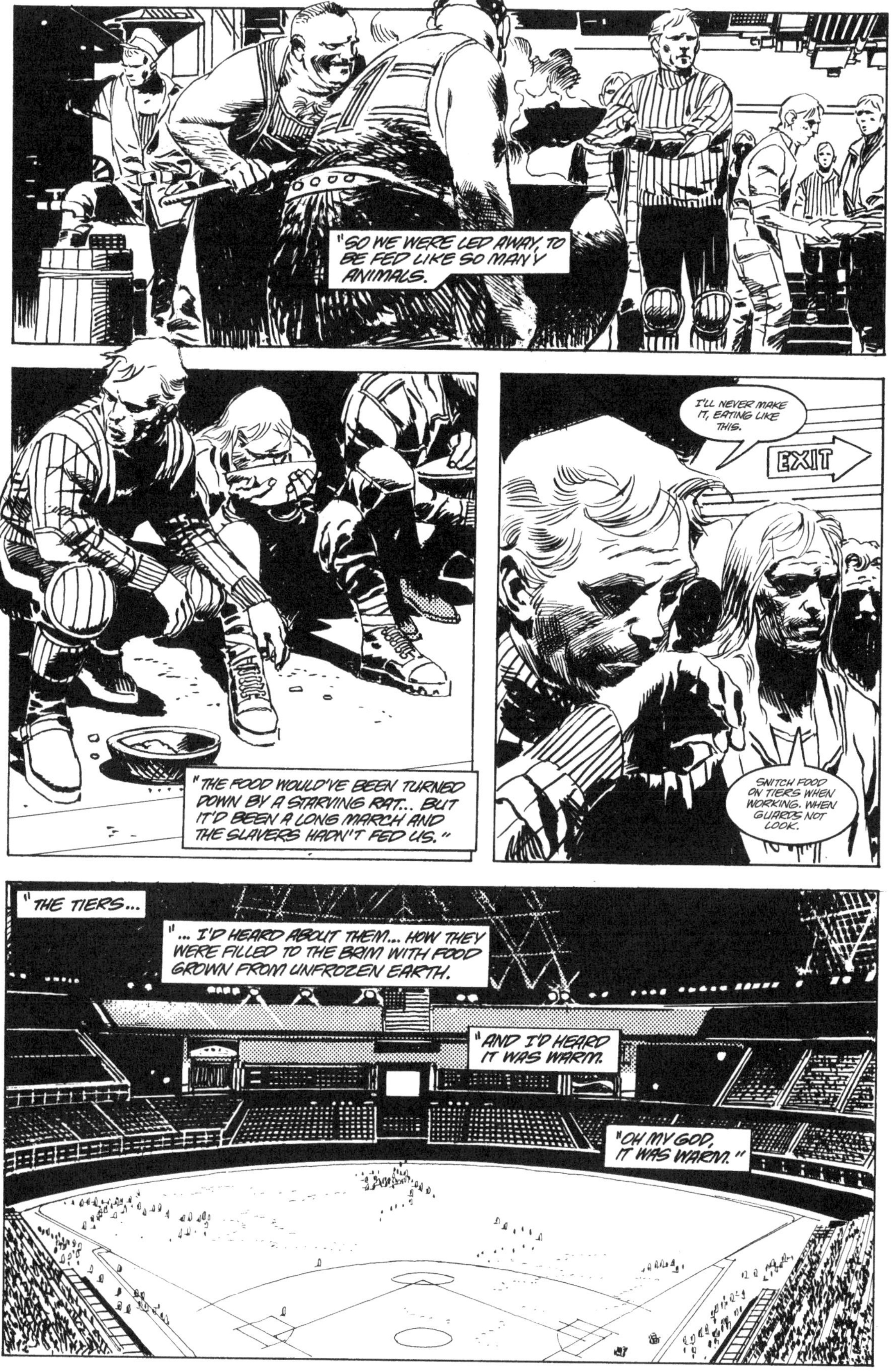
"SO WE WERE LED AWAY, TO BE FED LIKE SO MANY ANIMALS.
"THE FOOD WOULD'VE BEEN TURNED DOWN BY A STARVING RAT... BUT IT'D BEEN A LONG MARCH AND THE SLAVERS HADN'T FED US."
I'LL NEVER MAKE IT, EATING LIKE THIS.
EXIT
SNITCH FOOD ON TIERS WHEN WORKING. WHEN GUARDS NOT LOOK.
"THE TIERS...
"... I'D HEARD ABOUT THEM... HOW THEY WERE FILLED TO THE BRIM WITH FOOD GROWN FROM UNFROZEN EARTH.
"AND I'D HEARD IT WAS WARM.
"OH MY GOD, IT WAS WARM."

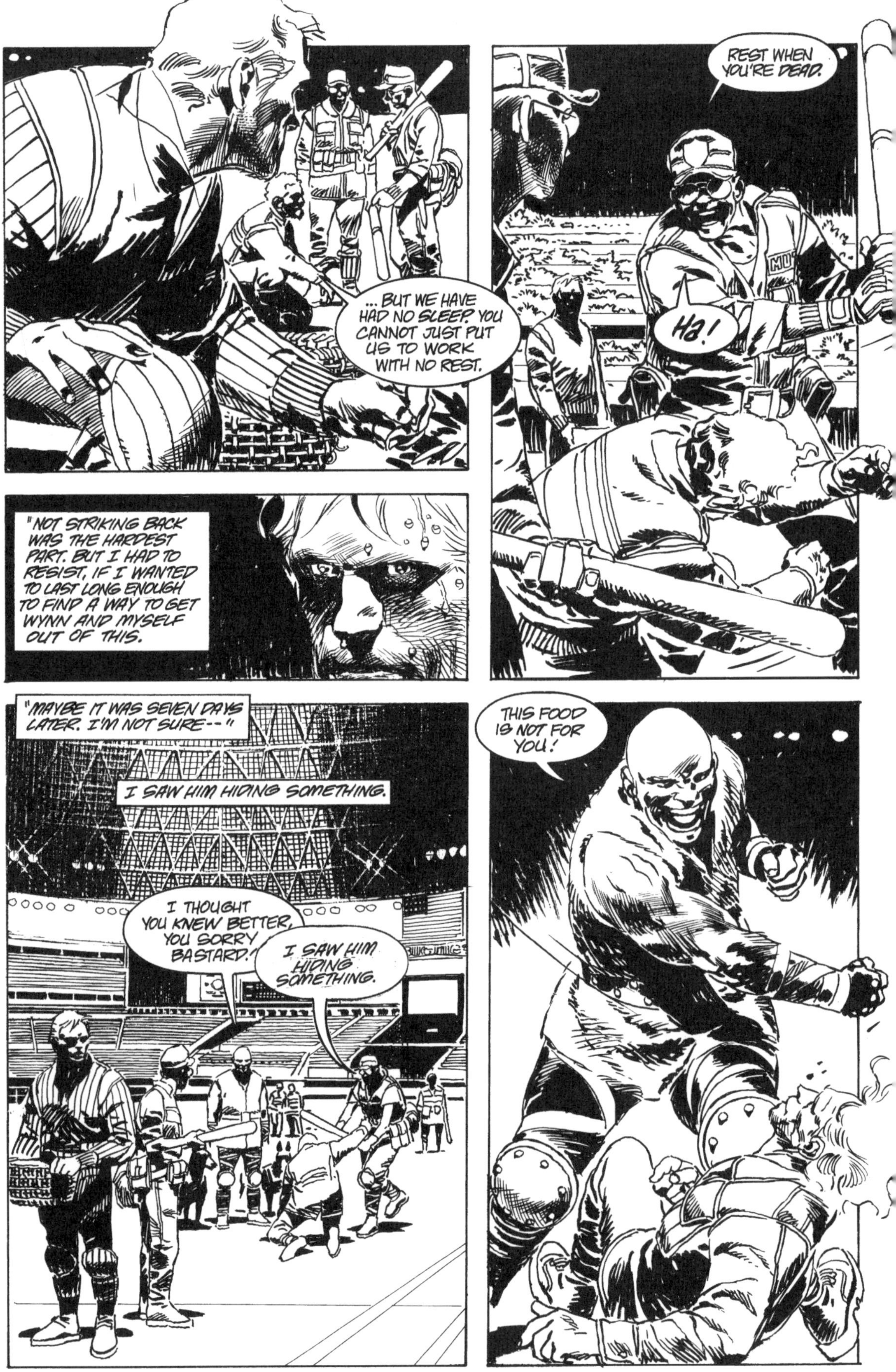

...BUT WE HAVE HAD NO SLEEP. YOU CANNOT JUST PUT US TO WORK WITH NO REST.
REST WHEN YOU'RE DEAD.
HA!
"NOT STRIKING BACK WAS THE HARDEST PART. BUT I HAD TO RESIST, IF I WANTED TO LAST LONG ENOUGH TO FIND A WAY TO GET WYNN AND MYSELF OUT OF THIS.
"MAYBE IT WAS SEVEN DAYS LATER. I'M NOT SURE--"
I SAW HIM HIDING SOMETHING.
I THOUGHT YOU KNEW BETTER, YOU SORRY BASTARD.!
I SAW HIM HIDING SOMETHING.
THIS FOOD IS NOT FOR YOU!

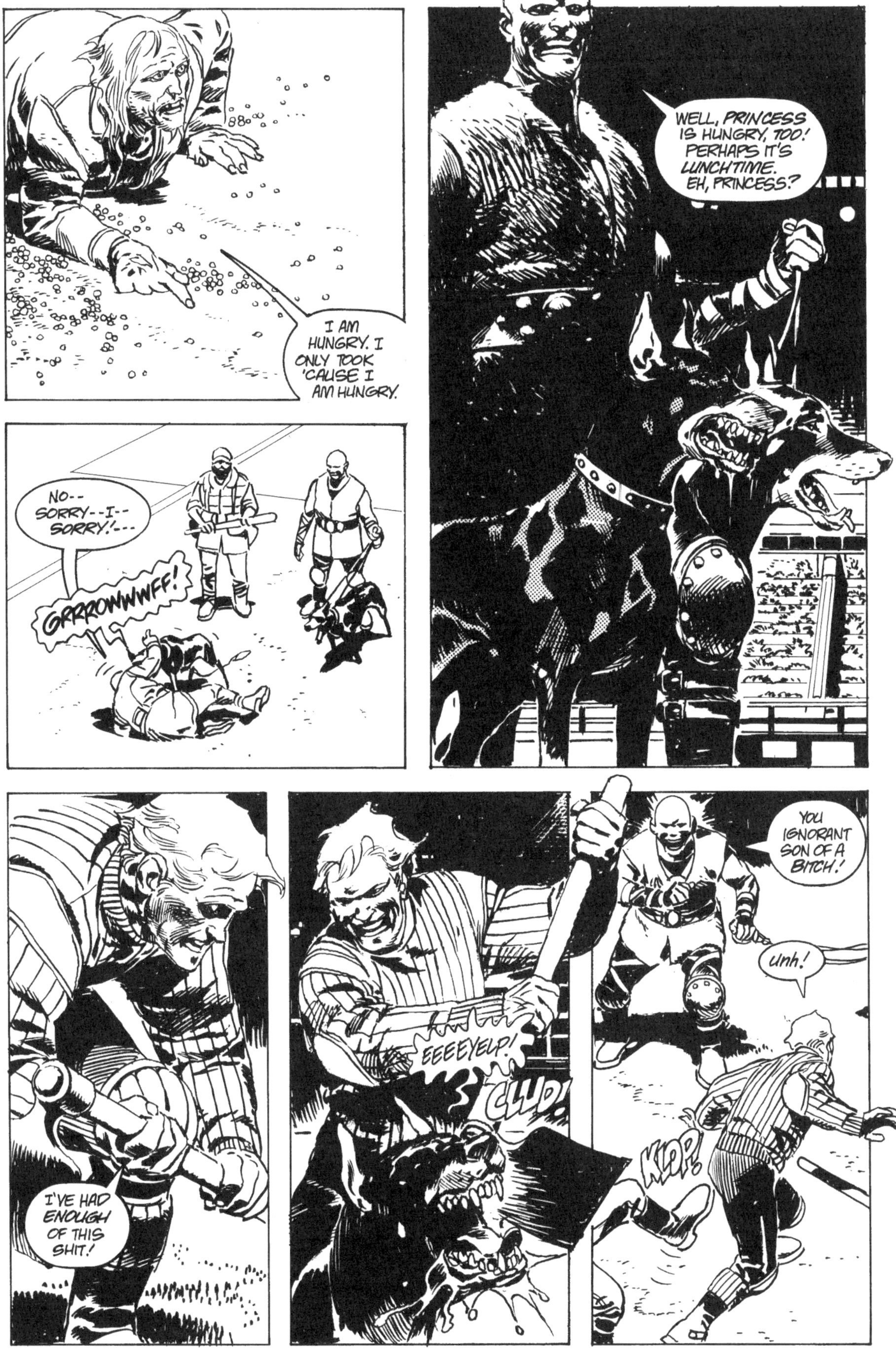
I AM HUNGRY. I ONLY TOOK 'CAUSE I AM HUNGRY.
WELL, PRINCESS IS HUNGRY, TOO! PERHAPS IT'S LUNCHTIME. EH, PRINCESS?
NO-- SORRY--I-- SORRY!---
GRRROWWWFF!
I'VE HAD ENOUGH OF THIS SHIT!
EEEEYELP!
CLUD!
YOU IGNORANT SON OF A BITCH!
Unh!
KLOP!

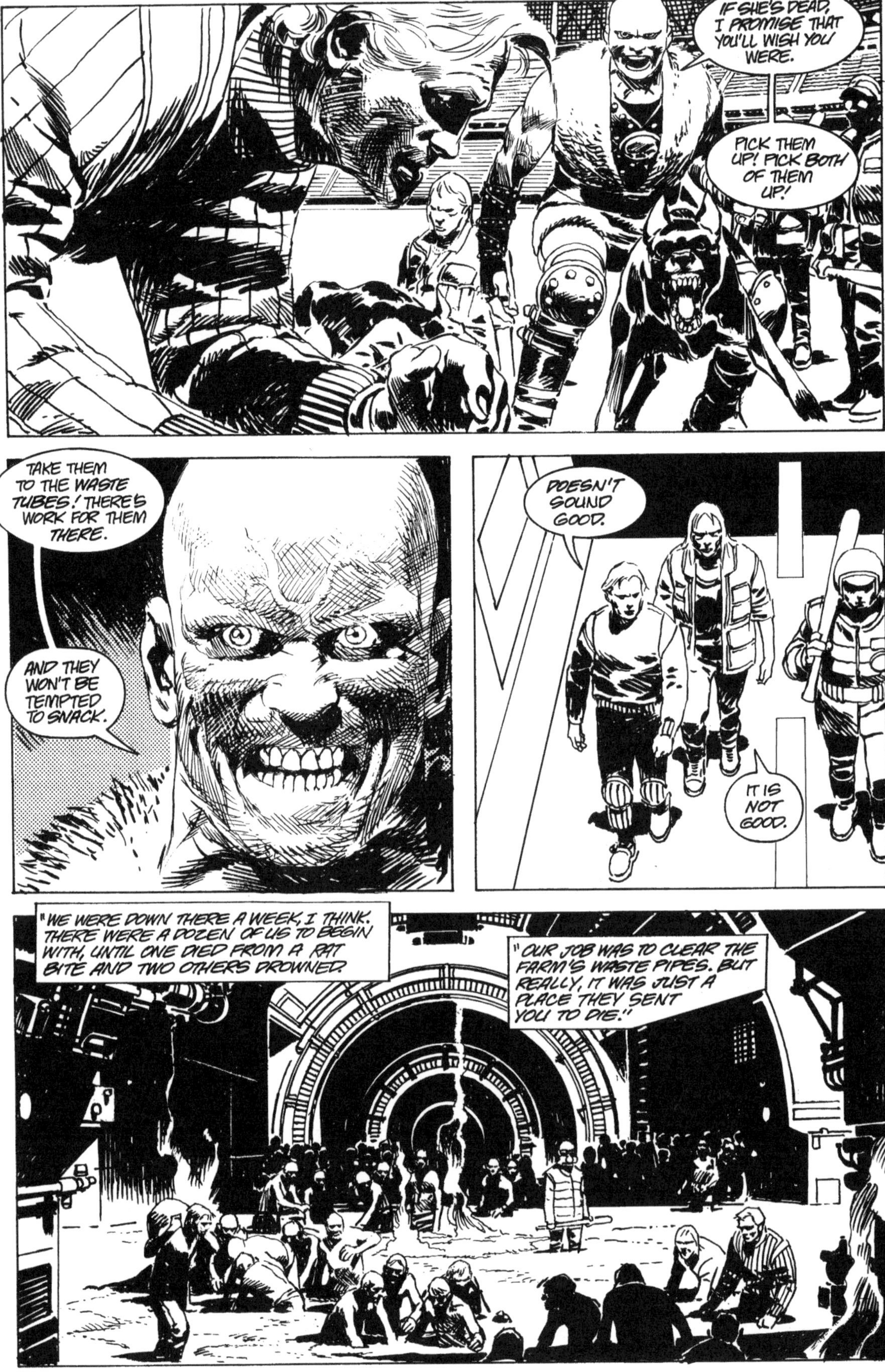
IF SHE'S DEAD, I PROMISE THAT YOU'LL WISH YOU WERE.
PICK THEM UP! PICK BOTH OF THEM UP!
TAKE THEM TO THE WASTE TUBES! THERE'S WORK FOR THEM THERE.
AND THEY WON'T BE TEMPTED TO SNACK.
DOESN'T SOUND GOOD.
IT IS NOT GOOD.
"WE WERE DOWN THERE A WEEK, I THINK. THERE WERE A DOZEN OF US TO BEGIN WITH, UNTIL ONE DIED FROM A RAT BITE AND TWO OTHERS DROWNED.
"OUR JOB WAS TO CLEAR THE FARM'S WASTE PIPES. BUT REALLY, IT WAS JUST A PLACE THEY SENT YOU TO DIE."

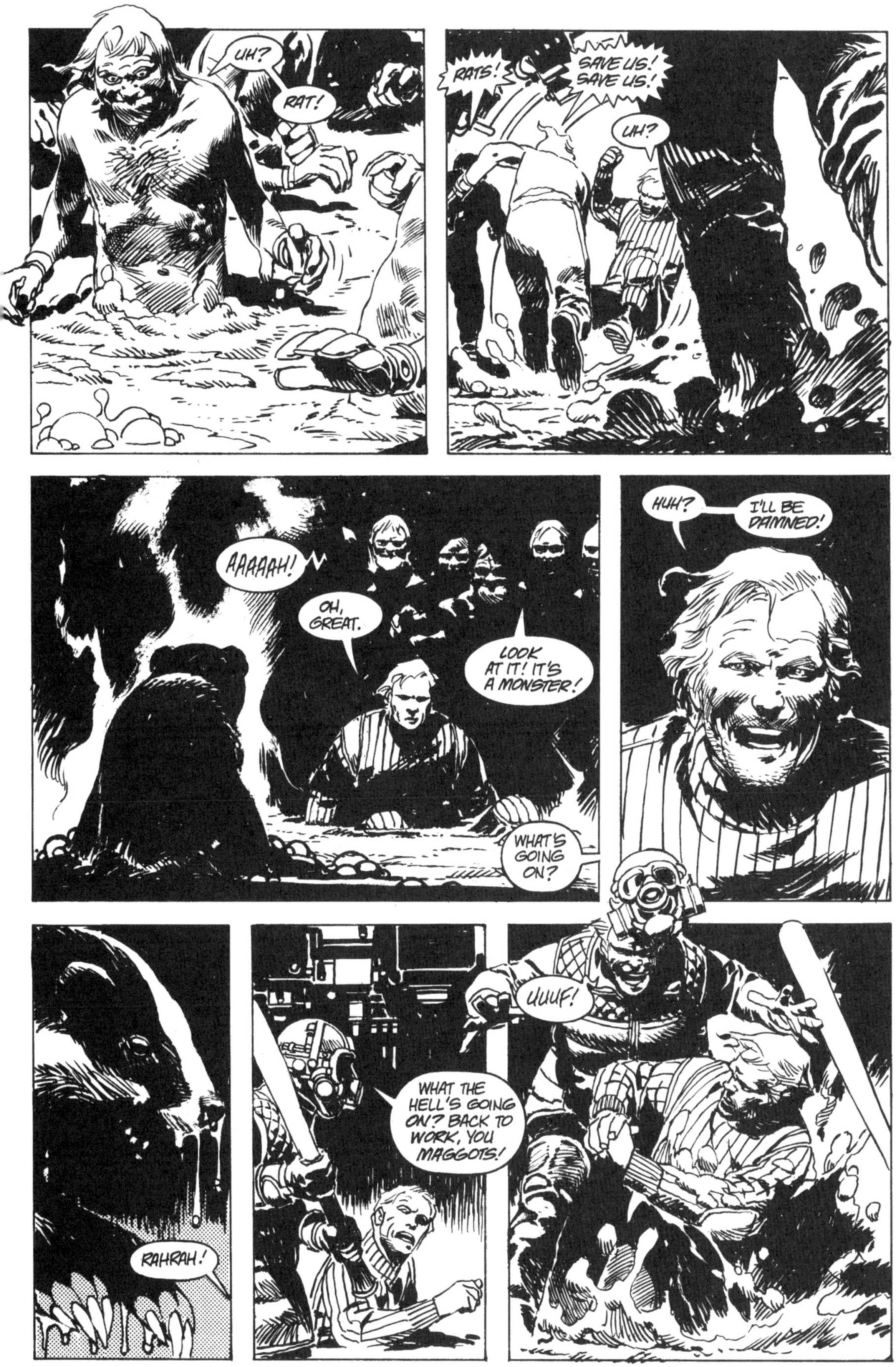
UH?
RAT!
RATS!
SAVE US! SAVE US!
UH?
AAAAAH!
OH, GREAT.
LOOK AT IT! IT'S A MONSTER!
WHAT'S GOING ON?
HUH?
I'LL BE DAMNED!
RAHRAH!
WHAT THE HELL'S GOING ON? BACK TO WORK, YOU MAGGOTS!
UUUF!

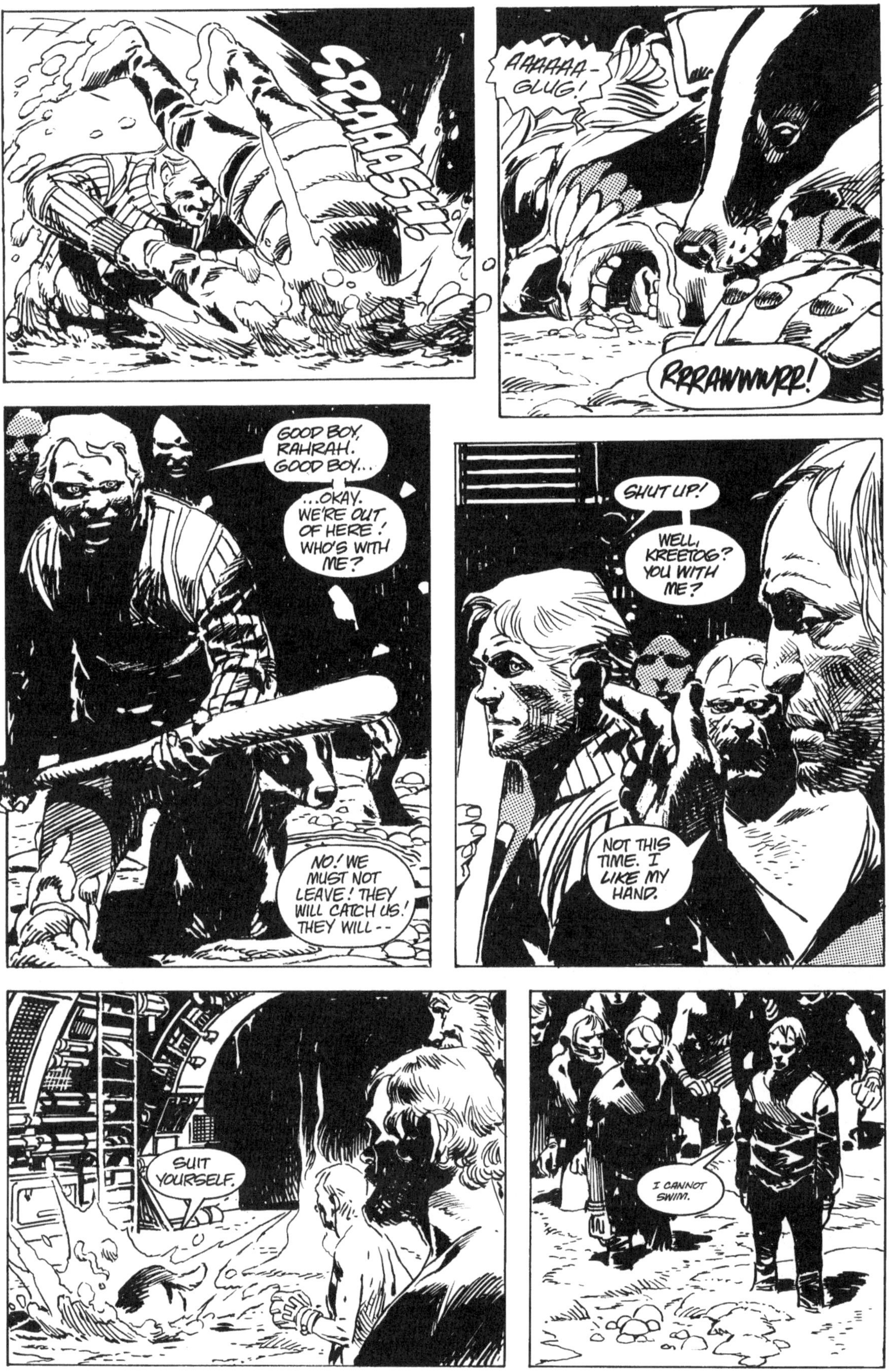
SPLAASH!
AAAAAA-GLUG!
RRRAWWWRR!
GOOD BOY, RAHRAH. GOOD BOY...
...OKAY. WE'RE OUT OF HERE! WHO'S WITH ME?
NO! WE MUST NOT LEAVE! THEY WILL CATCH US! THEY WILL--
SHUT UP!
WELL, KREETOG? YOU WITH ME?
NOT THIS TIME. I LIKE MY HAND.
SUIT YOURSELF.
I CANNOT SWIM.

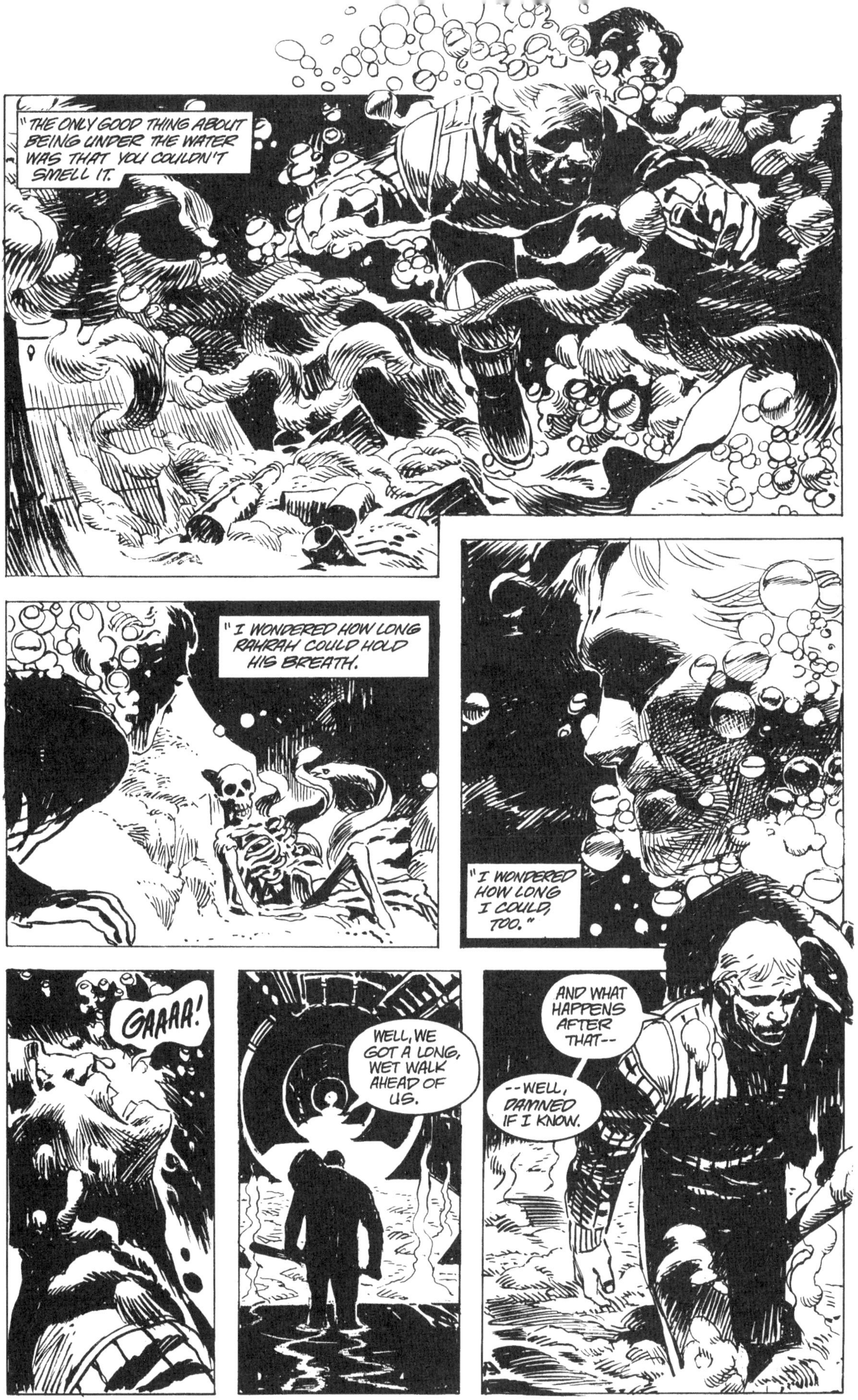
"THE ONLY GOOD THING ABOUT BEING UNDER THE WATER WAS THAT YOU COULDN'T SMELL IT.
"I WONDERED HOW LONG RAHRAH COULD HOLD HIS BREATH.
"I WONDERED HOW LONG I COULD, TOO."
GAAAA!
WELL, WE GOT A LONG, WET WALK AHEAD OF US.
AND WHAT HAPPENS AFTER THAT--
--WELL, DAMNED IF I KNOW.

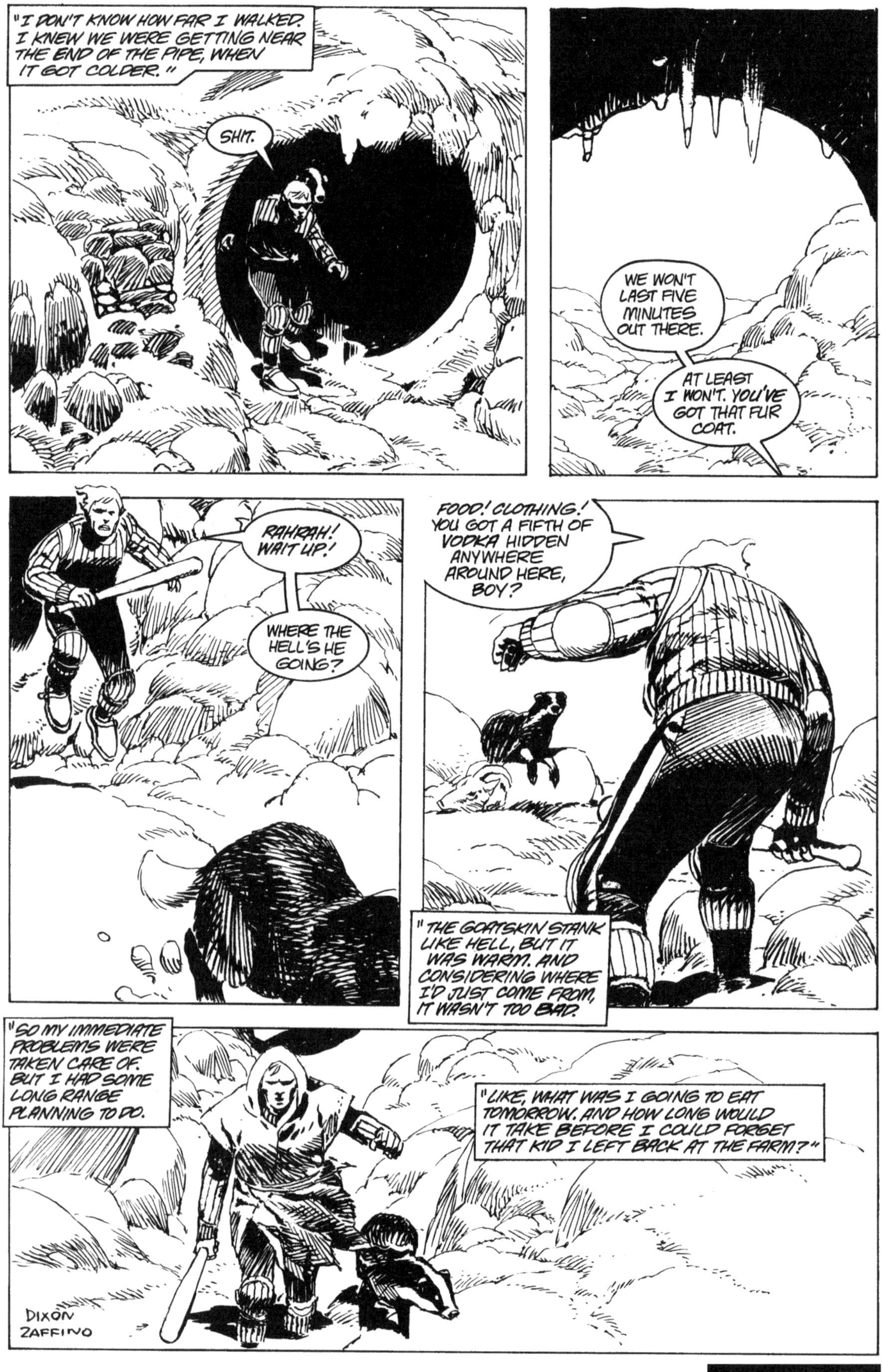
"I DON'T KNOW HOW FAR I WALKED. I KNEW WE WERE GETTING NEAR THE END OF THE PIPE, WHEN IT GOT COLDER."
SHIT.
WE WON'T LAST FIVE MINUTES OUT THERE.
AT LEAST I WON'T. YOU'VE GOT THAT FUR COAT.
RAHRAH! WAIT UP!
WHERE THE HELL'S HE GOING?
FOOD! CLOTHING! YOU GOT A FIFTH OF VODKA HIDDEN ANYWHERE AROUND HERE, BOY?
"THE GOATSKIN STANK LIKE HELL, BUT IT WAS WARM. AND CONSIDERING WHERE I'D JUST COME FROM, IT WASN'T TOO BAD.
"SO MY IMMEDIATE PROBLEMS WERE TAKEN CARE OF. BUT I HAD SOME LONG RANGE PLANNING TO DO.
"LIKE, WHAT WAS I GOING TO EAT TOMORROW. AND HOW LONG WOULD IT TAKE BEFORE I COULD FORGET THAT KID I LEFT BACK AT THE FARM?"
DIXON
ZAFFINO

END OF PART ONE

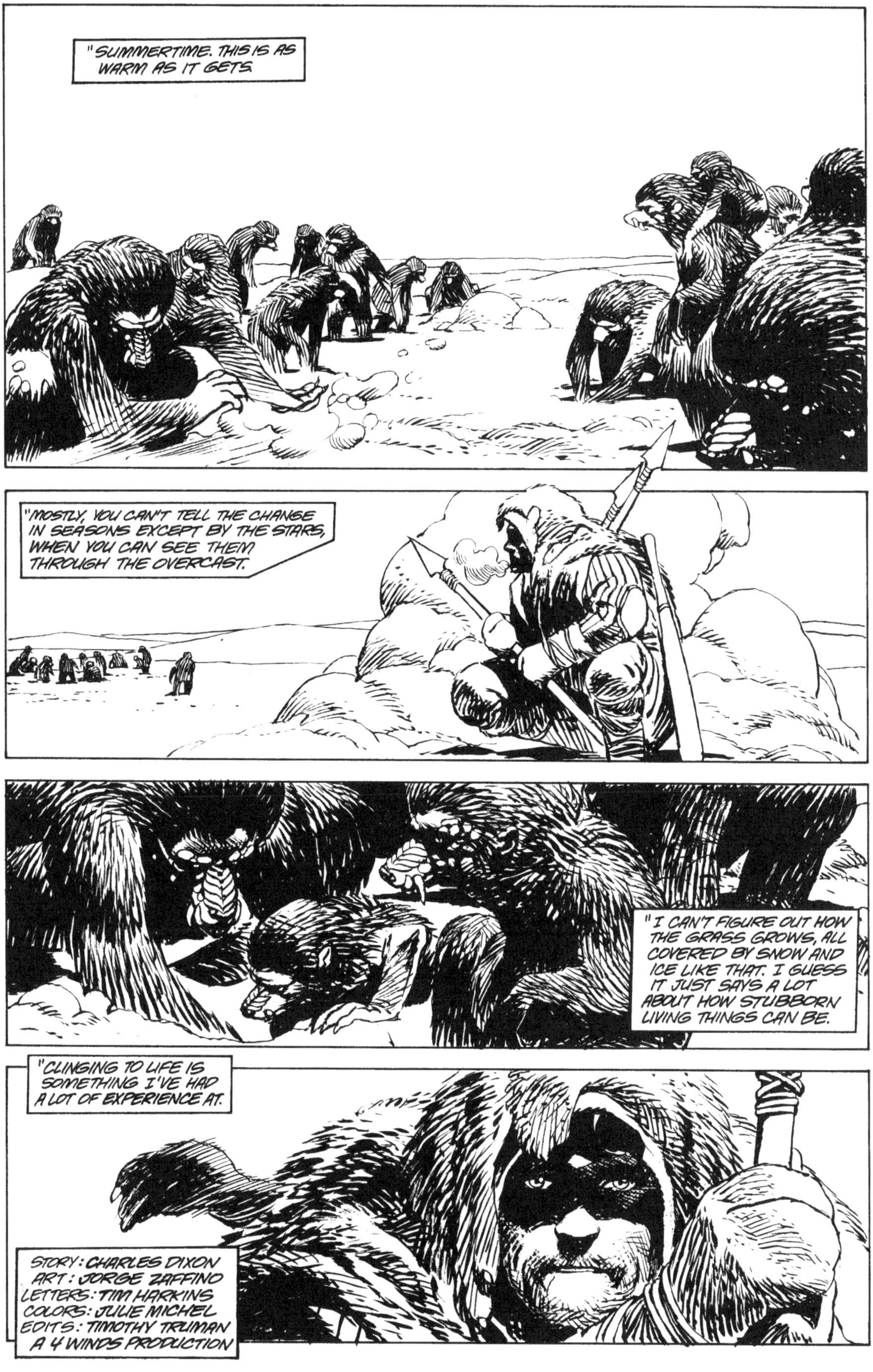
"SUMMERTIME. THIS IS AS WARM AS IT GETS.
"MOSTLY, YOU CAN'T TELL THE CHANGE IN SEASONS EXCEPT BY THE STARS, WHEN YOU CAN SEE THEM THROUGH THE OVERCAST.
"I CAN'T FIGURE OUT HOW THE GRASS GROWS, ALL COVERED BY SNOW AND ICE LIKE THAT. I GUESS IT JUST SAYS A LOT ABOUT HOW STUBBORN LIVING THINGS CAN BE.
"CLINGING TO LIFE IS SOMETHING I'VE HAD A LOT OF EXPERIENCE AT.
STORY: CHARLES DIXON
ART: JORGE ZAFFINO
LETTERS: TIM HARKINS
COLORS: JULIE MICHEL
EDITS: TIMOTHY TRUMAN
A 4 WINDS PRODUCTION

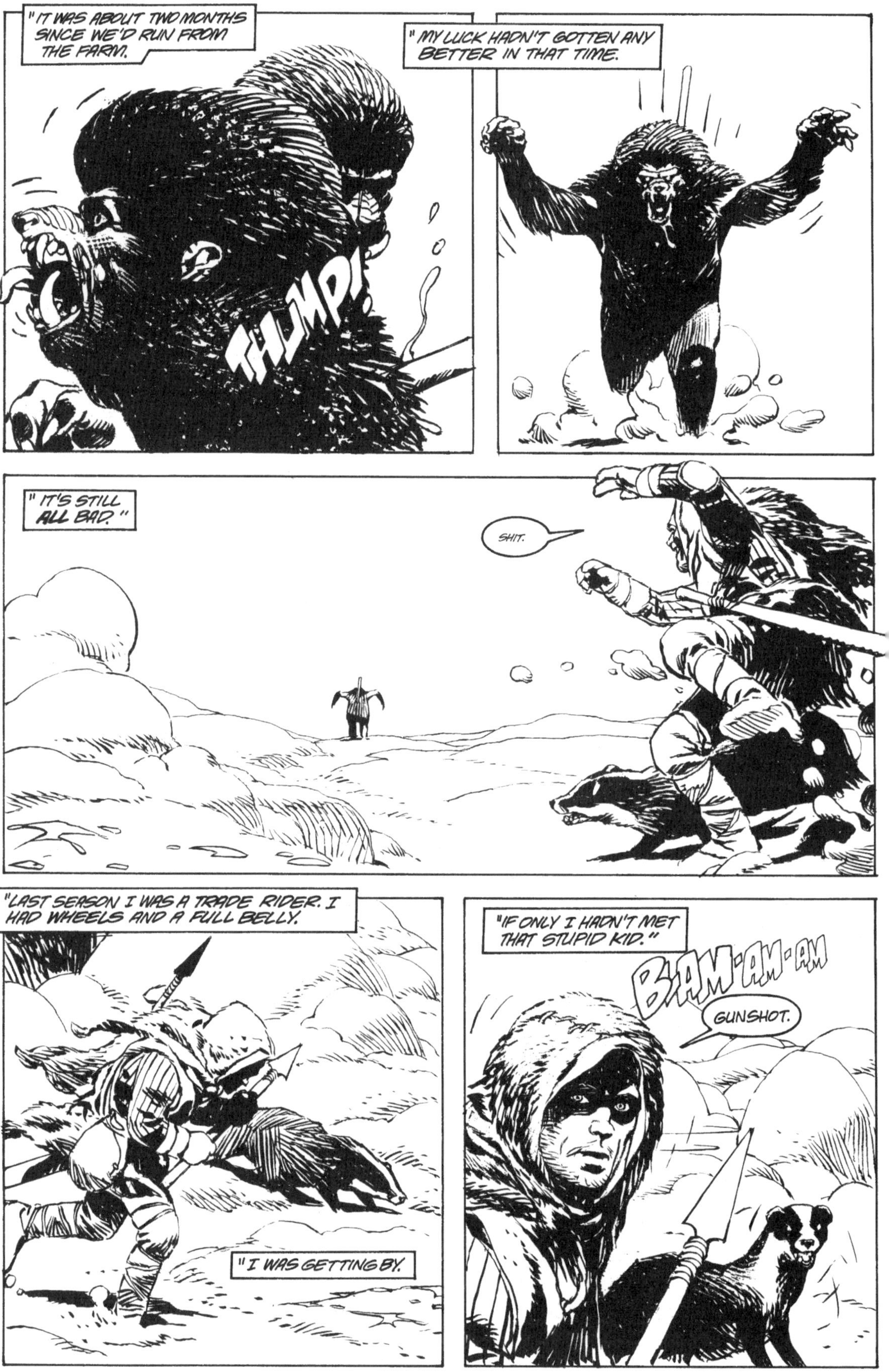
"IT WAS ABOUT TWO MONTHS SINCE WE'D RUN FROM THE FARM.
THUMP!
"MY LUCK HADN'T GOTTEN ANY BETTER IN THAT TIME.
"IT'S STILL ALL BAD."
SHIT.
"LAST SEASON I WAS A TRADE RIDER. I HAD WHEELS AND A FULL BELLY.
"I WAS GETTING BY.
"IF ONLY I HADN'T MET THAT STUPID KID."
B-AM-AM-AM
GUNSHOT.

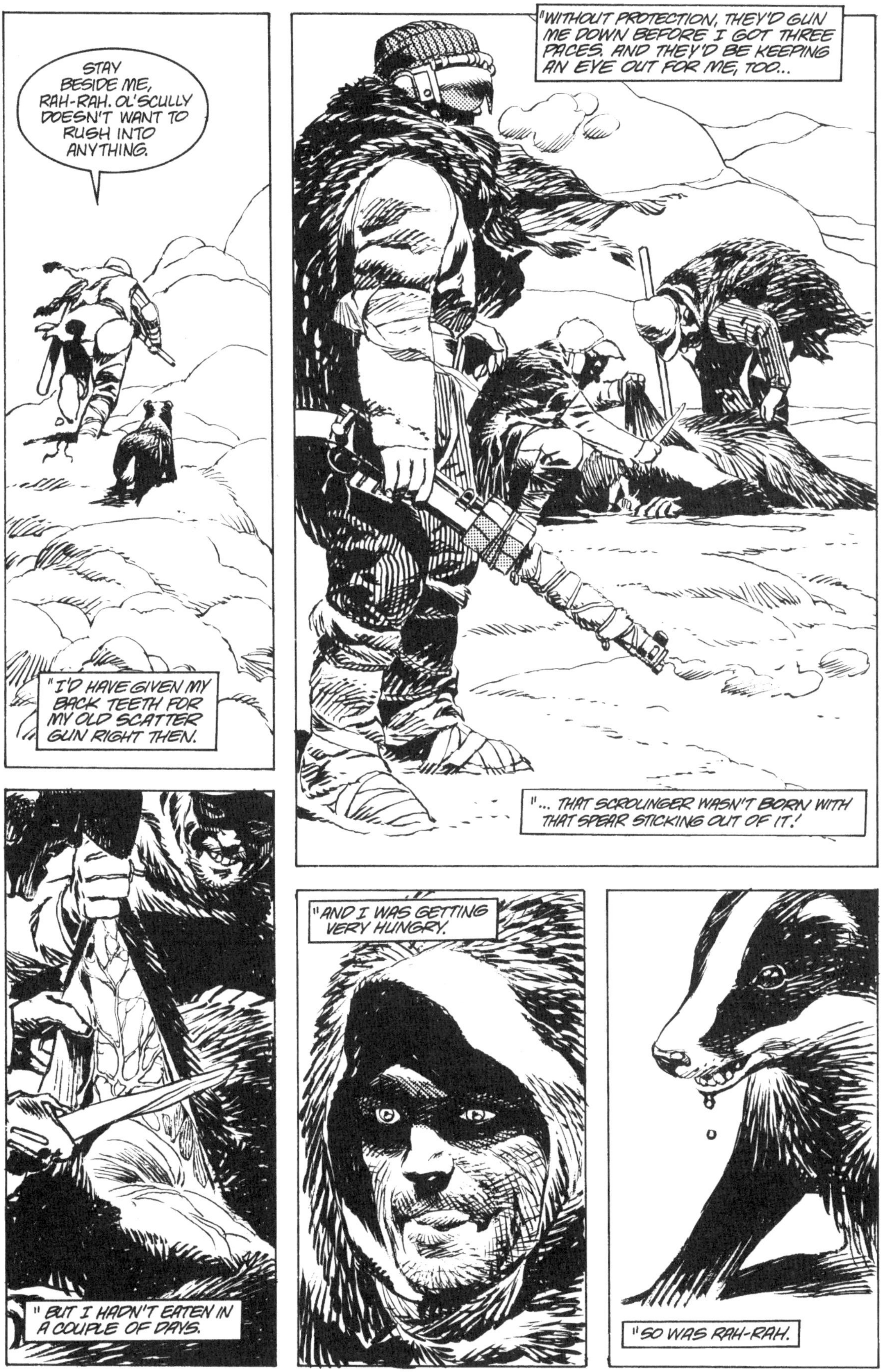
STAY BESIDE ME, RAH-RAH. OL'SCULLY DOESN'T WANT TO RUSH INTO ANYTHING.
"I'D HAVE GIVEN MY BACK TEETH FOR MY OLD SCATTER GUN RIGHT THEN.
"WITHOUT PROTECTION, THEY'D GUN ME DOWN BEFORE I GOT THREE PACES. AND THEY'D BE KEEPING AN EYE OUT FOR ME, TOO...
"... THAT SCROLINGER WASN'T BORN WITH THAT SPEAR STICKING OUT OF IT!
" BUT I HADN'T EATEN IN A COUPLE OF DAYS.
"AND I WAS GETTING VERY HUNGRY.
"SO WAS RAH-RAH.

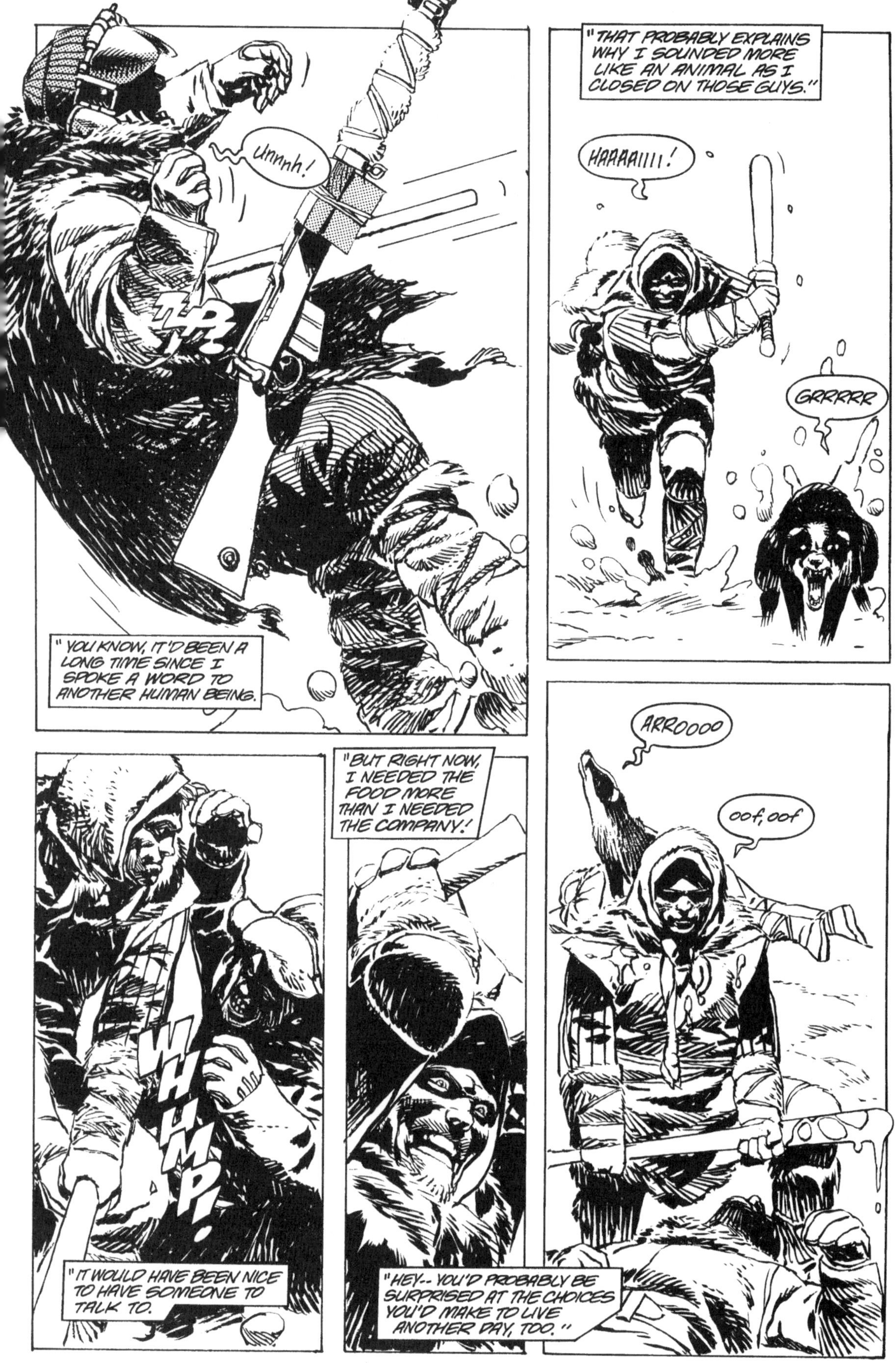
Unnnh!
"YOU KNOW, IT'D BEEN A LONG TIME SINCE I SPOKE A WORD TO ANOTHER HUMAN BEING.
"THAT PROBABLY EXPLAINS WHY I SOUNDED MORE LIKE AN ANIMAL AS I CLOSED ON THOSE GUYS."
HAAAAIIIII!
GRRRRR
WHUMP!
"IT WOULD HAVE BEEN NICE TO HAVE SOMEONE TO TALK TO.
"BUT RIGHT NOW, I NEEDED THE FOOD MORE THAN I NEEDED THE COMPANY!
ARROOOO
oof, oof
"HEY-- YOU'D PROBABLY BE SURPRISED AT THE CHOICES YOU'D MAKE TO LIVE ANOTHER DAY, TOO."

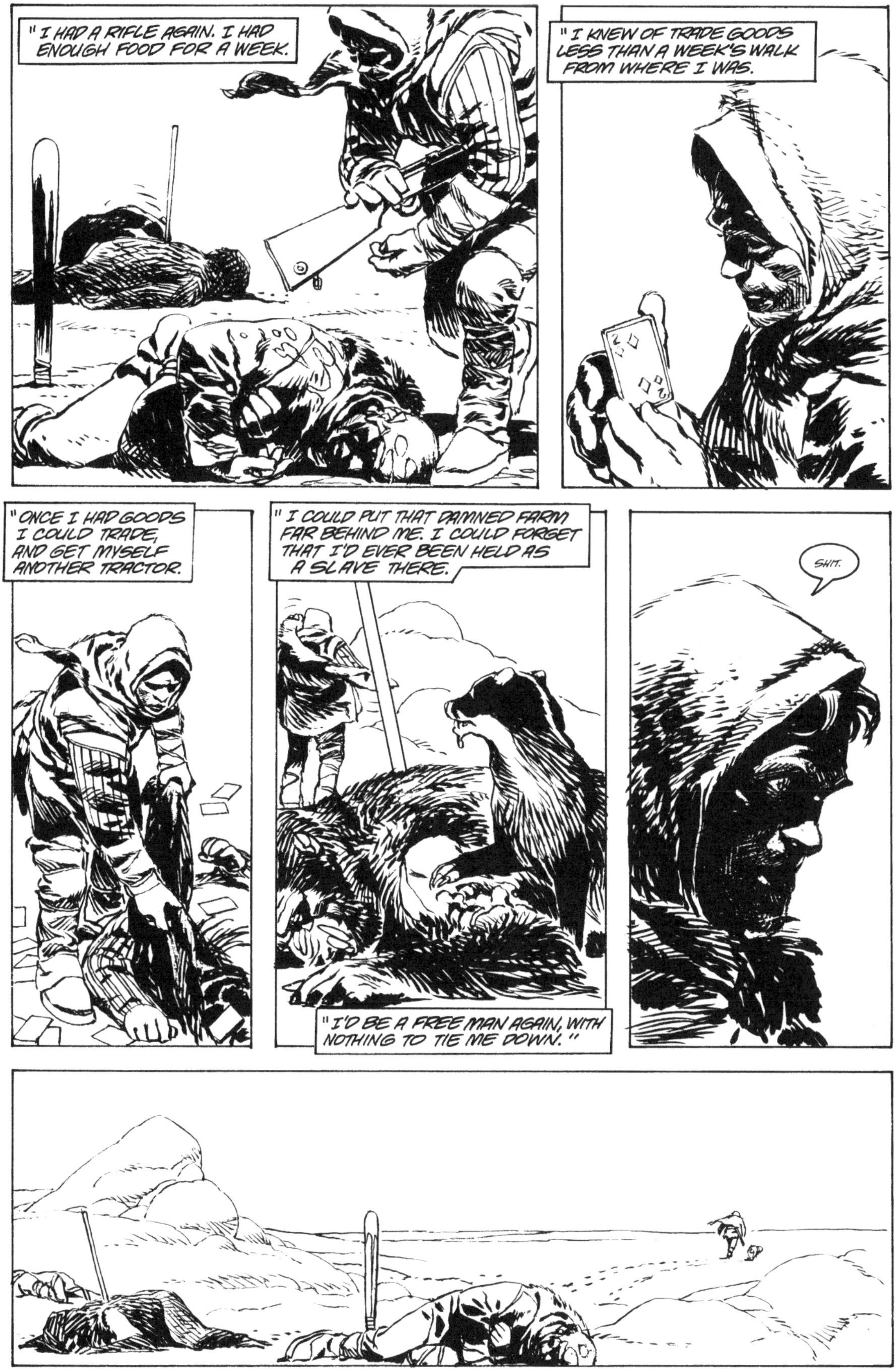
"I HAD A RIFLE AGAIN. I HAD ENOUGH FOOD FOR A WEEK.
"I KNEW OF TRADE GOODS LESS THAN A WEEK'S WALK FROM WHERE I WAS.
"ONCE I HAD GOODS I COULD TRADE, AND GET MYSELF ANOTHER TRACTOR.
"I COULD PUT THAT DAMNED FARM FAR BEHIND ME. I COULD FORGET THAT I'D EVER BEEN HELD AS A SLAVE THERE.
"I'D BE A FREE MAN AGAIN, WITH NOTHING TO TIE ME DOWN."
SHIT.

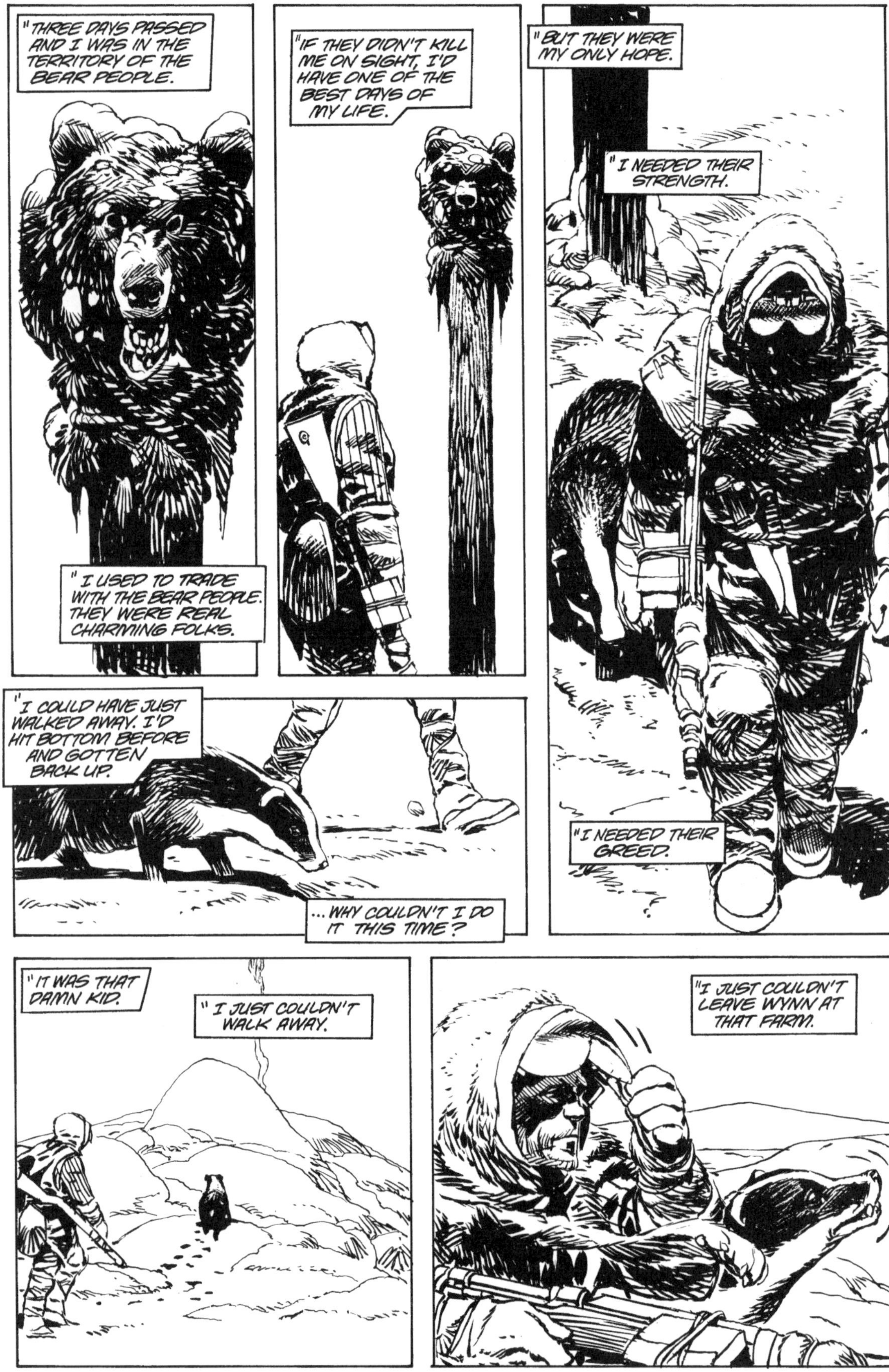
"THREE DAYS PASSED AND I WAS IN THE TERRITORY OF THE BEAR PEOPLE.
"I USED TO TRADE WITH THE BEAR PEOPLE. THEY WERE REAL CHARMING FOLKS.
"IF THEY DIDN'T KILL ME ON SIGHT, I'D HAVE ONE OF THE BEST DAYS OF MY LIFE.
"BUT THEY WERE MY ONLY HOPE.
"I NEEDED THEIR STRENGTH.
"I NEEDED THEIR GREED.
"I COULD HAVE JUST WALKED AWAY. I'D HIT BOTTOM BEFORE AND GOTTEN BACK UP.
...WHY COULDN'T I DO IT THIS TIME?
"IT WAS THAT DAMN KID.
"I JUST COULDN'T WALK AWAY.
"I JUST COULDN'T LEAVE WYNN AT THAT FARM.

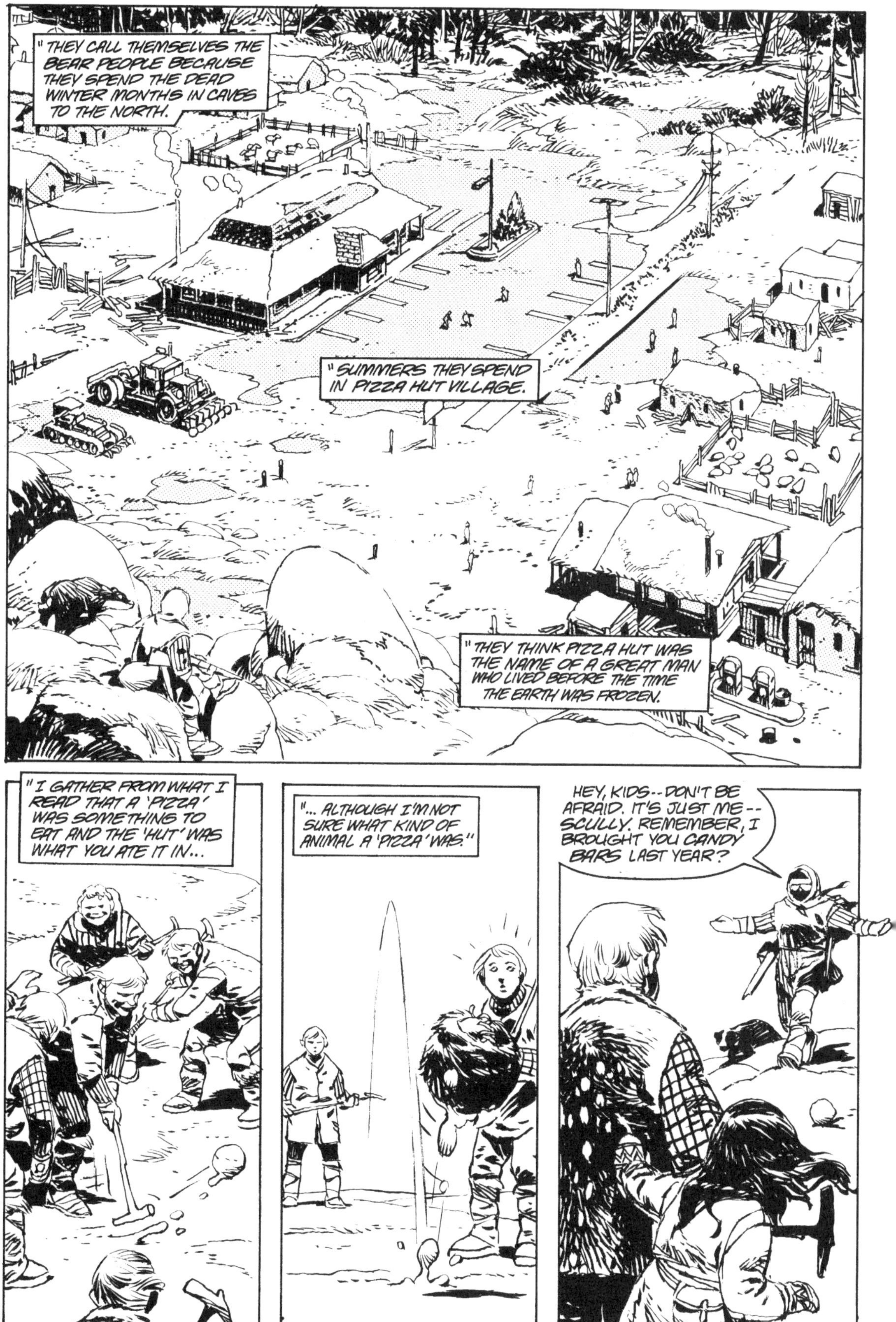
"THEY CALL THEMSELVES THE BEAR PEOPLE BECAUSE THEY SPEND THE DEAD WINTER MONTHS IN CAVES TO THE NORTH.
"SUMMERS THEY SPEND IN PIZZA HUT VILLAGE.
"THEY THINK PIZZA HUT WAS THE NAME OF A GREAT MAN WHO LIVED BEFORE THE TIME THE EARTH WAS FROZEN.
"I GATHER FROM WHAT I READ THAT A 'PIZZA' WAS SOMETHING TO EAT AND THE 'HUT' WAS WHAT YOU ATE IT IN...
"... ALTHOUGH I'M NOT SURE WHAT KIND OF ANIMAL A 'PIZZA' WAS."
HEY, KIDS--DON'T BE AFRAID. IT'S JUST ME--SCULLY. REMEMBER, I BROUGHT YOU CANDY BARS LAST YEAR?

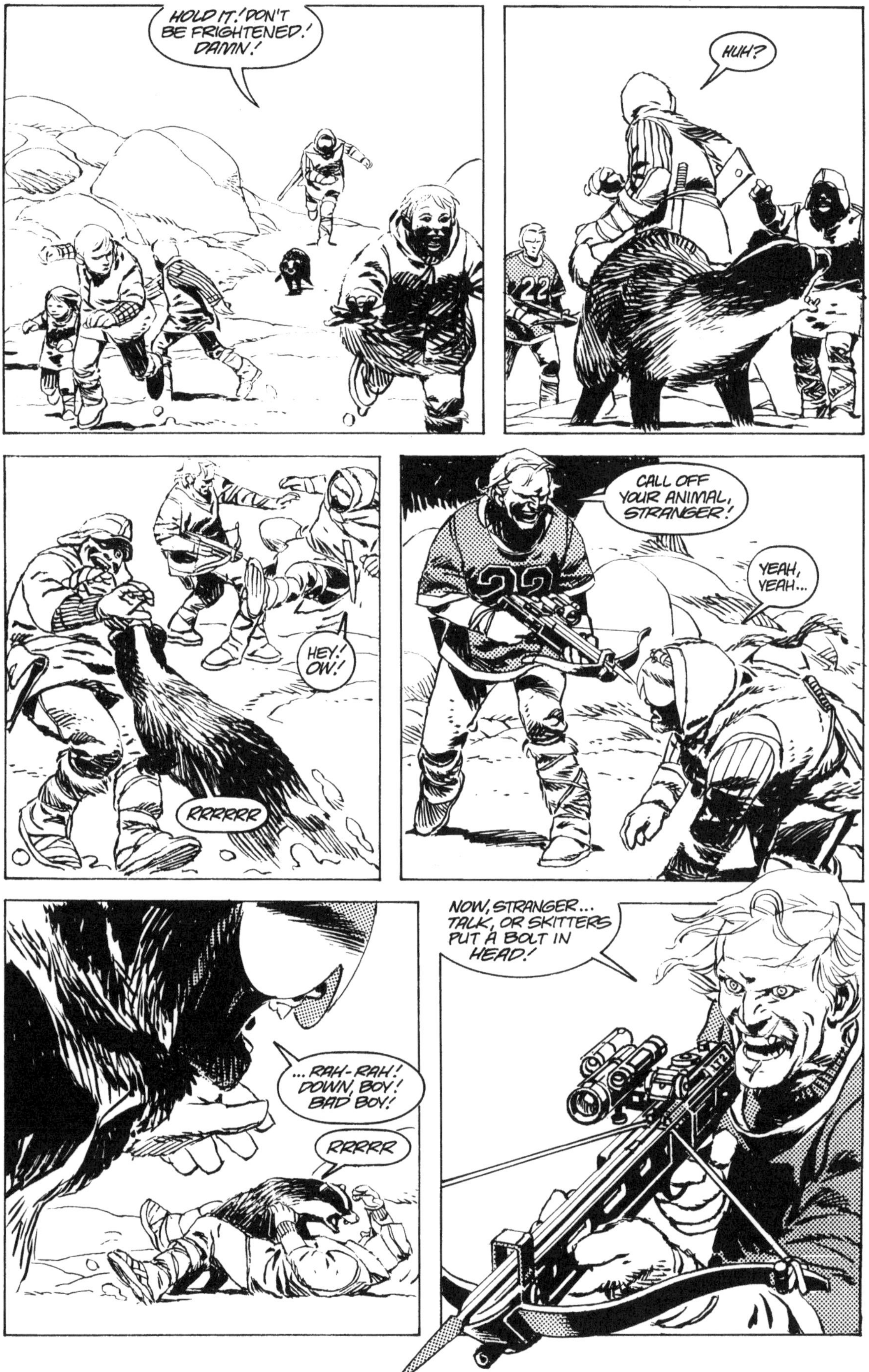
HOLD IT! DON'T BE FRIGHTENED! DAMN!
HUH?
HEY! OW!
RRRRRR
CALL OFF YOUR ANIMAL, STRANGER!
YEAH, YEAH...
...RAH-RAH! DOWN, BOY! BAD BOY!
RRRRR
NOW, STRANGER... TALK, OR SKITTERS PUT A BOLT IN HEAD!

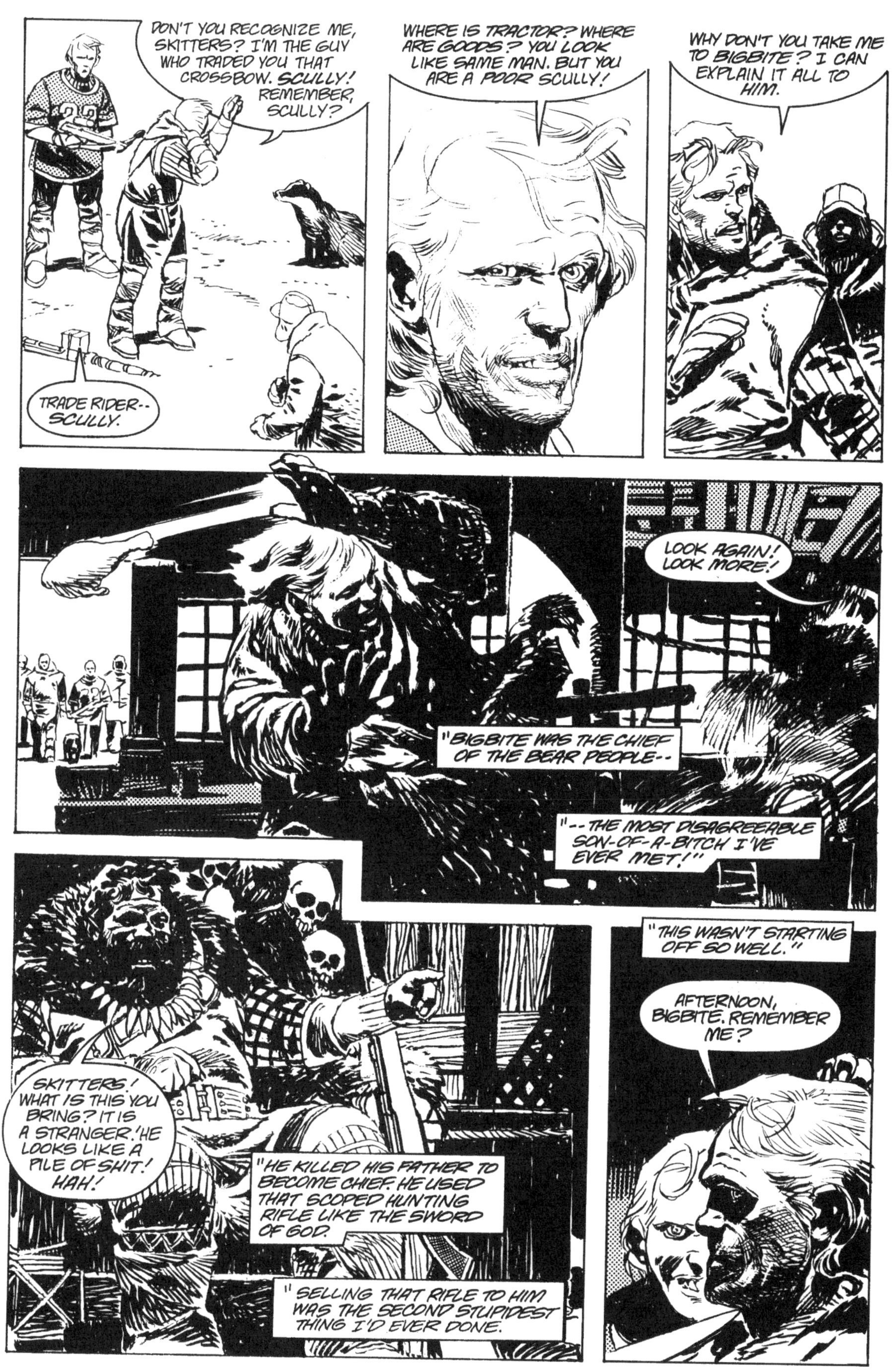
DON'T YOU RECOGNIZE ME, SKITTERS? I'M THE GUY WHO TRADED YOU THAT CROSSBOW. SCULLY! REMEMBER, SCULLY?
TRADE RIDER-- SCULLY.
WHERE IS TRACTOR? WHERE ARE GOODS? YOU LOOK LIKE SAME MAN. BUT YOU ARE A POOR SCULLY!
WHY DON'T YOU TAKE ME TO BIGBITE? I CAN EXPLAIN IT ALL TO HIM.
LOOK AGAIN! LOOK MORE!
"BIGBITE WAS THE CHIEF OF THE BEAR PEOPLE--
"--THE MOST DISAGREEABLE SON-OF-A-BITCH I'VE EVER MET!"
SKITTERS! WHAT IS THIS YOU BRING? IT IS A STRANGER! HE LOOKS LIKE A PILE OF SHIT! HAH!
"HE KILLED HIS FATHER TO BECOME CHIEF. HE USED THAT SCOPED HUNTING RIFLE LIKE THE SWORD OF GOD.
"SELLING THAT RIFLE TO HIM WAS THE SECOND STUPIDEST THING I'D EVER DONE.
"THIS WASN'T STARTING OFF SO WELL."
AFTERNOON, BIGBITE. REMEMBER ME?

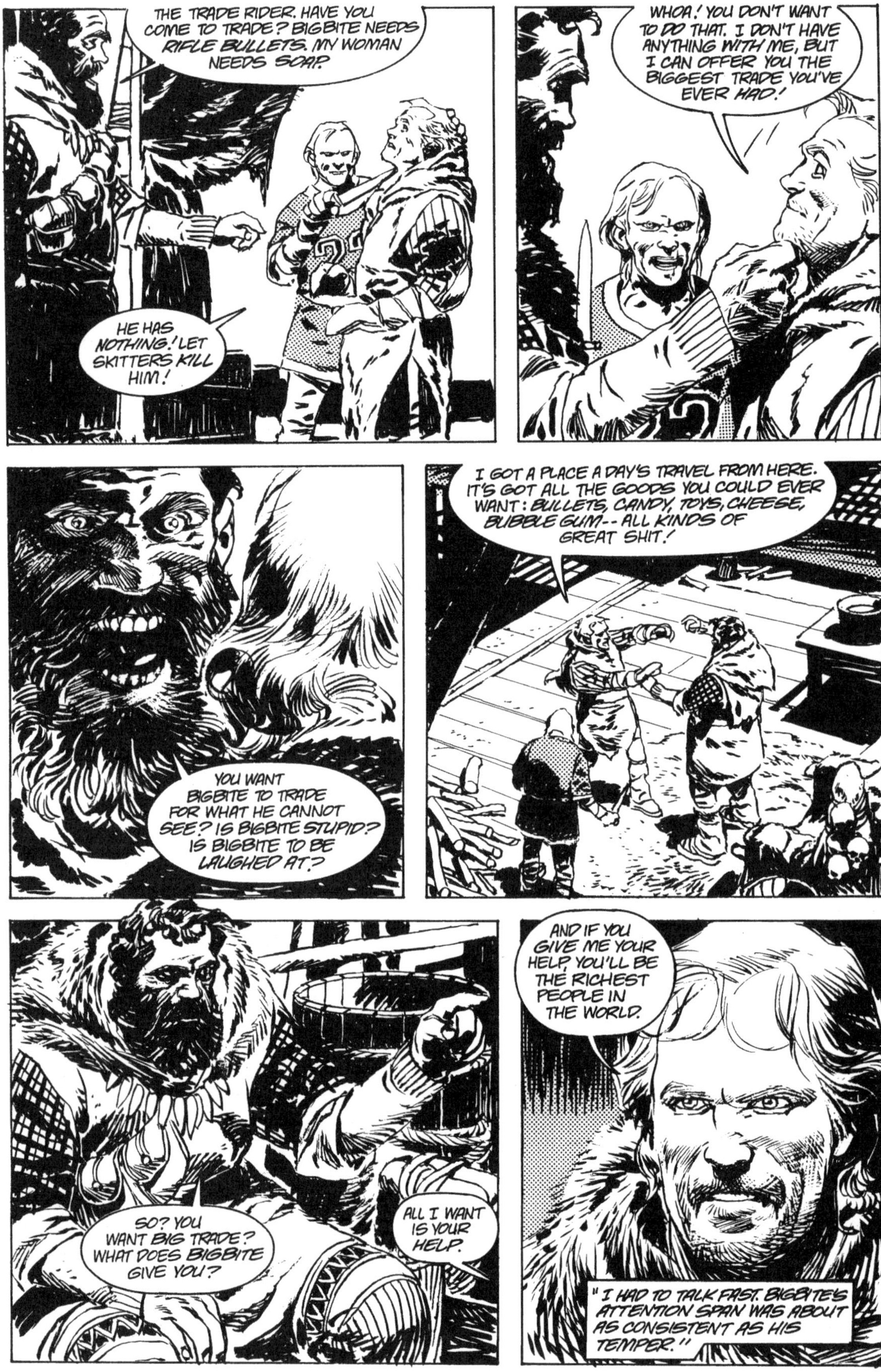
THE TRADE RIDER. HAVE YOU COME TO TRADE? BIGBITE NEEDS RIFLE BULLETS. MY WOMAN NEEDS SOAP.
HE HAS NOTHING! LET SKITTERS KILL HIM!
WHOA! YOU DON'T WANT TO DO THAT. I DON'T HAVE ANYTHING WITH ME, BUT I CAN OFFER YOU THE BIGGEST TRADE YOU'VE EVER HAD!
YOU WANT BIGBITE TO TRADE FOR WHAT HE CANNOT SEE? IS BIGBITE STUPID? IS BIGBITE TO BE LAUGHED AT?
I GOT A PLACE A DAY'S TRAVEL FROM HERE. IT'S GOT ALL THE GOODS YOU COULD EVER WANT: BULLETS, CANDY, TOYS, CHEESE, BUBBLE GUM-- ALL KINDS OF GREAT SHIT!
SO? YOU WANT BIG TRADE? WHAT DOES BIGBITE GIVE YOU?
ALL I WANT IS YOUR HELP.
AND IF YOU GIVE ME YOUR HELP, YOU'LL BE THE RICHEST PEOPLE IN THE WORLD.
"I HAD TO TALK FAST. BIGBITE'S ATTENTION SPAN WAS ABOUT AS CONSISTENT AS HIS TEMPER."

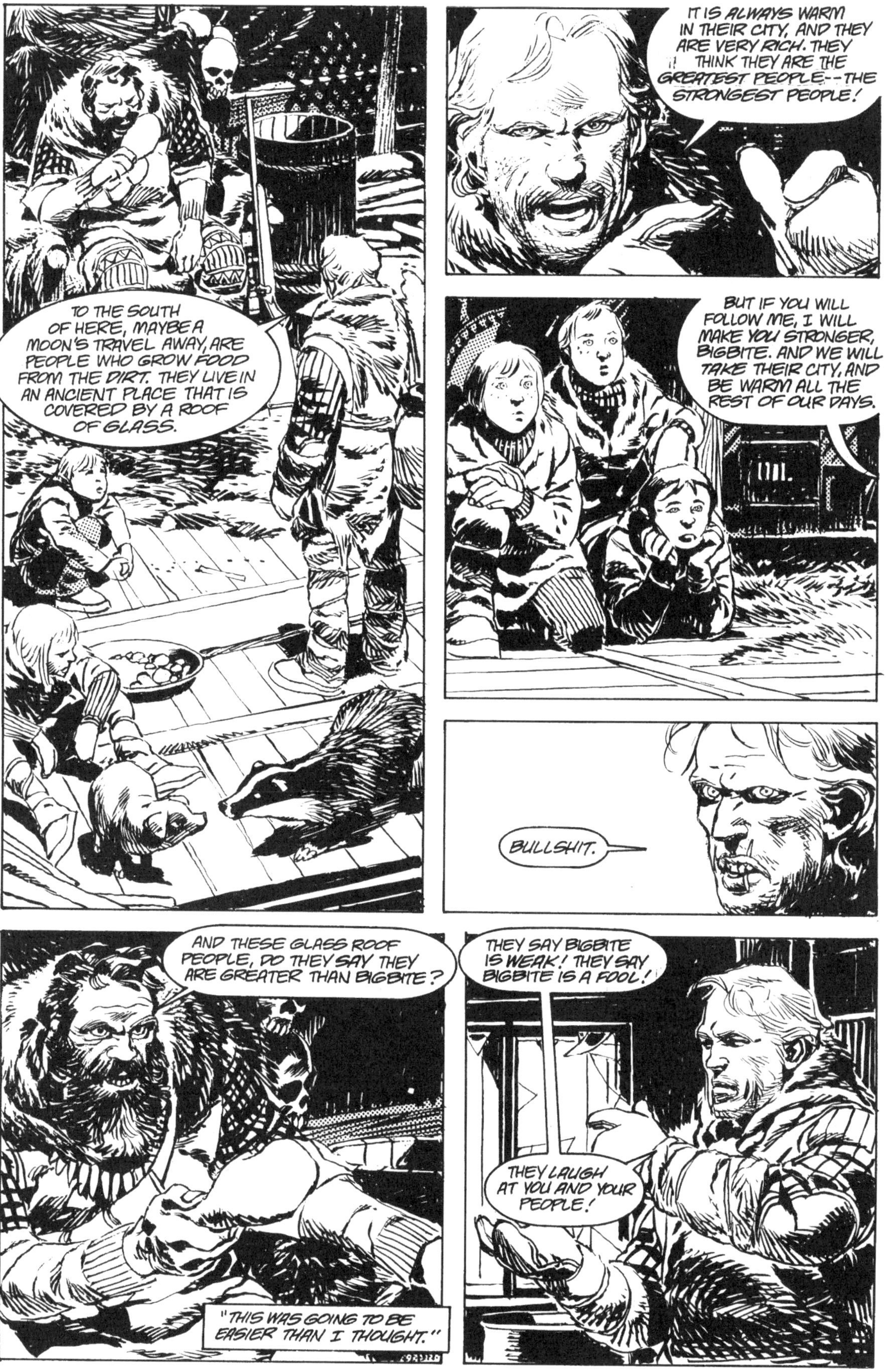

TO THE SOUTH OF HERE, MAYBE A MOON'S TRAVEL AWAY, ARE PEOPLE WHO GROW FOOD FROM THE DIRT. THEY LIVE IN AN ANCIENT PLACE THAT IS COVERED BY A ROOF OF GLASS.
IT IS ALWAYS WARM IN THEIR CITY, AND THEY ARE VERY RICH. THEY THINK THEY ARE THE GREATEST PEOPLE--THE STRONGEST PEOPLE!
BUT IF YOU WILL FOLLOW ME, I WILL MAKE YOU STRONGER, BIGBITE. AND WE WILL TAKE THEIR CITY, AND BE WARM ALL THE REST OF OUR DAYS.
BULLSHIT.
AND THESE GLASS ROOF PEOPLE, DO THEY SAY THEY ARE GREATER THAN BIGBITE?
"THIS WAS GOING TO BE EASIER THAN I THOUGHT."
THEY SAY BIGBITE IS WEAK! THEY SAY BIGBITE IS A FOOL!
THEY LAUGH AT YOU AND YOUR PEOPLE!

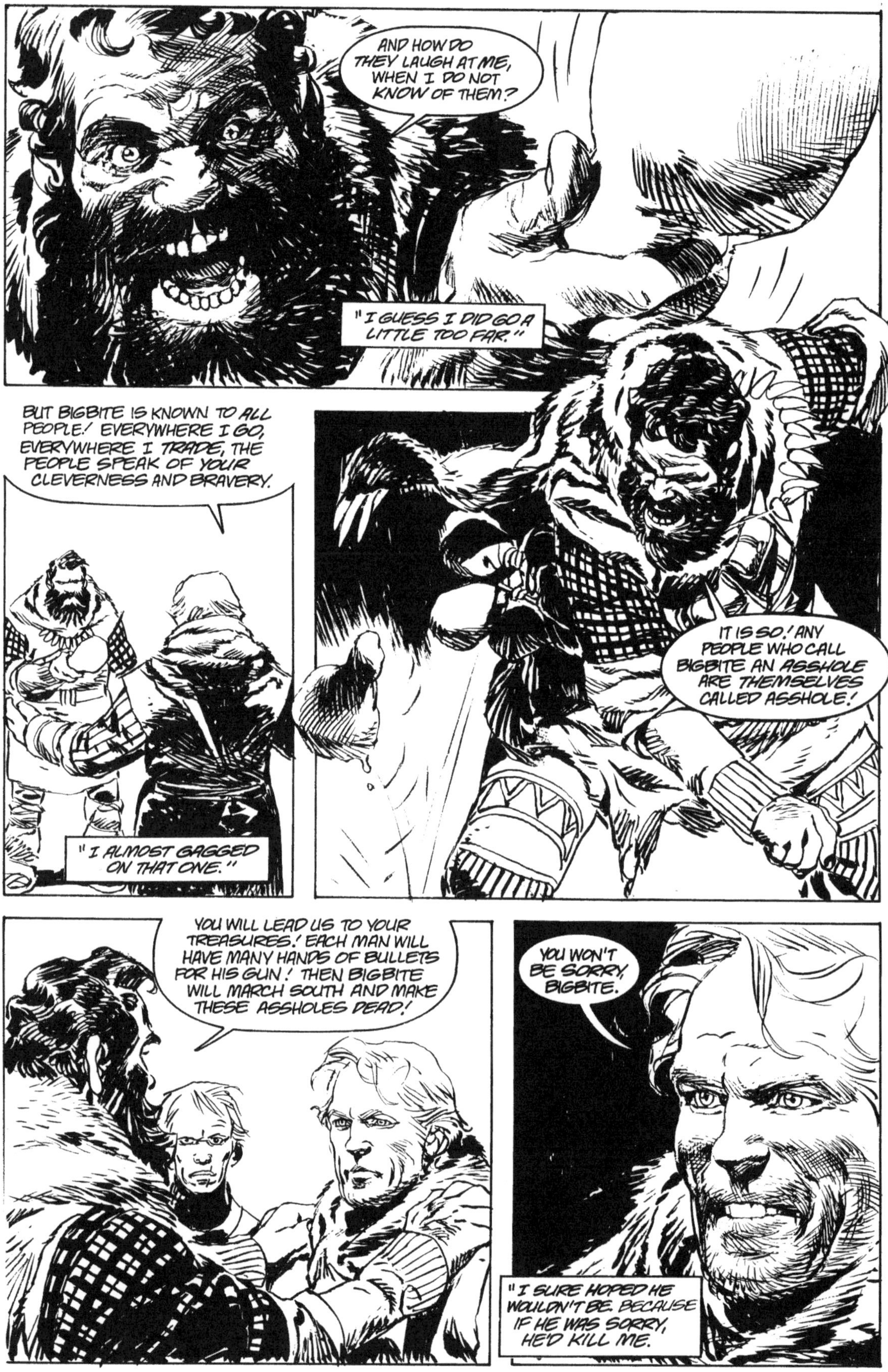
AND HOW DO THEY LAUGH AT ME, WHEN I DO NOT KNOW OF THEM?
"I GUESS I DID GO A LITTLE TOO FAR."
BUT BIGBITE IS KNOWN TO ALL PEOPLE! EVERYWHERE I GO, EVERYWHERE I TRADE, THE PEOPLE SPEAK OF YOUR CLEVERNESS AND BRAVERY.
"I ALMOST GAGGED ON THAT ONE."
IT IS SO! ANY PEOPLE WHO CALL BIGBITE AN ASSHOLE ARE THEMSELVES CALLED ASSHOLE!
YOU WILL LEAD US TO YOUR TREASURES! EACH MAN WILL HAVE MANY HANDS OF BULLETS FOR HIS GUN! THEN BIGBITE WILL MARCH SOUTH AND MAKE THESE ASSHOLES DEAD!
YOU WON'T BE SORRY, BIGBITE.
"I SURE HOPED HE WOULDN'T BE. BECAUSE IF HE WAS SORRY, HE'D KILL ME.

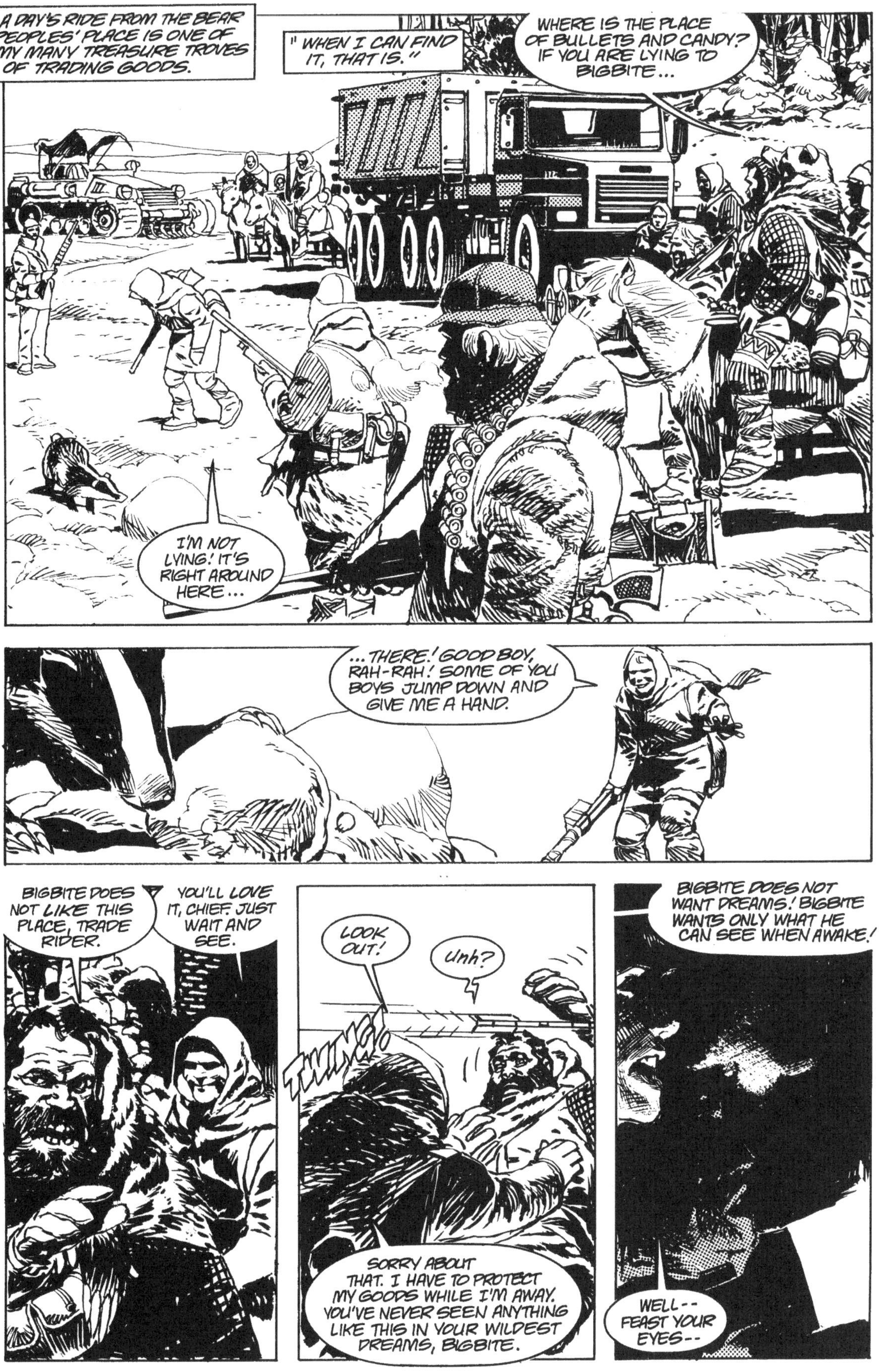
"A DAY'S RIDE FROM THE BEAR PEOPLES' PLACE IS ONE OF MY MANY TREASURE TROVES OF TRADING GOODS.
"WHEN I CAN FIND IT, THAT IS."
WHERE IS THE PLACE OF BULLETS AND CANDY? IF YOU ARE LYING TO BIGBITE...
I'M NOT LYING! IT'S RIGHT AROUND HERE...
...THERE! GOOD BOY, RAH-RAH! SOME OF YOU BOYS JUMP DOWN AND GIVE ME A HAND.
BIGBITE DOES NOT LIKE THIS PLACE, TRADE RIDER.
YOU'LL LOVE IT, CHIEF. JUST WAIT AND SEE.
LOOK OUT!
Unh?
TWING!
SORRY ABOUT THAT. I HAVE TO PROTECT MY GOODS WHILE I'M AWAY. YOU'VE NEVER SEEN ANYTHING LIKE THIS IN YOUR WILDEST DREAMS, BIGBITE.
BIGBITE DOES NOT WANT DREAMS! BIGBITE WANTS ONLY WHAT HE CAN SEE WHEN AWAKE!
WELL-- FEAST YOUR EYES--

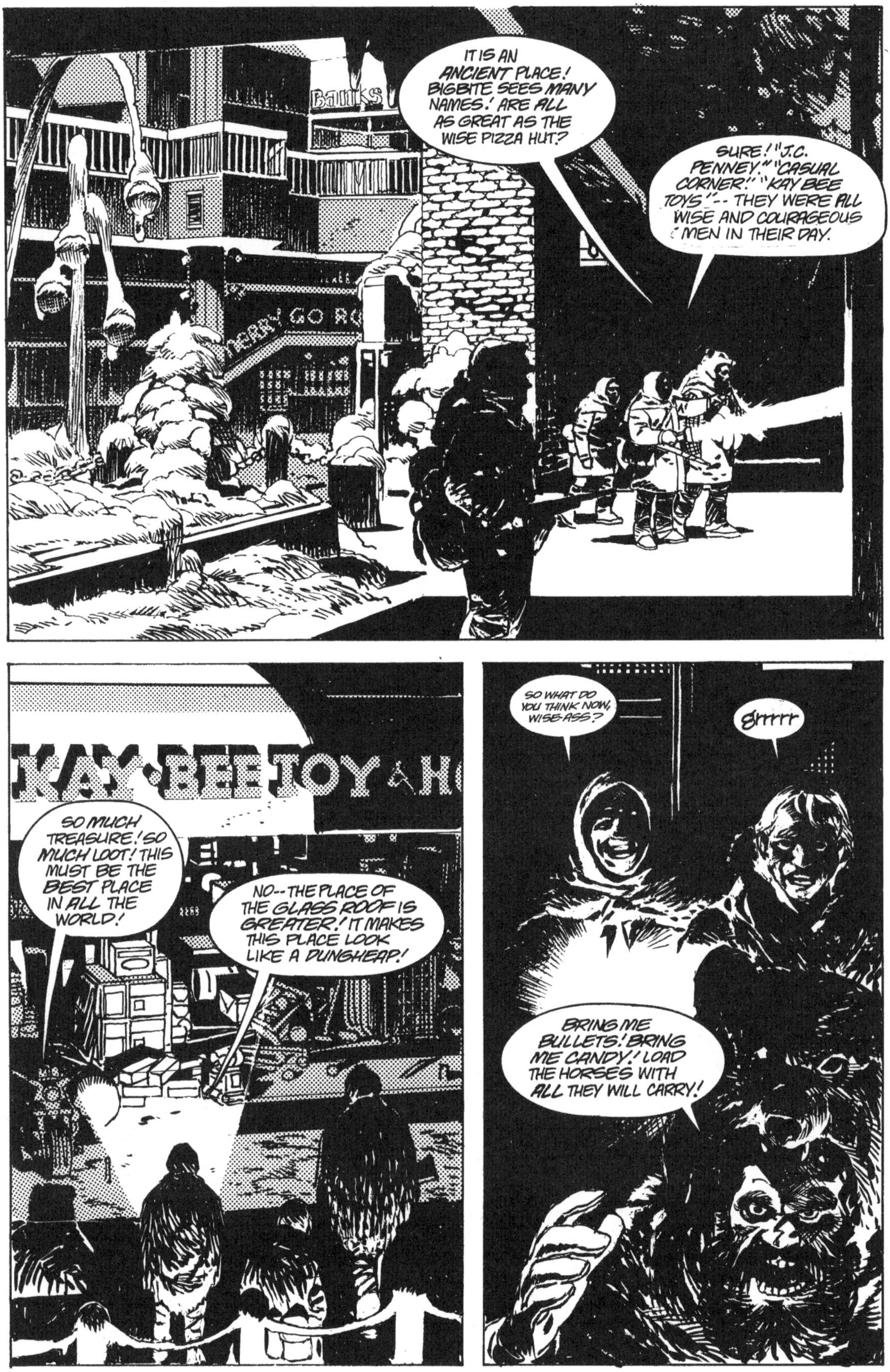
Banks
IT IS AN ANCIENT PLACE! BIGBITE SEES MANY NAMES! ARE ALL AS GREAT AS THE WISE PIZZA HUT?
SURE! "J.C. PENNEY," "CASUAL CORNER!" "KAY BEE TOYS"-- THEY WERE ALL WISE AND COURAGEOUS MEN IN THEIR DAY.
KAY BEE TOY
SO MUCH TREASURE! SO MUCH LOOT! THIS MUST BE THE BEST PLACE IN ALL THE WORLD!
NO--THE PLACE OF THE GLASS ROOF IS GREATER! IT MAKES THIS PLACE LOOK LIKE A DUNGHEAP!
SO WHAT DO YOU THINK NOW, WISE-ASS?
Grrrrr
BRING ME BULLETS! BRING ME CANDY! LOAD THE HORSES WITH ALL THEY WILL CARRY!

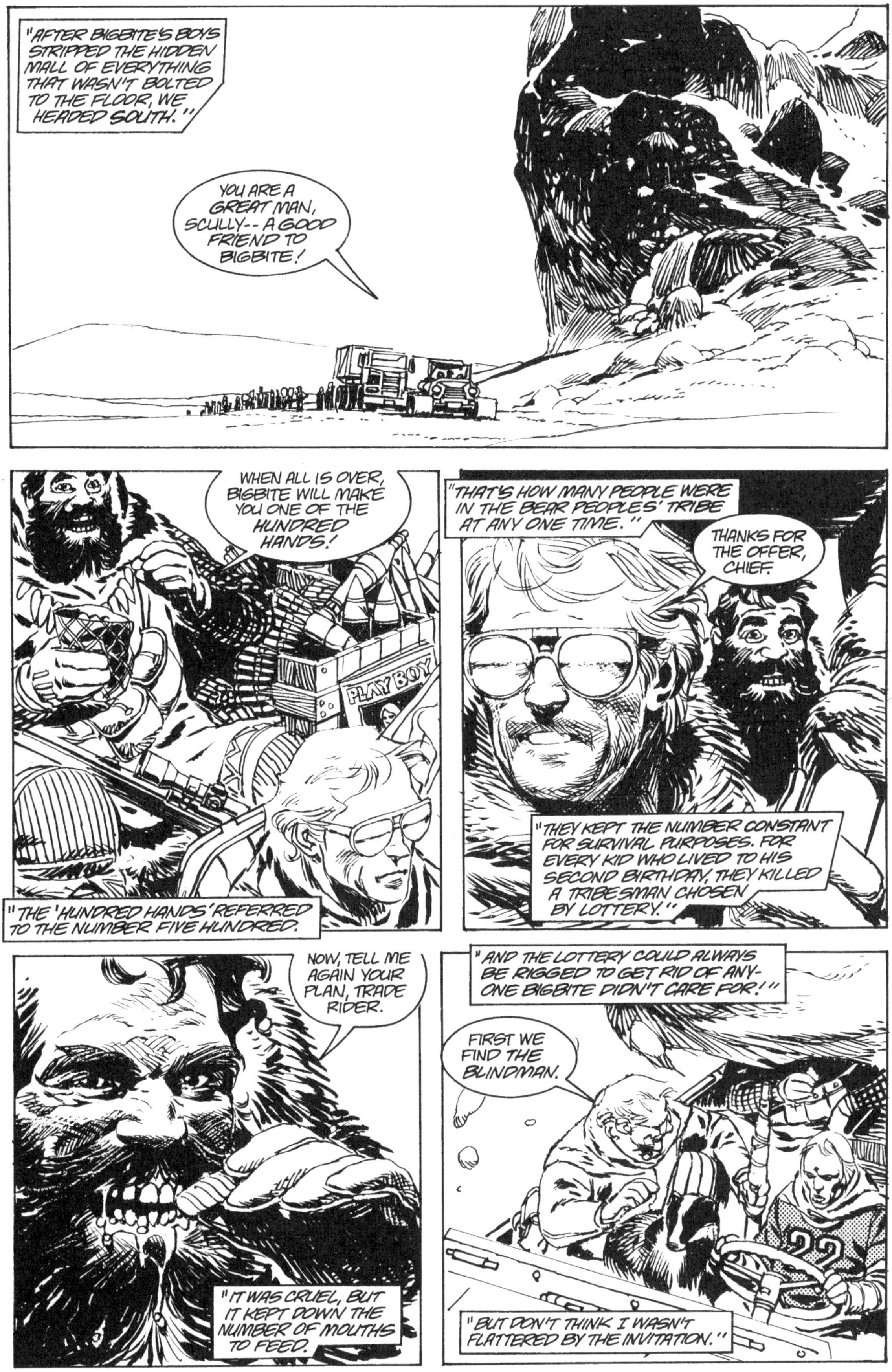
"AFTER BIGBITE'S BOYS STRIPPED THE HIDDEN MALL OF EVERYTHING THAT WASN'T BOLTED TO THE FLOOR, WE HEADED SOUTH."
YOU ARE A GREAT MAN, SCULLY-- A GOOD FRIEND TO BIGBITE!
WHEN ALL IS OVER, BIGBITE WILL MAKE YOU ONE OF THE HUNDRED HANDS!
PLAYBOY
"THE 'HUNDRED HANDS' REFERRED TO THE NUMBER FIVE HUNDRED.
"THAT'S HOW MANY PEOPLE WERE IN THE BEAR PEOPLES' TRIBE AT ANY ONE TIME."
THANKS FOR THE OFFER, CHIEF.
"THEY KEPT THE NUMBER CONSTANT FOR SURVIVAL PURPOSES. FOR EVERY KID WHO LIVED TO HIS SECOND BIRTHDAY, THEY KILLED A TRIBESMAN CHOSEN BY LOTTERY."
NOW, TELL ME AGAIN YOUR PLAN, TRADE RIDER.
"IT WAS CRUEL, BUT IT KEPT DOWN THE NUMBER OF MOUTHS TO FEED.
"AND THE LOTTERY COULD ALWAYS BE RIGGED TO GET RID OF ANY-ONE BIGBITE DIDN'T CARE FOR!"
FIRST WE FIND THE BLINDMAN.
"BUT DON'T THINK I WASN'T FLATTERED BY THE INVITATION."

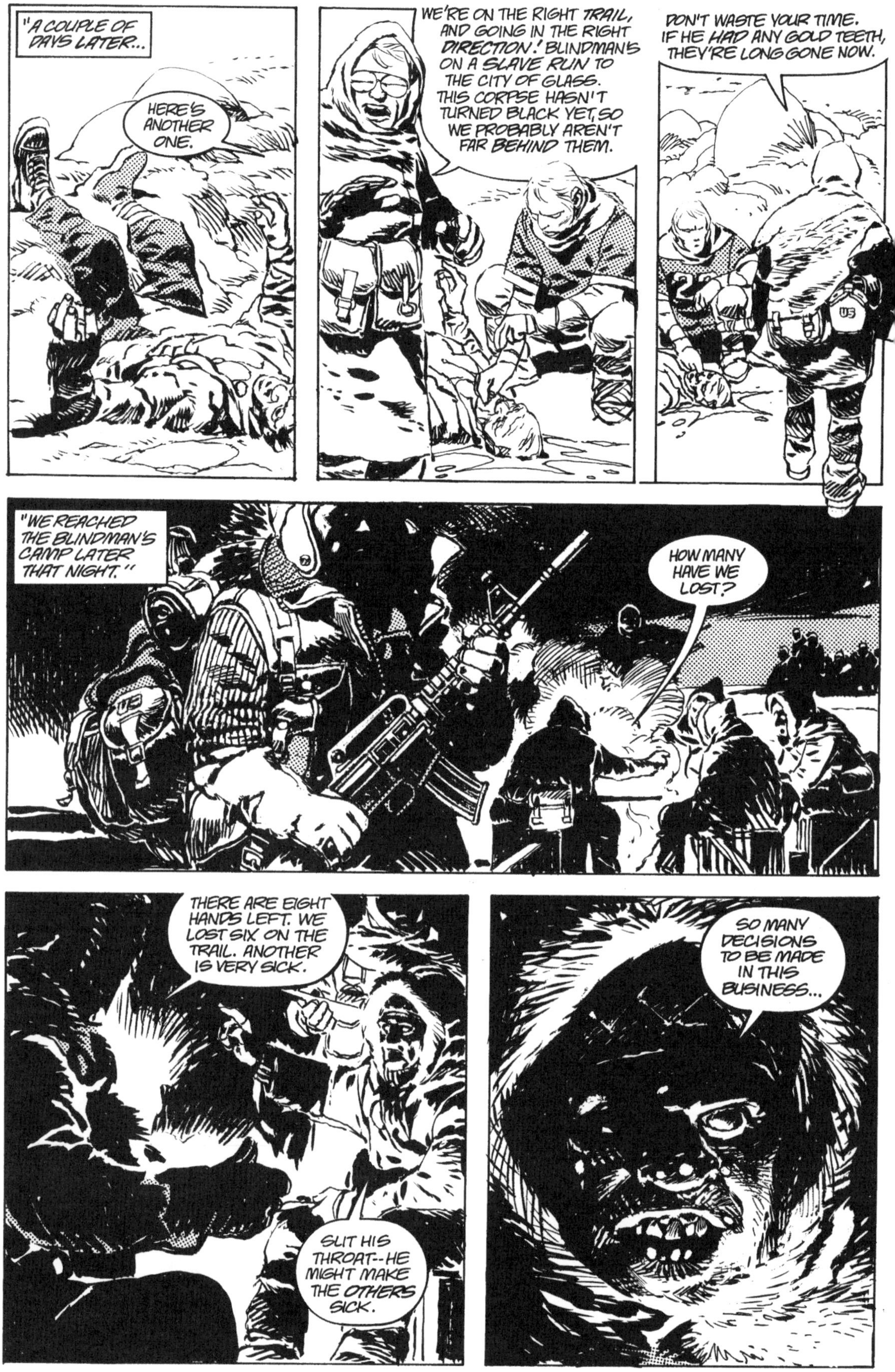
"A COUPLE OF DAYS LATER...
HERE'S ANOTHER ONE.
WE'RE ON THE RIGHT TRAIL, AND GOING IN THE RIGHT DIRECTION! BLINDMAN'S ON A SLAVE RUN TO THE CITY OF GLASS. THIS CORPSE HASN'T TURNED BLACK YET, SO WE PROBABLY AREN'T FAR BEHIND THEM.
DON'T WASTE YOUR TIME. IF HE HAD ANY GOLD TEETH, THEY'RE LONG GONE NOW.
"WE REACHED THE BLINDMAN'S CAMP LATER THAT NIGHT."
HOW MANY HAVE WE LOST?
THERE ARE EIGHT HANDS LEFT. WE LOST SIX ON THE TRAIL. ANOTHER IS VERY SICK.
SLIT HIS THROAT--HE MIGHT MAKE THE OTHERS SICK.
SO MANY DECISIONS TO BE MADE IN THIS BUSINESS...

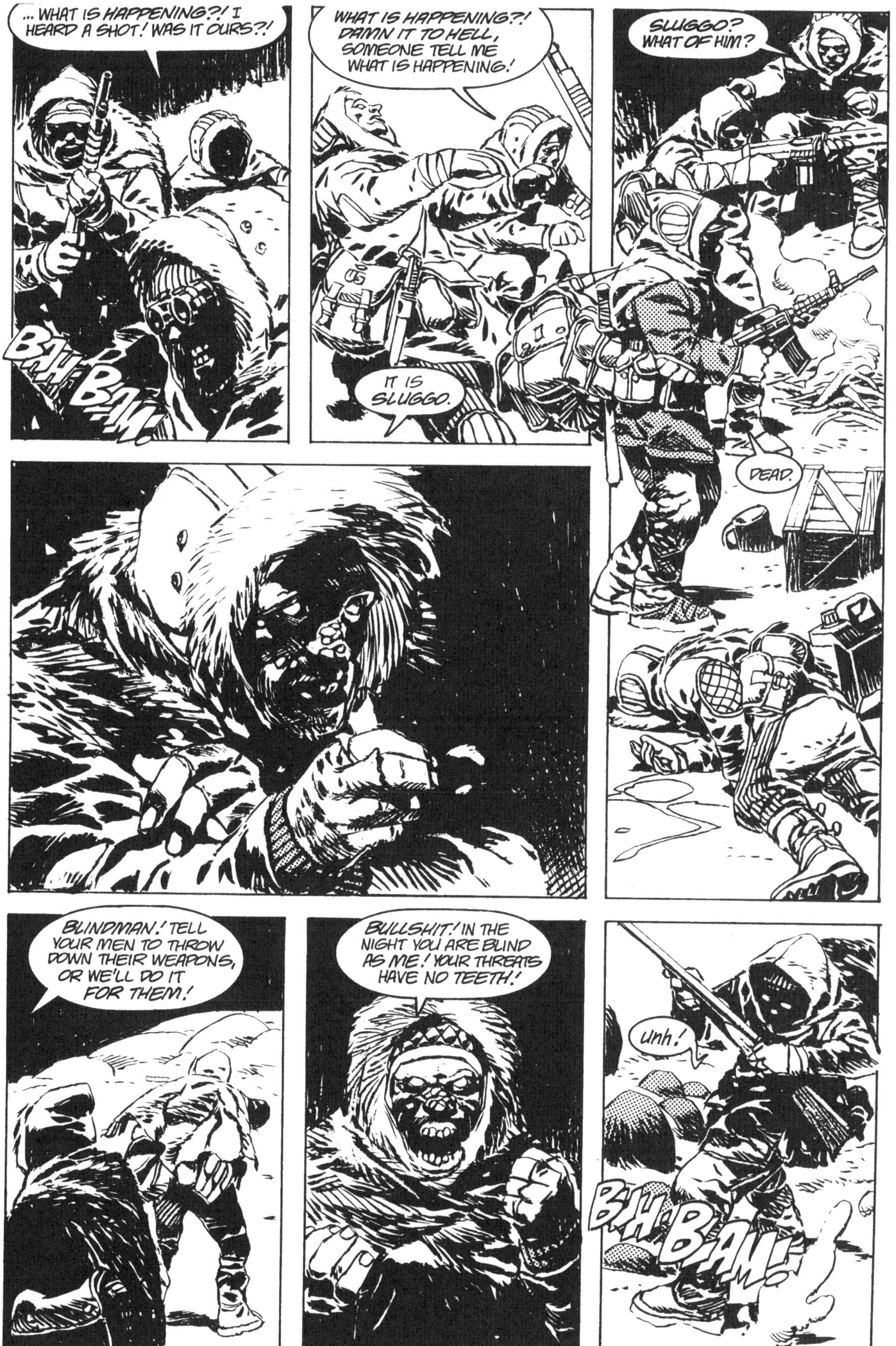
... WHAT IS HAPPENING?! I HEARD A SHOT! WAS IT OURS?!
BA-BAM!
WHAT IS HAPPENING?! DAMN IT TO HELL, SOMEONE TELL ME WHAT IS HAPPENING!
IT IS SLUGGO.
SLUGGO? WHAT OF HIM?
DEAD.
BLINDMAN! TELL YOUR MEN TO THROW DOWN THEIR WEAPONS, OR WE'LL DO IT FOR THEM!
BULLSHIT! IN THE NIGHT YOU ARE BLIND AS ME! YOUR THREATS HAVE NO TEETH!
Unh!
BA-BAM!

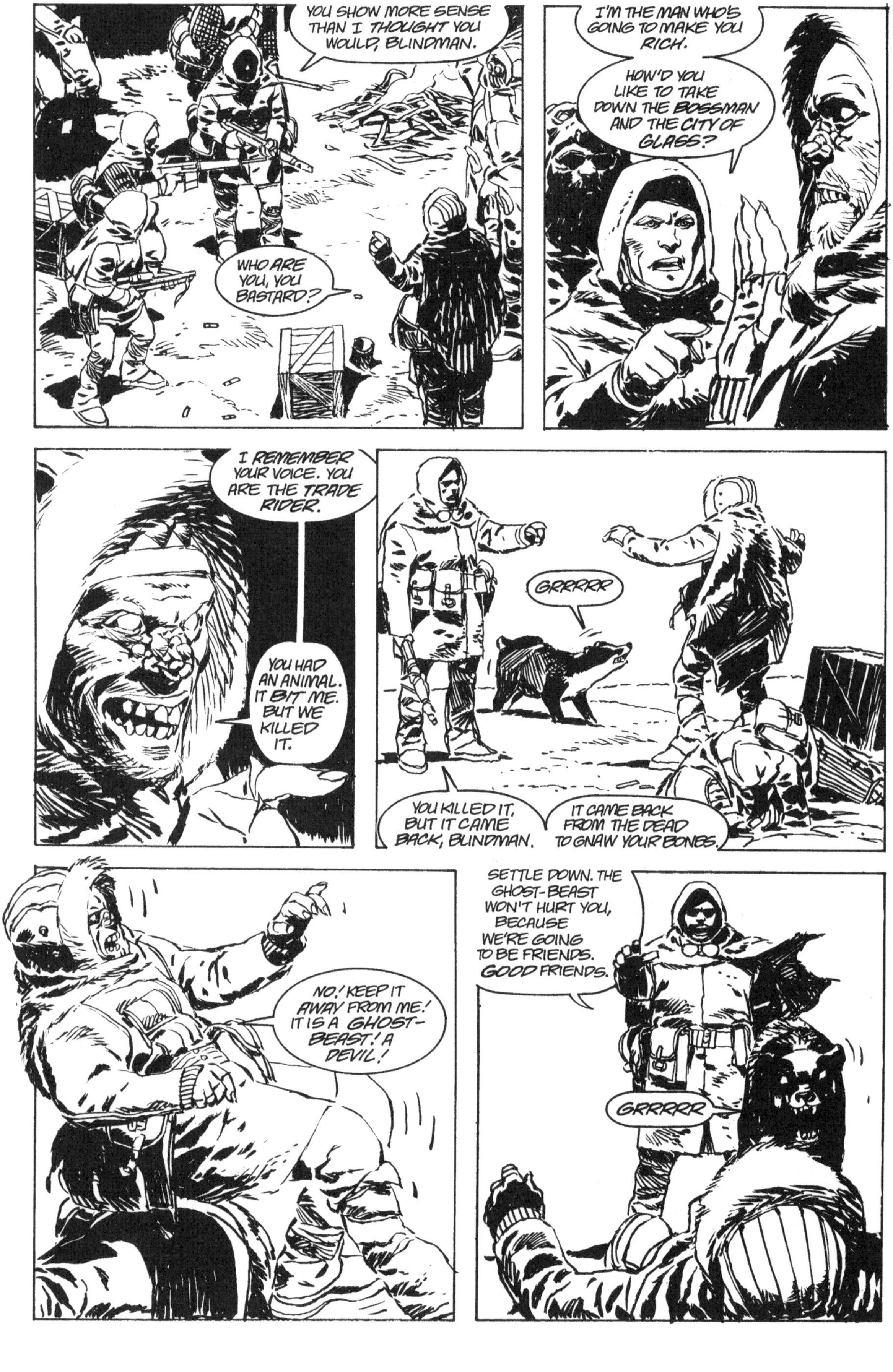
YOU SHOW MORE SENSE THAN I THOUGHT YOU WOULD, BLINDMAN.
WHO ARE YOU, YOU BASTARD?
I'M THE MAN WHO'S GOING TO MAKE YOU RICH.
HOW'D YOU LIKE TO TAKE DOWN THE BOSSMAN AND THE CITY OF GLASS?
I REMEMBER YOUR VOICE. YOU ARE THE TRADE RIDER.
YOU HAD AN ANIMAL. IT BIT ME. BUT WE KILLED IT.
GRRRRR
YOU KILLED IT, BUT IT CAME BACK, BLINDMAN.
IT CAME BACK FROM THE DEAD TO GNAW YOUR BONES.
NO! KEEP IT AWAY FROM ME! IT IS A GHOST-BEAST! A DEVIL!
SETTLE DOWN. THE GHOST-BEAST WON'T HURT YOU, BECAUSE WE'RE GOING TO BE FRIENDS. GOOD FRIENDS.
GRRRRR

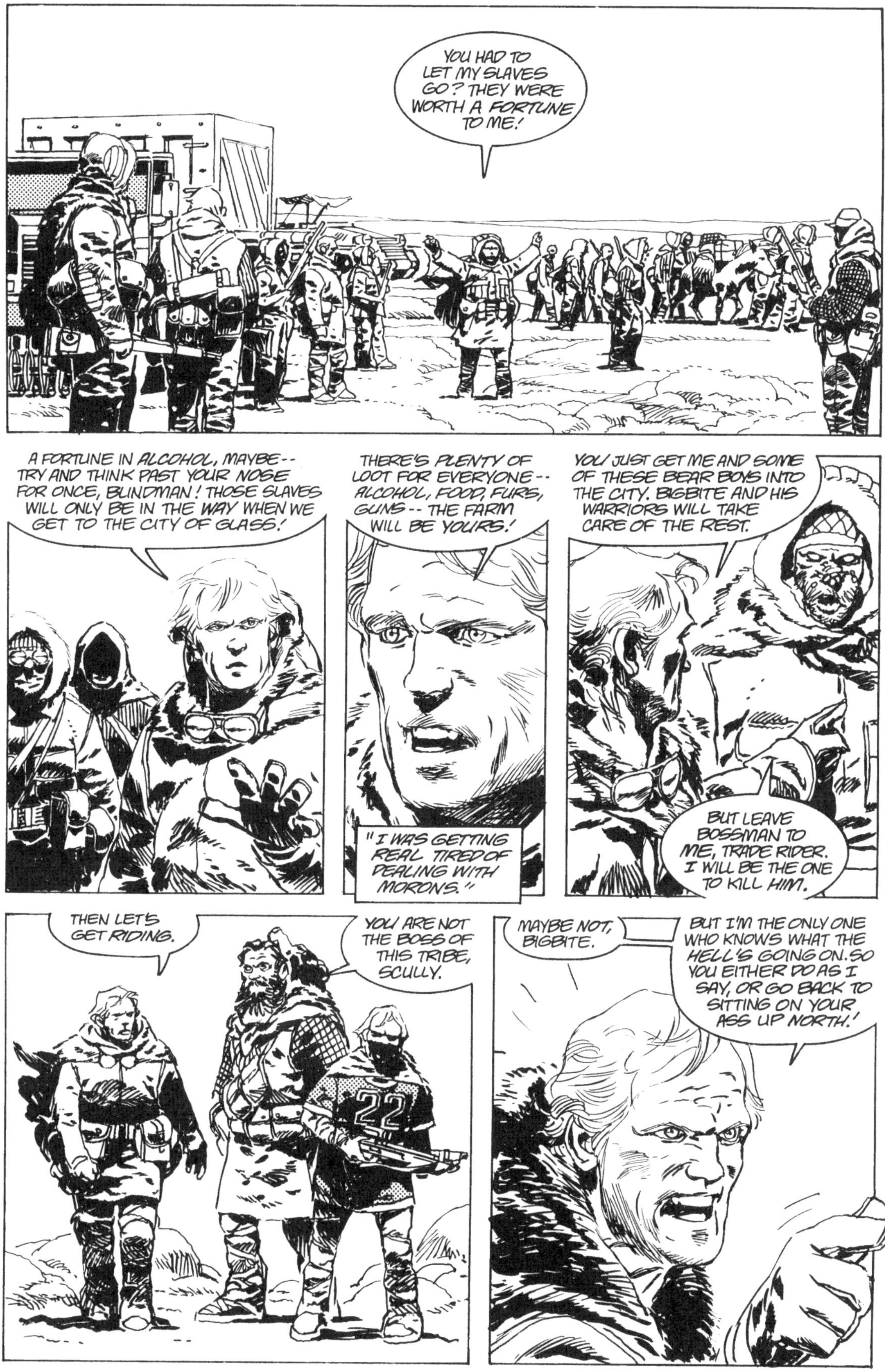
YOU HAD TO LET MY SLAVES GO? THEY WERE WORTH A FORTUNE TO ME!
A FORTUNE IN ALCOHOL, MAYBE-- TRY AND THINK PAST YOUR NOSE FOR ONCE, BLINDMAN! THOSE SLAVES WILL ONLY BE IN THE WAY WHEN WE GET TO THE CITY OF GLASS!
THERE'S PLENTY OF LOOT FOR EVERYONE-- ALCOHOL, FOOD, FURS, GUNS-- THE FARM WILL BE YOURS!
"I WAS GETTING REAL TIRED OF DEALING WITH MORONS."
YOU JUST GET ME AND SOME OF THESE BEAR BOYS INTO THE CITY. BIGBITE AND HIS WARRIORS WILL TAKE CARE OF THE REST.
BUT LEAVE BOSSMAN TO ME, TRADE RIDER. I WILL BE THE ONE TO KILL HIM.
THEN LET'S GET RIDING.
YOU ARE NOT THE BOSS OF THIS TRIBE, SCULLY.
MAYBE NOT, BIGBITE.
BUT I'M THE ONLY ONE WHO KNOWS WHAT THE HELL'S GOING ON. SO YOU EITHER DO AS I SAY, OR GO BACK TO SITTING ON YOUR ASS UP NORTH!
22

"THE CITY OF GLASS CAME IN SIGHT A FEW DAYS LATER."

HO!

"I WAS BACK. I CAN'T SAY I WAS REAL HAPPY ABOUT IT."

MORE SLAVES FOR THE BOSSMAN! MORE GALLONS FOR ME!

I WANT TO SEE BOSSMAN!

GO GET WILEY.

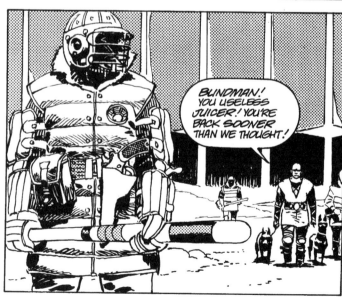

BLINDMAN! YOU USELESS JUICER! YOU'RE BACK SOONER THAN WE THOUGHT!

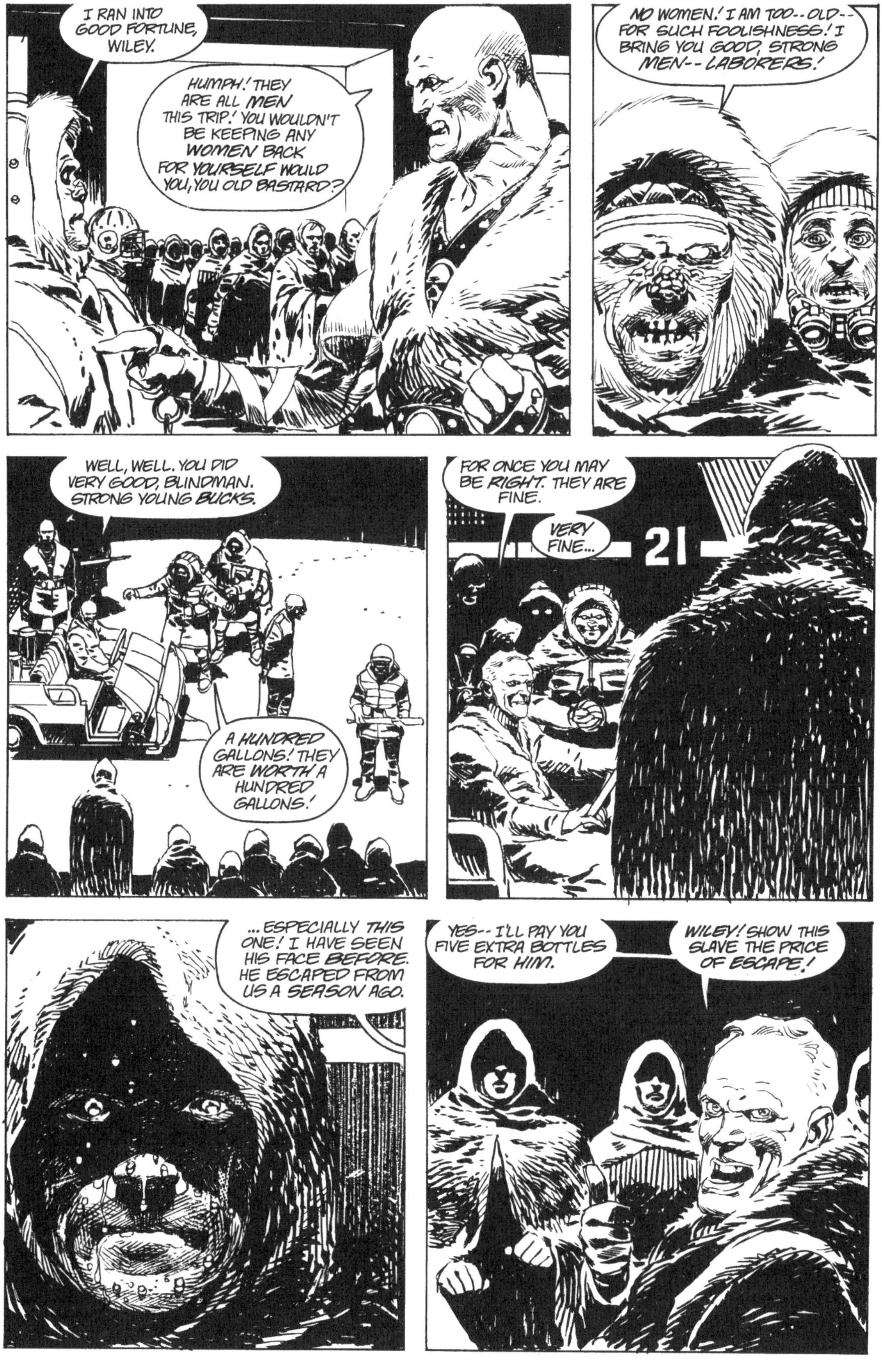

I RAN INTO GOOD FORTUNE, WILEY.
HUMPH! THEY ARE ALL MEN THIS TRIP! YOU WOULDN'T BE KEEPING ANY WOMEN BACK FOR YOURSELF WOULD YOU, YOU OLD BASTARD?
NO WOMEN! I AM TOO--OLD--FOR SUCH FOOLISHNESS! I BRING YOU GOOD, STRONG MEN--LABORERS!
WELL, WELL. YOU DID VERY GOOD, BLINDMAN. STRONG YOUNG BUCKS.
A HUNDRED GALLONS! THEY ARE WORTH A HUNDRED GALLONS!
FOR ONCE YOU MAY BE RIGHT. THEY ARE FINE.
VERY FINE...
21
...ESPECIALLY THIS ONE! I HAVE SEEN HIS FACE BEFORE. HE ESCAPED FROM US A SEASON AGO.
YES--I'LL PAY YOU FIVE EXTRA BOTTLES FOR HIM.
WILEY! SHOW THIS SLAVE THE PRICE OF ESCAPE!

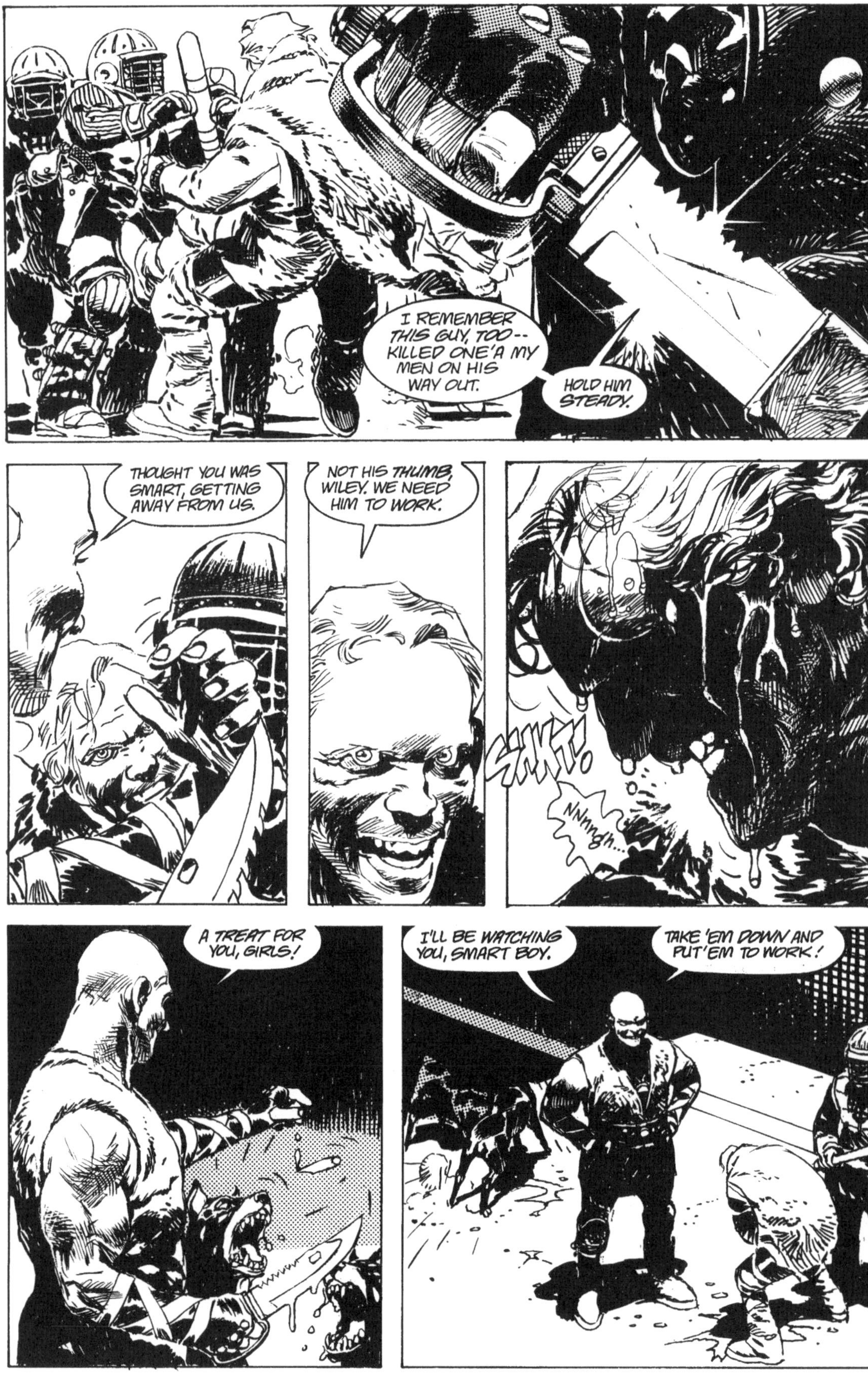
I REMEMBER THIS GUY, TOO-- KILLED ONE'A MY MEN ON HIS WAY OUT.
HOLD HIM STEADY.
THOUGHT YOU WAS SMART, GETTING AWAY FROM US.
NOT HIS THUMB, WILEY. WE NEED HIM TO WORK.
SHKT!
NNnmgh...
A TREAT FOR YOU, GIRLS!
I'LL BE WATCHING YOU, SMART BOY.
TAKE 'EM DOWN AND PUT'EM TO WORK!

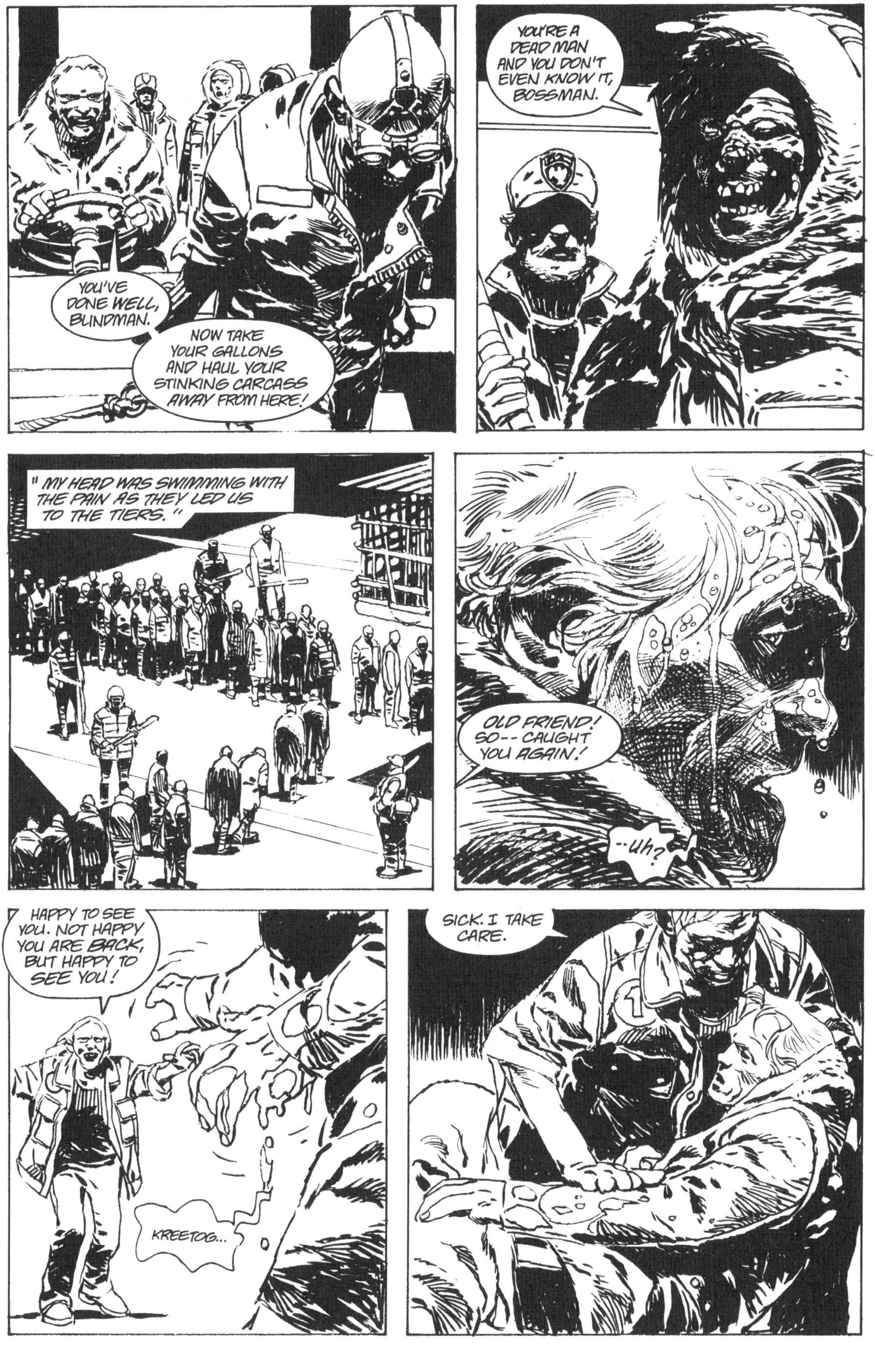
YOU'VE DONE WELL, BLINDMAN.
NOW TAKE YOUR GALLONS AND HAUL YOUR STINKING CARCASS AWAY FROM HERE!
YOU'RE A DEAD MAN AND YOU DON'T EVEN KNOW IT, BOSSMAN.
" MY HEAD WAS SWIMMING WITH THE PAIN AS THEY LED US TO THE TIERS."
OLD FRIEND! SO-- CAUGHT YOU AGAIN!
--UH?
HAPPY TO SEE YOU. NOT HAPPY YOU ARE BACK, BUT HAPPY TO SEE YOU!
KREETOG...
SICK. I TAKE CARE.

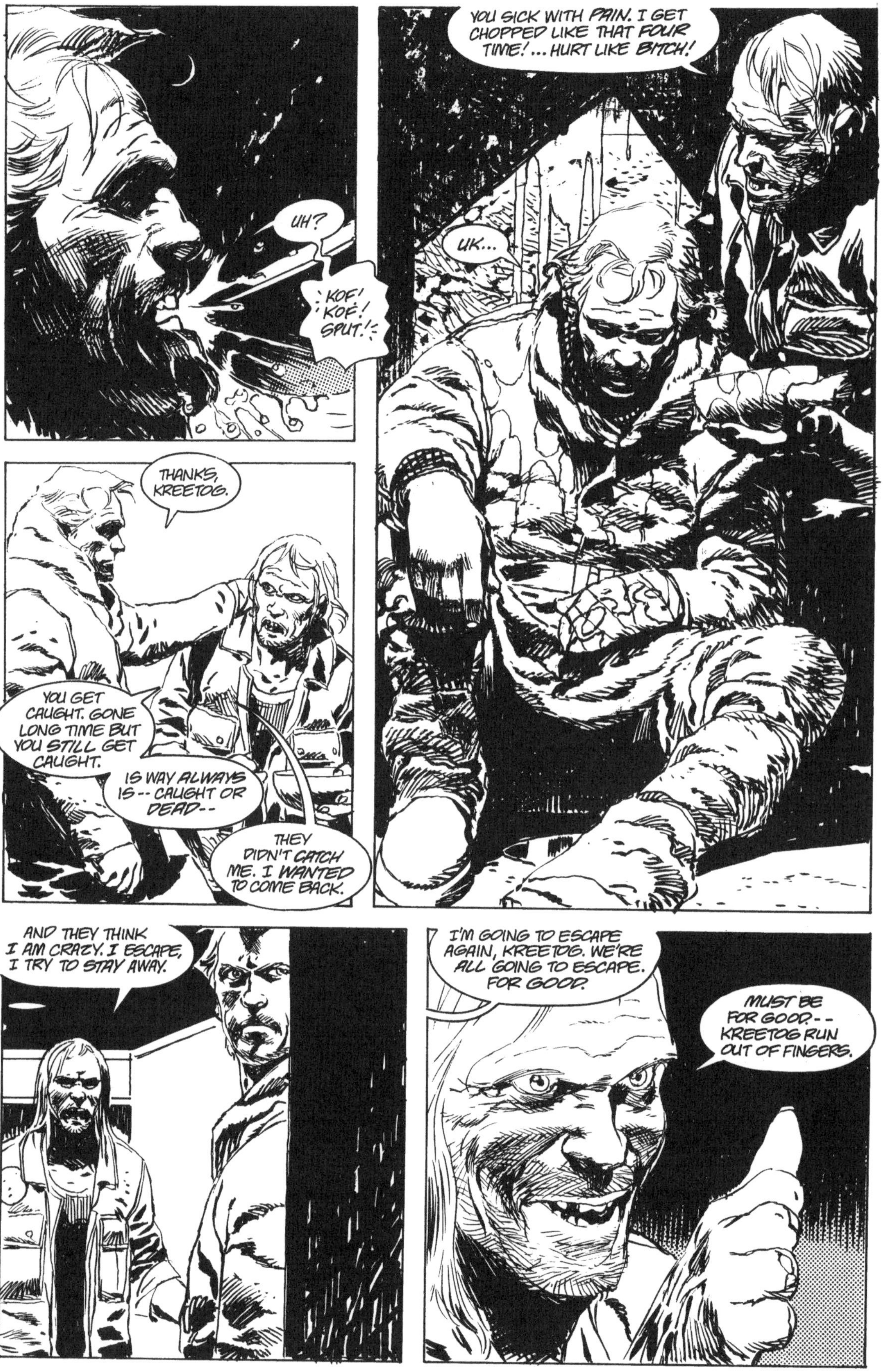
UH?
KOF! KOF! SPUT!
YOU SICK WITH PAIN. I GET CHOPPED LIKE THAT FOUR TIME! ... HURT LIKE BITCH!
UK...
THANKS, KREETOG.
YOU GET CAUGHT. GONE LONG TIME BUT YOU STILL GET CAUGHT.
IS WAY ALWAYS IS -- CAUGHT OR DEAD--
THEY DIDN'T CATCH ME. I WANTED TO COME BACK.
AND THEY THINK I AM CRAZY. I ESCAPE, I TRY TO STAY AWAY.
I'M GOING TO ESCAPE AGAIN, KREETOG. WE'RE ALL GOING TO ESCAPE. FOR GOOD.
MUST BE FOR GOOD-- KREETOG RUN OUT OF FINGERS.

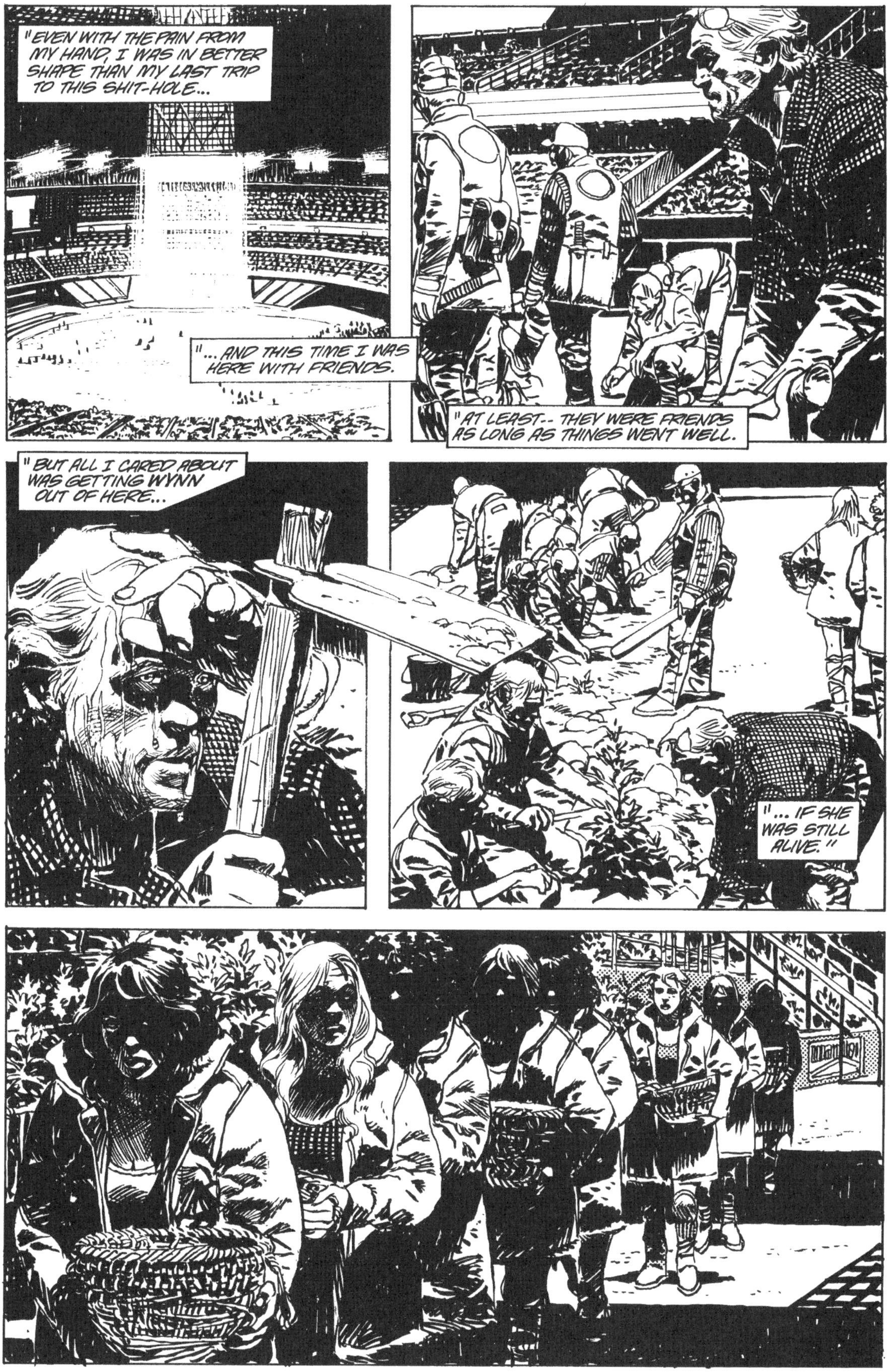
"EVEN WITH THE PAIN FROM MY HAND, I WAS IN BETTER SHAPE THAN MY LAST TRIP TO THIS SHIT-HOLE...
"...AND THIS TIME I WAS HERE WITH FRIENDS.
"AT LEAST-- THEY WERE FRIENDS AS LONG AS THINGS WENT WELL.
"BUT ALL I CARED ABOUT WAS GETTING WYNN OUT OF HERE...
"...IF SHE WAS STILL ALIVE."

END OF PART TWO

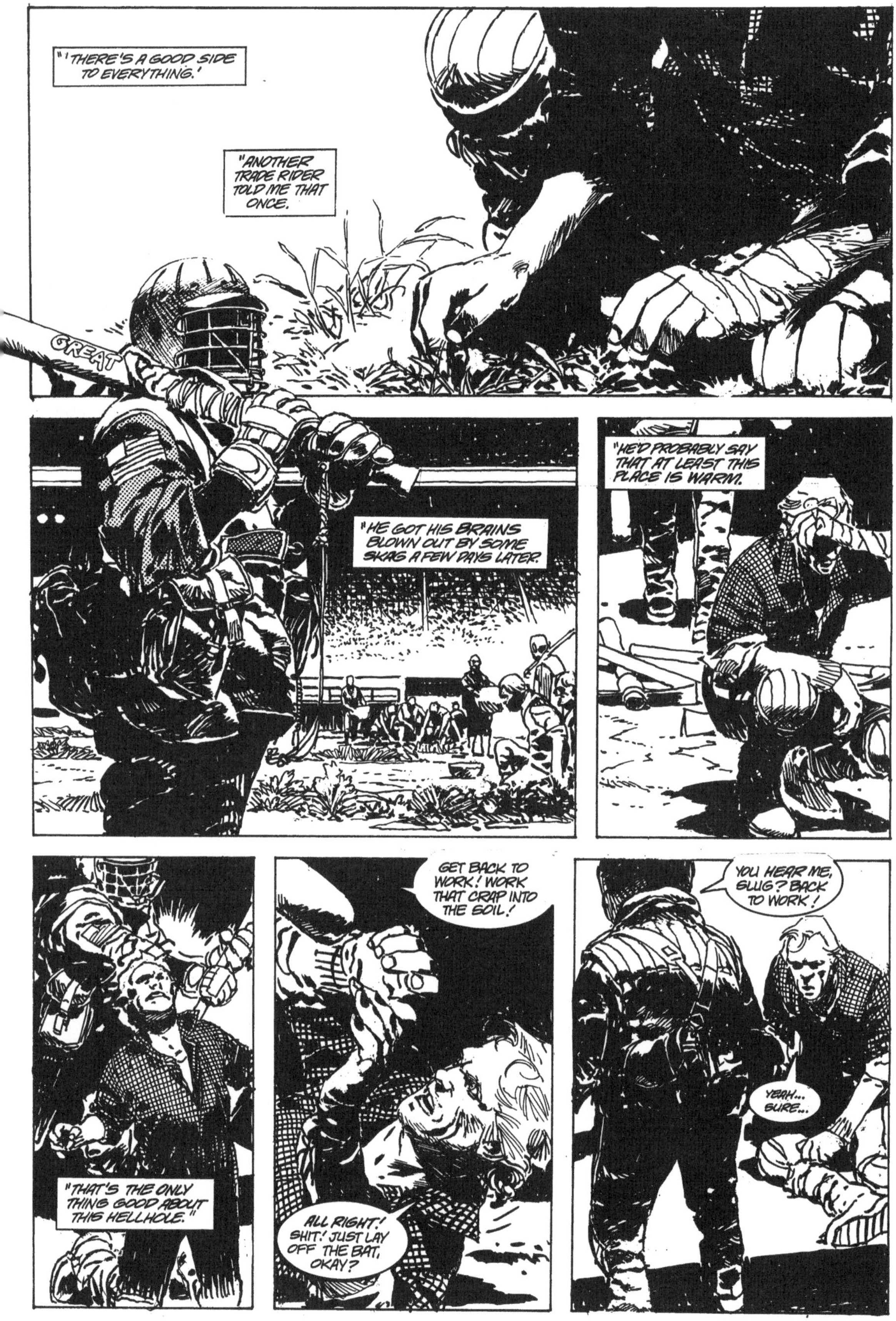
"'THERE'S A GOOD SIDE TO EVERYTHING.'
"ANOTHER TRADE RIDER TOLD ME THAT ONCE.
GREAT
"HE GOT HIS BRAINS BLOWN OUT BY SOME SKAG A FEW DAYS LATER.
"HE'D PROBABLY SAY THAT AT LEAST THIS PLACE IS WARM.
"THAT'S THE ONLY THING GOOD ABOUT THIS HELLHOLE."
GET BACK TO WORK! WORK THAT CRAP INTO THE SOIL!
ALL RIGHT! SHIT! JUST LAY OFF THE BAT, OKAY?
YOU HEAR ME, SLUG? BACK TO WORK!
YEAH... SURE...

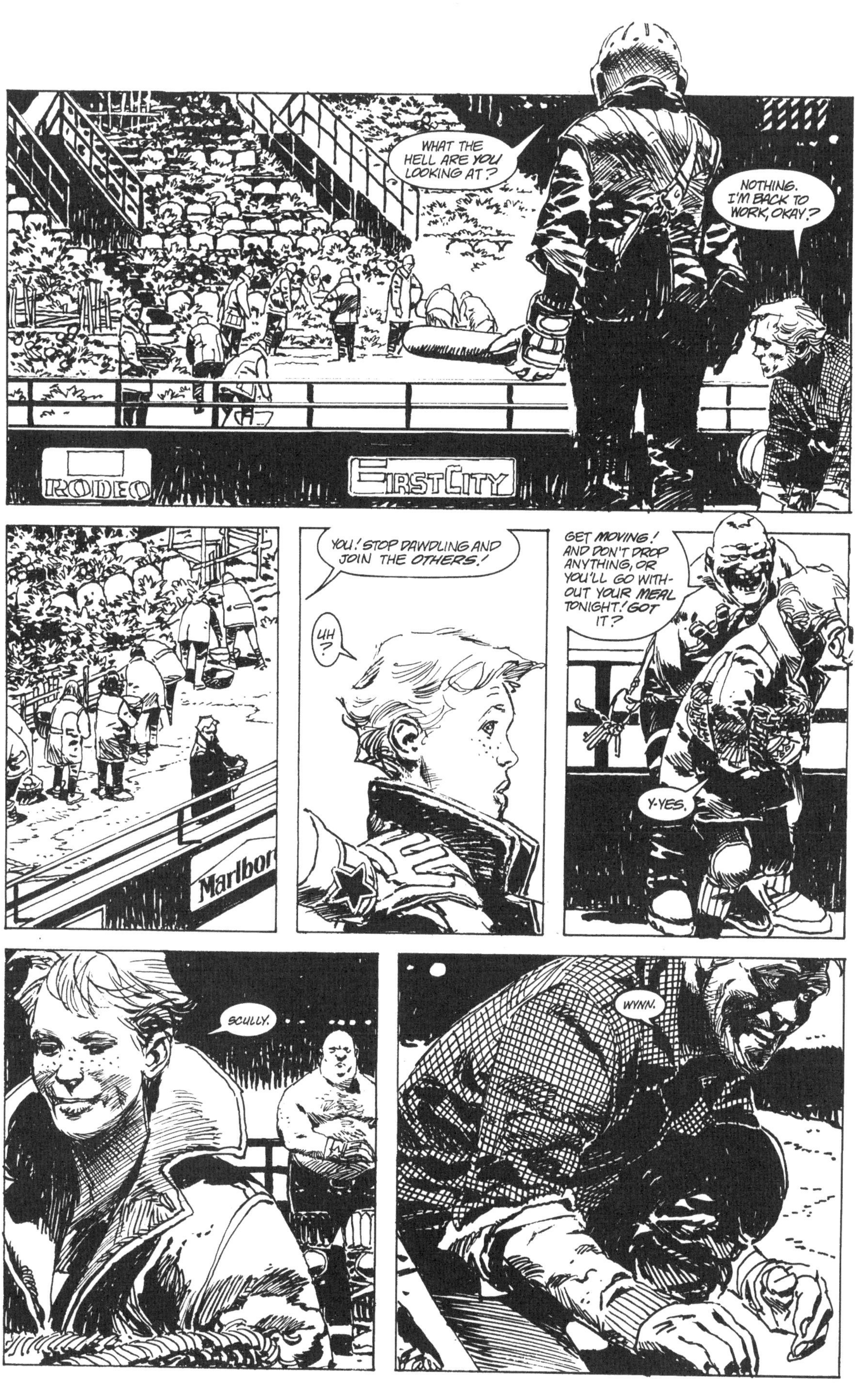

WHAT THE HELL ARE YOU LOOKING AT?
NOTHING. I'M BACK TO WORK, OKAY?
RODEO
FIRST CITY
Marlbor
YOU! STOP DAWDLING AND JOIN THE OTHERS!
UH?
GET MOVING! AND DON'T DROP ANYTHING, OR YOU'LL GO WITHOUT YOUR MEAL TONIGHT! GOT IT?
Y-YES.
SCULLY.
WYNN.

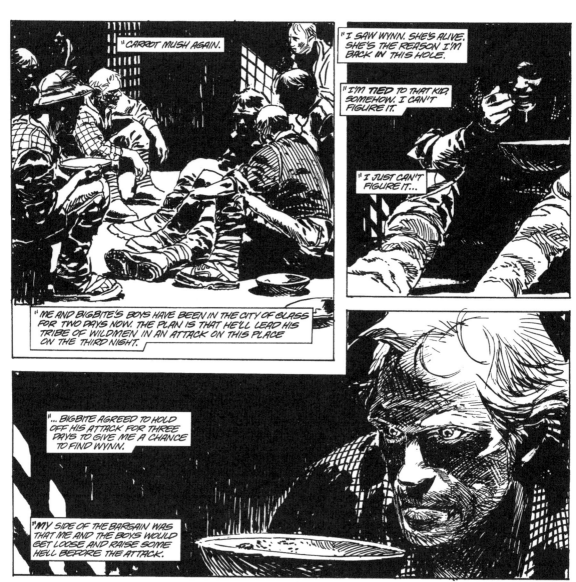

"CARROT MUSH AGAIN.

"ME AND BIGBITE'S BOYS HAVE BEEN IN THE CITY OF GLASS FOR TWO DAYS NOW. THE PLAN IS THAT HE'LL LEAD HIS TRIBE OF WILDMEN IN AN ATTACK ON THIS PLACE ON THE THIRD NIGHT.

"I SAW WYNN. SHE'S ALIVE. SHE'S THE REASON I'M BACK IN THIS HOLE.

"I'M TIED TO THAT KID, SOMEHOW. I CAN'T FIGURE IT.

"I JUST CAN'T FIGURE IT...

"...BIGBITE AGREED TO HOLD OFF HIS ATTACK FOR THREE DAYS TO GIVE ME A CHANCE TO FIND WYNN.

"MY SIDE OF THE BARGAIN WAS THAT ME AND THE BOYS WOULD GET LOOSE AND RAISE SOME HELL BEFORE THE ATTACK.

"AFTER THREE DAYS OF NOTHING BUT VEGETABLE PORRIDGE, THESE GUYS WERE MORE THAN READY FOR SOME WHOLESALE DESTRUCTION.

"ALL WE HAD TO DO WAS PUT UP WITH ONE MORE DAY OF COW DUNG AND CORN STALKS.

"SHOULDN'T BE TOO HARD. AT LEAST IT WAS WARM HERE."

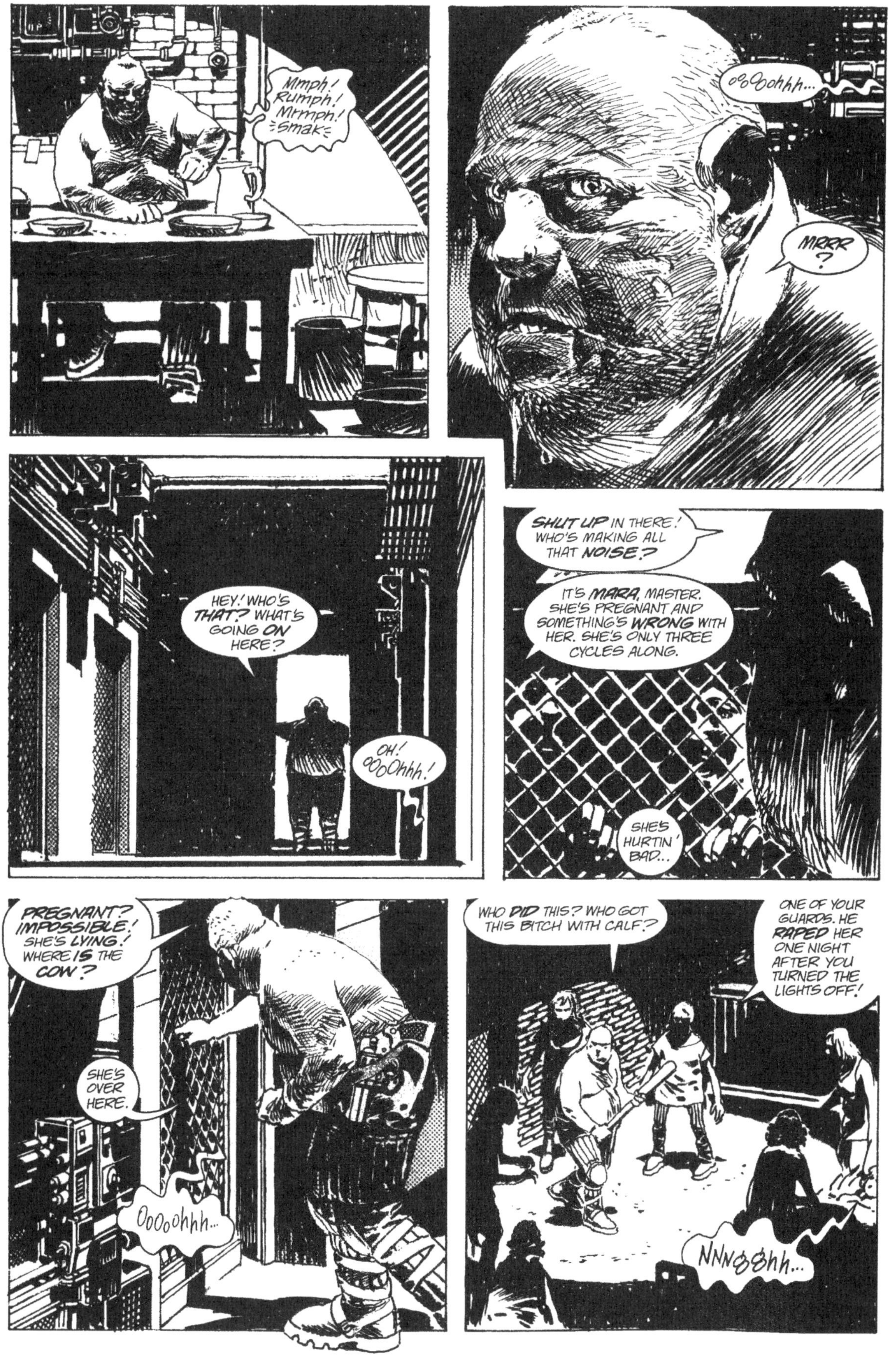
Mmph! Rumph! Mrmph! Smak
oo0ohhh...
MRRR ?
HEY! WHO'S THAT? WHAT'S GOING ON HERE?
OH! oooOhhh!
SHUT UP IN THERE! WHO'S MAKING ALL THAT NOISE?
IT'S MARA, MASTER. SHE'S PREGNANT AND SOMETHING'S WRONG WITH HER. SHE'S ONLY THREE CYCLES ALONG.
SHE'S HURTIN' BAD...
PREGNANT? IMPOSSIBLE! SHE'S LYING! WHERE IS THE COW?
SHE'S OVER HERE.
Ooooohhh...
WHO DID THIS? WHO GOT THIS BITCH WITH CALF?
ONE OF YOUR GUARDS. HE RAPED HER ONE NIGHT AFTER YOU TURNED THE LIGHTS OFF!
NNNooohh...

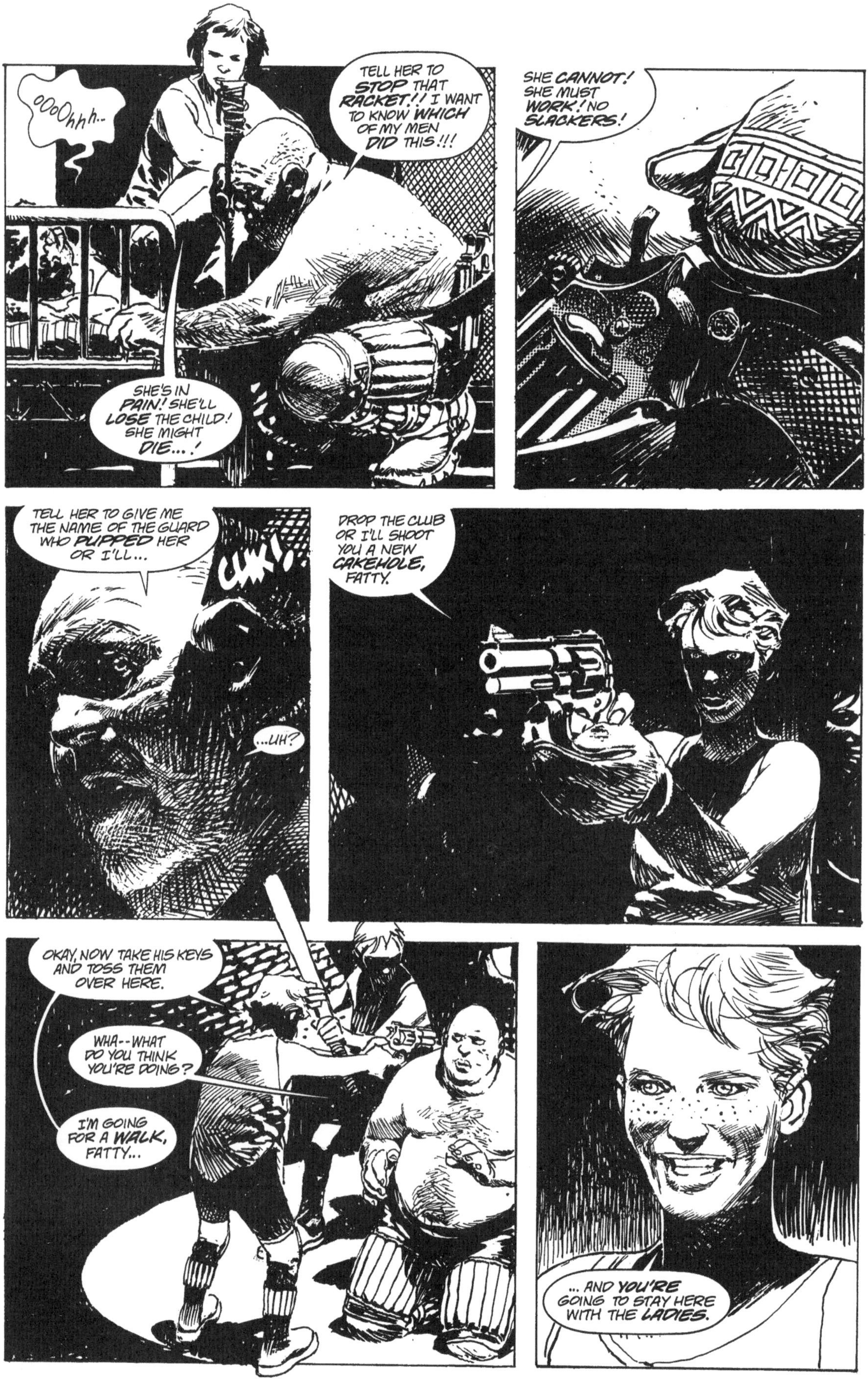
oOoOhhh...
TELL HER TO STOP THAT RACKET!! I WANT TO KNOW WHICH OF MY MEN DID THIS!!!
SHE'S IN PAIN! SHE'LL LOSE THE CHILD! SHE MIGHT DIE...!
SHE CANNOT! SHE MUST WORK! NO SLACKERS!
TELL HER TO GIVE ME THE NAME OF THE GUARD WHO PUPPED HER OR I'LL...
CLIK!
...UH?
DROP THE CLUB OR I'LL SHOOT YOU A NEW CAKEHOLE, FATTY.
OKAY, NOW TAKE HIS KEYS AND TOSS THEM OVER HERE.
WHA--WHAT DO YOU THINK YOU'RE DOING?
I'M GOING FOR A WALK, FATTY...
... AND YOU'RE GOING TO STAY HERE WITH THE LADIES.

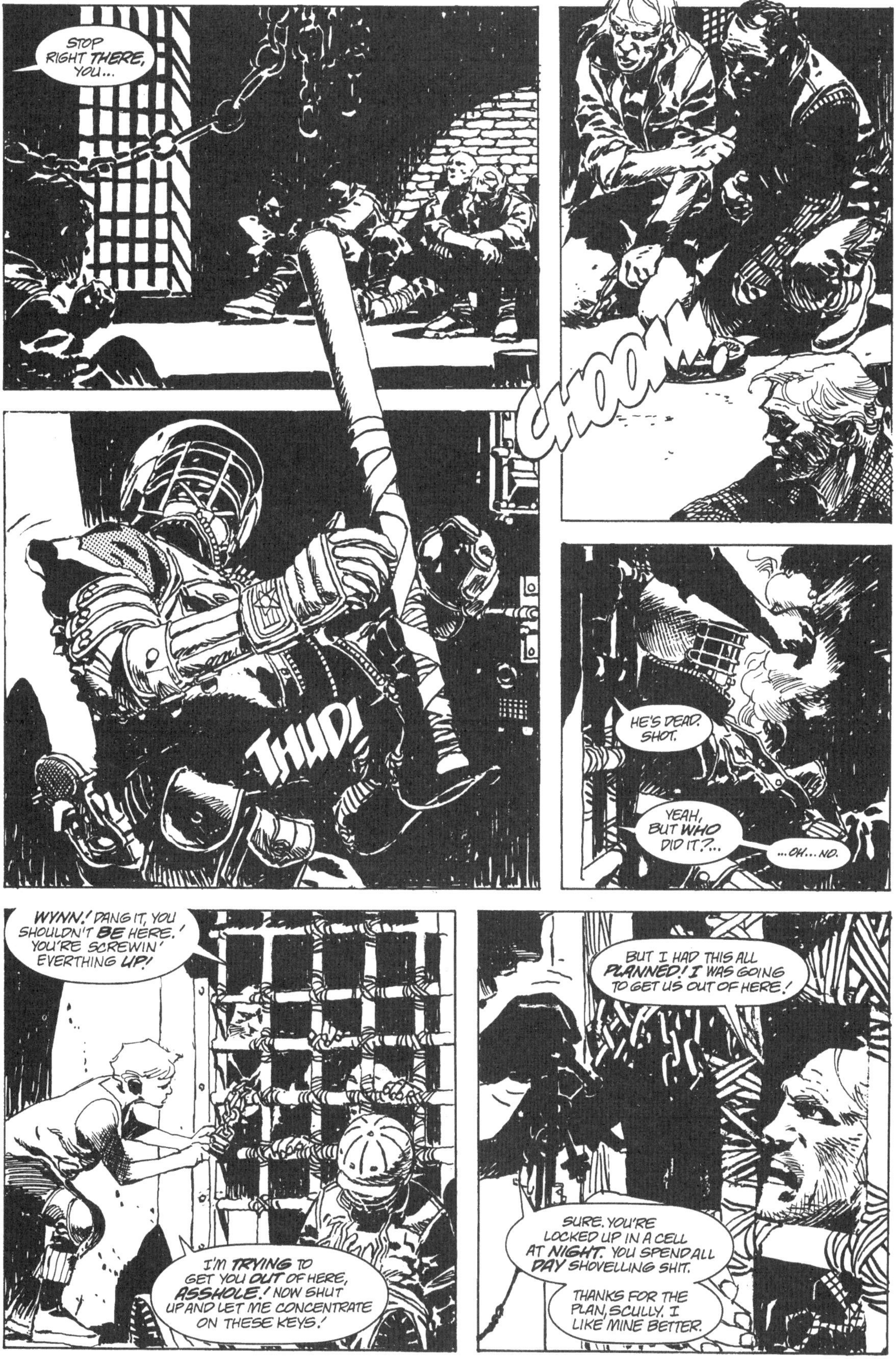

STOP RIGHT THERE, YOU...
CHOOM
THUD!
HE'S DEAD. SHOT.
YEAH, BUT WHO DID IT?...
...OH... NO.
WYNN! DANG IT, YOU SHOULDN'T BE HERE! YOU'RE SCREWIN' EVERTHING UP!
I'M TRYING TO GET YOU OUT OF HERE, ASSHOLE! NOW SHUT UP AND LET ME CONCENTRATE ON THESE KEYS!
BUT I HAD THIS ALL PLANNED! I WAS GOING TO GET US OUT OF HERE!
SURE. YOU'RE LOCKED UP IN A CELL AT NIGHT. YOU SPEND ALL DAY SHOVELLING SHIT.
THANKS FOR THE PLAN, SCULLY. I LIKE MINE BETTER.

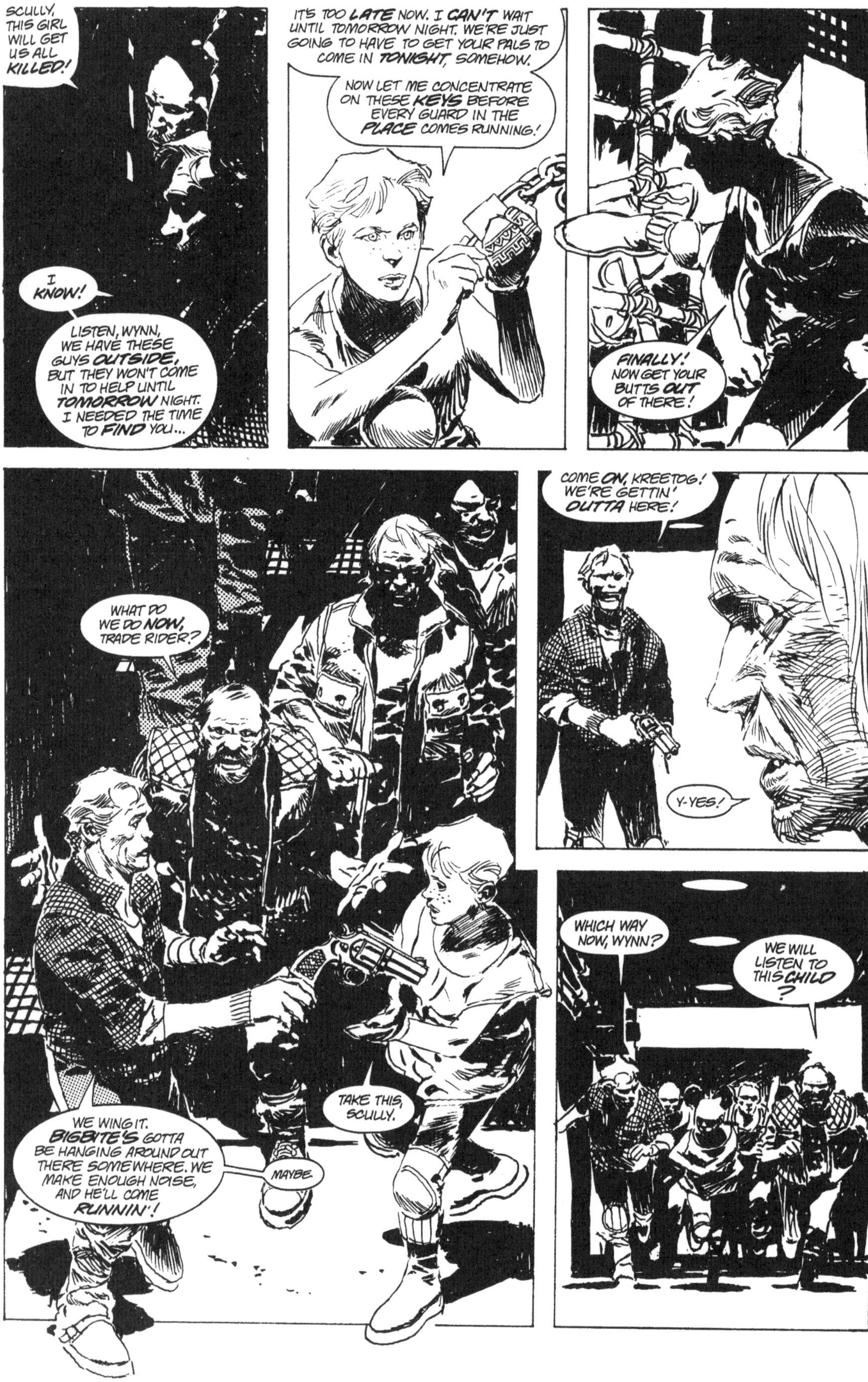
SCULLY, THIS GIRL WILL GET US ALL KILLED!
I KNOW!
LISTEN, WYNN, WE HAVE THESE GUYS OUTSIDE, BUT THEY WON'T COME IN TO HELP UNTIL TOMORROW NIGHT. I NEEDED THE TIME TO FIND YOU...
IT'S TOO LATE NOW. I CAN'T WAIT UNTIL TOMORROW NIGHT. WE'RE JUST GOING TO HAVE TO GET YOUR PALS TO COME IN TONIGHT, SOMEHOW.
NOW LET ME CONCENTRATE ON THESE KEYS BEFORE EVERY GUARD IN THE PLACE COMES RUNNING!
FINALLY! NOW GET YOUR BUTTS OUT OF THERE!
WHAT DO WE DO NOW, TRADE RIDER?
TAKE THIS, SCULLY.
WE WING IT. BIGBITE'S GOTTA BE HANGING AROUND OUT THERE SOMEWHERE. WE MAKE ENOUGH NOISE, AND HE'LL COME RUNNIN'!
MAYBE.
COME ON, KREETOG! WE'RE GETTIN' OUTTA HERE!
Y-YES!
WHICH WAY NOW, WYNN?
WE WILL LISTEN TO THIS CHILD ?

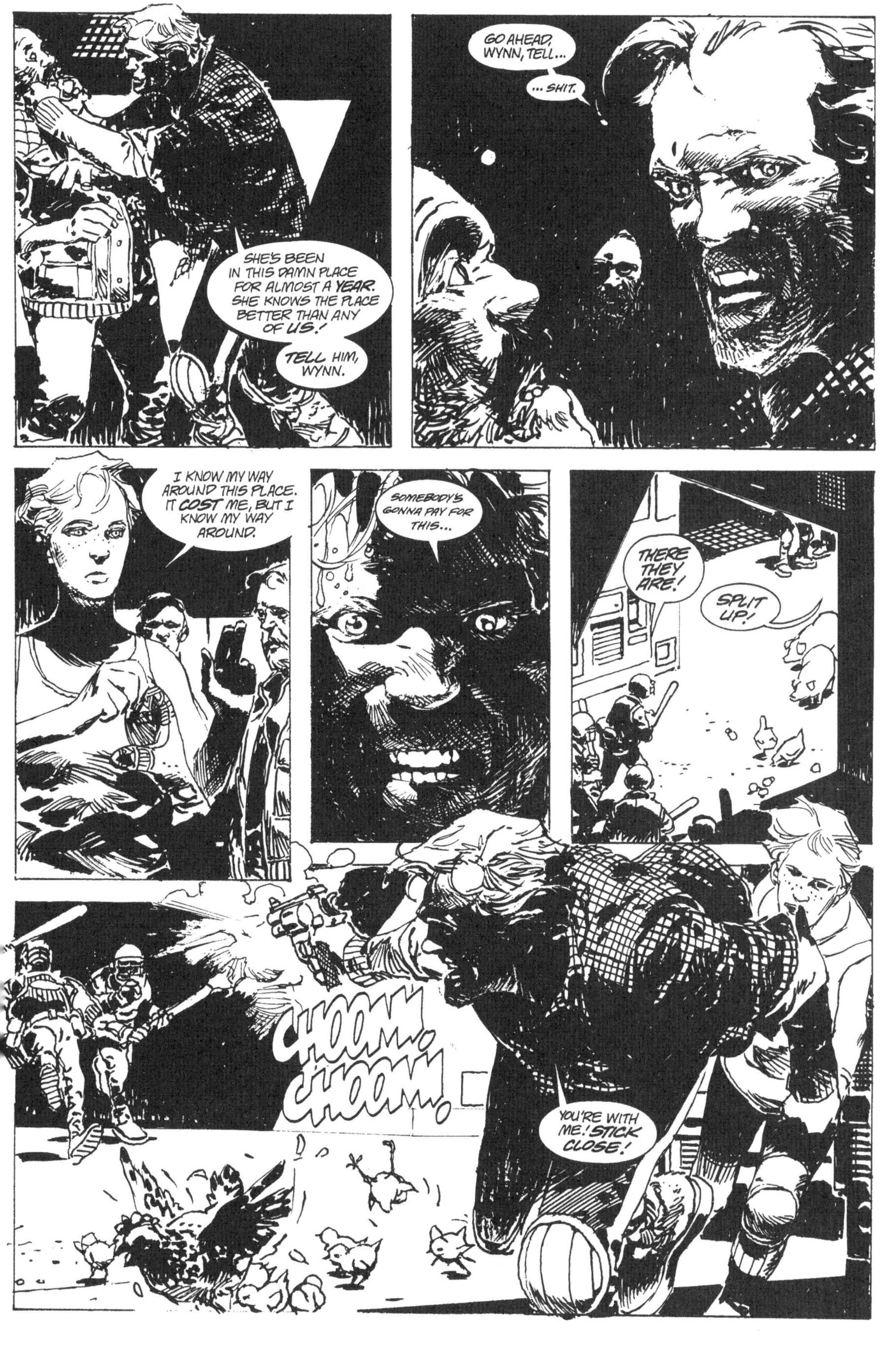
SHE'S BEEN IN THIS DAMN PLACE FOR ALMOST A YEAR. SHE KNOWS THE PLACE BETTER THAN ANY OF US!
TELL HIM, WYNN.
GO AHEAD, WYNN, TELL...
...SHIT.
I KNOW MY WAY AROUND THIS PLACE. IT COST ME, BUT I KNOW MY WAY AROUND.
SOMEBODY'S GONNA PAY FOR THIS...
THERE THEY ARE!
SPLIT UP!
CHOOM! CHOOM!
YOU'RE WITH ME! STICK CLOSE!

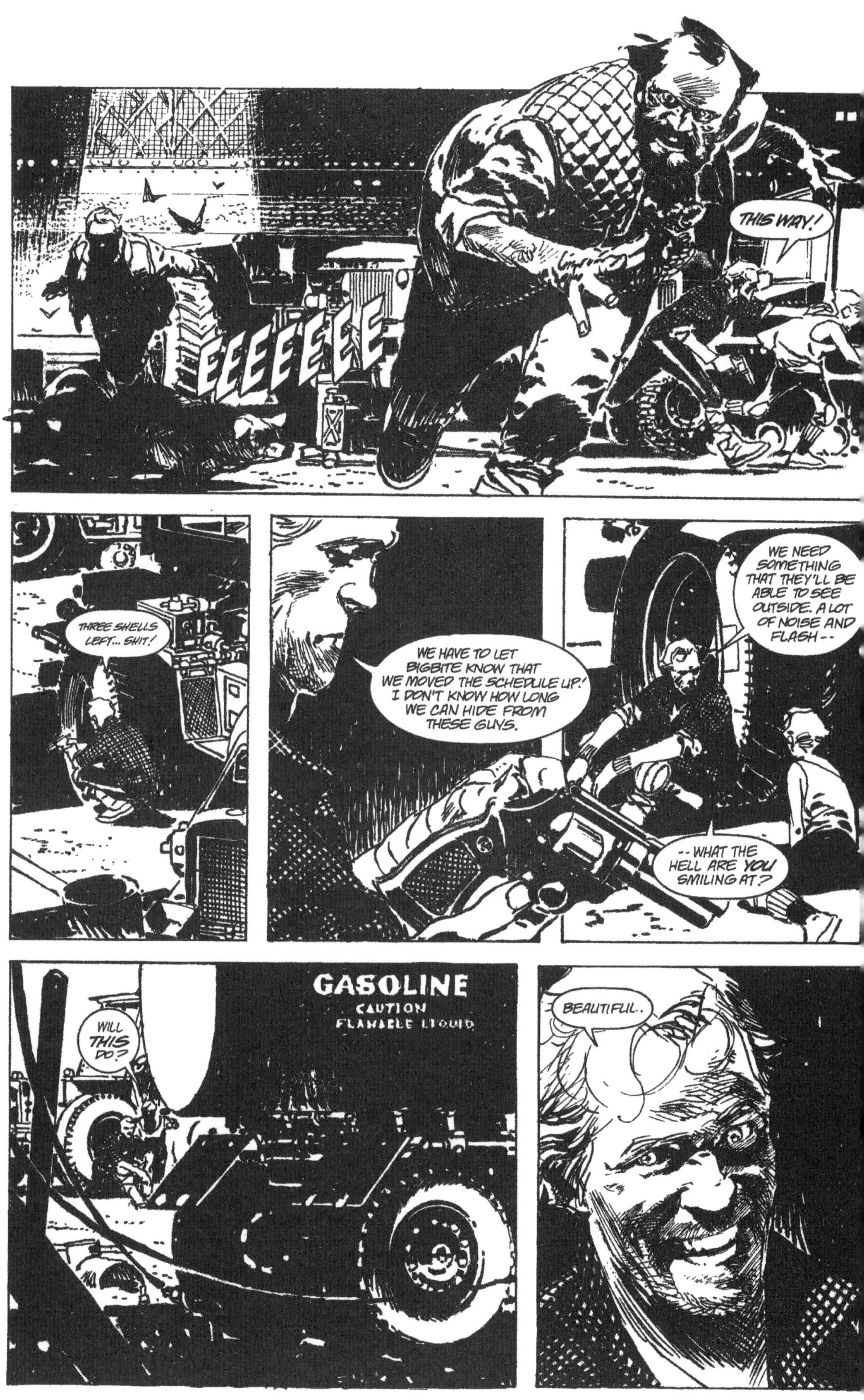
EEEEEEE
THIS WAY!
THREE SHELLS LEFT... SHIT!
WE HAVE TO LET BIGBITE KNOW THAT WE MOVED THE SCHEDULE UP! I DON'T KNOW HOW LONG WE CAN HIDE FROM THESE GUYS.
WE NEED SOMETHING THAT THEY'LL BE ABLE TO SEE OUTSIDE. A LOT OF NOISE AND FLASH--
--WHAT THE HELL ARE YOU SMILING AT?
GASOLINE
CAUTION
FLAMABLE LIQUID
WILL THIS DO?
BEAUTIFUL..

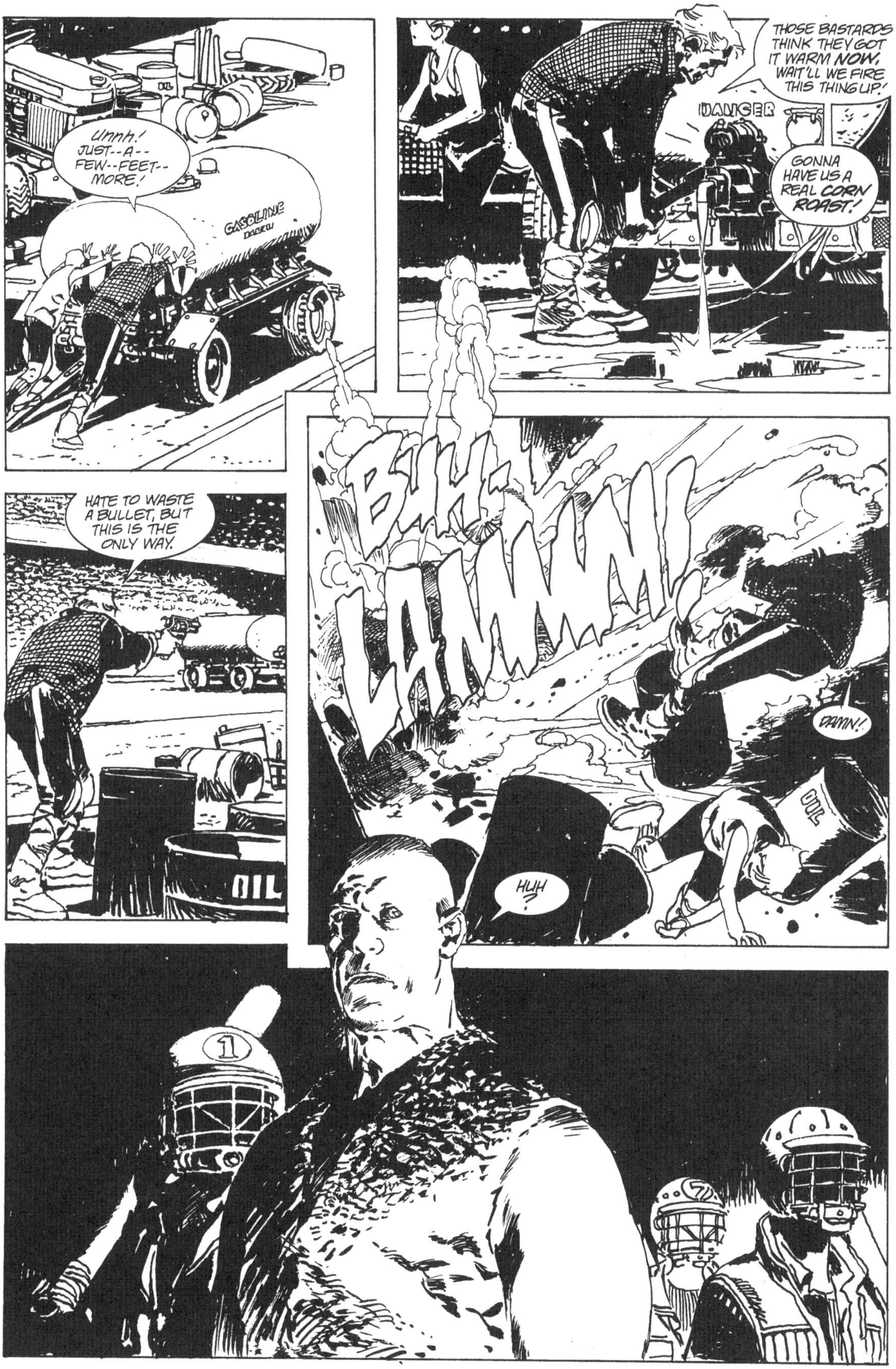
UNNH! JUST--A--FEW--FEET--MORE!
GASOLINE
THOSE BASTARDS THINK THEY GOT IT WARM NOW. WAIT'LL WE FIRE THIS THING UP!
DANGER
GONNA HAVE US A REAL CORN ROAST!
HATE TO WASTE A BULLET, BUT THIS IS THE ONLY WAY.
OIL
BLAMMM!
DAMN!
OIL
HUH?

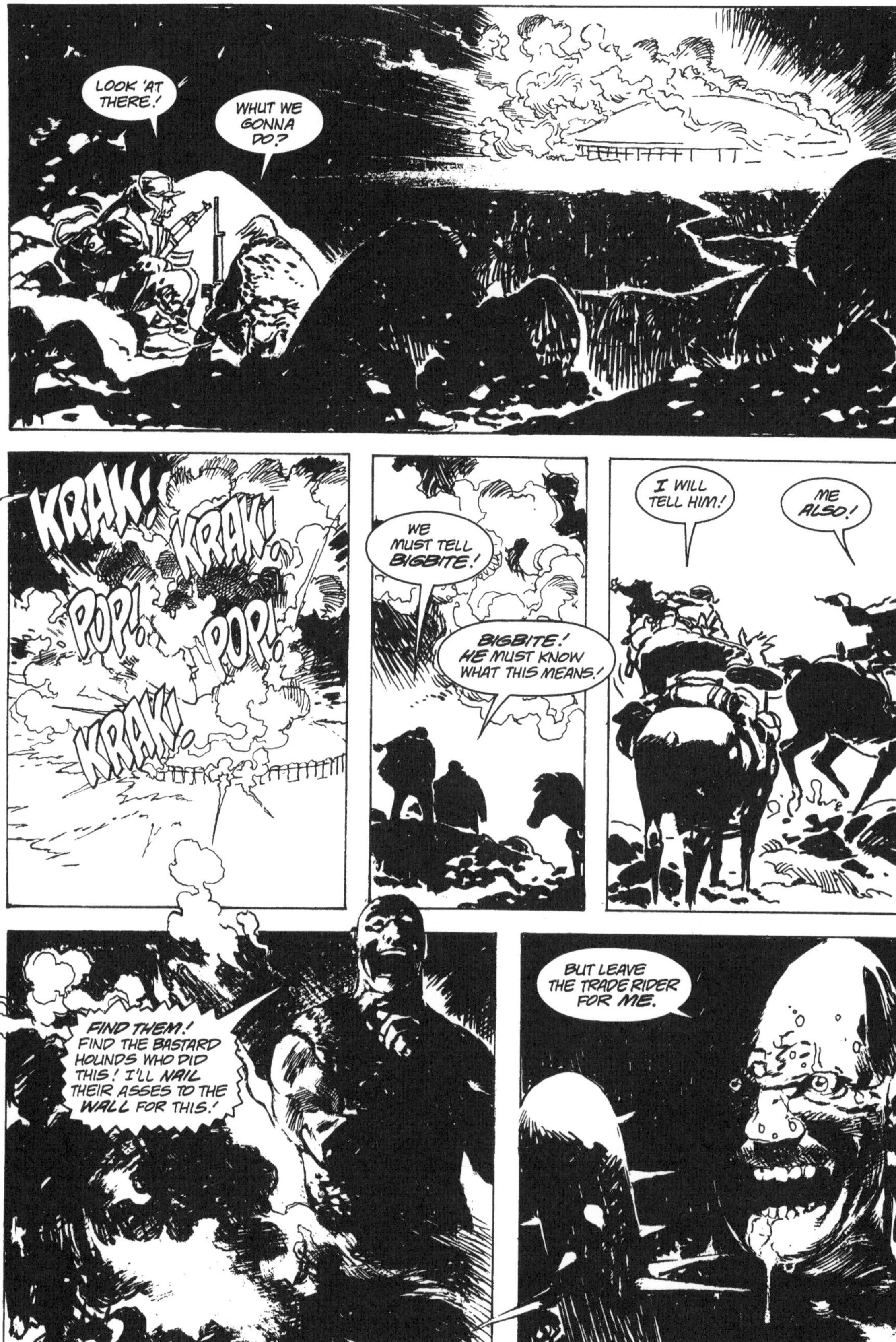
LOOK 'AT THERE!
WHUT WE GONNA DO?
KRAK!
KRAK!
POP!
POP!
KRAK!
WE MUST TELL BIGBITE!
BIGBITE! HE MUST KNOW WHAT THIS MEANS!
I WILL TELL HIM!
ME ALSO!
FIND THEM! FIND THE BASTARD HOUNDS WHO DID THIS! I'LL NAIL THEIR ASSES TO THE WALL FOR THIS!
BUT LEAVE THE TRADE RIDER FOR ME.

THAT OUGHTA GET BIGBITE MOVIN'!

ALL WE HAVE TO DO IS STAY OUTTA SIGHT 'TIL HE BRINGS THAT HOWLING MOB HE CALLS A TRIBE IN HERE!

I HOPE HE BRINGS IT SOON!

HELL.

SCULLY!

CHOOM

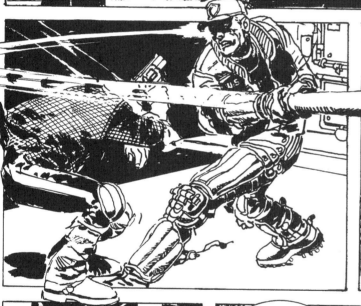

Unhh!

CLUD!

TWELVE GALIGE. PRETTY FAIR SHAPE.

"LOUISVILLE SLUGGER."

WHAT WAS LOUISVILLE?

IT WAS IN KENTUCKY. SAW IT ON A MAP ONCE.

WHAT'S KENTUCKY?

CAN WE SAVE THE GEOGRAPHY LESSON FOR LATER?

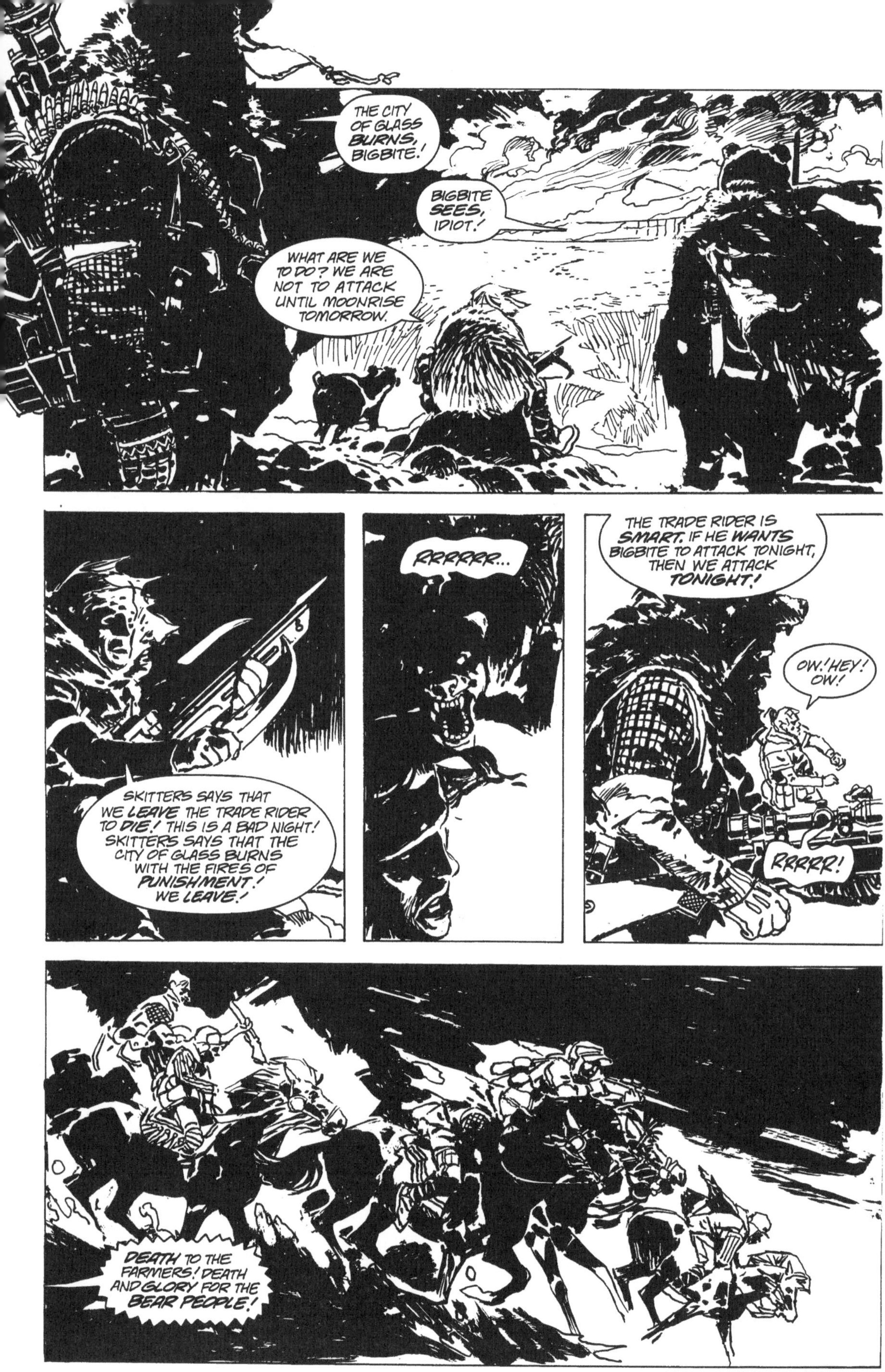
THE CITY OF GLASS BURNS, BIGBITE!
BIGBITE SEES, IDIOT!
WHAT ARE WE TO DO? WE ARE NOT TO ATTACK UNTIL MOONRISE TOMORROW.
SKITTERS SAYS THAT WE LEAVE THE TRADE RIDER TO DIE! THIS IS A BAD NIGHT! SKITTERS SAYS THAT THE CITY OF GLASS BURNS WITH THE FIRES OF PUNISHMENT! WE LEAVE!
RRRRRR...
THE TRADE RIDER IS SMART. IF HE WANTS BIGBITE TO ATTACK TONIGHT, THEN WE ATTACK TONIGHT!
OW! HEY! OW!
RRRRR!
DEATH TO THE FARMERS! DEATH AND GLORY FOR THE BEAR PEOPLE!

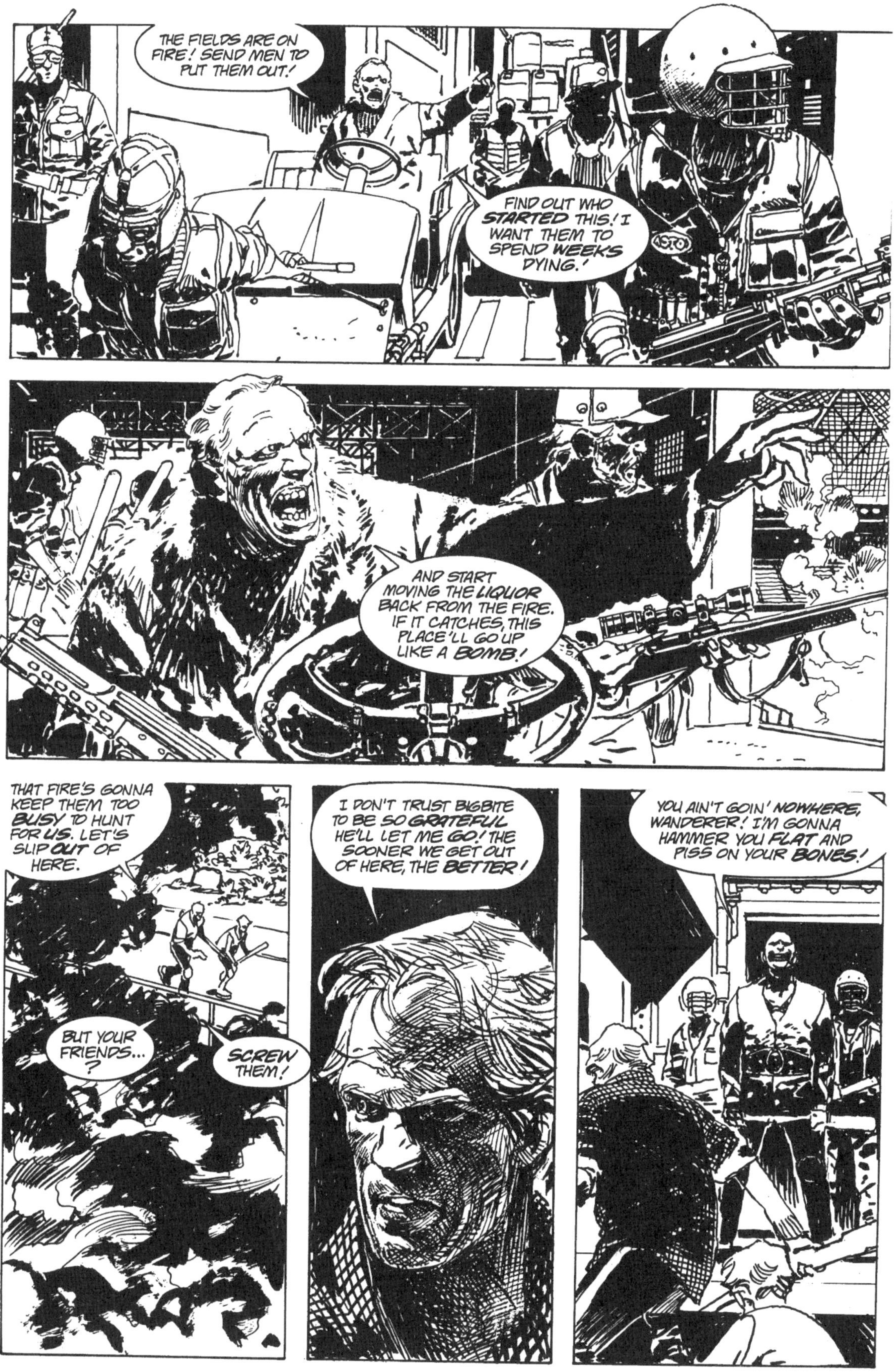
THE FIELDS ARE ON FIRE! SEND MEN TO PUT THEM OUT!
FIND OUT WHO STARTED THIS! I WANT THEM TO SPEND WEEKS DYING!
AND START MOVING THE LIQUOR BACK FROM THE FIRE. IF IT CATCHES, THIS PLACE'LL GO UP LIKE A BOMB!
THAT FIRE'S GONNA KEEP THEM TOO BUSY TO HUNT FOR US. LET'S SLIP OUT OF HERE.
BUT YOUR FRIENDS...?
SCREW THEM!
I DON'T TRUST BIGBITE TO BE SO GRATEFUL HE'LL LET ME GO! THE SOONER WE GET OUT OF HERE, THE BETTER!
YOU AIN'T GOIN' NOWHERE, WANDERER! I'M GONNA HAMMER YOU FLAT AND PISS ON YOUR BONES!

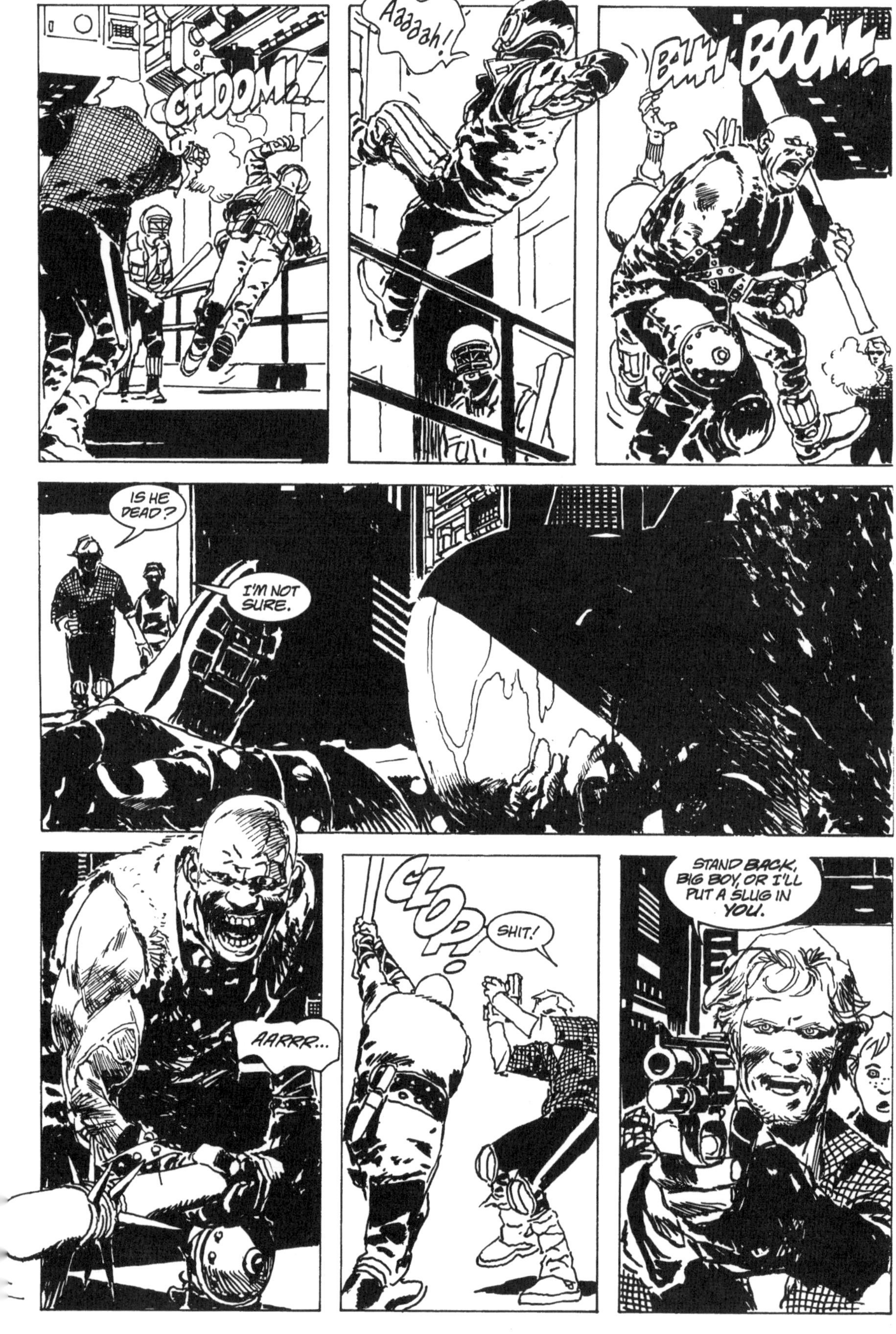
CHOOM!
Aaaaah!
BLAM BOOM!
IS HE DEAD?
I'M NOT SURE.
AARRR...
CLOP!
SHIT!
STAND BACK, BIG BOY, OR I'LL PUT A SLUG IN YOU.

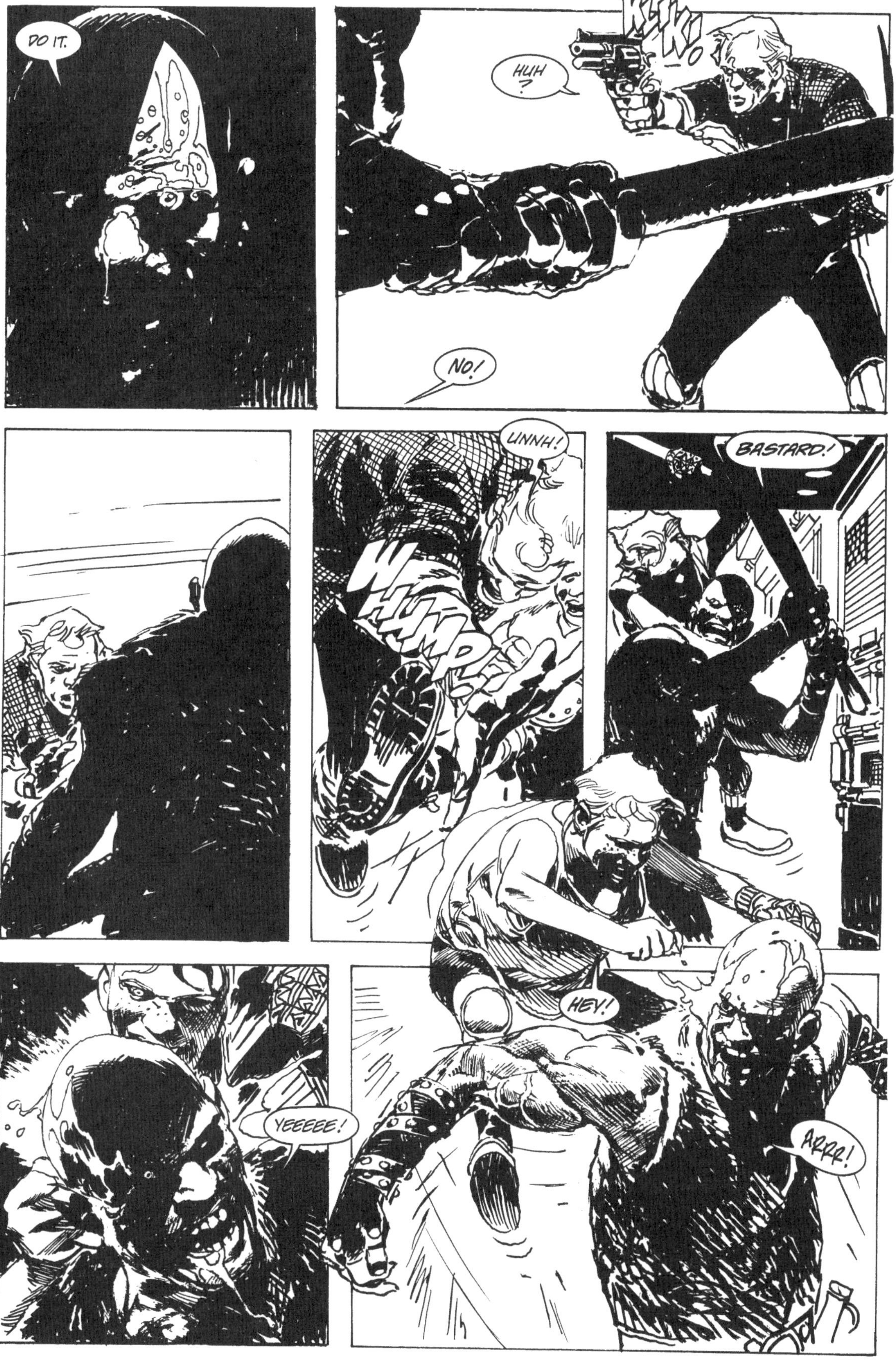
DO IT.
KLIK!
HUH
?
NO!
UNNH!
WHUMP!
BASTARD!
HEY!
YEEEEE!
ARRR!

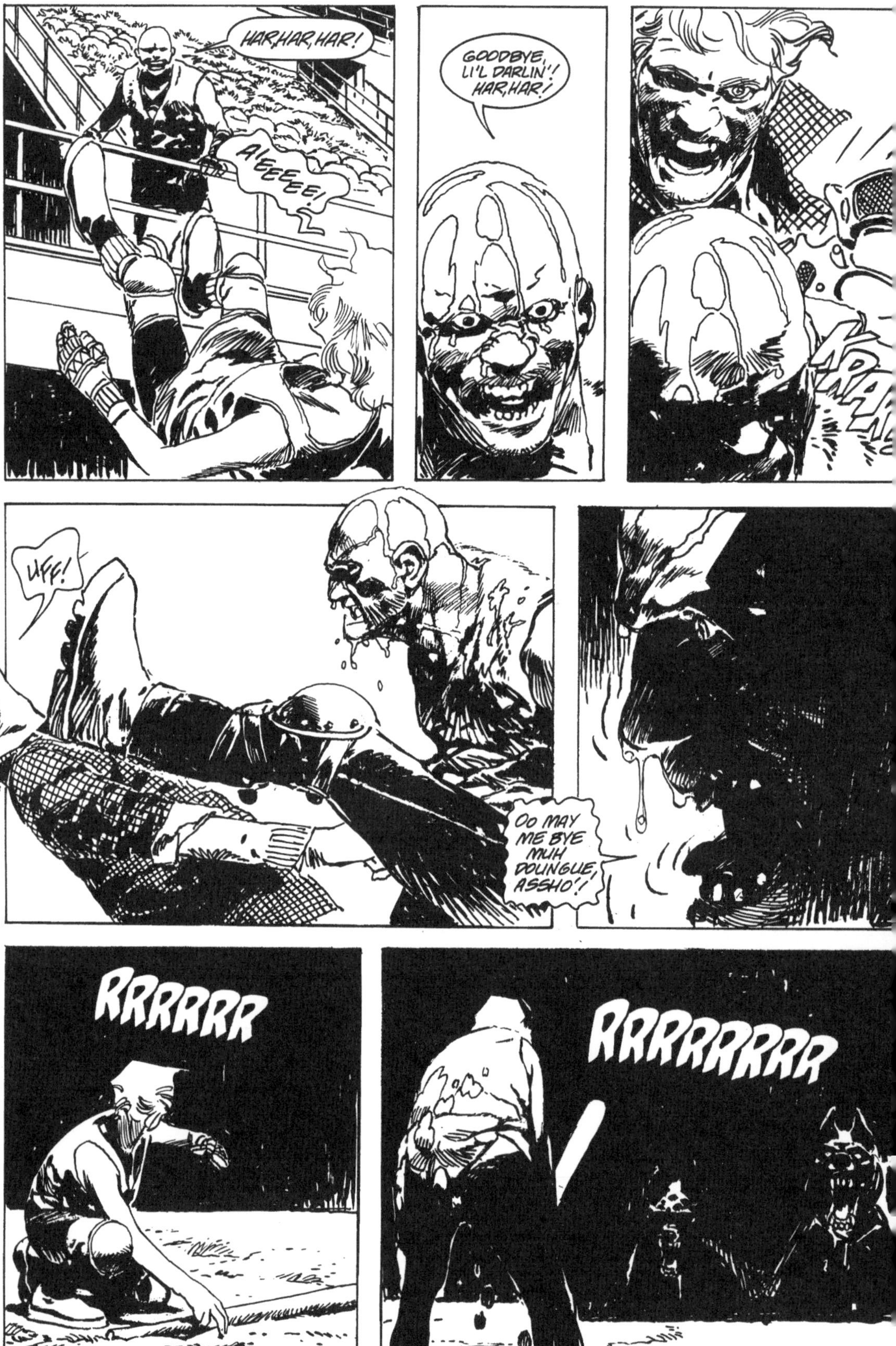

HAR,HAR,HAR!
AIEEEEE!
GOODBYE, LI'L DARLIN'! HAR,HAR!
UFF!
OO MAY ME BYE MUH DOUNGUE, ASSHO'!
RRRRRR
RRRRRRRR

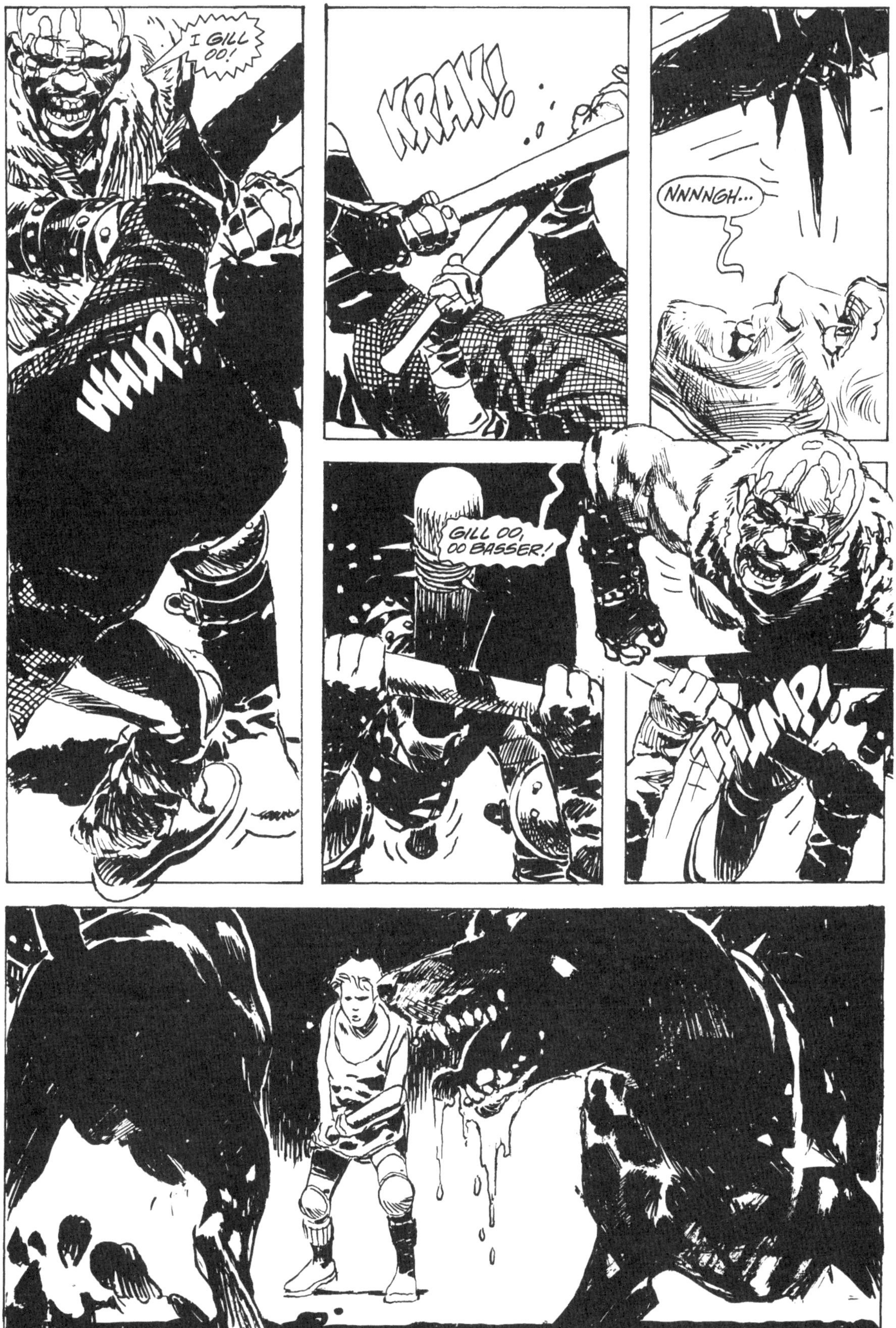

I GILL OO!
WHUP!
KRAK!
NNNNGH...
GILL OO, OO BASSER!
THUMP!

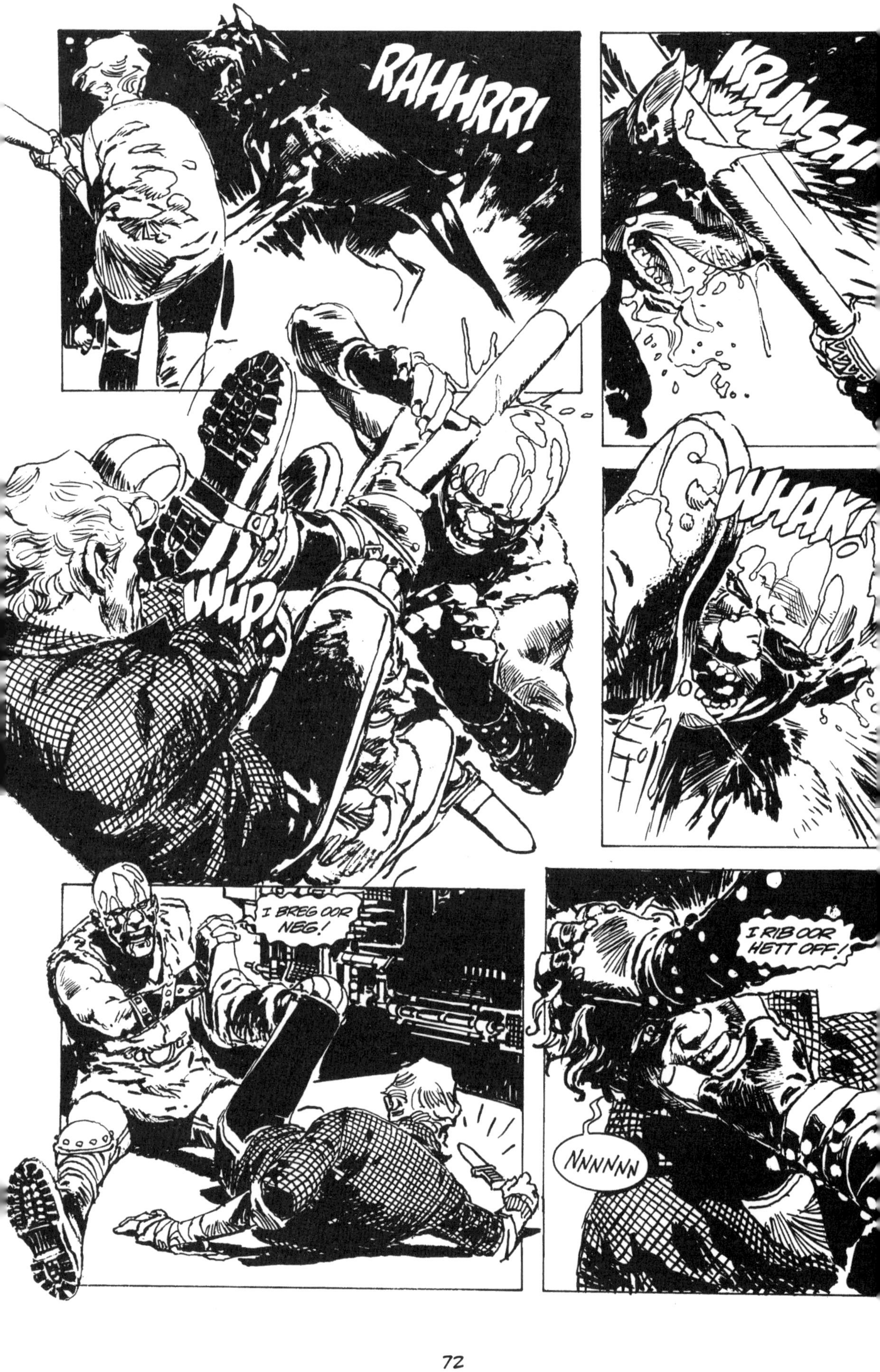

RAHHRR!
KRUNSH!
WUP!
WHAK!
I BREG OOR NEG!
I RIB OOR HETT OFF!
NNNNNN

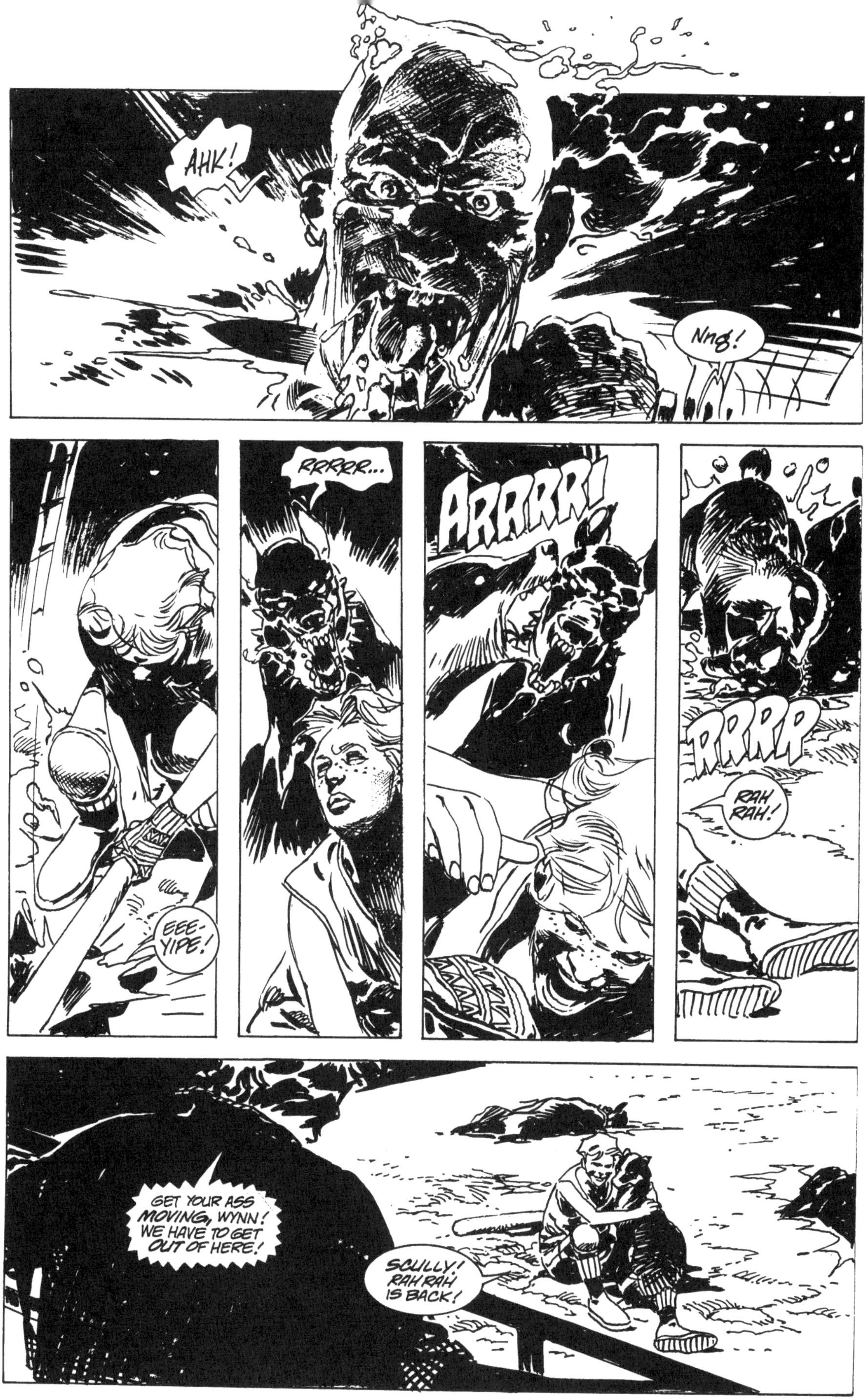
AHK!
Nng!
EEE-YIPE!
RRRRR...
ARRRR!
RRRR
RAH RAH!
GET YOUR ASS MOVING, WYNN! WE HAVE TO GET OUT OF HERE!
SCULLY! RAH RAH IS BACK!

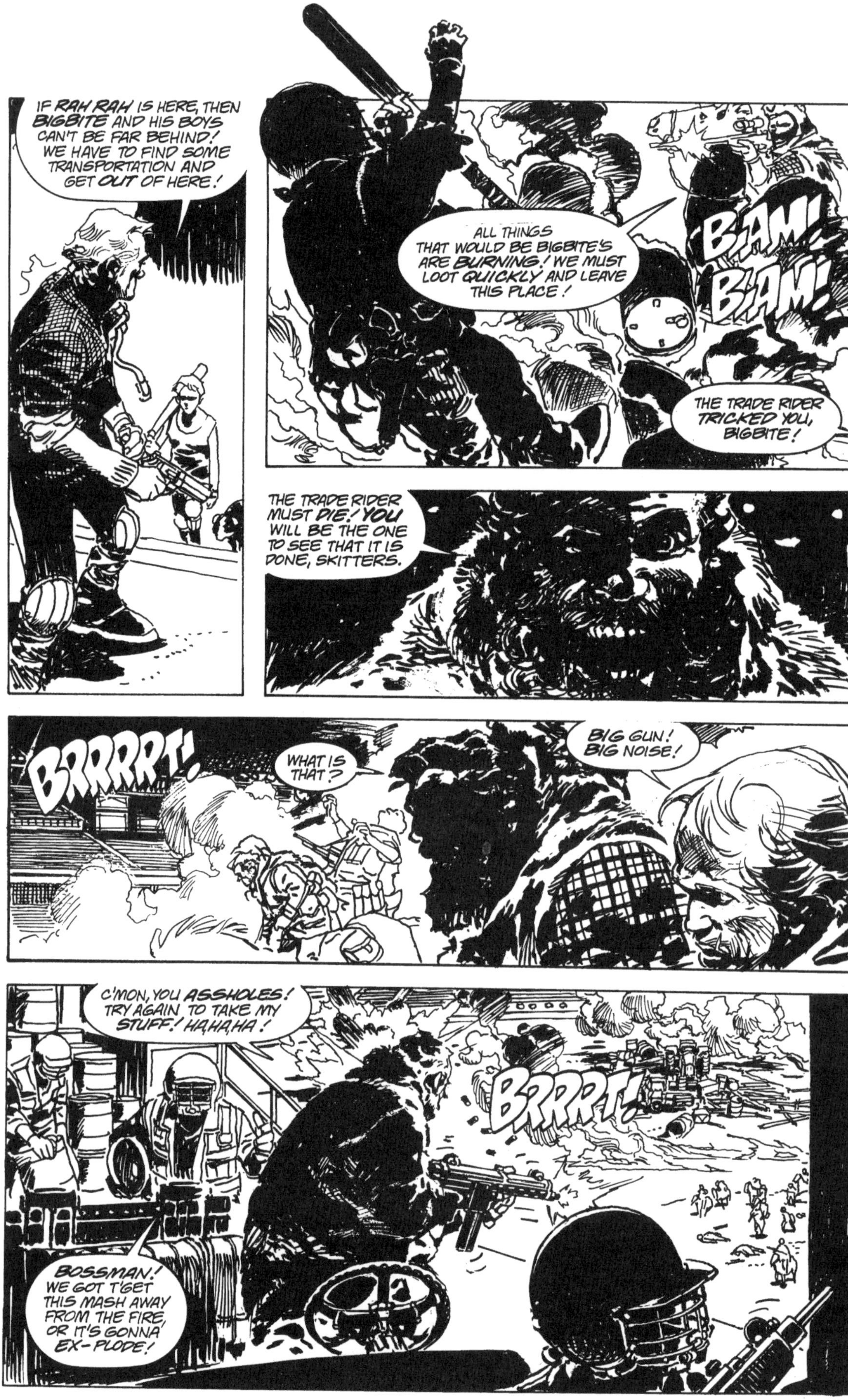
IF RAH RAH IS HERE, THEN BIGBITE AND HIS BOYS CAN'T BE FAR BEHIND! WE HAVE TO FIND SOME TRANSPORTATION AND GET OUT OF HERE!
ALL THINGS THAT WOULD BE BIGBITE'S ARE BURNING! WE MUST LOOT QUICKLY AND LEAVE THIS PLACE!
BLAM! BLAM!
THE TRADE RIDER TRICKED YOU, BIGBITE!
THE TRADE RIDER MUST DIE! YOU WILL BE THE ONE TO SEE THAT IT IS DONE, SKITTERS.
BRRRRT!
WHAT IS THAT?
BIG GUN! BIG NOISE!
C'MON, YOU ASSHOLES! TRY AGAIN TO TAKE MY STUFF! HA,HA,HA!
BRRRT!
BOSSMAN! WE GOT T'GET THIS MASH AWAY FROM THE FIRE OR IT'S GONNA EX-PLODE!

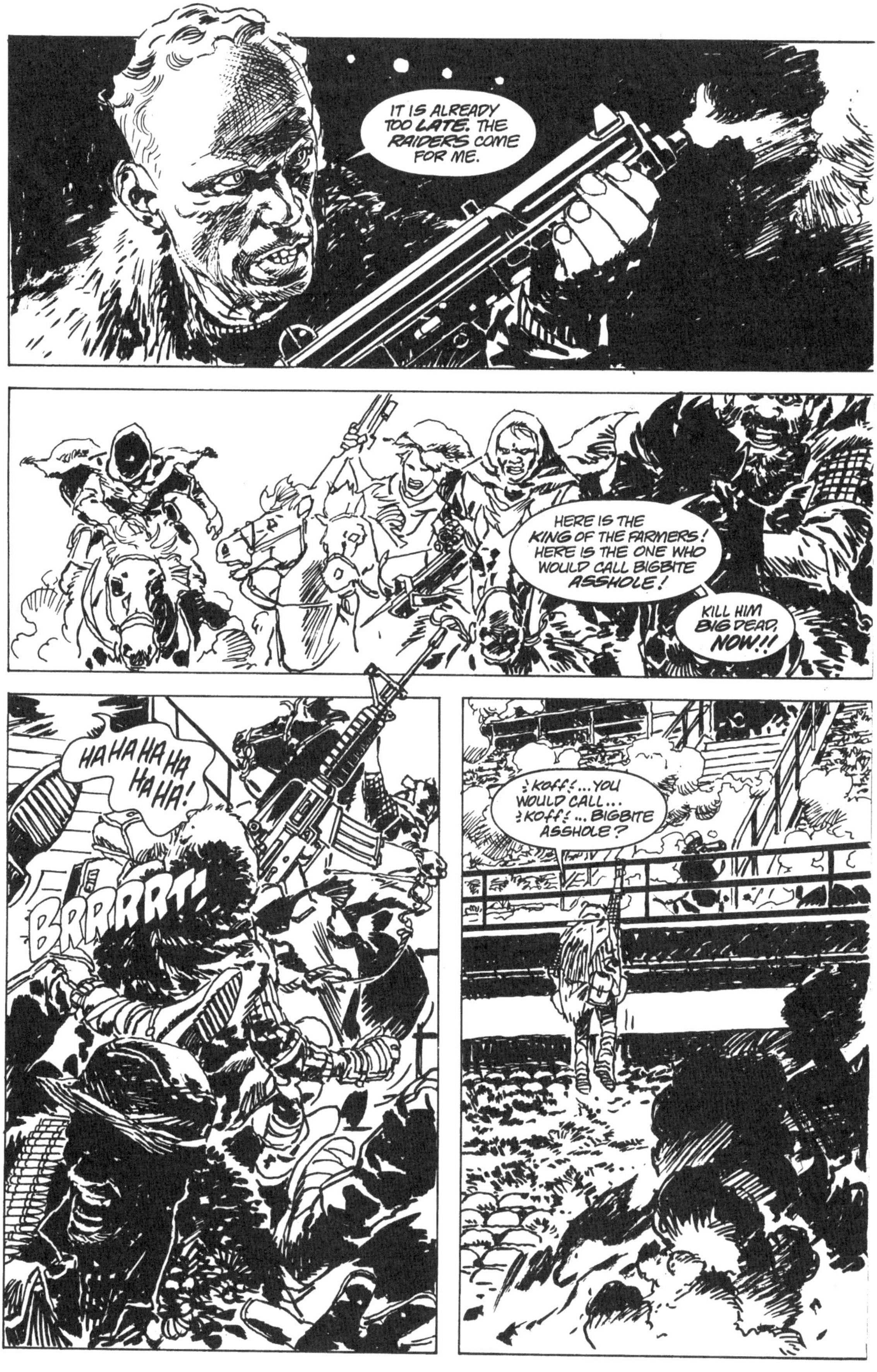
IT IS ALREADY TOO LATE. THE RAIDERS COME FOR ME.
HERE IS THE KING OF THE FARMERS! HERE IS THE ONE WHO WOULD CALL BIGBITE ASSHOLE!
KILL HIM BIG DEAD, NOW!!
HAHAHAHA HAHA!
BRRRRT!
KOFF!...YOU WOULD CALL... *KOFF!*... BIGBITE ASSHOLE?

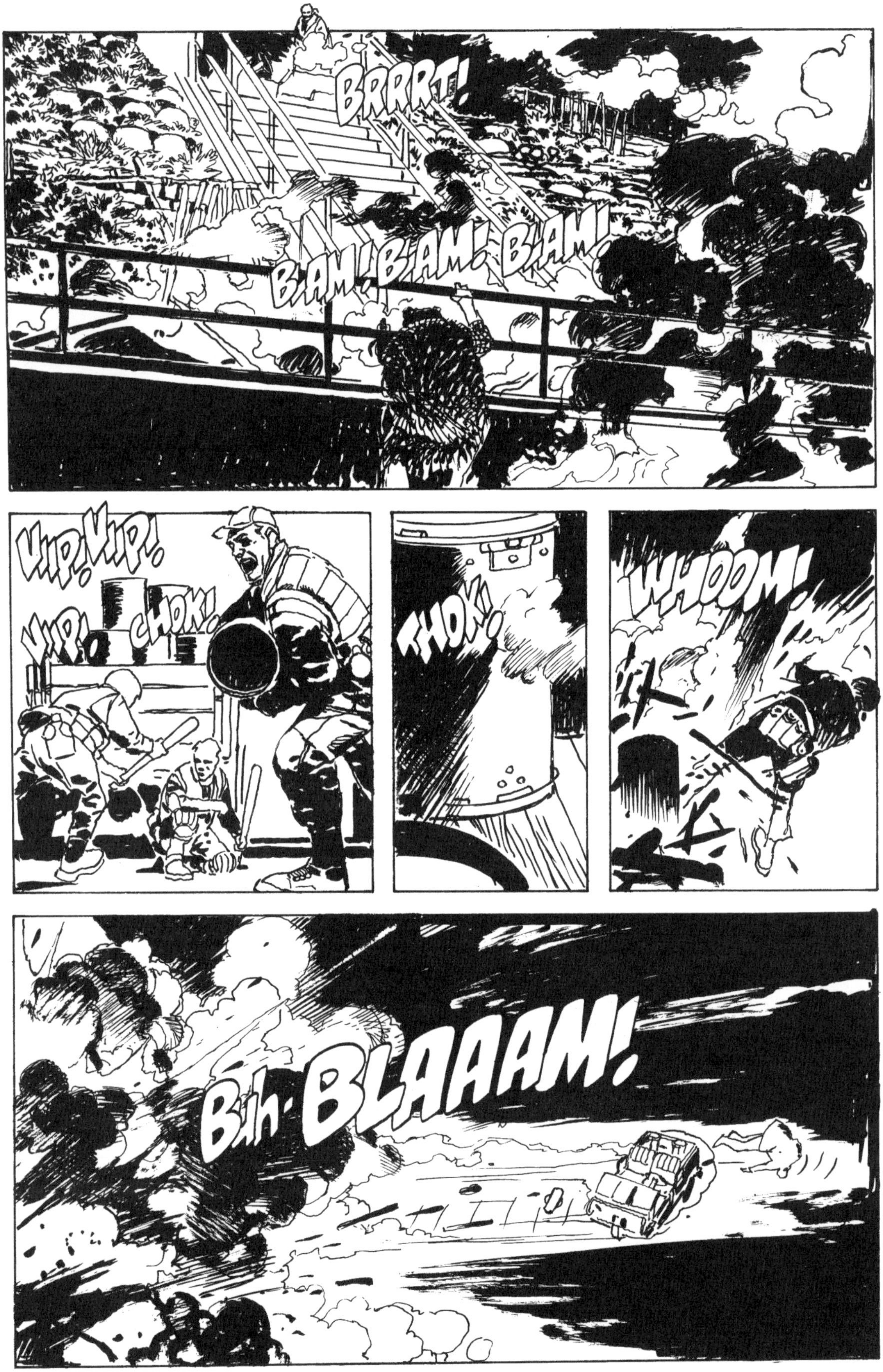
BRRRT!
BAM! BAM! BAM!
VIP! VIP!
VIP!
CHOK!
THOK!
WHOOM!
Buh-BLAAAM!

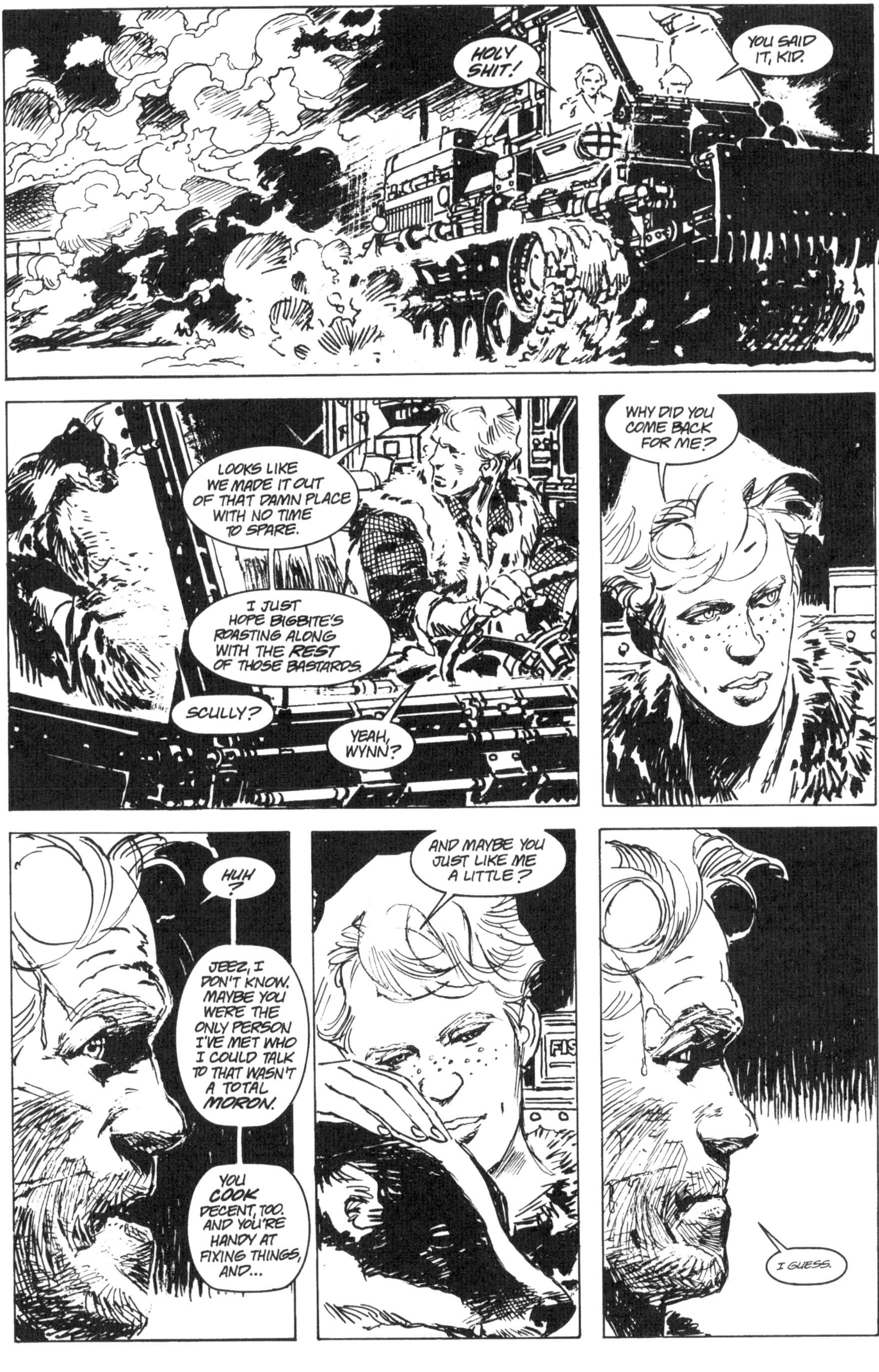
HOLY SHIT!
YOU SAID IT, KID.
LOOKS LIKE WE MADE IT OUT OF THAT DAMN PLACE WITH NO TIME TO SPARE.
I JUST HOPE BIGBITE'S ROASTING ALONG WITH THE REST OF THOSE BASTARDS.
SCULLY?
YEAH, WYNN?
WHY DID YOU COME BACK FOR ME?
HUH?
JEEZ, I DON'T KNOW. MAYBE YOU WERE THE ONLY PERSON I'VE MET WHO I COULD TALK TO THAT WASN'T A TOTAL MORON.
YOU COOK DECENT, TOO. AND YOU'RE HANDY AT FIXING THINGS, AND...
AND MAYBE YOU JUST LIKE ME A LITTLE?
I GUESS.

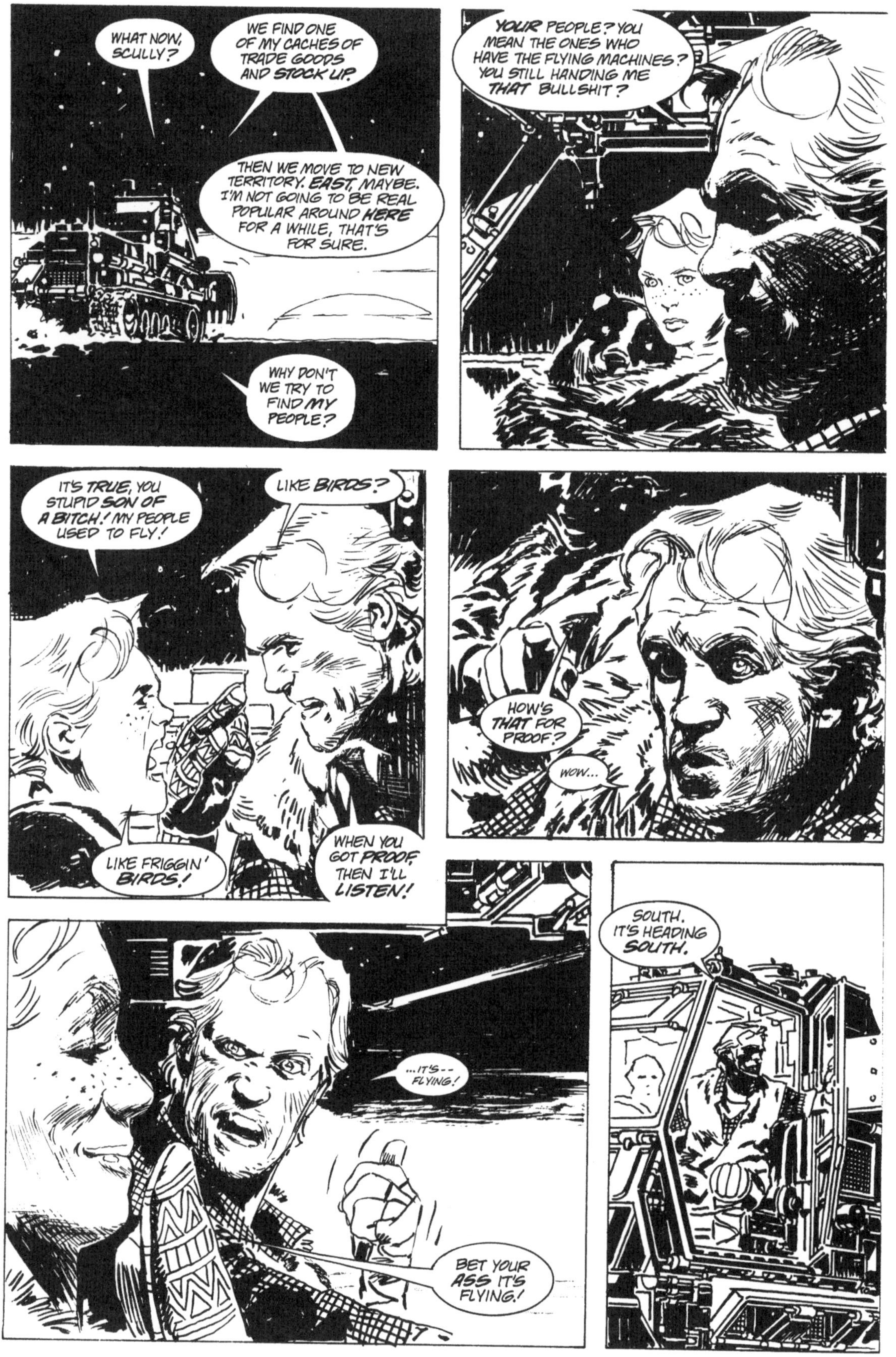
WHAT NOW, SCULLY?
WE FIND ONE OF MY CACHES OF TRADE GOODS AND STOCK UP.
THEN WE MOVE TO NEW TERRITORY. EAST, MAYBE. I'M NOT GOING TO BE REAL POPULAR AROUND HERE FOR A WHILE, THAT'S FOR SURE.
WHY DON'T WE TRY TO FIND MY PEOPLE?
YOUR PEOPLE? YOU MEAN THE ONES WHO HAVE THE FLYING MACHINES? YOU STILL HANDING ME THAT BULLSHIT?
IT'S TRUE, YOU STUPID SON OF A BITCH! MY PEOPLE USED TO FLY!
LIKE BIRDS?
LIKE FRIGGIN' BIRDS!
WHEN YOU GOT PROOF, THEN I'LL LISTEN!
HOW'S THAT FOR PROOF?
WOW...
...IT'S--FLYING!
BET YOUR ASS IT'S FLYING!
SOUTH. IT'S HEADING SOUTH.

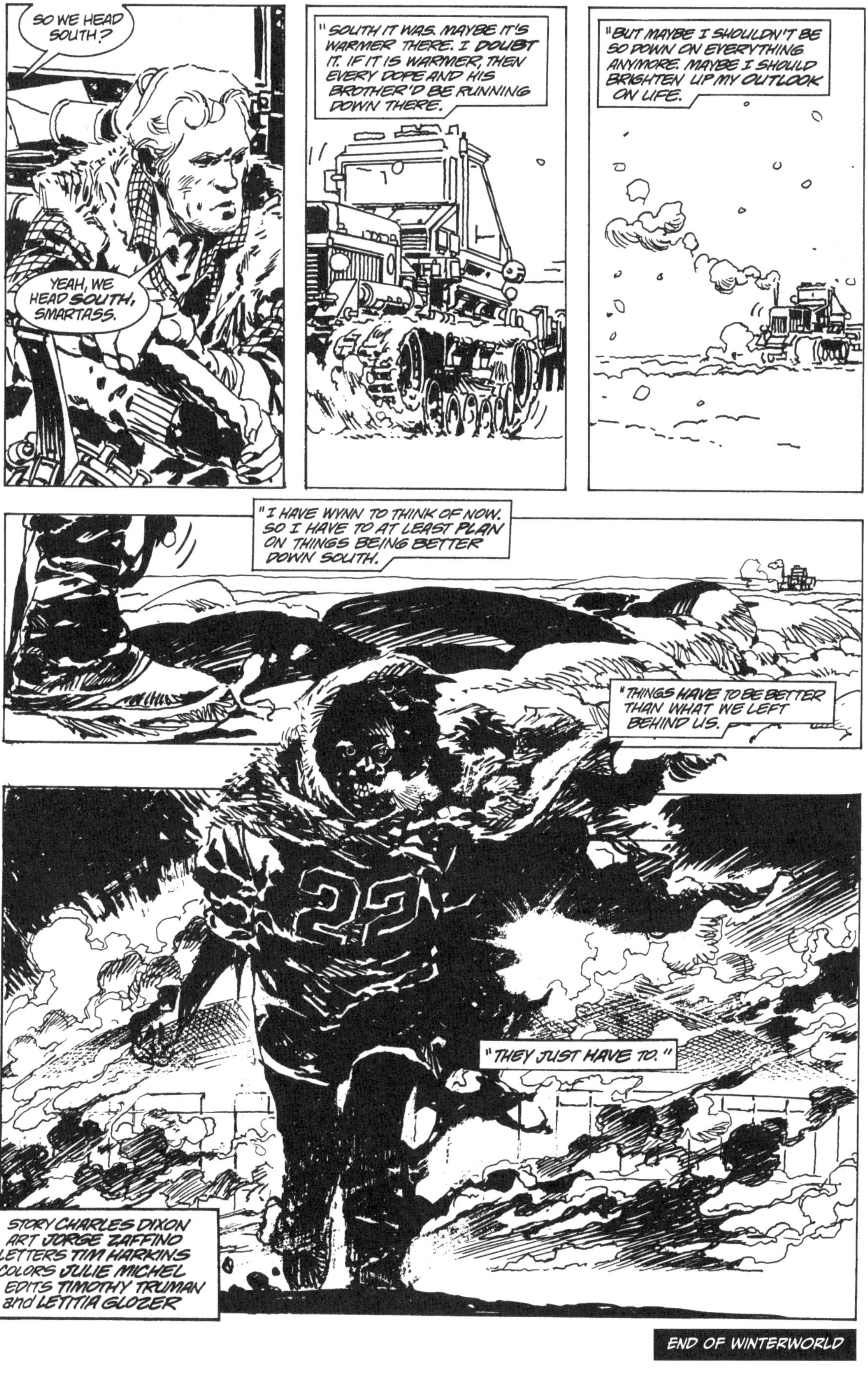
SO WE HEAD SOUTH?
YEAH, WE HEAD SOUTH, SMARTASS.
"SOUTH IT WAS. MAYBE IT'S WARMER THERE. I DOUBT IT. IF IT IS WARMER, THEN EVERY DOPE AND HIS BROTHER'D BE RUNNING DOWN THERE.
"BUT MAYBE I SHOULDN'T BE SO DOWN ON EVERYTHING ANYMORE. MAYBE I SHOULD BRIGHTEN UP MY OUTLOOK ON LIFE.
"I HAVE WYNN TO THINK OF NOW. SO I HAVE TO AT LEAST PLAN ON THINGS BEING BETTER DOWN SOUTH.
"THINGS HAVE TO BE BETTER THAN WHAT WE LEFT BEHIND US.
"THEY JUST HAVE TO."
STORY CHARLES DIXON
ART JORGE ZAFFINO
LETTERS TIM HARKINS
COLORS JULIE MICHEL
EDITS TIMOTHY TRUMAN
and LETITIA GLOZER
END OF WINTERWORLD

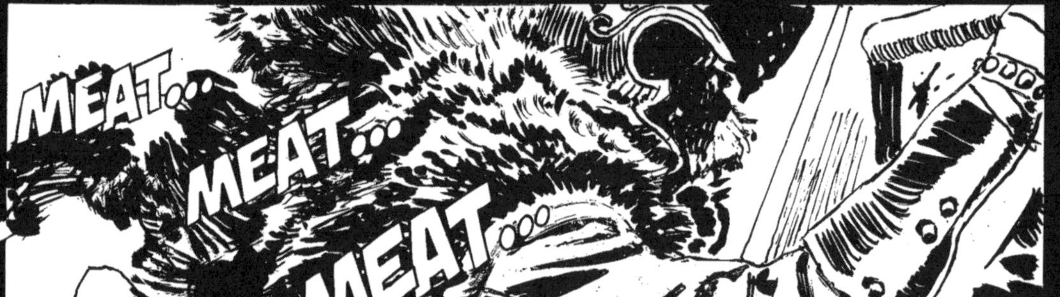
MEAT...
MEAT...
MEAT...
MEAT...

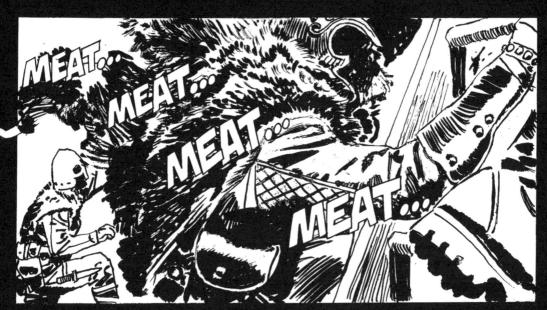

WINTERSEA

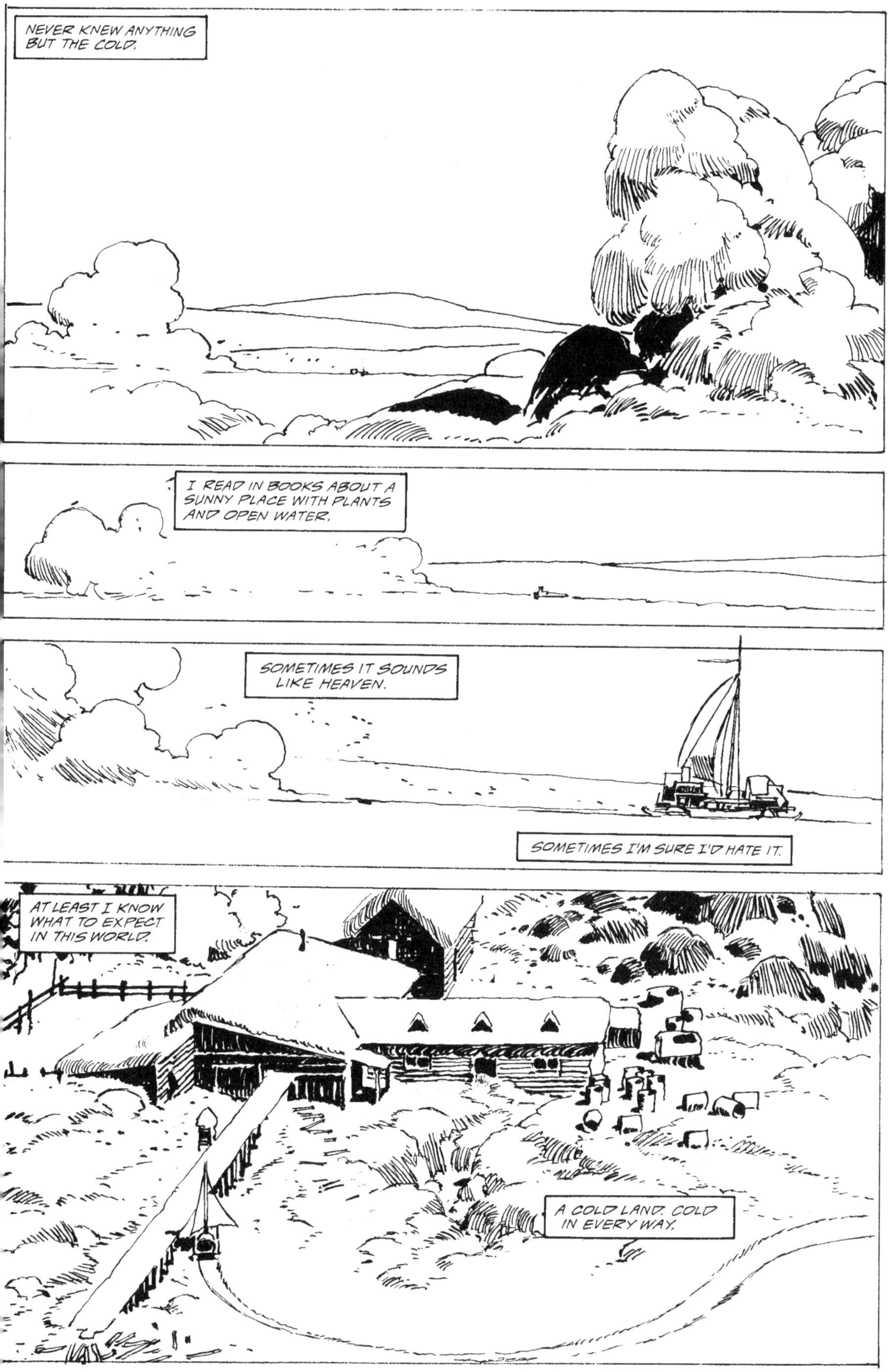
NEVER KNEW ANYTHING BUT THE COLD.
I READ IN BOOKS ABOUT A SUNNY PLACE WITH PLANTS AND OPEN WATER.
SOMETIMES IT SOUNDS LIKE HEAVEN.
SOMETIMES I'M SURE I'D HATE IT.
AT LEAST I KNOW WHAT TO EXPECT IN THIS WORLD.
A COLD LAND. COLD IN EVERY WAY.

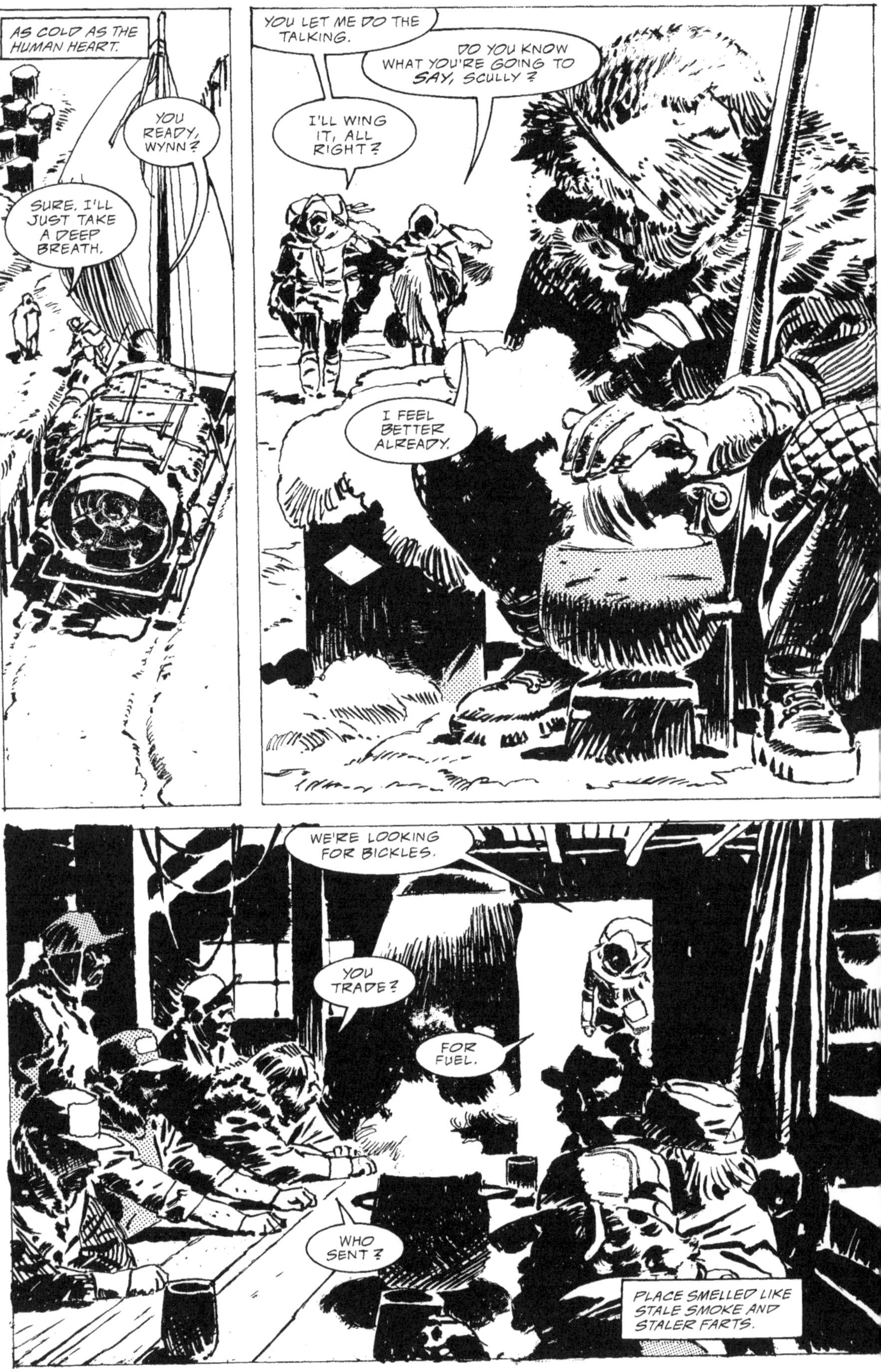
AS COLD AS THE HUMAN HEART.
YOU READY, WYNN?
SURE. I'LL JUST TAKE A DEEP BREATH.
YOU LET ME DO THE TALKING.
DO YOU KNOW WHAT YOU'RE GOING TO SAY, SCULLY?
I'LL WING IT, ALL RIGHT?
I FEEL BETTER ALREADY.
WE'RE LOOKING FOR BICKLES.
YOU TRADE?
FOR FUEL.
WHO SENT?
PLACE SMELLED LIKE STALE SMOKE AND STALER FARTS.

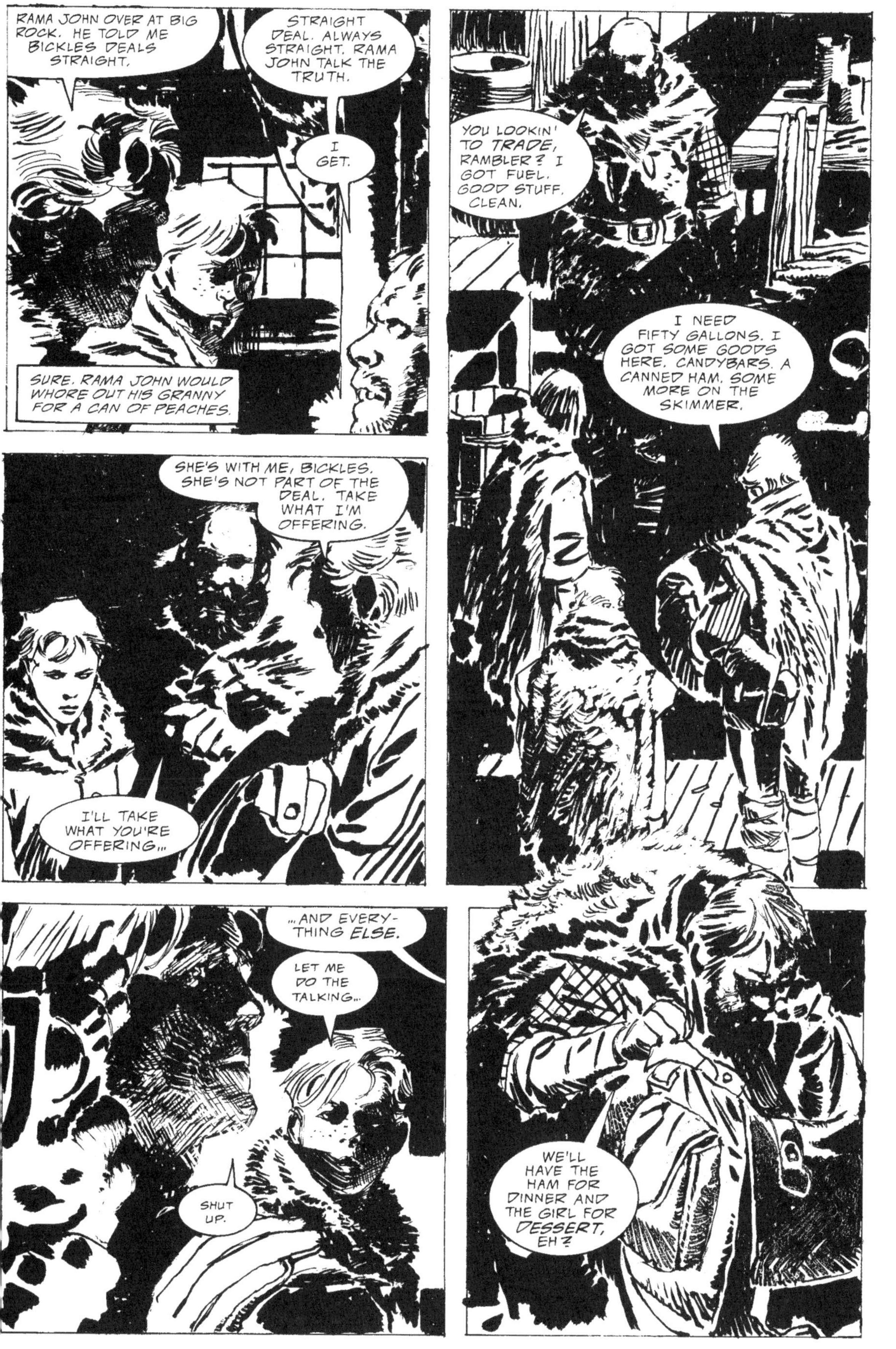
RAMA JOHN OVER AT BIG ROCK. HE TOLD ME BICKLES DEALS STRAIGHT.
STRAIGHT DEAL. ALWAYS STRAIGHT. RAMA JOHN TALK THE TRUTH.
I GET.
SURE. RAMA JOHN WOULD WHORE OUT HIS GRANNY FOR A CAN OF PEACHES.
YOU LOOKIN' TO TRADE, RAMBLER? I GOT FUEL. GOOD STUFF. CLEAN.
I NEED FIFTY GALLONS. I GOT SOME GOODS HERE. CANDYBARS. A CANNED HAM. SOME MORE ON THE SKIMMER.
SHE'S WITH ME, BICKLES. SHE'S NOT PART OF THE DEAL. TAKE WHAT I'M OFFERING.
I'LL TAKE WHAT YOU'RE OFFERING...
...AND EVERY-THING ELSE.
LET ME DO THE TALKING...
SHUT UP.
WE'LL HAVE THE HAM FOR DINNER AND THE GIRL FOR DESSERT, EH?

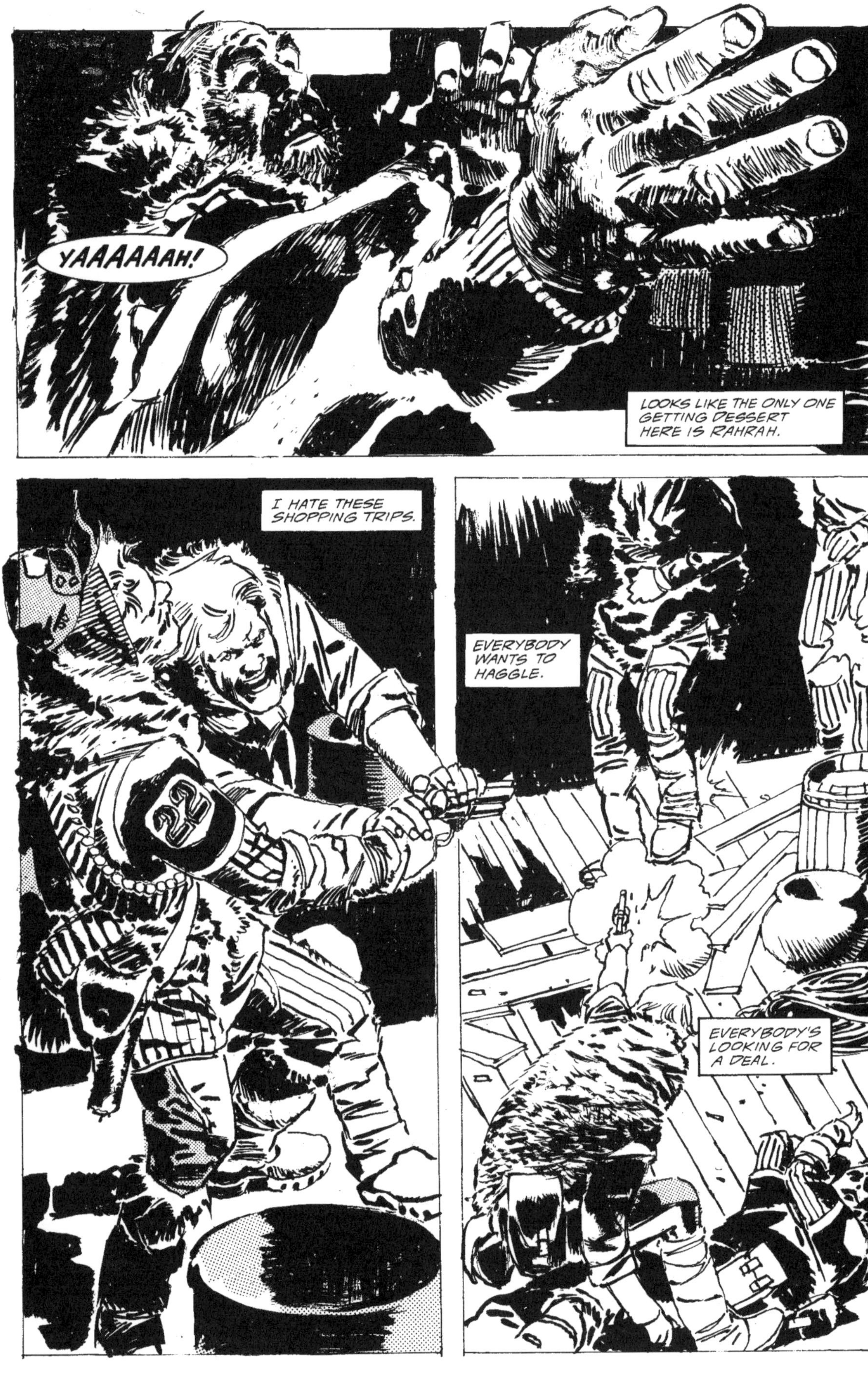
YAAAAAAH!
LOOKS LIKE THE ONLY ONE GETTING DESSERT HERE IS RAHRAH.
I HATE THESE SHOPPING TRIPS.
EVERYBODY WANTS TO HAGGLE.
EVERYBODY'S LOOKING FOR A DEAL.

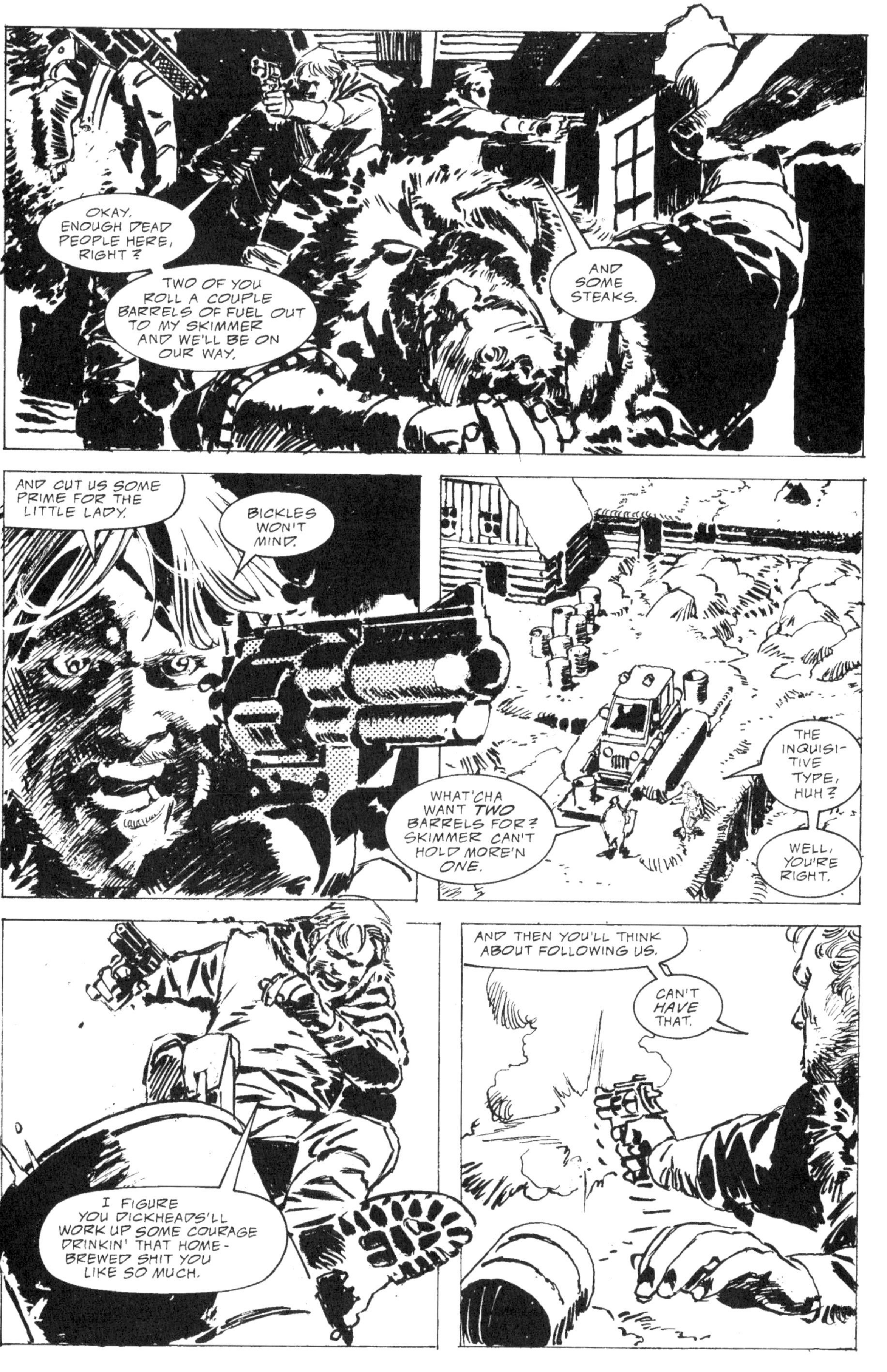

OKAY. ENOUGH DEAD PEOPLE HERE, RIGHT?
TWO OF YOU ROLL A COUPLE BARRELS OF FUEL OUT TO MY SKIMMER AND WE'LL BE ON OUR WAY.
AND SOME STEAKS.
AND CUT US SOME PRIME FOR THE LITTLE LADY.
BICKLES WON'T MIND.
WHAT'CHA WANT TWO BARRELS FOR? SKIMMER CAN'T HOLD MORE'N ONE.
THE INQUISI-TIVE TYPE, HUH?
WELL, YOU'RE RIGHT.
I FIGURE YOU DICKHEADS'LL WORK UP SOME COURAGE DRINKIN' THAT HOME-BREWED SHIT YOU LIKE SO MUCH.
AND THEN YOU'LL THINK ABOUT FOLLOWING US.
CAN'T HAVE THAT.

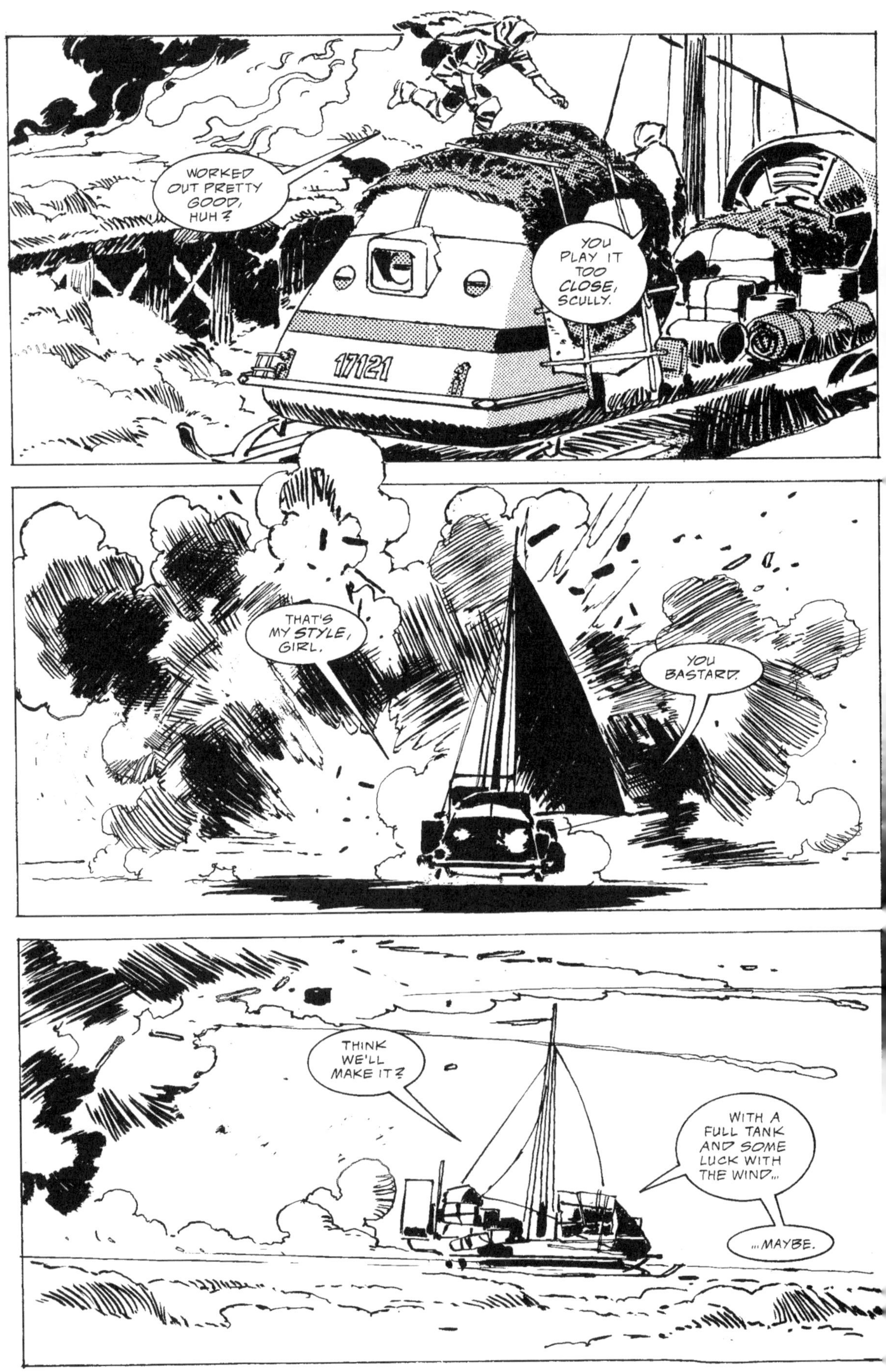
WORKED OUT PRETTY GOOD, HUH?
YOU PLAY IT TOO CLOSE, SCULLY.
17121
THAT'S MY STYLE, GIRL.
YOU BASTARD.
THINK WE'LL MAKE IT?
WITH A FULL TANK AND SOME LUCK WITH THE WIND...
...MAYBE.

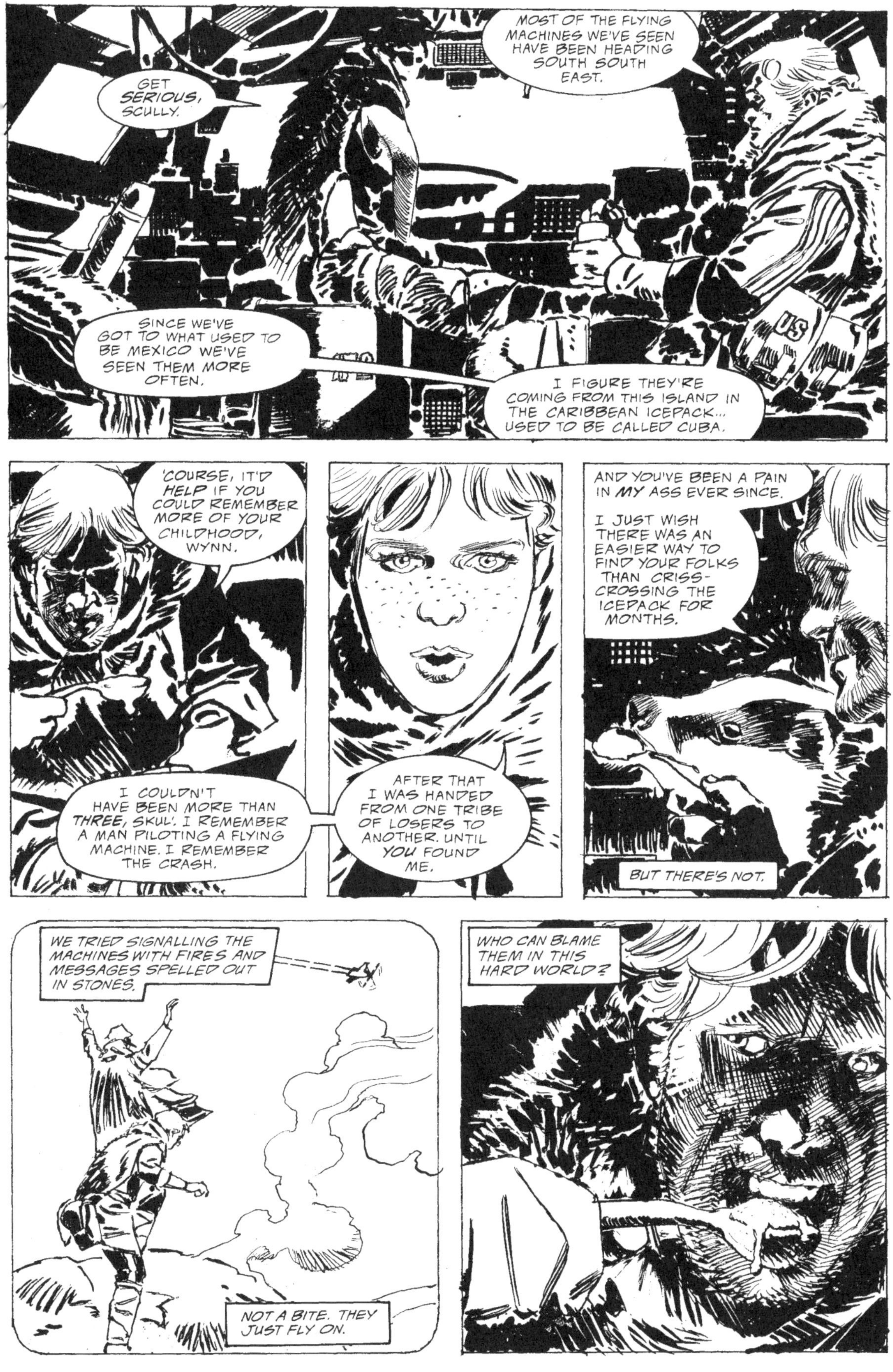
GET SERIOUS, SCULLY.
MOST OF THE FLYING MACHINES WE'VE SEEN HAVE BEEN HEADING SOUTH SOUTH EAST.
SINCE WE'VE GOT TO WHAT USED TO BE MEXICO WE'VE SEEN THEM MORE OFTEN.
I FIGURE THEY'RE COMING FROM THIS ISLAND IN THE CARIBBEAN ICEPACK... USED TO BE CALLED CUBA.
US
'COURSE, IT'D HELP IF YOU COULD REMEMBER MORE OF YOUR CHILDHOOD, WYNN.
I COULDN'T HAVE BEEN MORE THAN THREE, SKUL'. I REMEMBER A MAN PILOTING A FLYING MACHINE. I REMEMBER THE CRASH.
AFTER THAT I WAS HANDED FROM ONE TRIBE OF LOSERS TO ANOTHER. UNTIL YOU FOUND ME.
AND YOU'VE BEEN A PAIN IN MY ASS EVER SINCE.
I JUST WISH THERE WAS AN EASIER WAY TO FIND YOUR FOLKS THAN CRISS-CROSSING THE ICEPACK FOR MONTHS.
BUT THERE'S NOT.
WE TRIED SIGNALLING THE MACHINES WITH FIRES AND MESSAGES SPELLED OUT IN STONES.
NOT A BITE. THEY JUST FLY ON.
WHO CAN BLAME THEM IN THIS HARD WORLD?

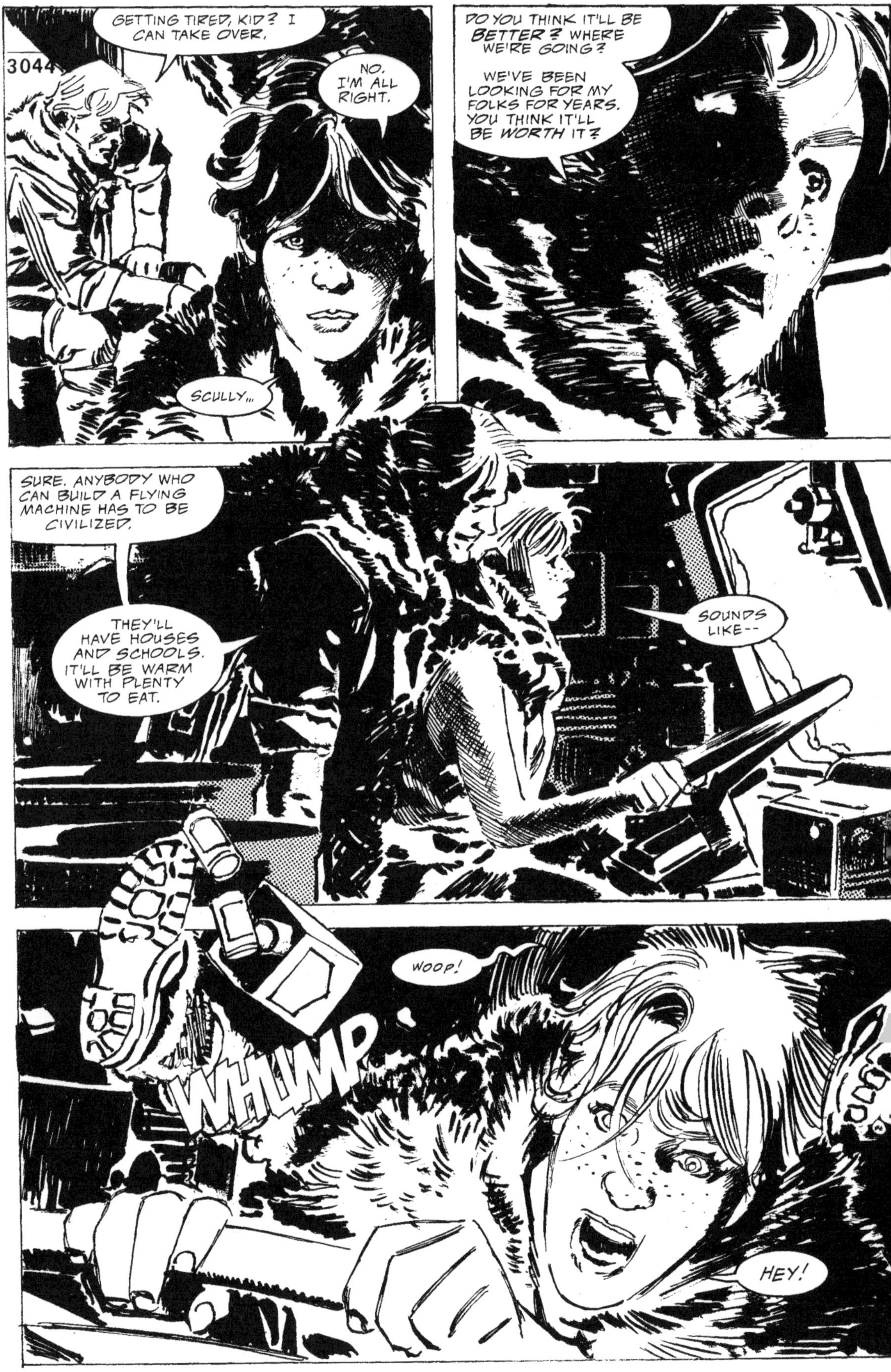

3044
GETTING TIRED, KID? I CAN TAKE OVER.
NO. I'M ALL RIGHT.
SCULLY...
DO YOU THINK IT'LL BE BETTER? WHERE WE'RE GOING?
WE'VE BEEN LOOKING FOR MY FOLKS FOR YEARS. YOU THINK IT'LL BE WORTH IT?
SURE. ANYBODY WHO CAN BUILD A FLYING MACHINE HAS TO BE CIVILIZED.
THEY'LL HAVE HOUSES AND SCHOOLS. IT'LL BE WARM WITH PLENTY TO EAT.
SOUNDS LIKE--
WOOP!
WHUMP
HEY!

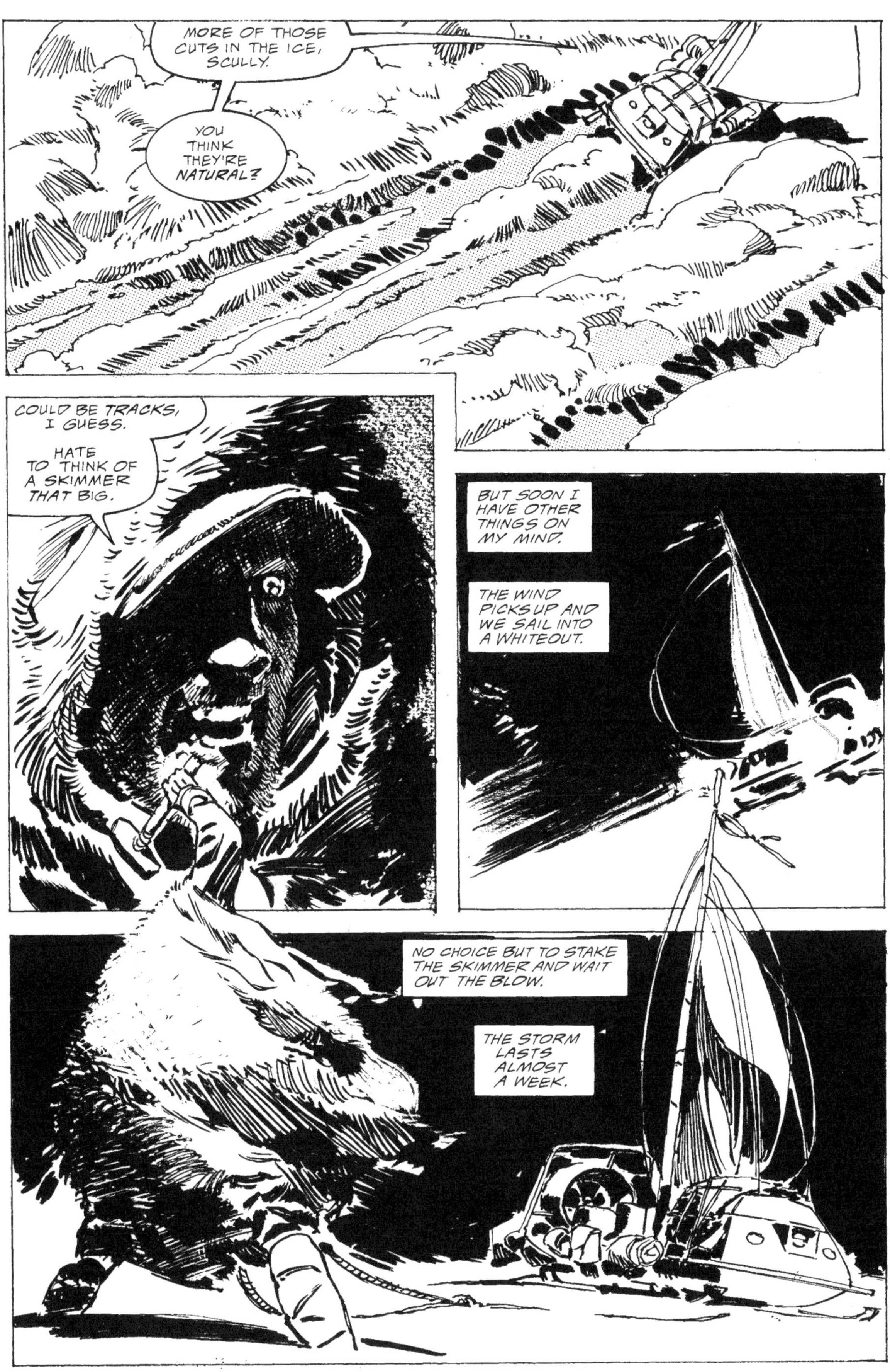
MORE OF THOSE CUTS IN THE ICE, SCULLY.
YOU THINK THEY'RE NATURAL?
COULD BE TRACKS, I GUESS.
HATE TO THINK OF A SKIMMER THAT BIG.
BUT SOON I HAVE OTHER THINGS ON MY MIND.
THE WIND PICKS UP AND WE SAIL INTO A WHITEOUT.
NO CHOICE BUT TO STAKE THE SKIMMER AND WAIT OUT THE BLOW.
THE STORM LASTS ALMOST A WEEK.

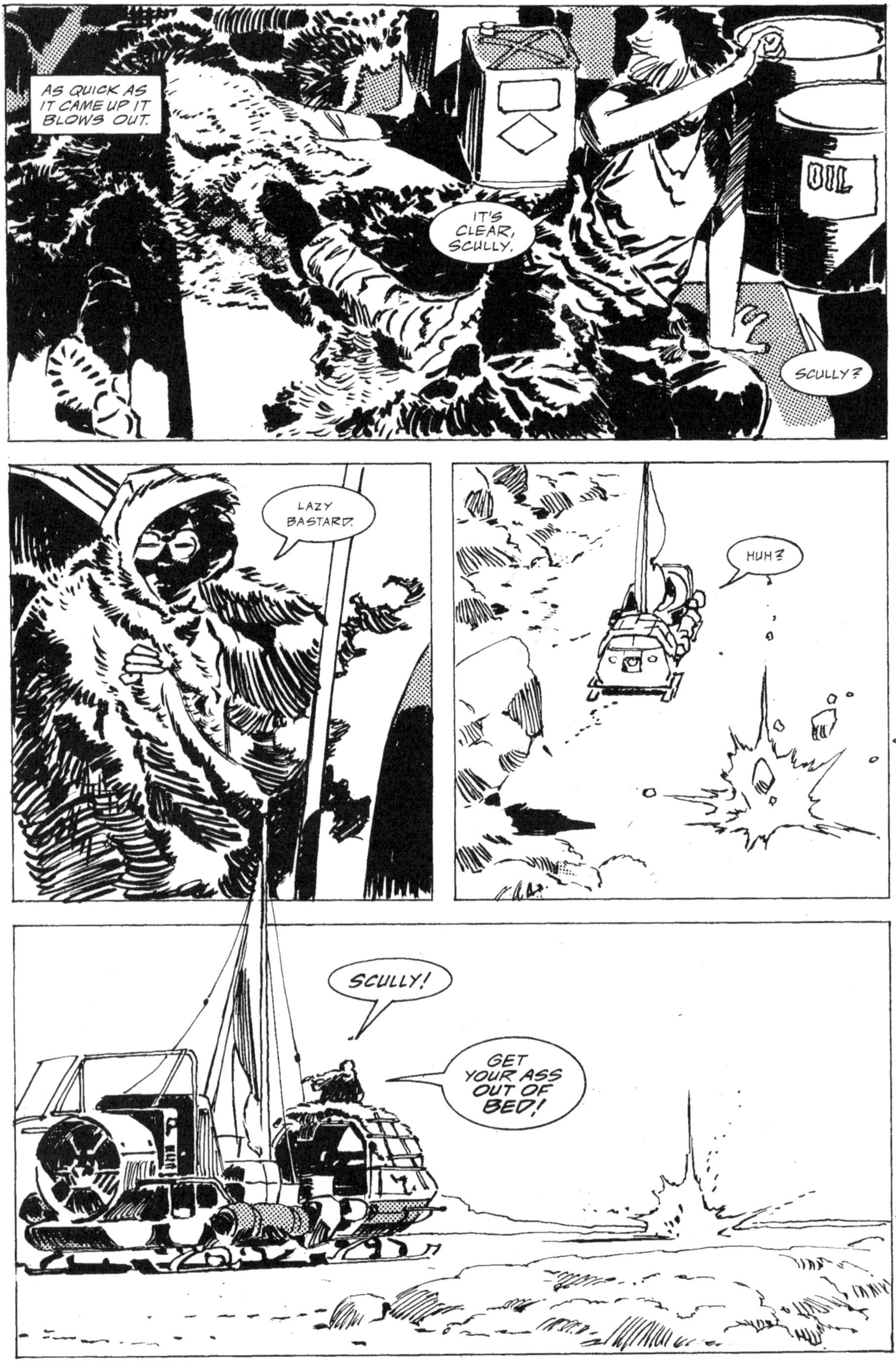
AS QUICK AS IT CAME UP IT BLOWS OUT.
IT'S CLEAR, SCULLY.
SCULLY?
LAZY BASTARD.
HUH?
SCULLY!
GET YOUR ASS OUT OF BED!

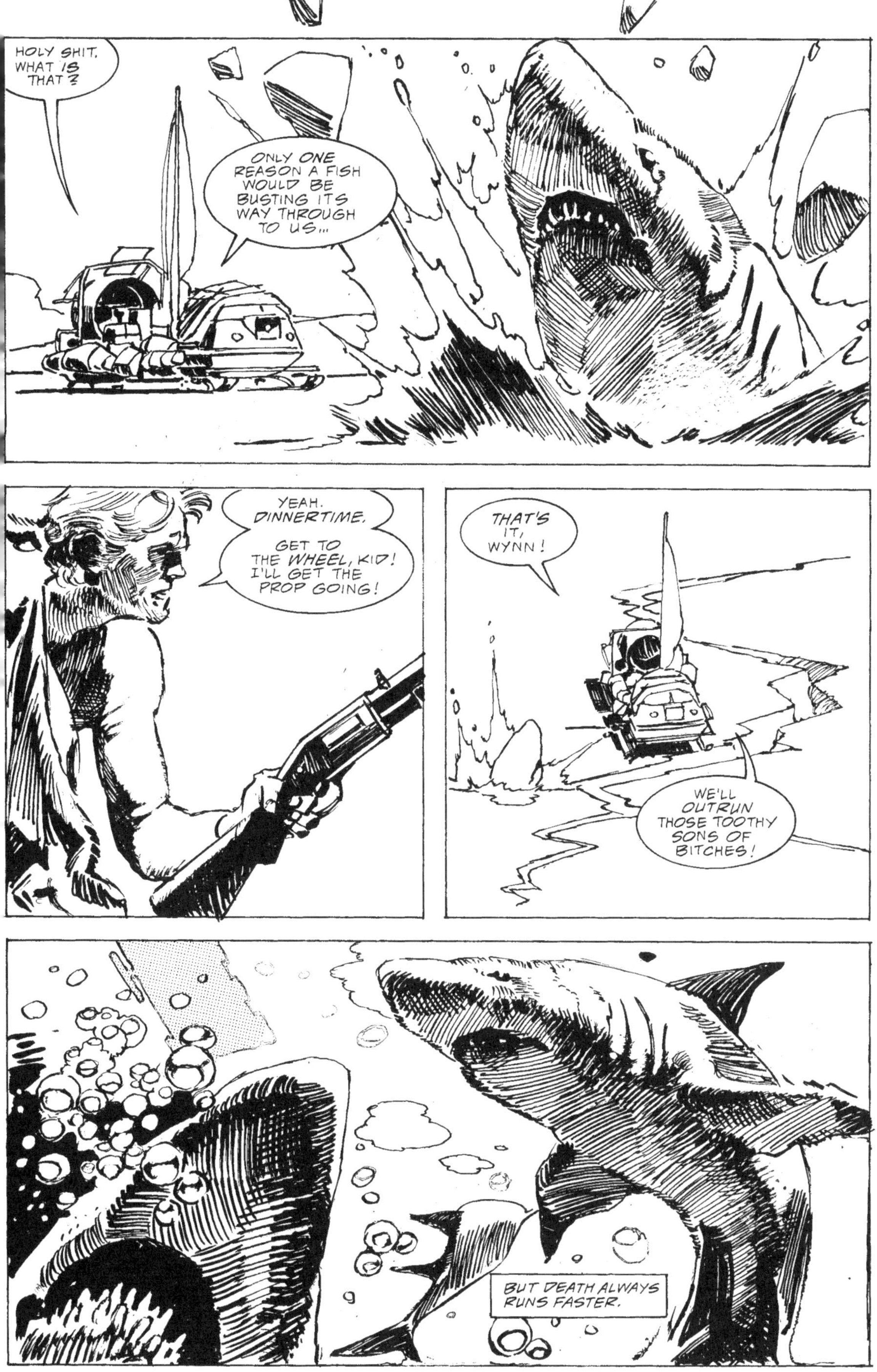
HOLY SHIT. WHAT IS THAT?
ONLY ONE REASON A FISH WOULD BE BUSTING ITS WAY THROUGH TO US...
YEAH. DINNERTIME.
GET TO THE WHEEL, KID! I'LL GET THE PROP GOING!
THAT'S IT, WYNN!
WE'LL OUTRUN THOSE TOOTHY SONS OF BITCHES!
BUT DEATH ALWAYS RUNS FASTER.

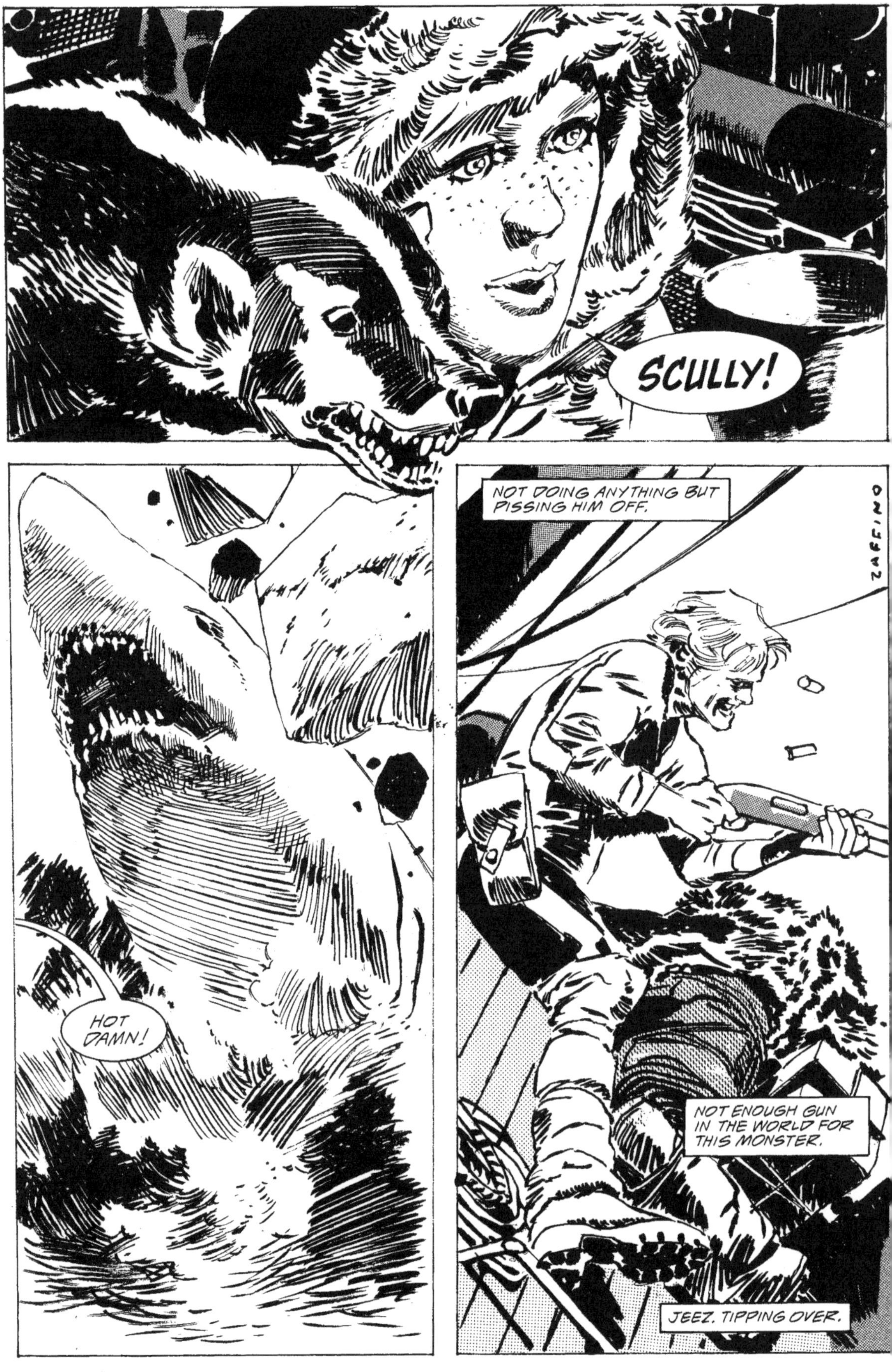
SCULLY!
HOT DAMN!
NOT DOING ANYTHING BUT PISSING HIM OFF.
ZAFFINO
NOT ENOUGH GUN IN THE WORLD FOR THIS MONSTER.
JEEZ. TIPPING OVER.

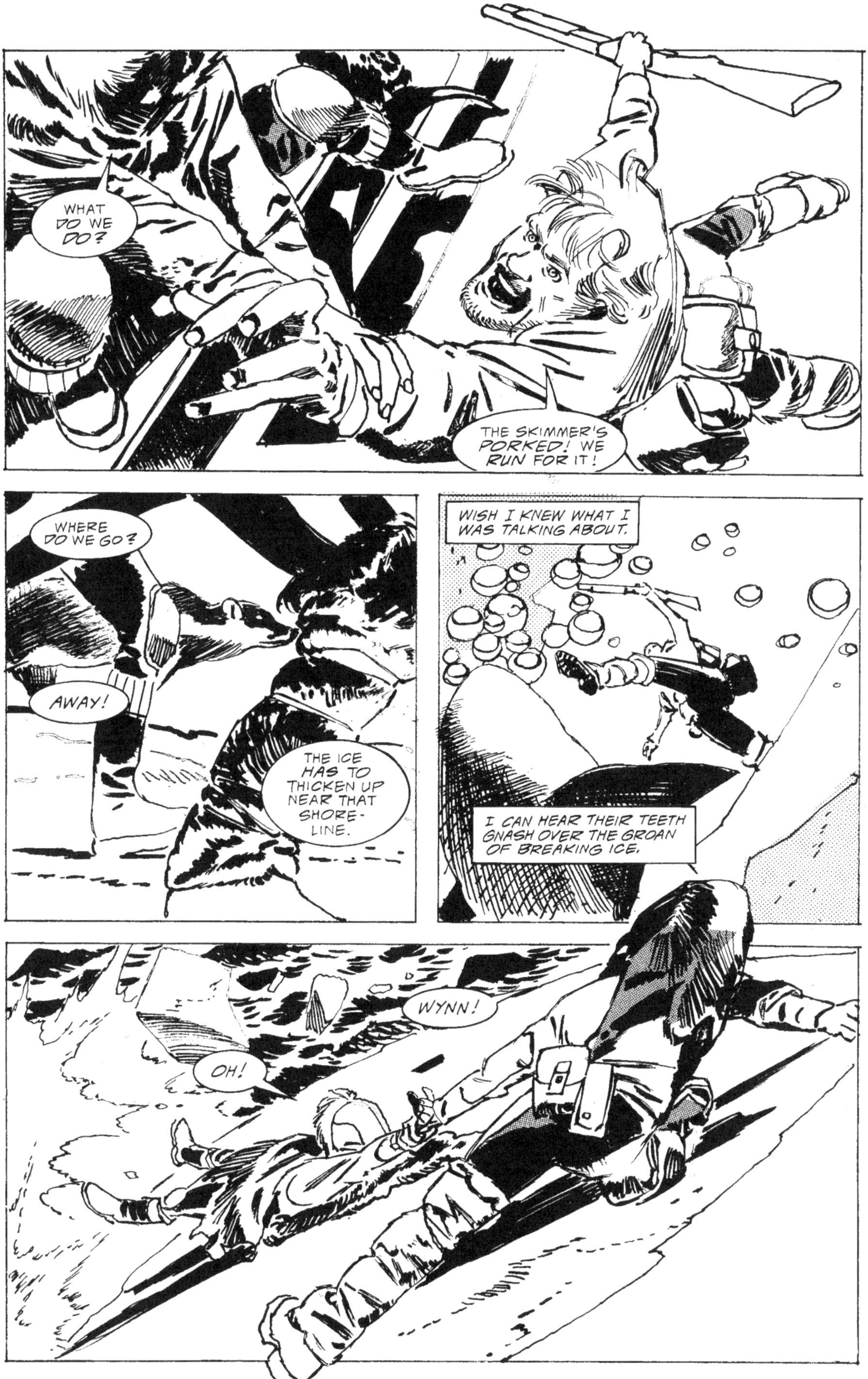
WHAT DO WE DO?
THE SKIMMER'S PORKED! WE RUN FOR IT!
WHERE DO WE GO?
AWAY!
THE ICE HAS TO THICKEN UP NEAR THAT SHORE-LINE.
WISH I KNEW WHAT I WAS TALKING ABOUT.
I CAN HEAR THEIR TEETH GNASH OVER THE GROAN OF BREAKING ICE.
WYNN!
OH!

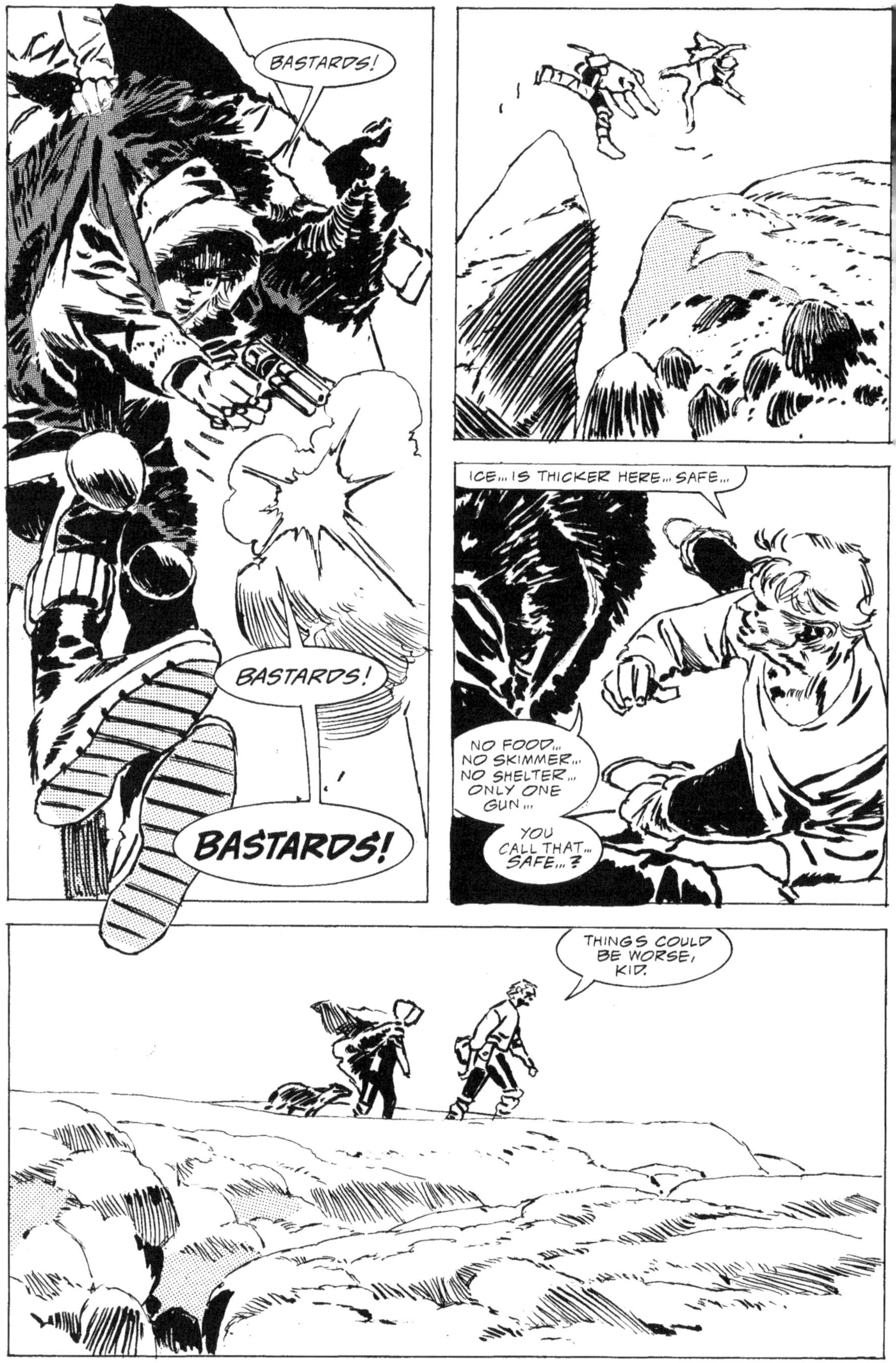

BASTARDS!
BASTARDS!
BASTARDS!
ICE... IS THICKER HERE... SAFE...
NO FOOD... NO SKIMMER... NO SHELTER... ONLY ONE GUN...
YOU CALL THAT... SAFE...?
THINGS COULD BE WORSE, KID.

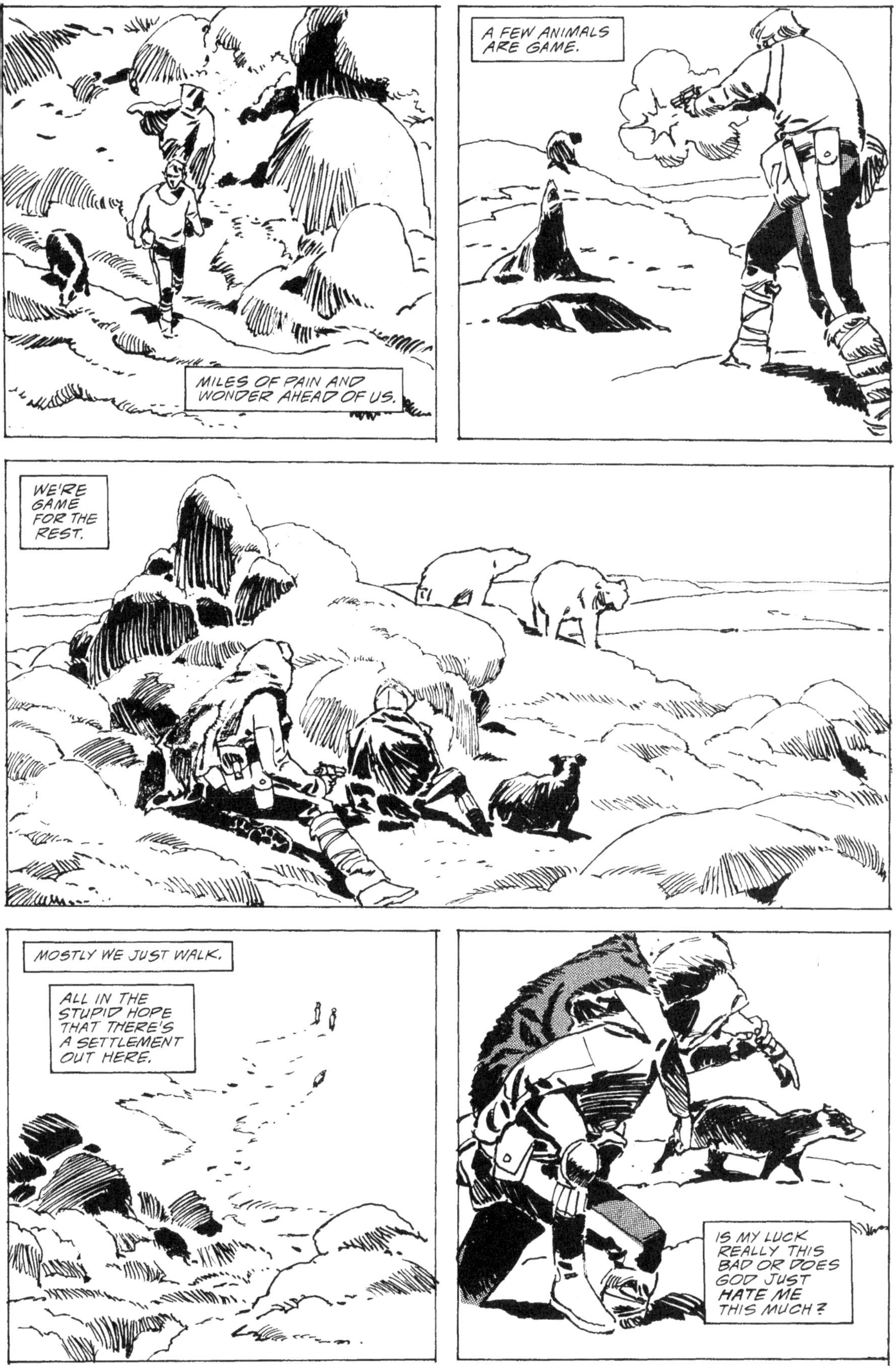
MILES OF PAIN AND WONDER AHEAD OF US.
A FEW ANIMALS ARE GAME.
WE'RE GAME FOR THE REST.
MOSTLY WE JUST WALK.
ALL IN THE STUPID HOPE THAT THERE'S A SETTLEMENT OUT HERE.
IS MY LUCK REALLY THIS BAD OR DOES GOD JUST HATE ME THIS MUCH?

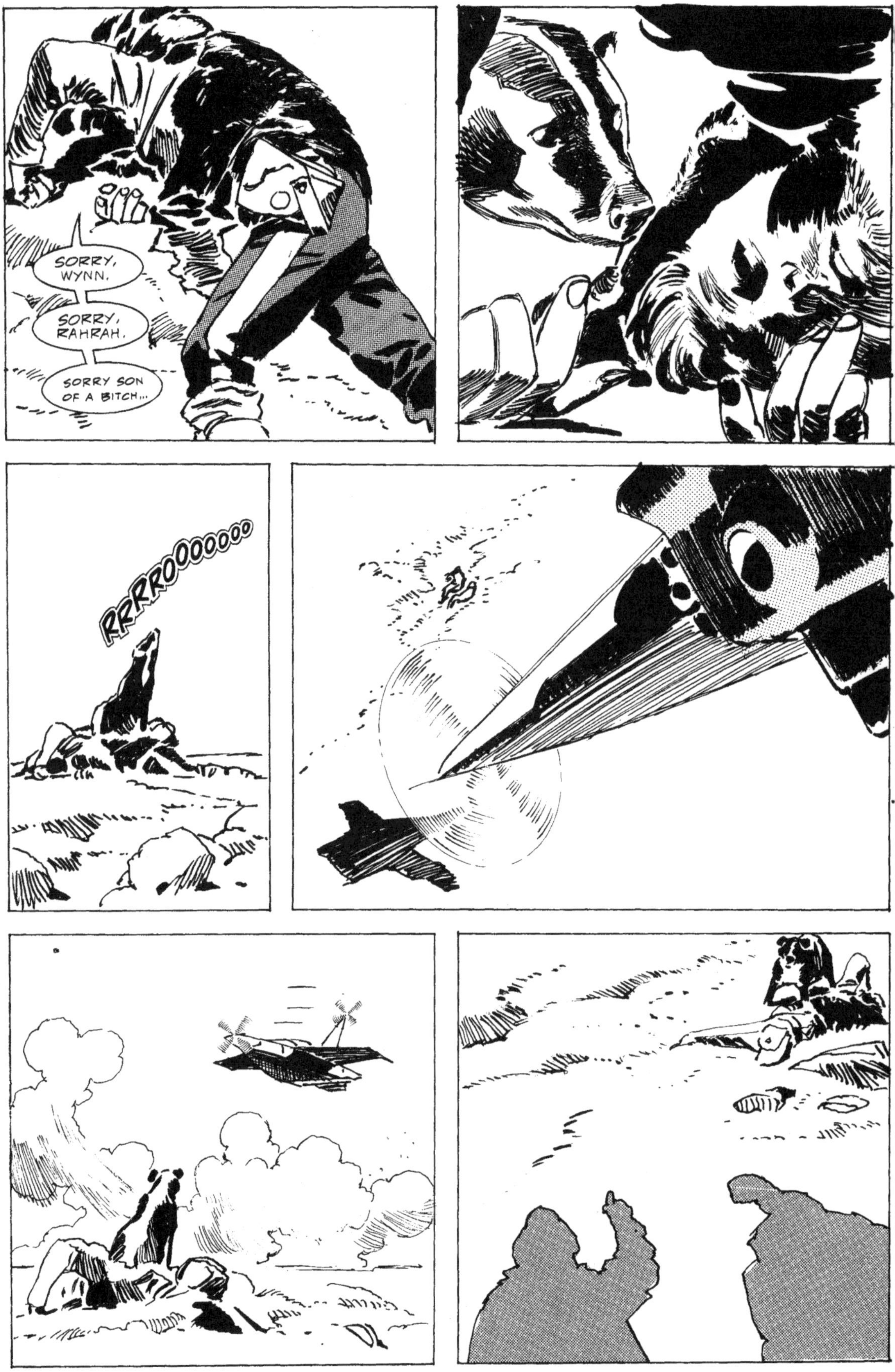
SORRY, WYNN.
SORRY, RAHRAH.
SORRY SON OF A BITCH...
RRRROOOOOOOO

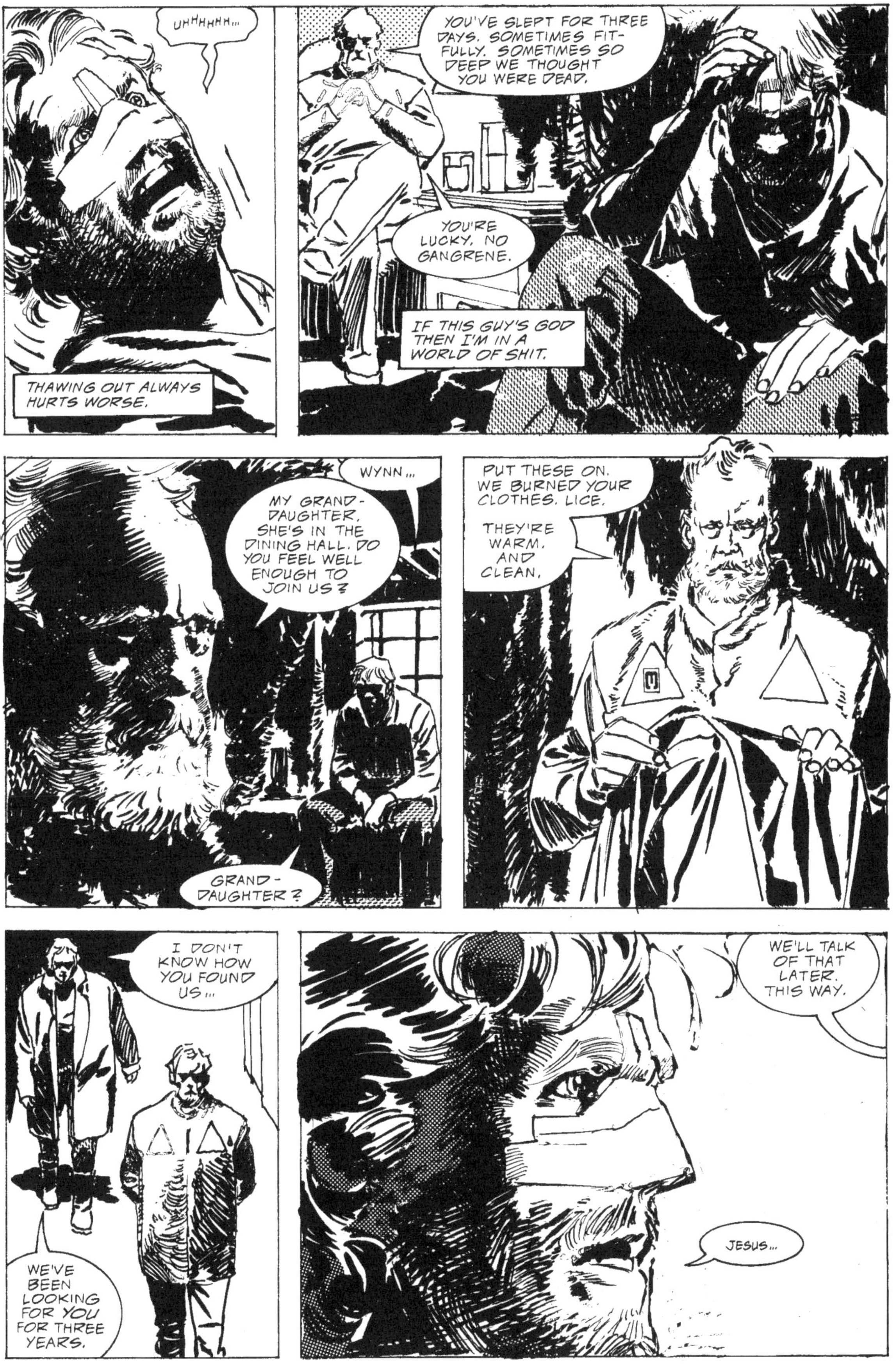
UHHHHHH...
THAWING OUT ALWAYS HURTS WORSE.
YOU'VE SLEPT FOR THREE DAYS. SOMETIMES FITFULLY. SOMETIMES SO DEEP WE THOUGHT YOU WERE DEAD.
YOU'RE LUCKY. NO GANGRENE.
IF THIS GUY'S GOD THEN I'M IN A WORLD OF SHIT.
WYNN...
MY GRAND-DAUGHTER, SHE'S IN THE DINING HALL. DO YOU FEEL WELL ENOUGH TO JOIN US?
GRAND-DAUGHTER?
PUT THESE ON. WE BURNED YOUR CLOTHES. LICE.
THEY'RE WARM. AND CLEAN.
I DON'T KNOW HOW YOU FOUND US...
WE'VE BEEN LOOKING FOR YOU FOR THREE YEARS.
WE'LL TALK OF THAT LATER. THIS WAY.
JESUS...

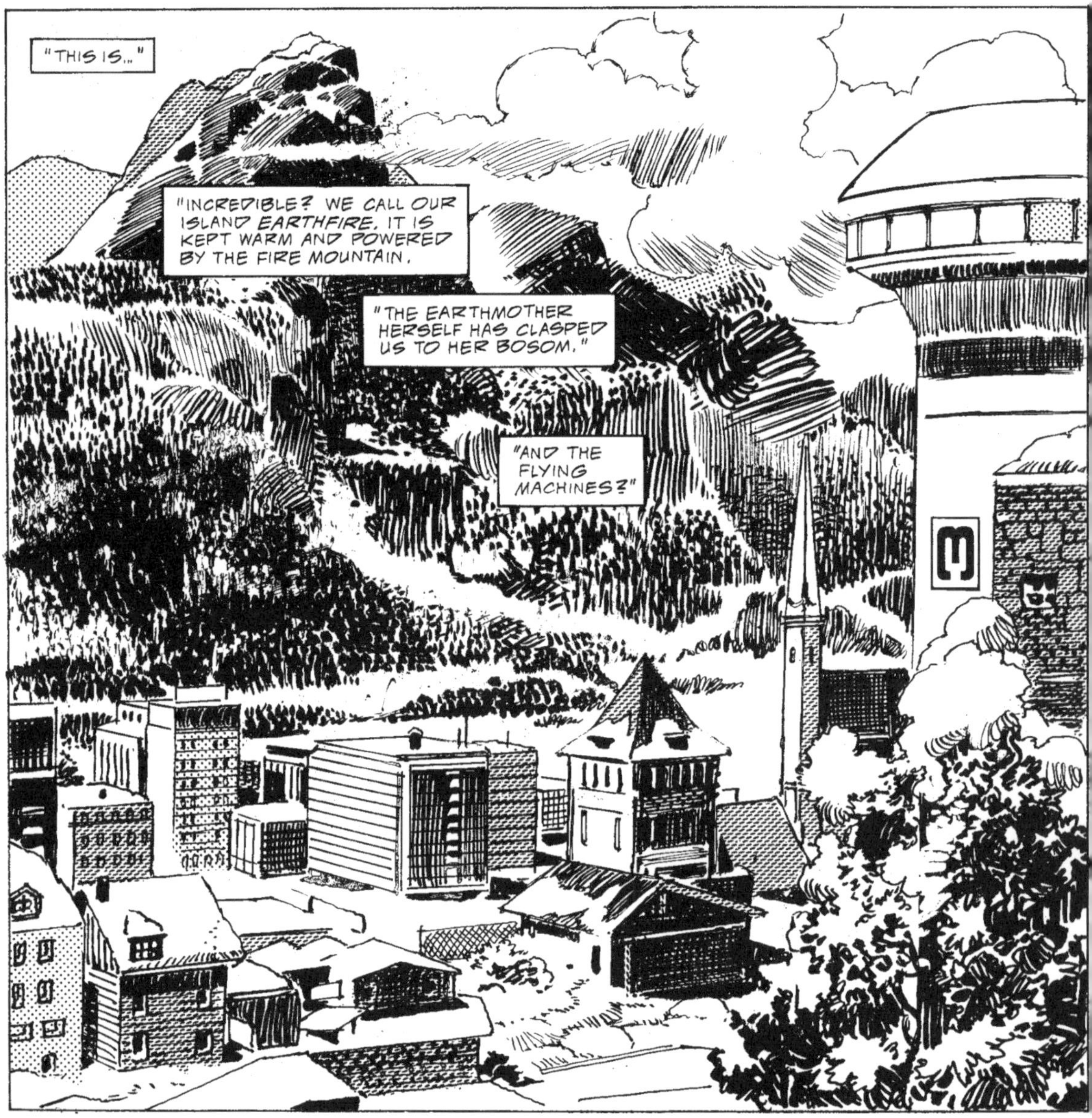
"THIS IS..."
"INCREDIBLE? WE CALL OUR ISLAND EARTHFIRE. IT IS KEPT WARM AND POWERED BY THE FIRE MOUNTAIN.
"THE EARTHMOTHER HERSELF HAS CLASPED US TO HER BOSOM."
"AND THE FLYING MACHINES?"

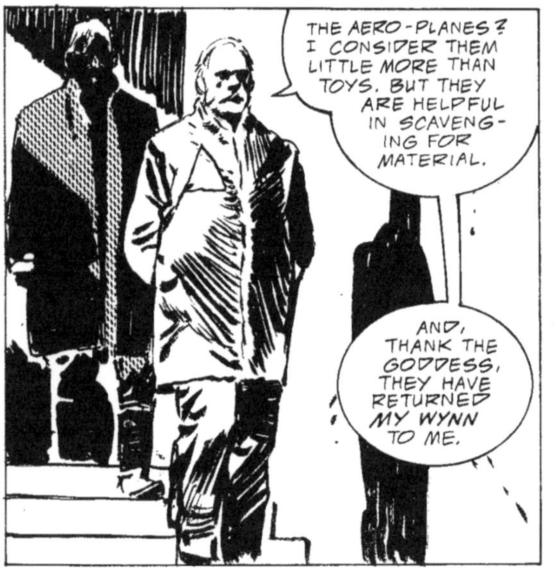
THE AERO-PLANES? I CONSIDER THEM LITTLE MORE THAN TOYS. BUT THEY ARE HELPFUL IN SCAVENG-ING FOR MATERIAL.
AND, THANK THE GODDESS, THEY HAVE RETURNED MY WYNN TO ME.

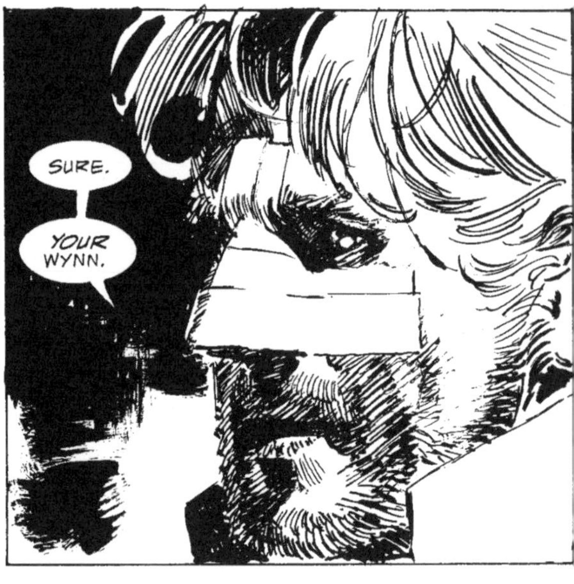
SURE.
YOUR WYNN.

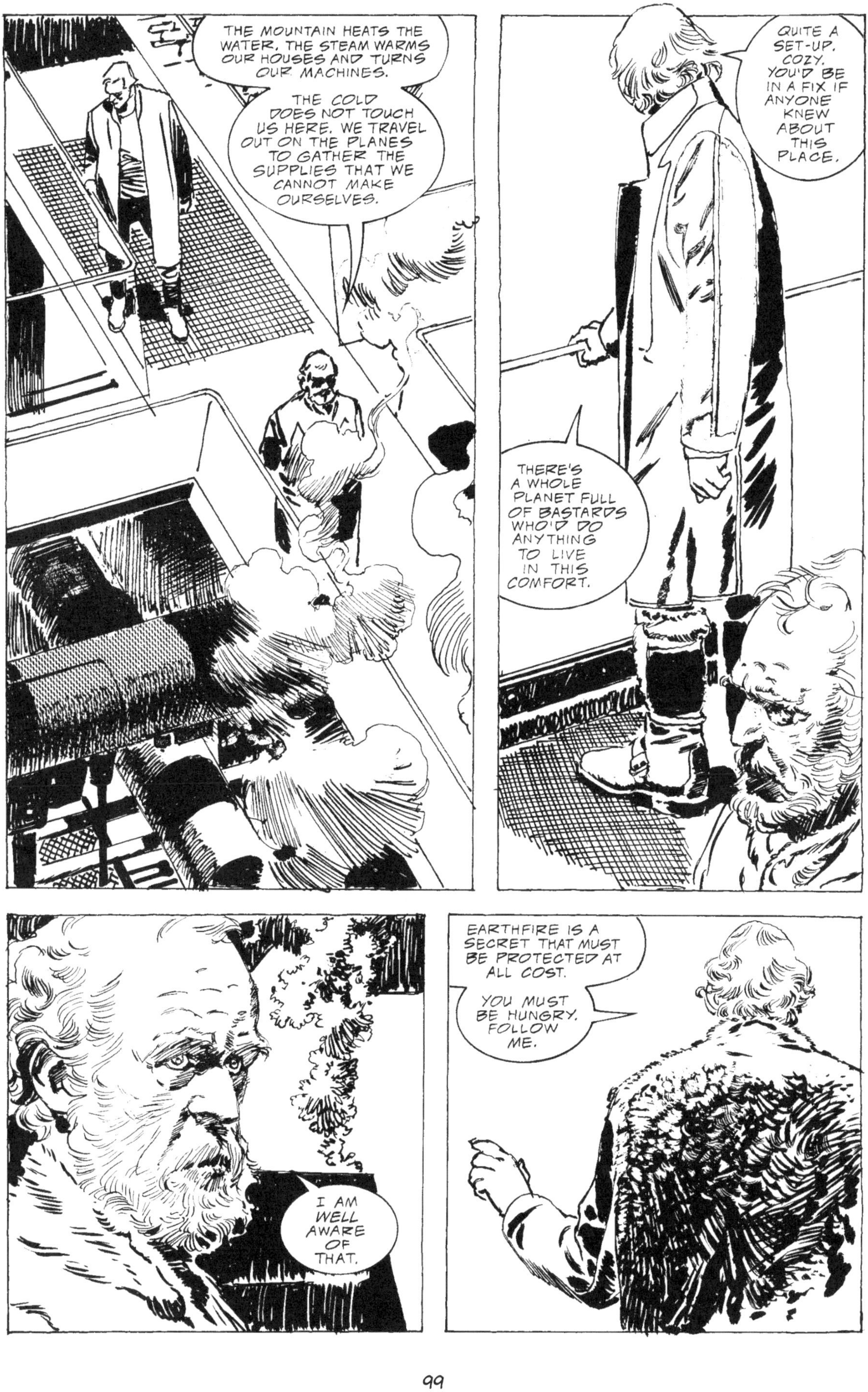
THE MOUNTAIN HEATS THE WATER. THE STEAM WARMS OUR HOUSES AND TURNS OUR MACHINES.
THE COLD DOES NOT TOUCH US HERE. WE TRAVEL OUT ON THE PLANES TO GATHER THE SUPPLIES THAT WE CANNOT MAKE OURSELVES.
QUITE A SET-UP. COZY. YOU'D BE IN A FIX IF ANYONE KNEW ABOUT THIS PLACE.
THERE'S A WHOLE PLANET FULL OF BASTARDS WHO'D DO ANYTHING TO LIVE IN THIS COMFORT.
I AM WELL AWARE OF THAT.
EARTHFIRE IS A SECRET THAT MUST BE PROTECTED AT ALL COST.
YOU MUST BE HUNGRY. FOLLOW ME.

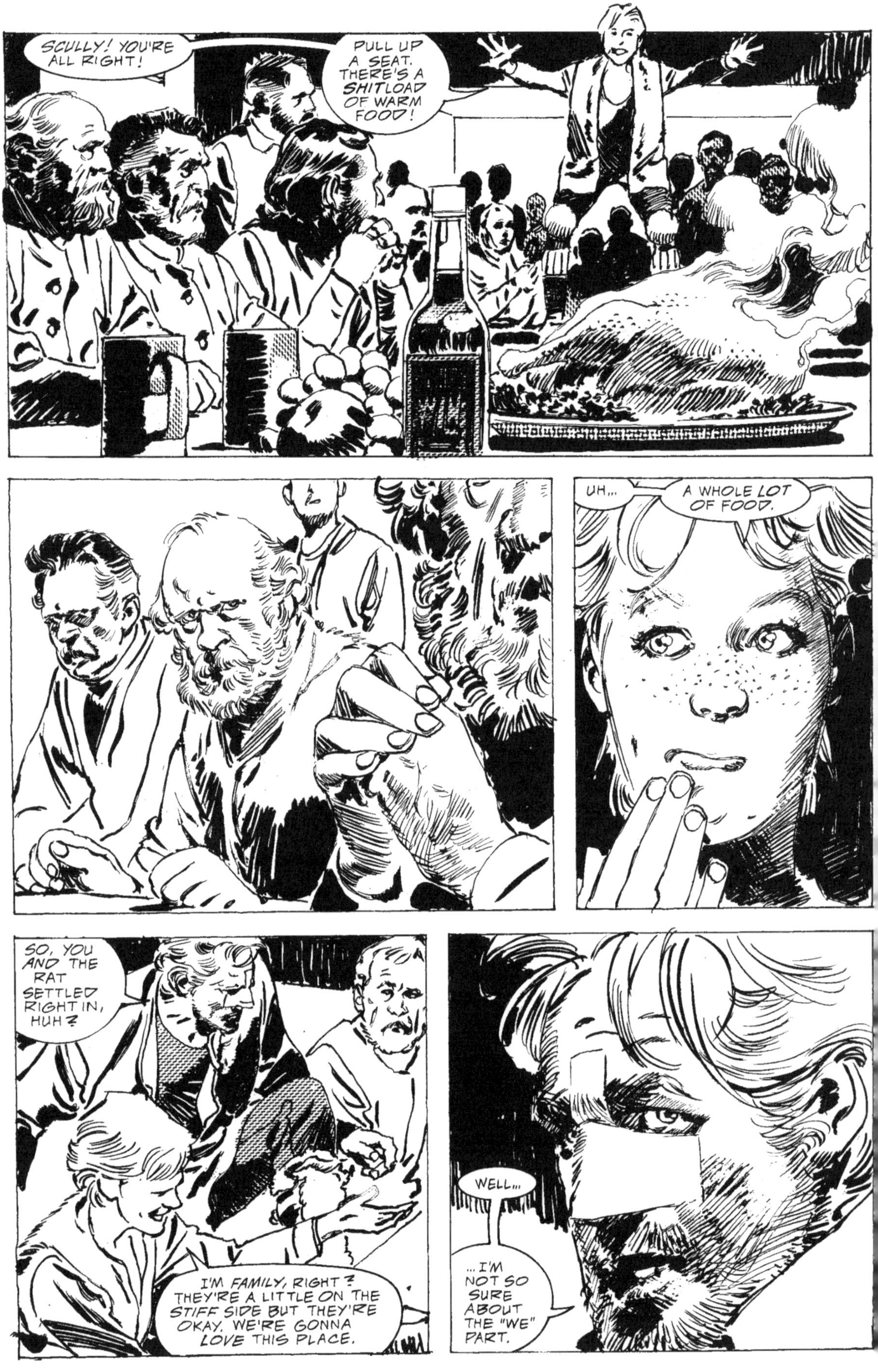
SCULLY! YOU'RE ALL RIGHT!
PULL UP A SEAT. THERE'S A SHITLOAD OF WARM FOOD!
UH...
A WHOLE LOT OF FOOD.
SO, YOU AND THE RAT SETTLED RIGHT IN, HUH?
I'M FAMILY, RIGHT? THEY'RE A LITTLE ON THE STIFF SIDE BUT THEY'RE OKAY. WE'RE GONNA LOVE THIS PLACE.
WELL...
...I'M NOT SO SURE ABOUT THE "WE" PART.

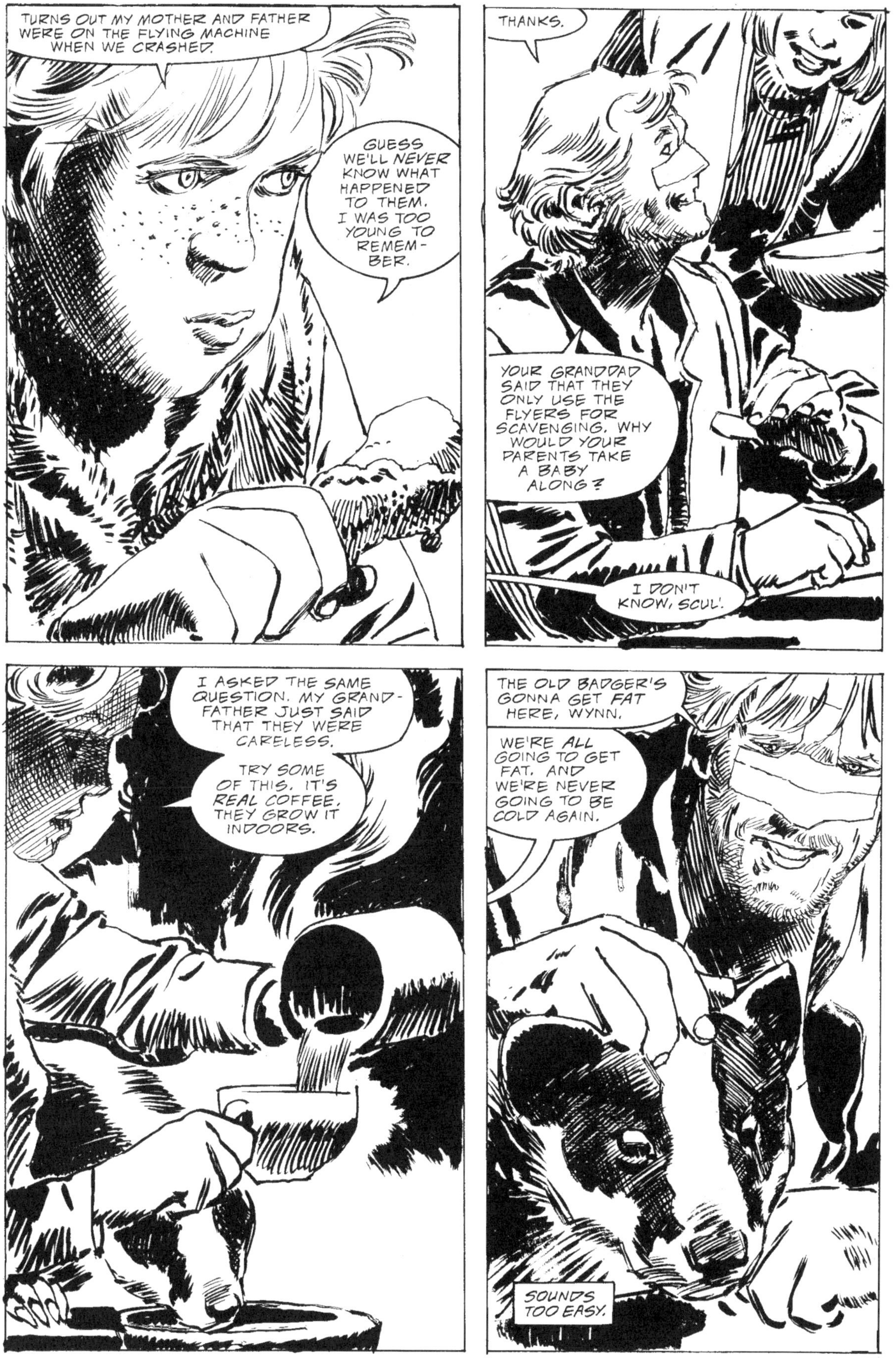
TURNS OUT MY MOTHER AND FATHER WERE ON THE FLYING MACHINE WHEN WE CRASHED.
GUESS WE'LL NEVER KNOW WHAT HAPPENED TO THEM. I WAS TOO YOUNG TO REMEM-BER.
THANKS.
YOUR GRANDDAD SAID THAT THEY ONLY USE THE FLYERS FOR SCAVENGING. WHY WOULD YOUR PARENTS TAKE A BABY ALONG?
I DON'T KNOW, SCUL'.
I ASKED THE SAME QUESTION. MY GRAND-FATHER JUST SAID THAT THEY WERE CARELESS.
TRY SOME OF THIS. IT'S REAL COFFEE. THEY GROW IT INDOORS.
THE OLD BADGER'S GONNA GET FAT HERE, WYNN.
WE'RE ALL GOING TO GET FAT. AND WE'RE NEVER GOING TO BE COLD AGAIN.
SOUNDS TOO EASY.

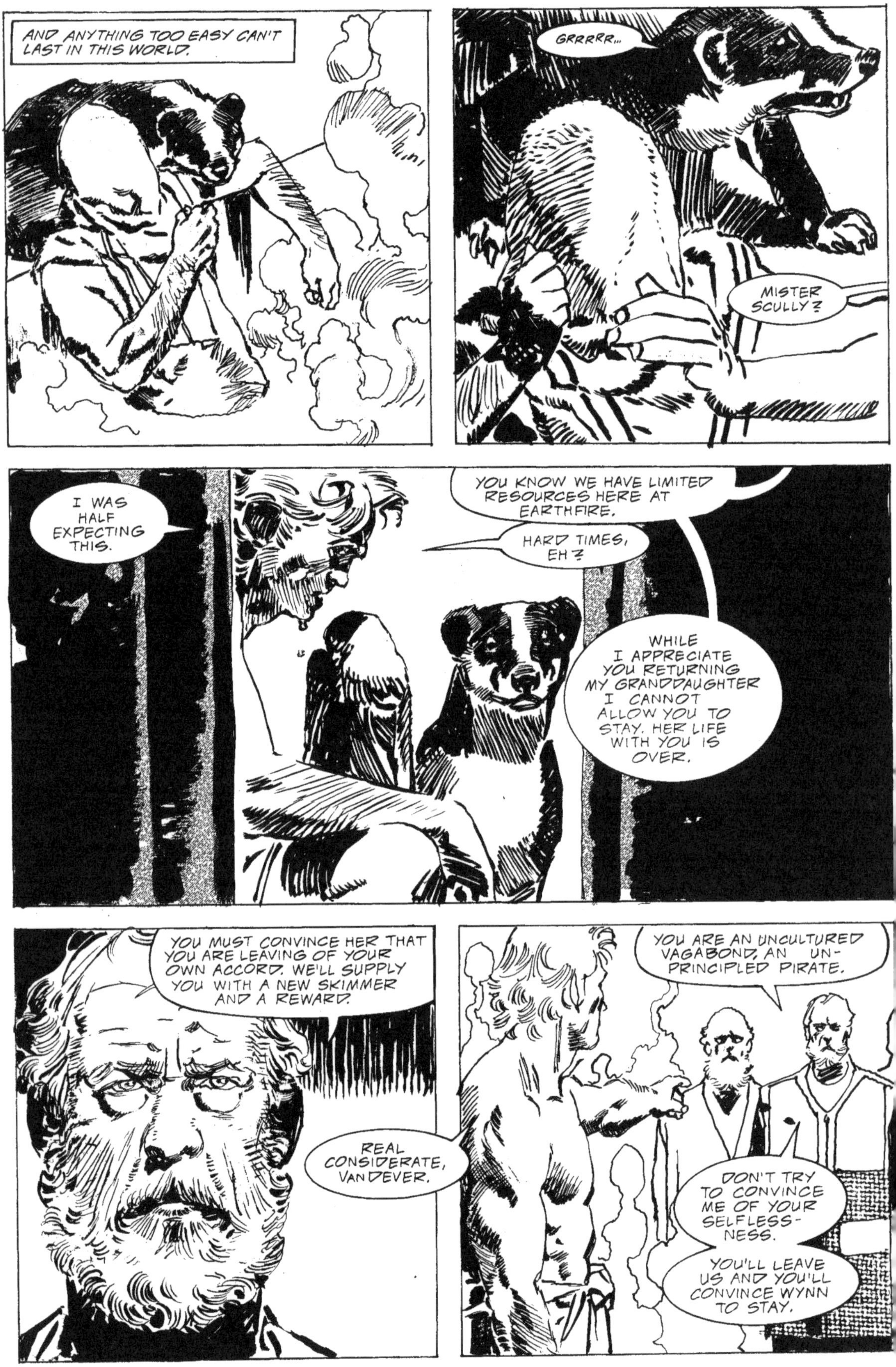
AND ANYTHING TOO EASY CAN'T LAST IN THIS WORLD.
GRRRRR...
MISTER SCULLY?
I WAS HALF EXPECTING THIS.
YOU KNOW WE HAVE LIMITED RESOURCES HERE AT EARTHFIRE.
HARD TIMES, EH?
WHILE I APPRECIATE YOU RETURNING MY GRANDDAUGHTER I CANNOT ALLOW YOU TO STAY. HER LIFE WITH YOU IS OVER.
YOU MUST CONVINCE HER THAT YOU ARE LEAVING OF YOUR OWN ACCORD. WE'LL SUPPLY YOU WITH A NEW SKIMMER AND A REWARD.
REAL CONSIDERATE, VANDEVER.
YOU ARE AN UNCULTURED VAGABOND, AN UNPRINCIPLED PIRATE.
DON'T TRY TO CONVINCE ME OF YOUR SELFLESSNESS.
YOU'LL LEAVE US AND YOU'LL CONVINCE WYNN TO STAY.

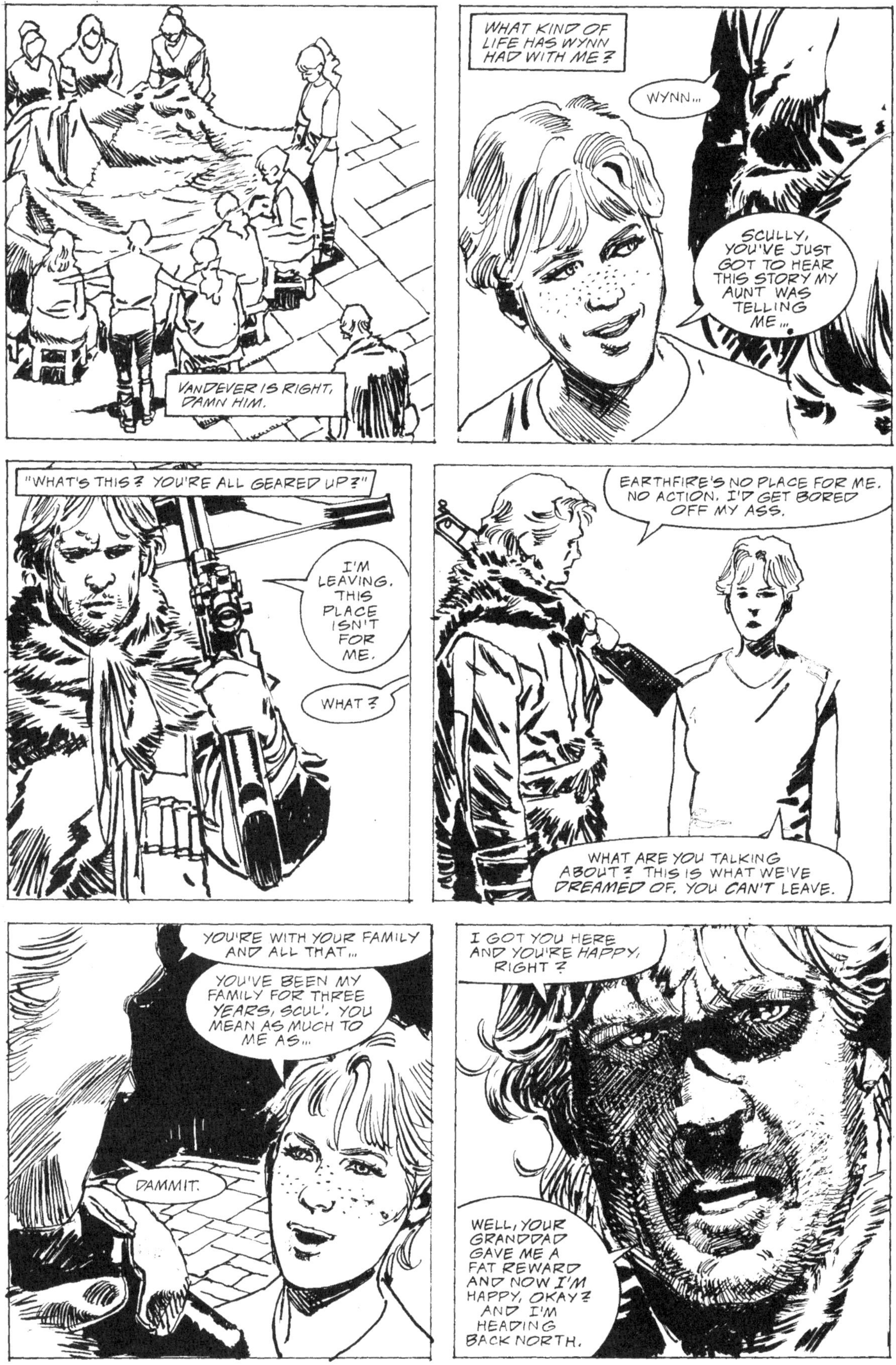
VANDEVER IS RIGHT, DAMN HIM.
WHAT KIND OF LIFE HAS WYNN HAD WITH ME?
WYNN...
SCULLY, YOU'VE JUST GOT TO HEAR THIS STORY MY AUNT WAS TELLING ME...
"WHAT'S THIS? YOU'RE ALL GEARED UP?"
I'M LEAVING. THIS PLACE ISN'T FOR ME.
WHAT?
EARTHFIRE'S NO PLACE FOR ME. NO ACTION. I'D GET BORED OFF MY ASS.
WHAT ARE YOU TALKING ABOUT? THIS IS WHAT WE'VE DREAMED OF. YOU CAN'T LEAVE.
YOU'RE WITH YOUR FAMILY AND ALL THAT...
YOU'VE BEEN MY FAMILY FOR THREE YEARS, SCUL'. YOU MEAN AS MUCH TO ME AS...
DAMMIT.
I GOT YOU HERE AND YOU'RE HAPPY, RIGHT?
WELL, YOUR GRANDDAD GAVE ME A FAT REWARD AND NOW I'M HAPPY, OKAY? AND I'M HEADING BACK NORTH.

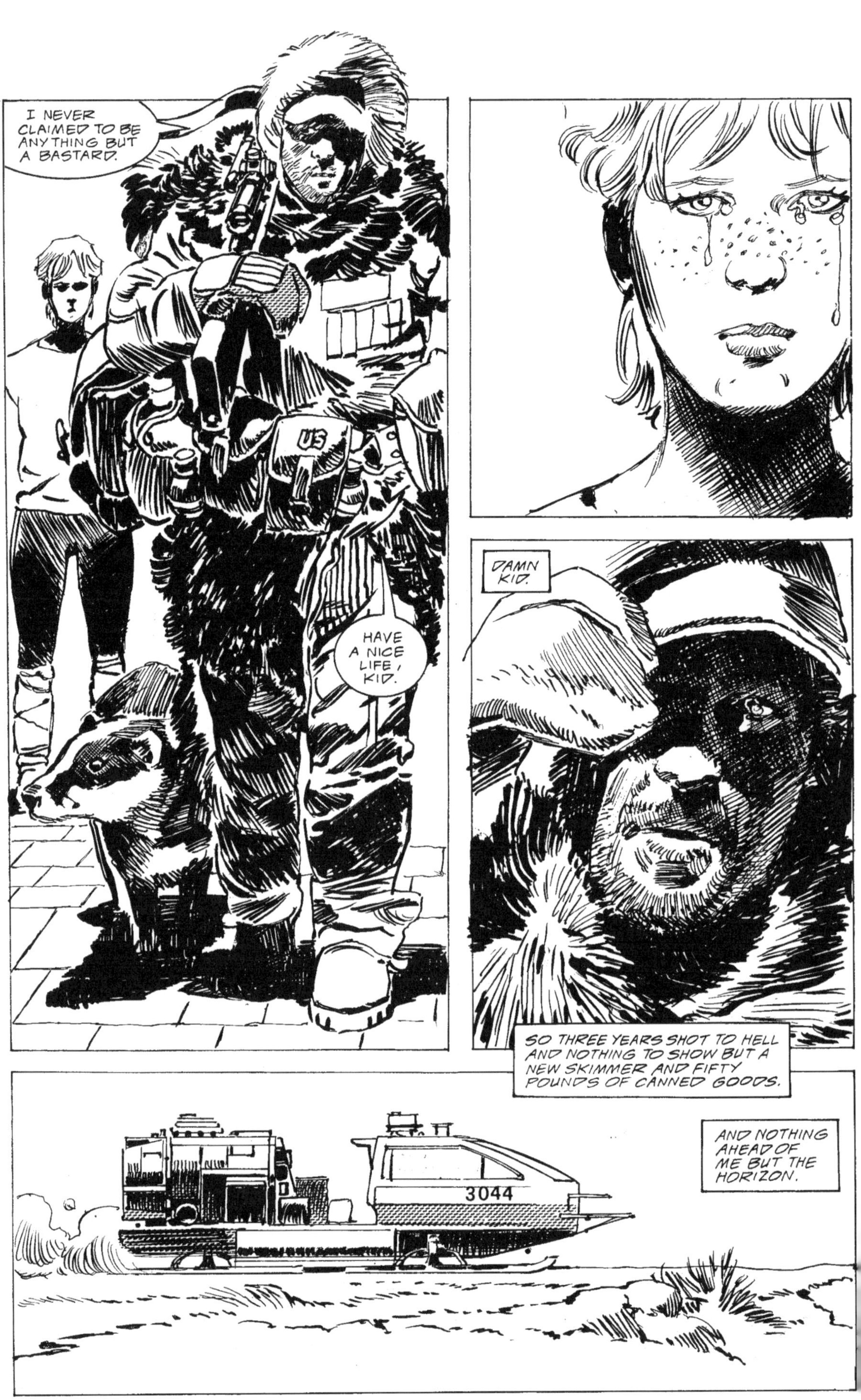

I NEVER CLAIMED TO BE ANYTHING BUT A BASTARD.
HAVE A NICE LIFE, KID.
DAMN KID.
SO THREE YEARS SHOT TO HELL AND NOTHING TO SHOW BUT A NEW SKIMMER AND FIFTY POUNDS OF CANNED GOODS.
AND NOTHING AHEAD OF ME BUT THE HORIZON.
3044

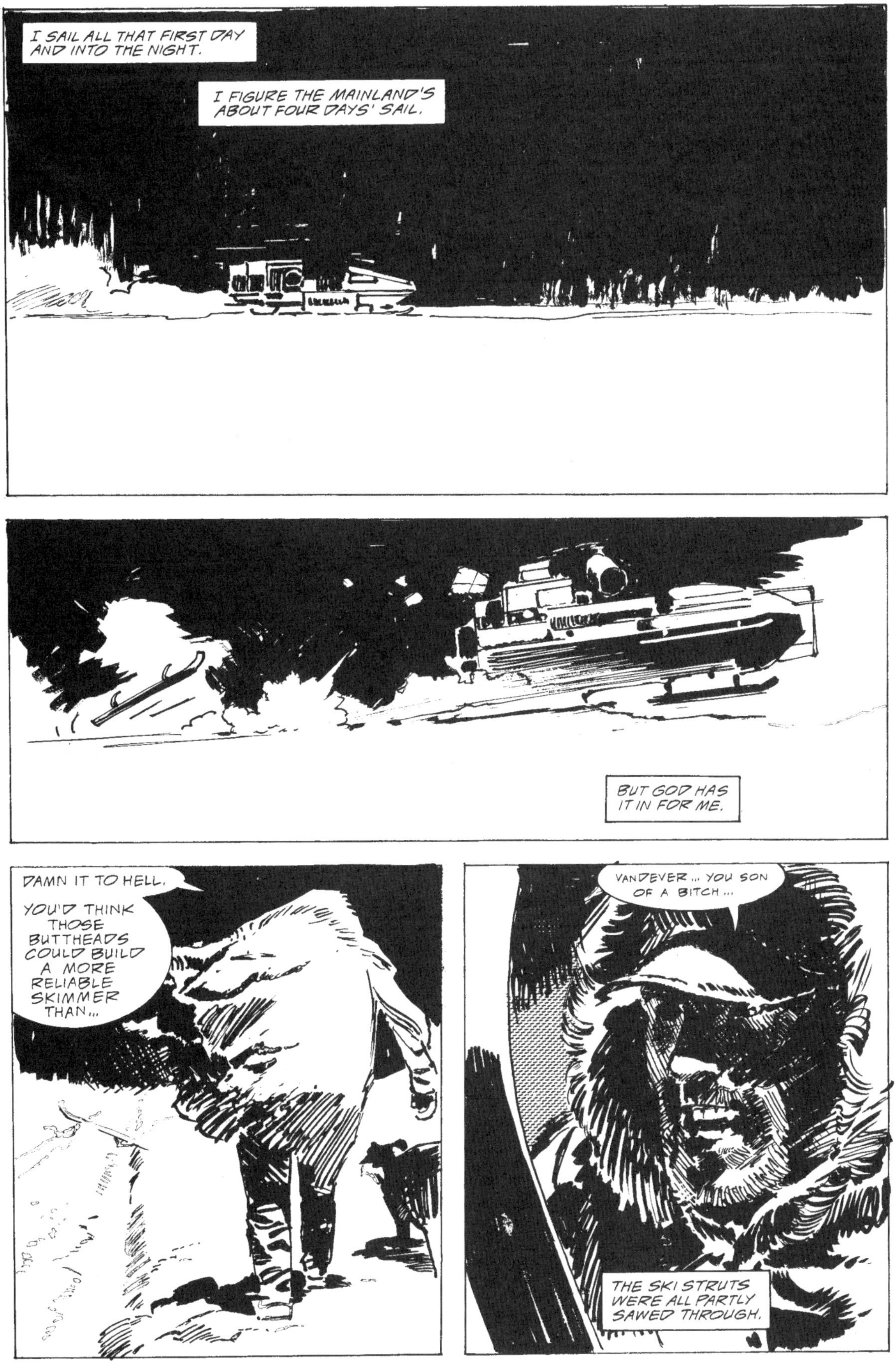
I SAIL ALL THAT FIRST DAY AND INTO THE NIGHT.
I FIGURE THE MAINLAND'S ABOUT FOUR DAYS' SAIL.
BUT GOD HAS IT IN FOR ME.
DAMN IT TO HELL.
YOU'D THINK THOSE BUTTHEADS COULD BUILD A MORE RELIABLE SKIMMER THAN...
VANDEVER... YOU SON OF A BITCH...
THE SKI STRUTS WERE ALL PARTLY SAWED THROUGH.

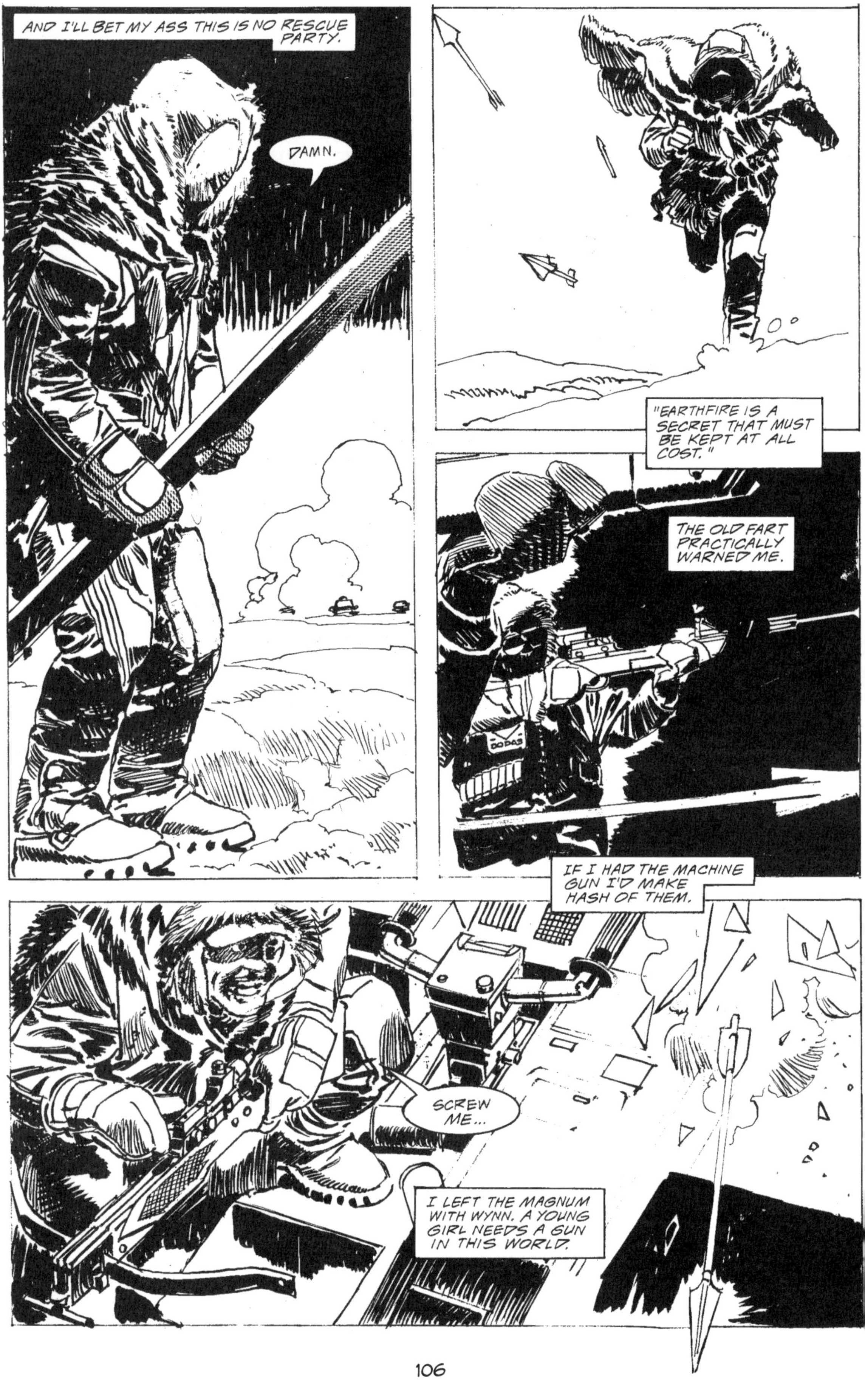
AND I'LL BET MY ASS THIS IS NO RESCUE PARTY.
DAMN.
"EARTHFIRE IS A SECRET THAT MUST BE KEPT AT ALL COST."
THE OLD FART PRACTICALLY WARNED ME.
IF I HAD THE MACHINE GUN I'D MAKE HASH OF THEM.
SCREW ME...
I LEFT THE MAGNUM WITH WYNN. A YOUNG GIRL NEEDS A GUN IN THIS WORLD.

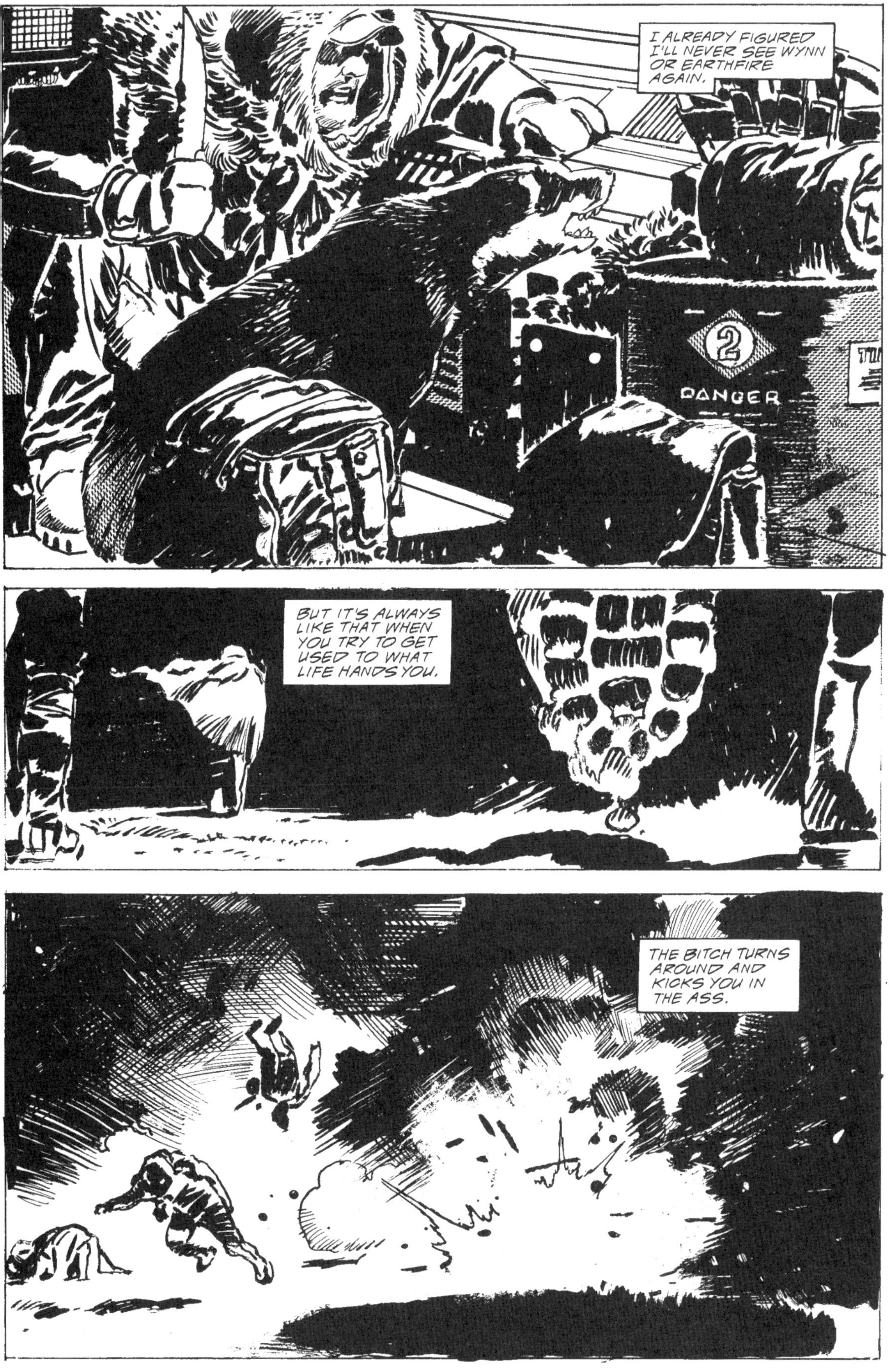
I ALREADY FIGURED I'LL NEVER SEE WYNN OR EARTHFIRE AGAIN.
2
DANGER
BUT IT'S ALWAYS LIKE THAT WHEN YOU TRY TO GET USED TO WHAT LIFE HANDS YOU.
THE BITCH TURNS AROUND AND KICKS YOU IN THE ASS.

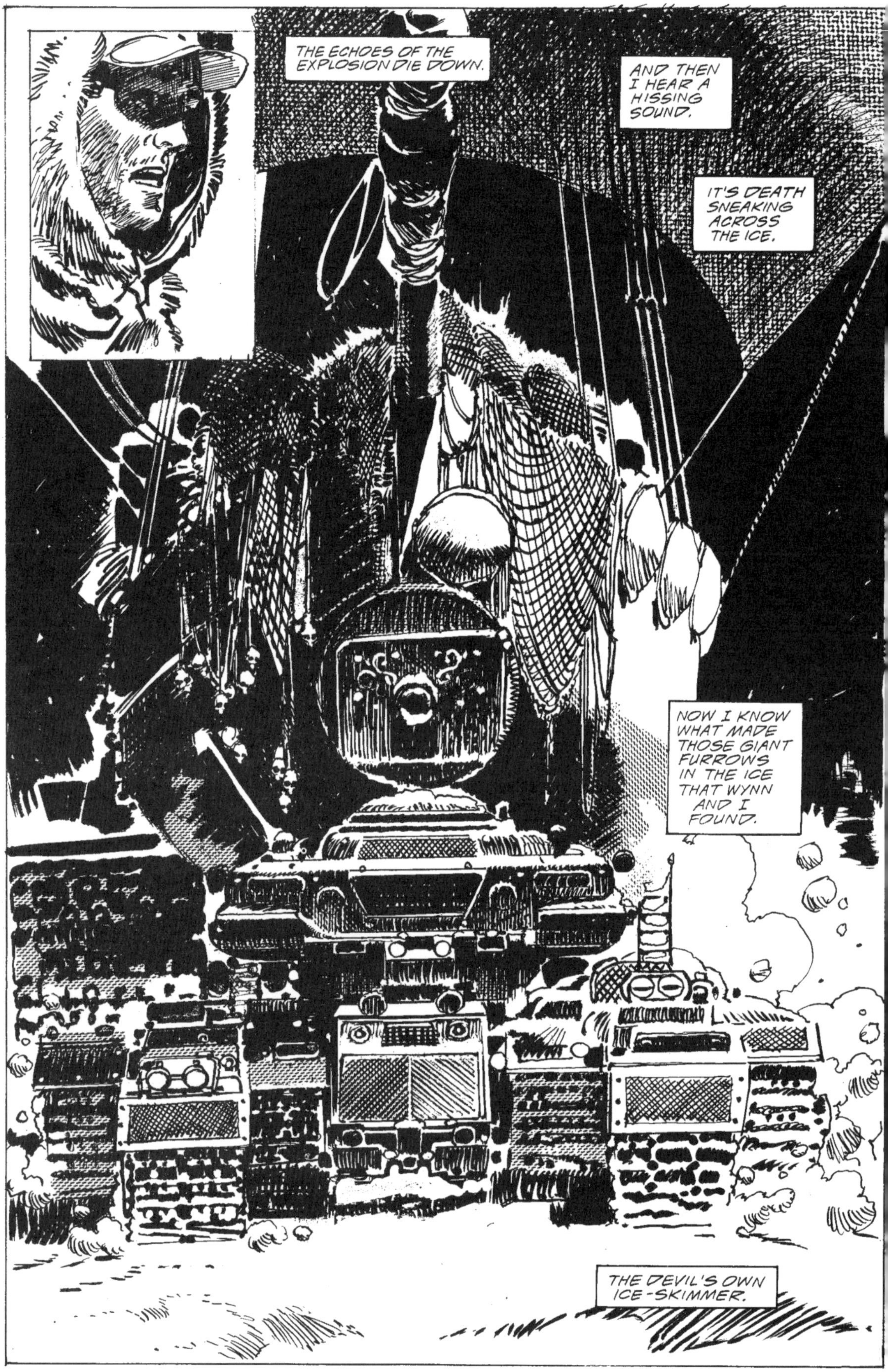
THE ECHOES OF THE EXPLOSION DIE DOWN.
AND THEN I HEAR A HISSING SOUND.
IT'S DEATH SNEAKING ACROSS THE ICE.
NOW I KNOW WHAT MADE THOSE GIANT FURROWS IN THE ICE THAT WYNN AND I FOUND.
THE DEVIL'S OWN ICE-SKIMMER.

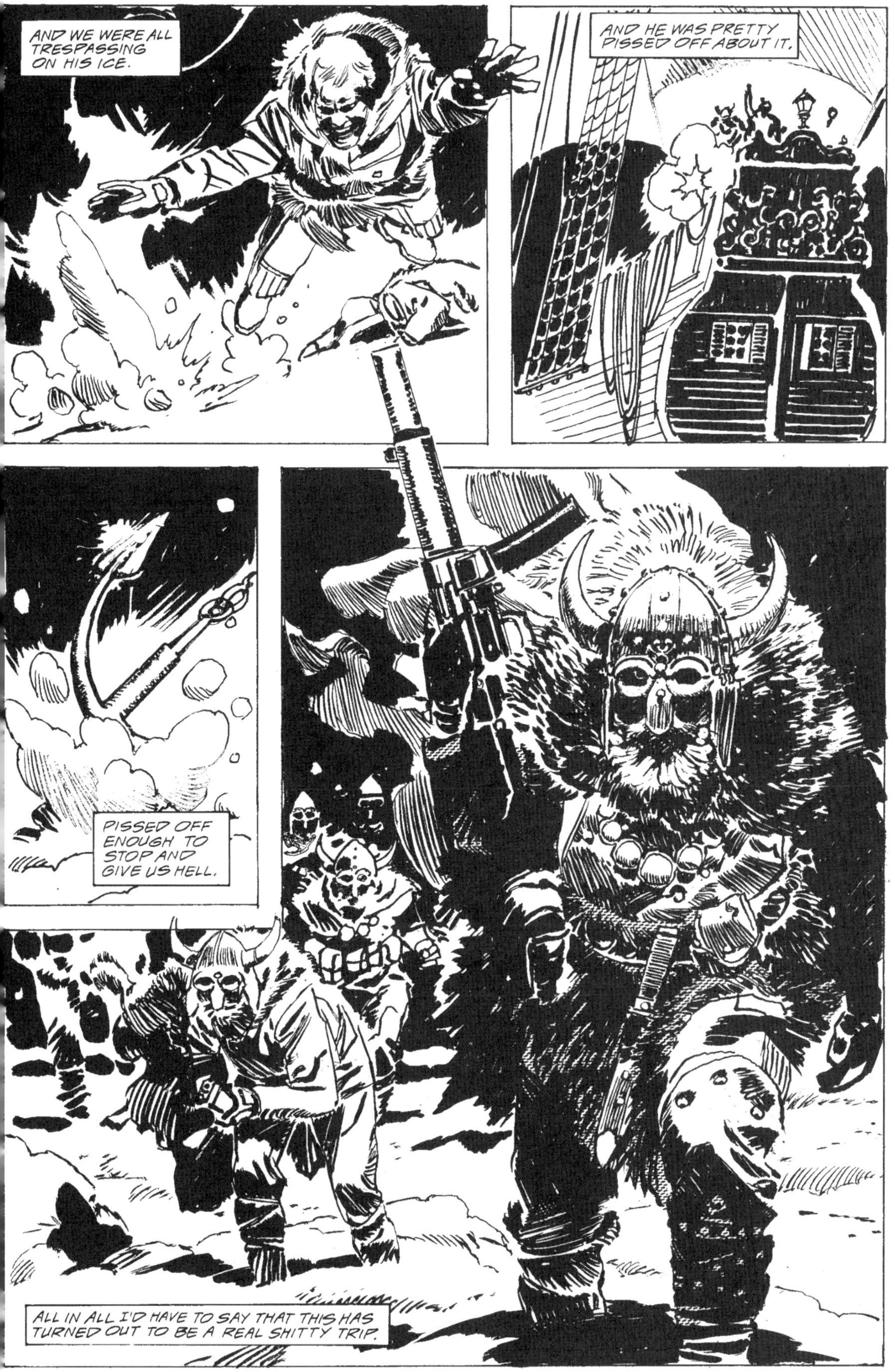
AND WE WERE ALL TRESPASSING ON HIS ICE.
AND HE WAS PRETTY PISSED OFF ABOUT IT.
PISSED OFF ENOUGH TO STOP AND GIVE US HELL.
ALL IN ALL I'D HAVE TO SAY THAT THIS HAS TURNED OUT TO BE A REAL SHITTY TRIP.

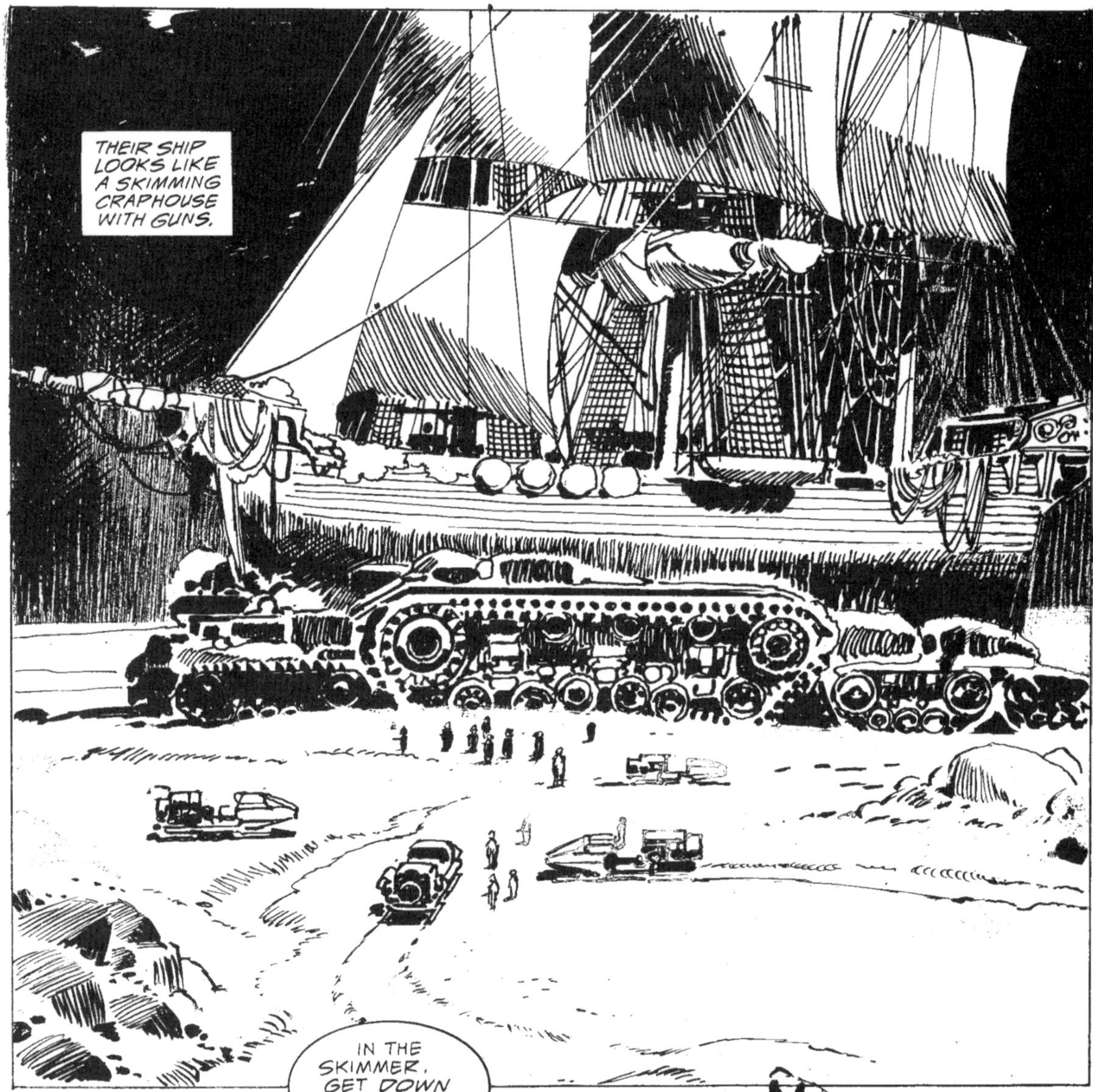
THEIR SHIP LOOKS LIKE A SKIMMING CRAPHOUSE WITH GUNS.

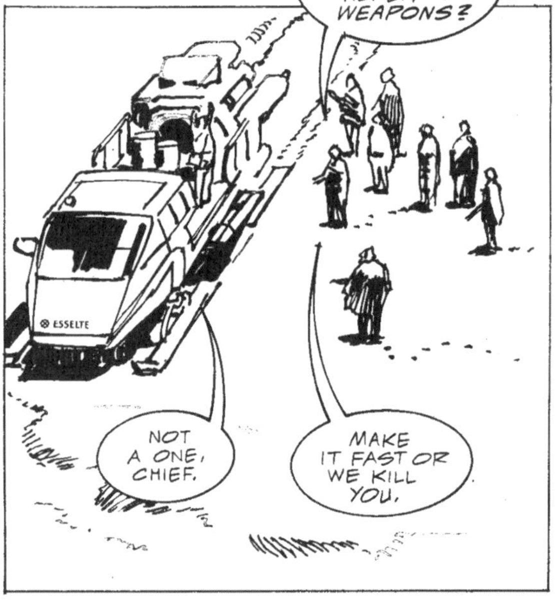
IN THE SKIMMER. GET DOWN HERE. ANY WEAPONS?
ESSELTE
NOT A ONE, CHIEF.
MAKE IT FAST OR WE KILL YOU.

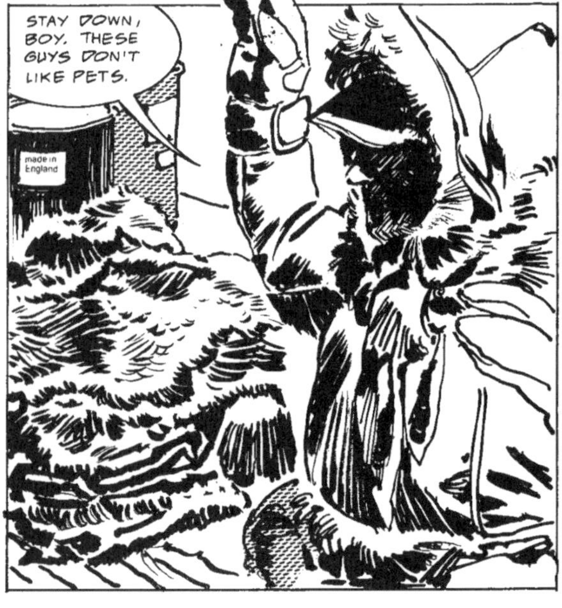
STAY DOWN, BOY. THESE GUYS DON'T LIKE PETS.
made in England

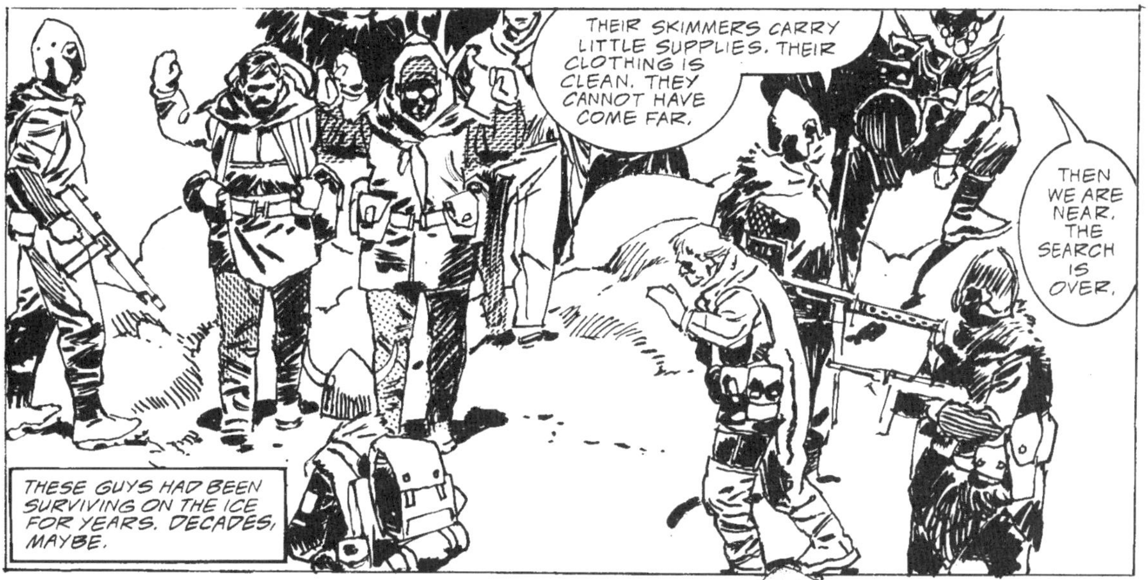
THESE GUYS HAD BEEN SURVIVING ON THE ICE FOR YEARS. DECADES, MAYBE.
THEIR SKIMMERS CARRY LITTLE SUPPLIES. THEIR CLOTHING IS CLEAN. THEY CANNOT HAVE COME FAR.
THEN WE ARE NEAR. THE SEARCH IS OVER.

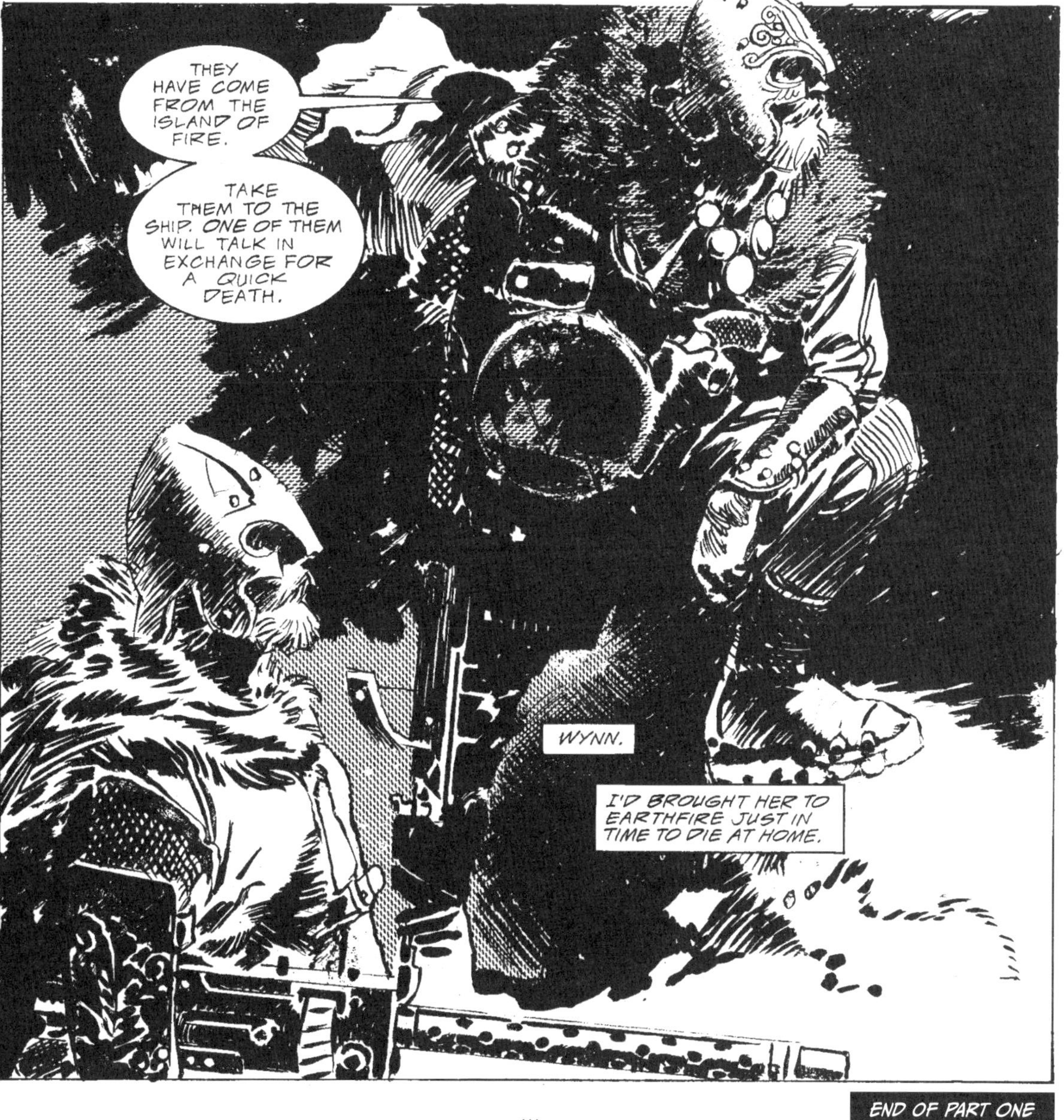
THEY HAVE COME FROM THE ISLAND OF FIRE.
TAKE THEM TO THE SHIP. ONE OF THEM WILL TALK IN EXCHANGE FOR A QUICK DEATH.
WYNN.
I'D BROUGHT HER TO EARTHFIRE JUST IN TIME TO DIE AT HOME.

END OF PART ONE

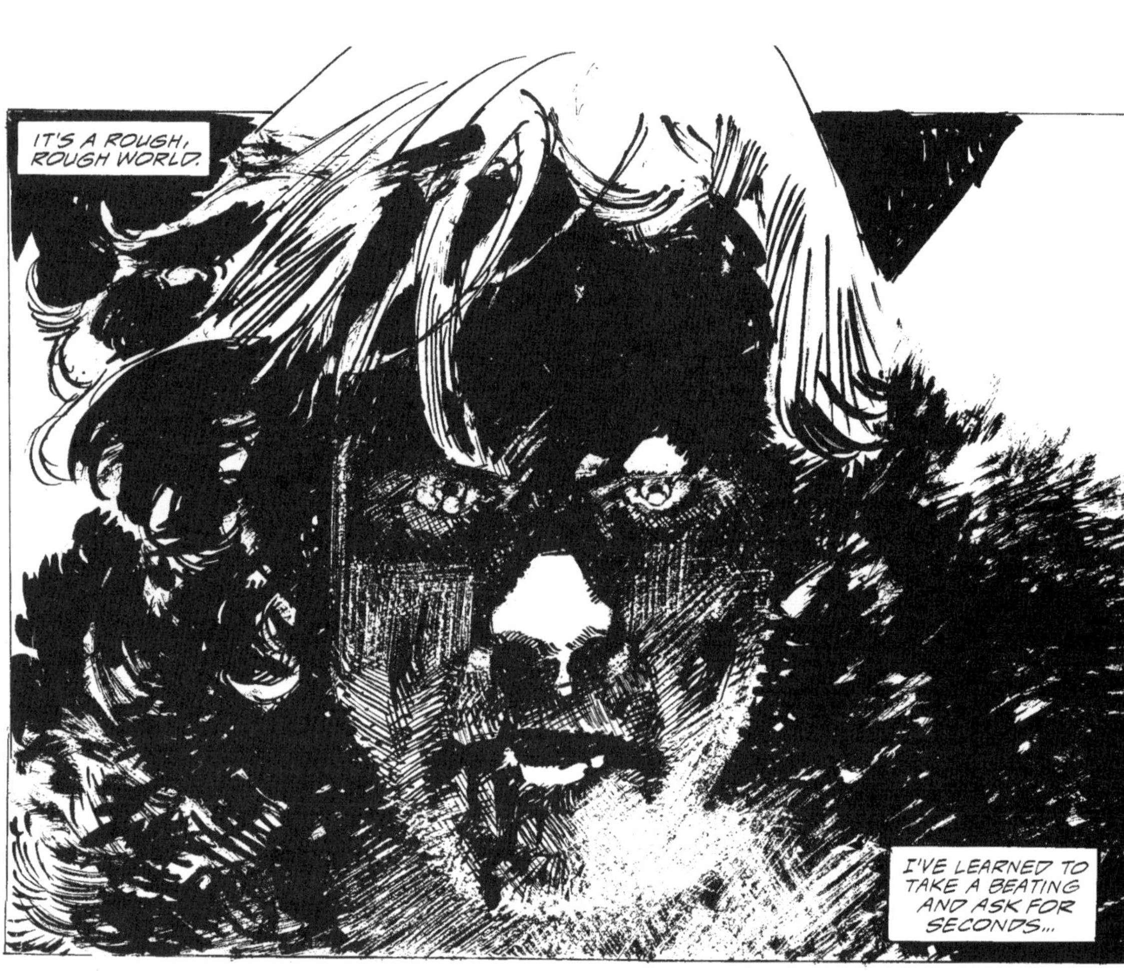
IT'S A ROUGH, ROUGH WORLD.
I'VE LEARNED TO TAKE A BEATING AND ASK FOR SECONDS...

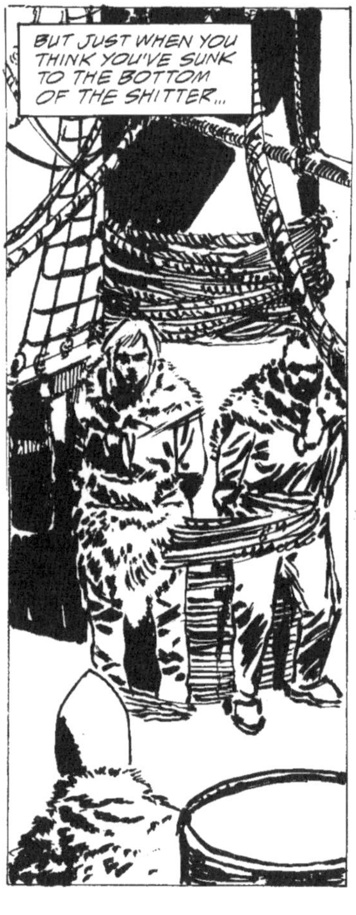
BUT JUST WHEN YOU THINK YOU'VE SUNK TO THE BOTTOM OF THE SHITTER...

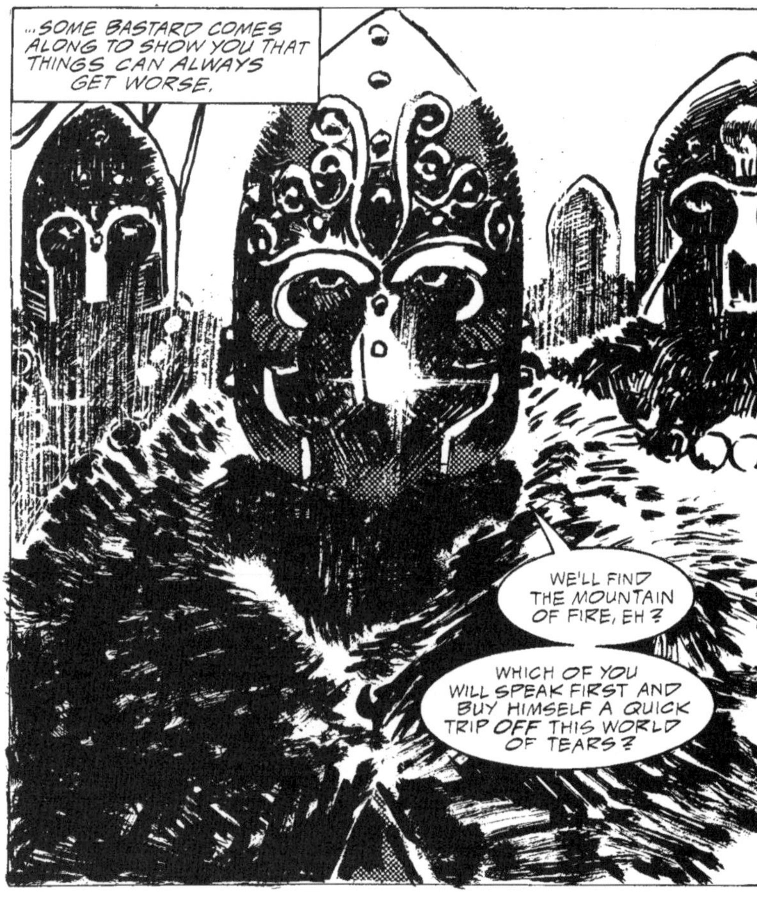
...SOME BASTARD COMES ALONG TO SHOW YOU THAT THINGS CAN ALWAYS GET WORSE.
WE'LL FIND THE MOUNTAIN OF FIRE, EH?
WHICH OF YOU WILL SPEAK FIRST AND BUY HIMSELF A QUICK TRIP OFF THIS WORLD OF TEARS?

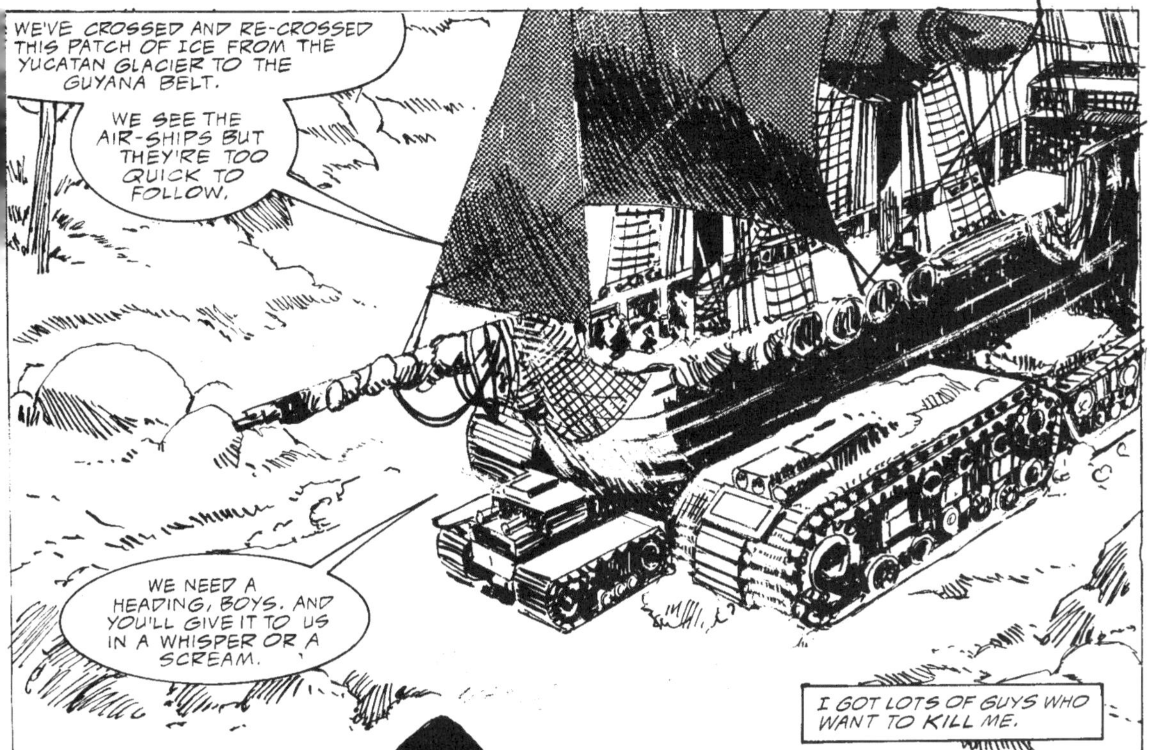
WE'VE CROSSED AND RE-CROSSED THIS PATCH OF ICE FROM THE YUCATAN GLACIER TO THE GUYANA BELT.
WE SEE THE AIR-SHIPS BUT THEY'RE TOO QUICK TO FOLLOW.
WE NEED A HEADING, BOYS. AND YOU'LL GIVE IT TO US IN A WHISPER OR A SCREAM.
I GOT LOTS OF GUYS WHO WANT TO KILL ME.

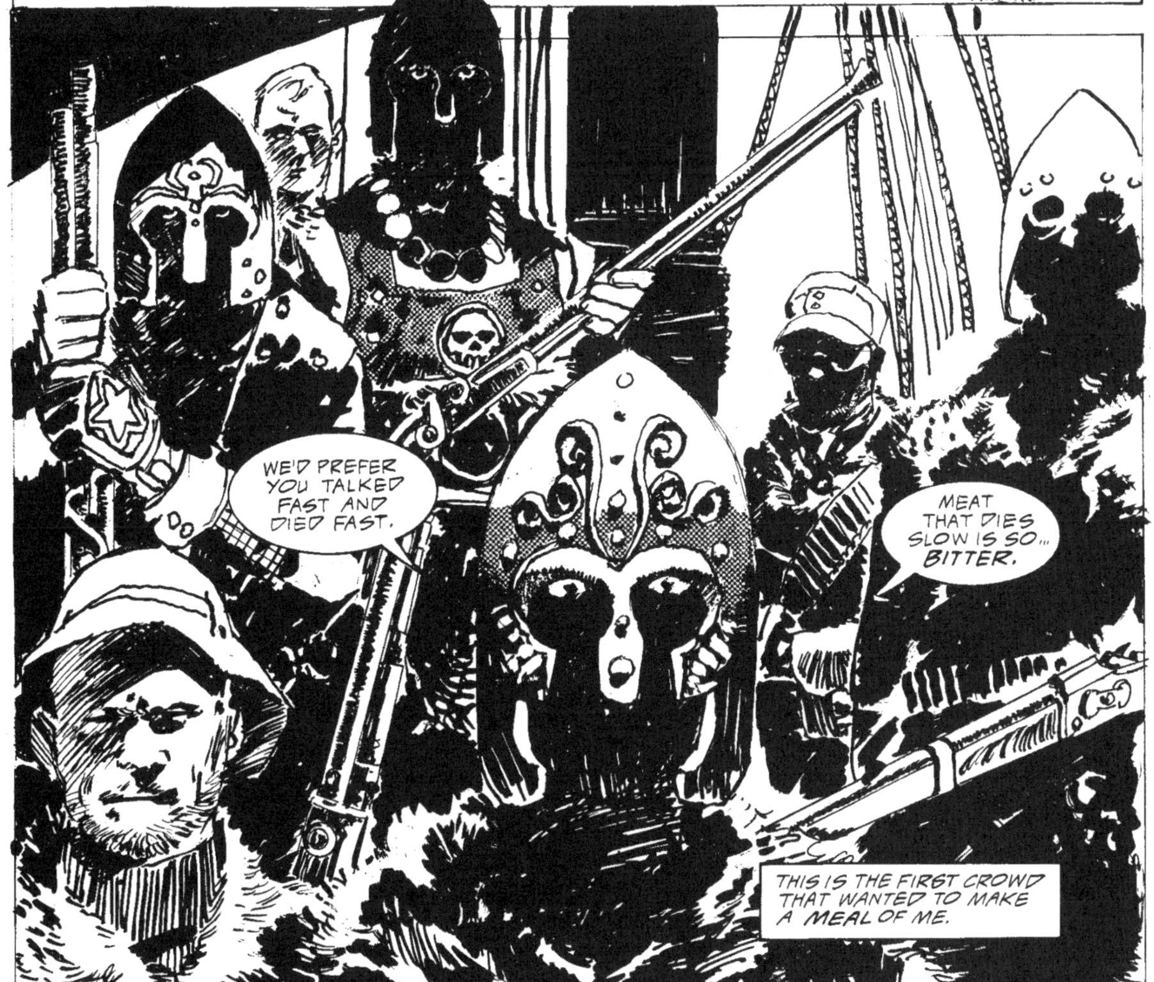
WE'D PREFER YOU TALKED FAST AND DIED FAST.
MEAT THAT DIES SLOW IS SO... BITTER.
THIS IS THE FIRST CROWD THAT WANTED TO MAKE A MEAL OF ME.

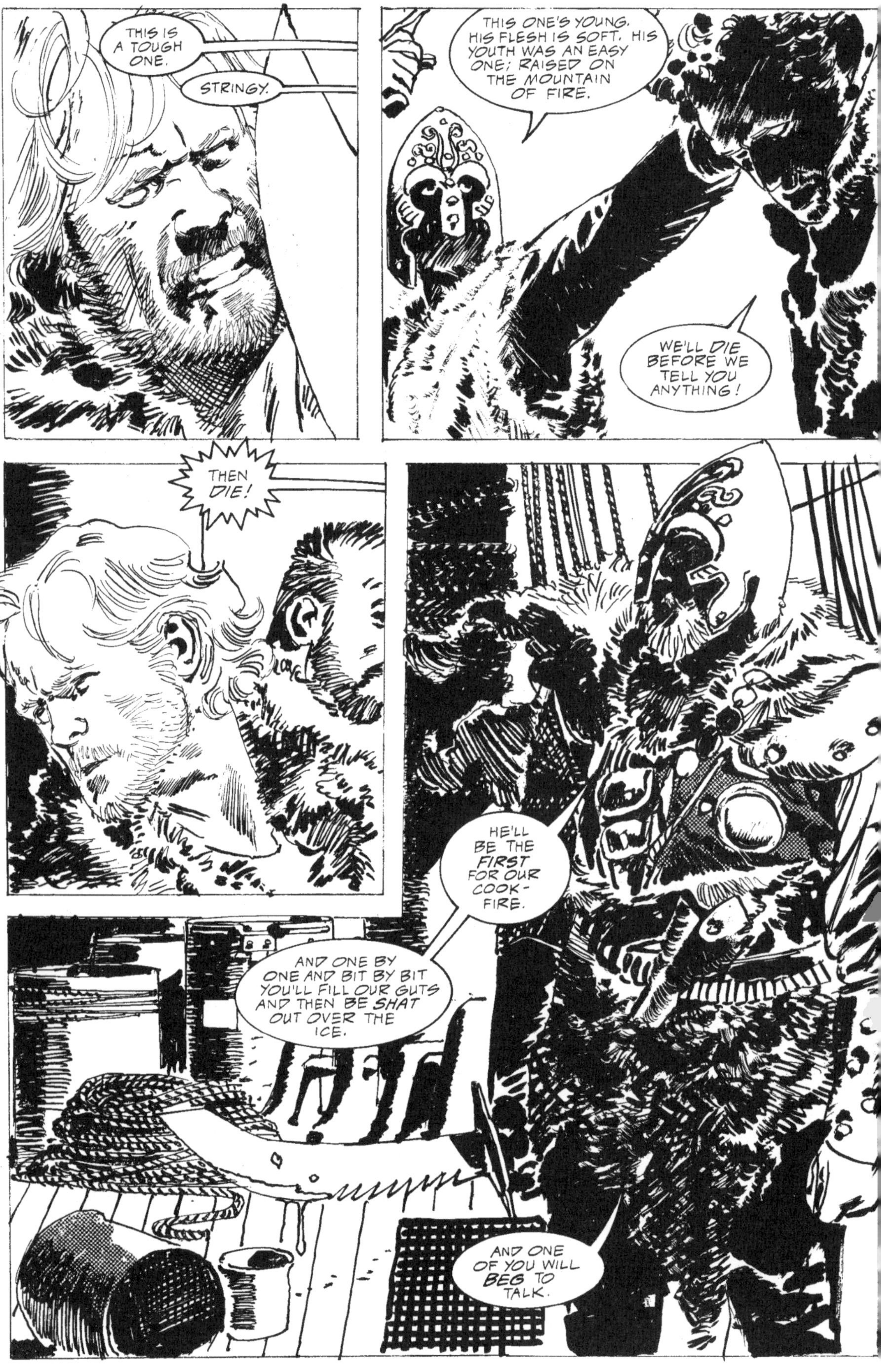
THIS IS A TOUGH ONE.
STRINGY.
THIS ONE'S YOUNG. HIS FLESH IS SOFT. HIS YOUTH WAS AN EASY ONE; RAISED ON THE MOUNTAIN OF FIRE.
WE'LL DIE BEFORE WE TELL YOU ANYTHING!
THEN DIE!
HE'LL BE THE FIRST FOR OUR COOK-FIRE.
AND ONE BY ONE AND BIT BY BIT YOU'LL FILL OUR GUTS AND THEN BE SHAT OUT OVER THE ICE.
AND ONE OF YOU WILL BEG TO TALK.

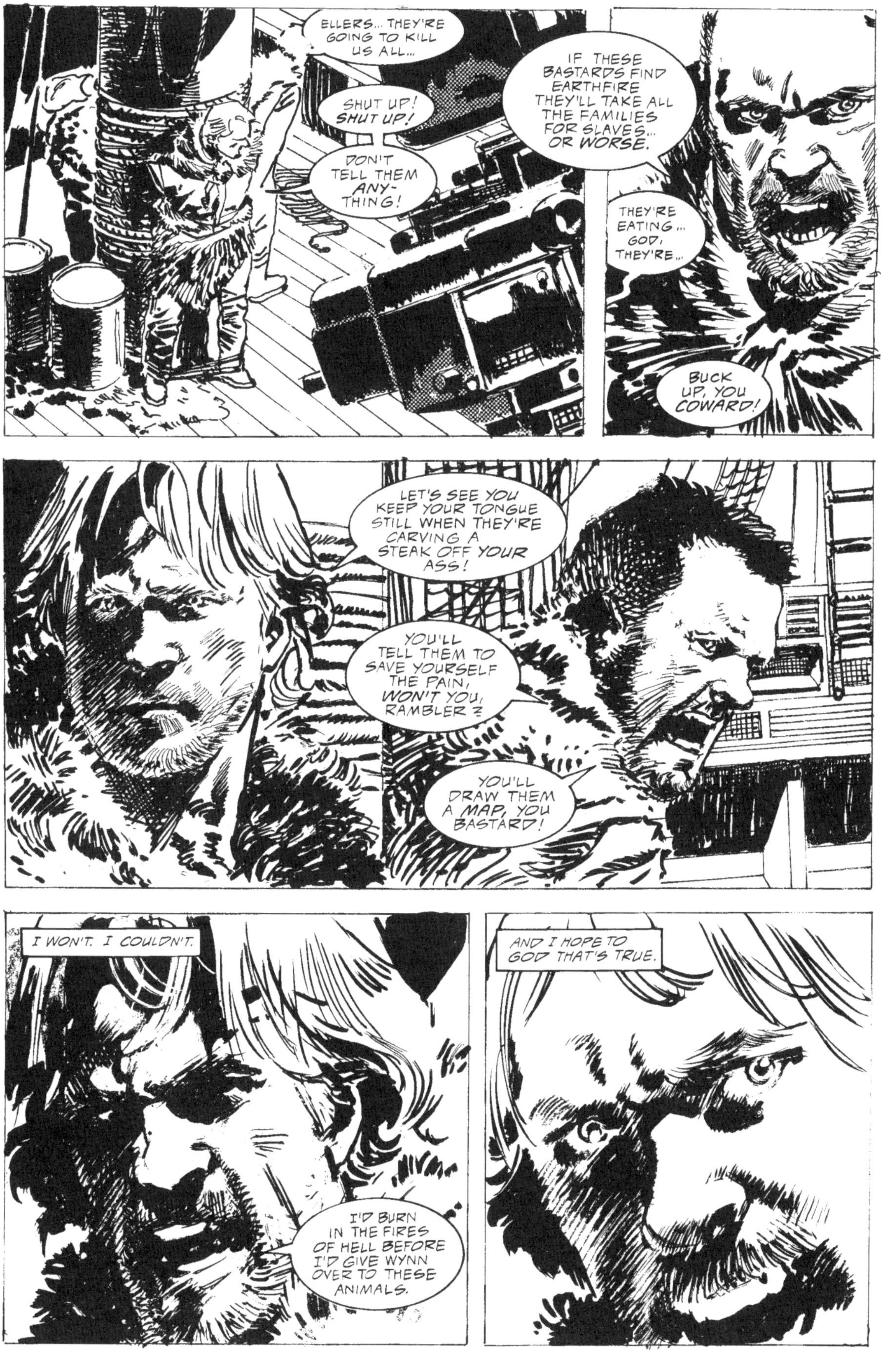
ELLERS... THEY'RE GOING TO KILL US ALL...
SHUT UP! SHUT UP!
DON'T TELL THEM ANY-THING!
IF THESE BASTARDS FIND EARTHFIRE THEY'LL TAKE ALL THE FAMILIES FOR SLAVES... OR WORSE.
THEY'RE EATING... GOD, THEY'RE...
BUCK UP, YOU COWARD!
LET'S SEE YOU KEEP YOUR TONGUE STILL WHEN THEY'RE CARVING A STEAK OFF YOUR ASS!
YOU'LL TELL THEM TO SAVE YOURSELF THE PAIN, WON'T YOU, RAMBLER?
YOU'LL DRAW THEM A MAP, YOU BASTARD!
I WON'T. I COULDN'T.
I'D BURN IN THE FIRES OF HELL BEFORE I'D GIVE WYNN OVER TO THESE ANIMALS.
AND I HOPE TO GOD THAT'S TRUE.

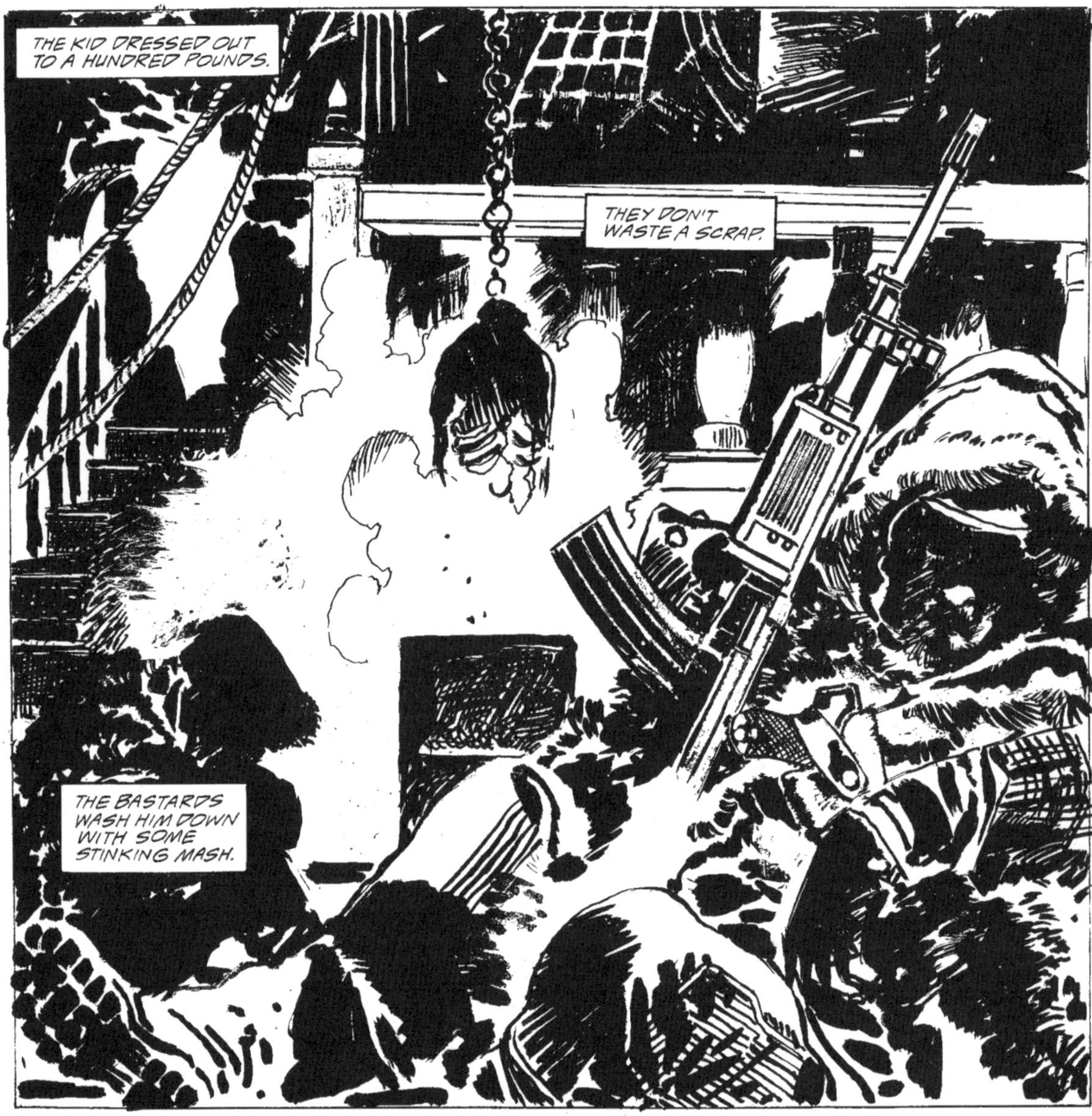
THE KID DRESSED OUT TO A HUNDRED POUNDS.
THEY DON'T WASTE A SCRAP.
THE BASTARDS WASH HIM DOWN WITH SOME STINKING MASH.

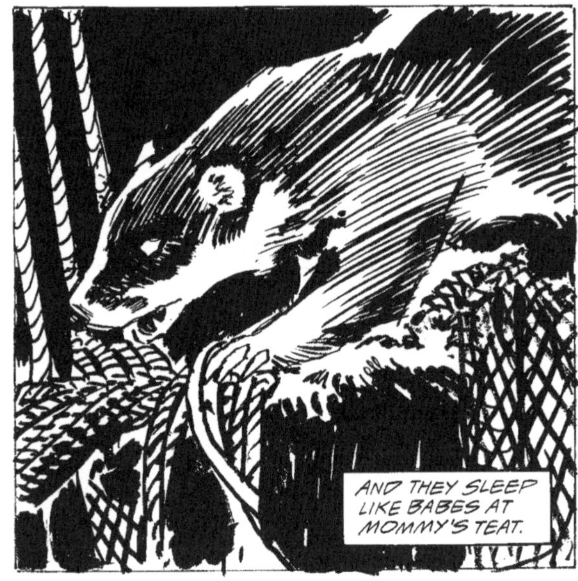
AND THEY SLEEP LIKE BABES AT MOMMY'S TEAT.

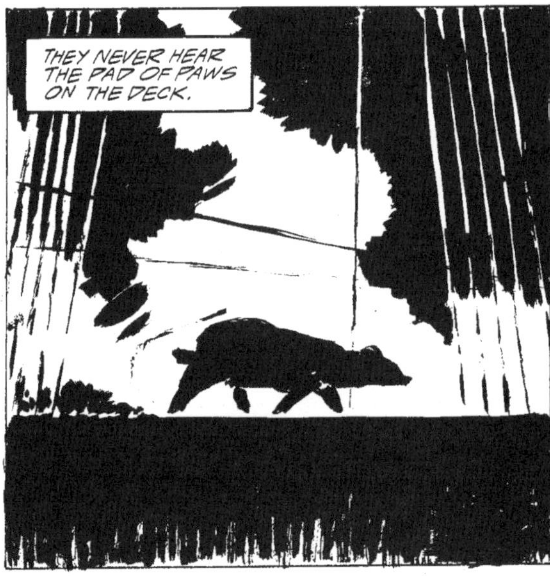
THEY NEVER HEAR THE PAD OF PAWS ON THE DECK.

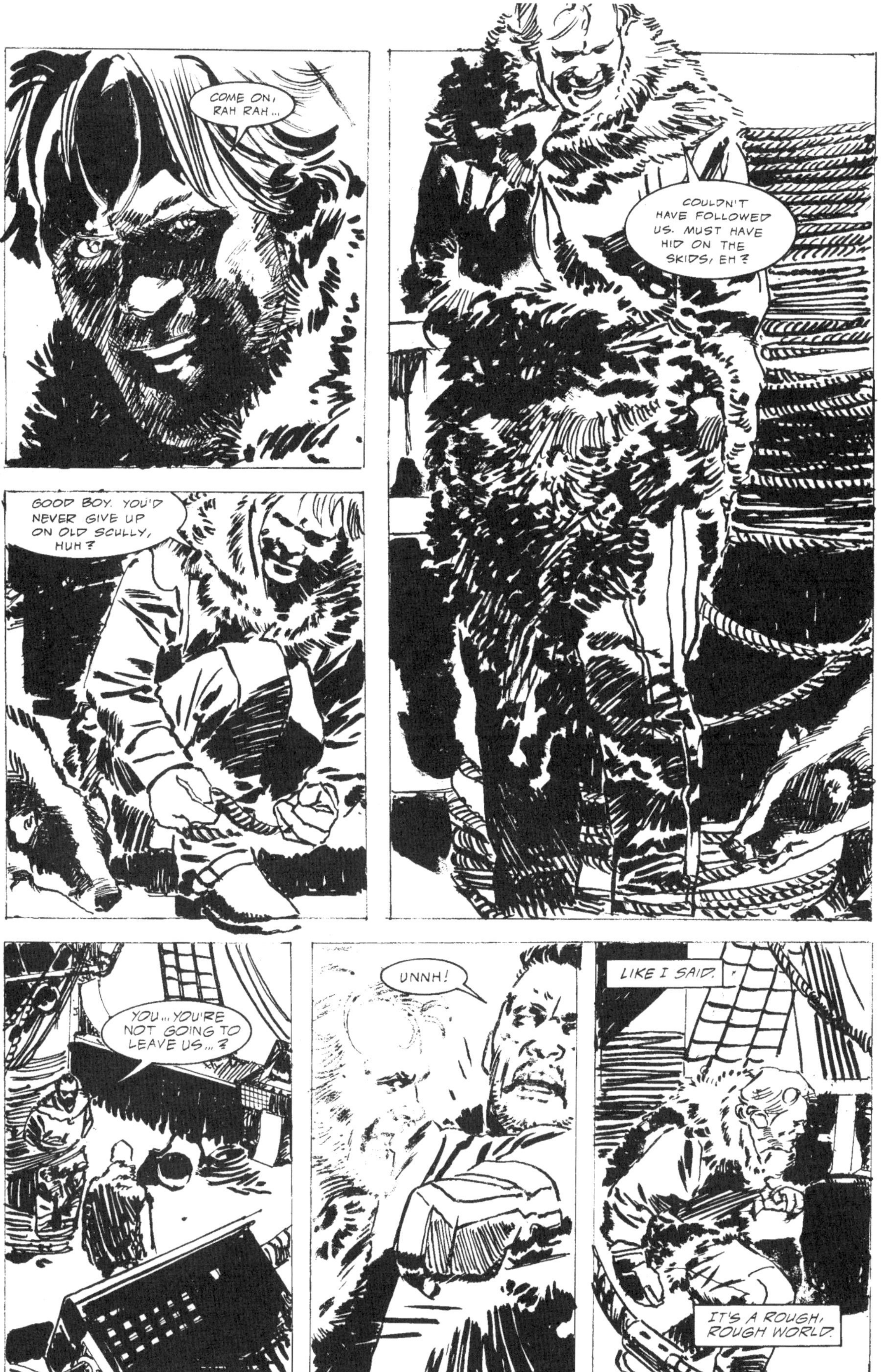
COME ON, RAH RAH...
COULDN'T HAVE FOLLOWED US. MUST HAVE HID ON THE SKIDS, EH?
GOOD BOY. YOU'D NEVER GIVE UP ON OLD SCULLY, HUH?
YOU... YOU'RE NOT GOING TO LEAVE US...?
UNNH!
LIKE I SAID.
IT'S A ROUGH, ROUGH WORLD.

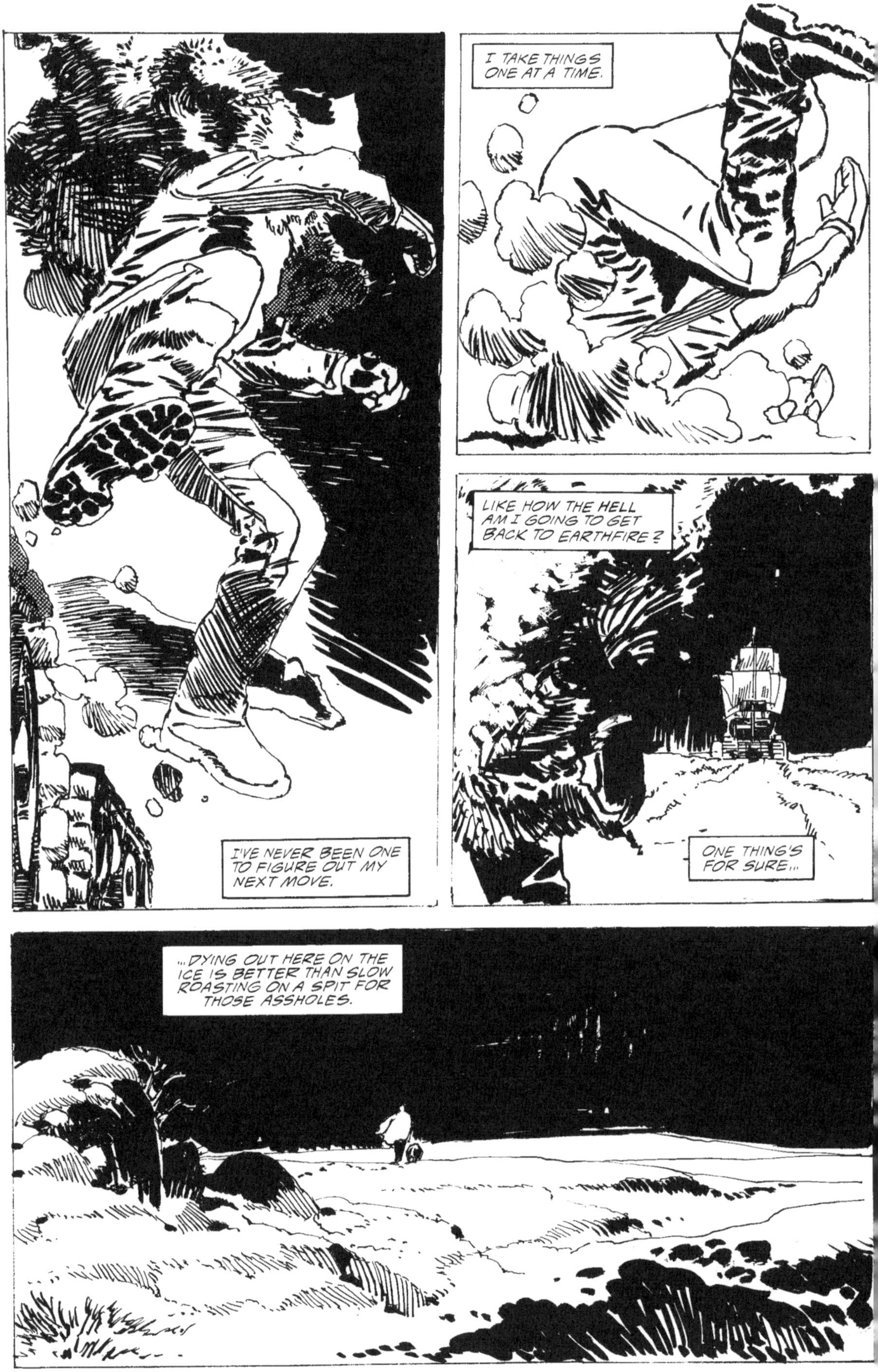
I'VE NEVER BEEN ONE TO FIGURE OUT MY NEXT MOVE.
I TAKE THINGS ONE AT A TIME.
LIKE HOW THE HELL AM I GOING TO GET BACK TO EARTHFIRE?
ONE THING'S FOR SURE...
...DYING OUT HERE ON THE ICE IS BETTER THAN SLOW ROASTING ON A SPIT FOR THOSE ASSHOLES.

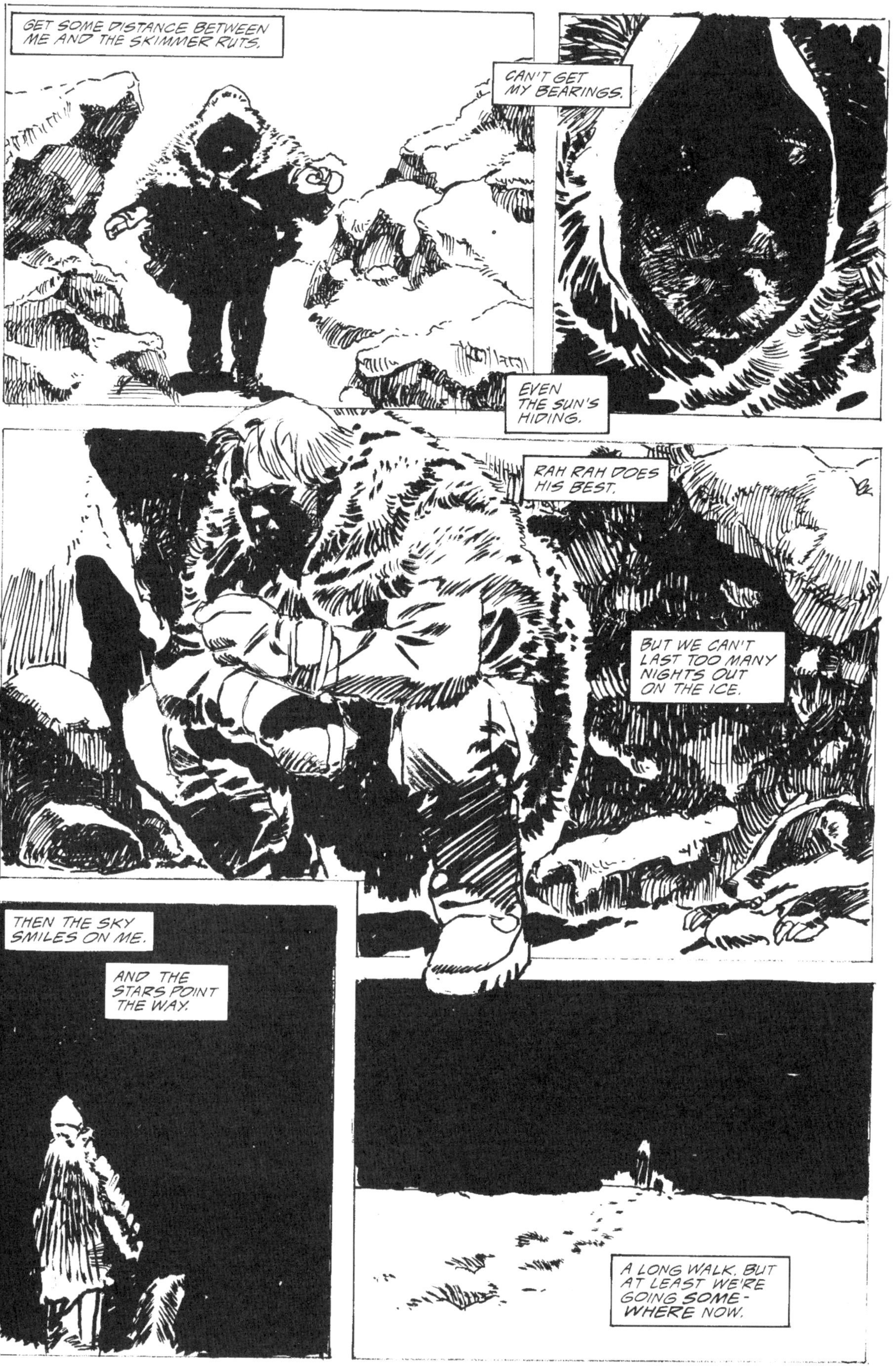
GET SOME DISTANCE BETWEEN ME AND THE SKIMMER RUTS.
CAN'T GET MY BEARINGS.
EVEN THE SUN'S HIDING.
RAH RAH DOES HIS BEST.
BUT WE CAN'T LAST TOO MANY NIGHTS OUT ON THE ICE.
THEN THE SKY SMILES ON ME.
AND THE STARS POINT THE WAY.
A LONG WALK, BUT AT LEAST WE'RE GOING SOME-WHERE NOW.

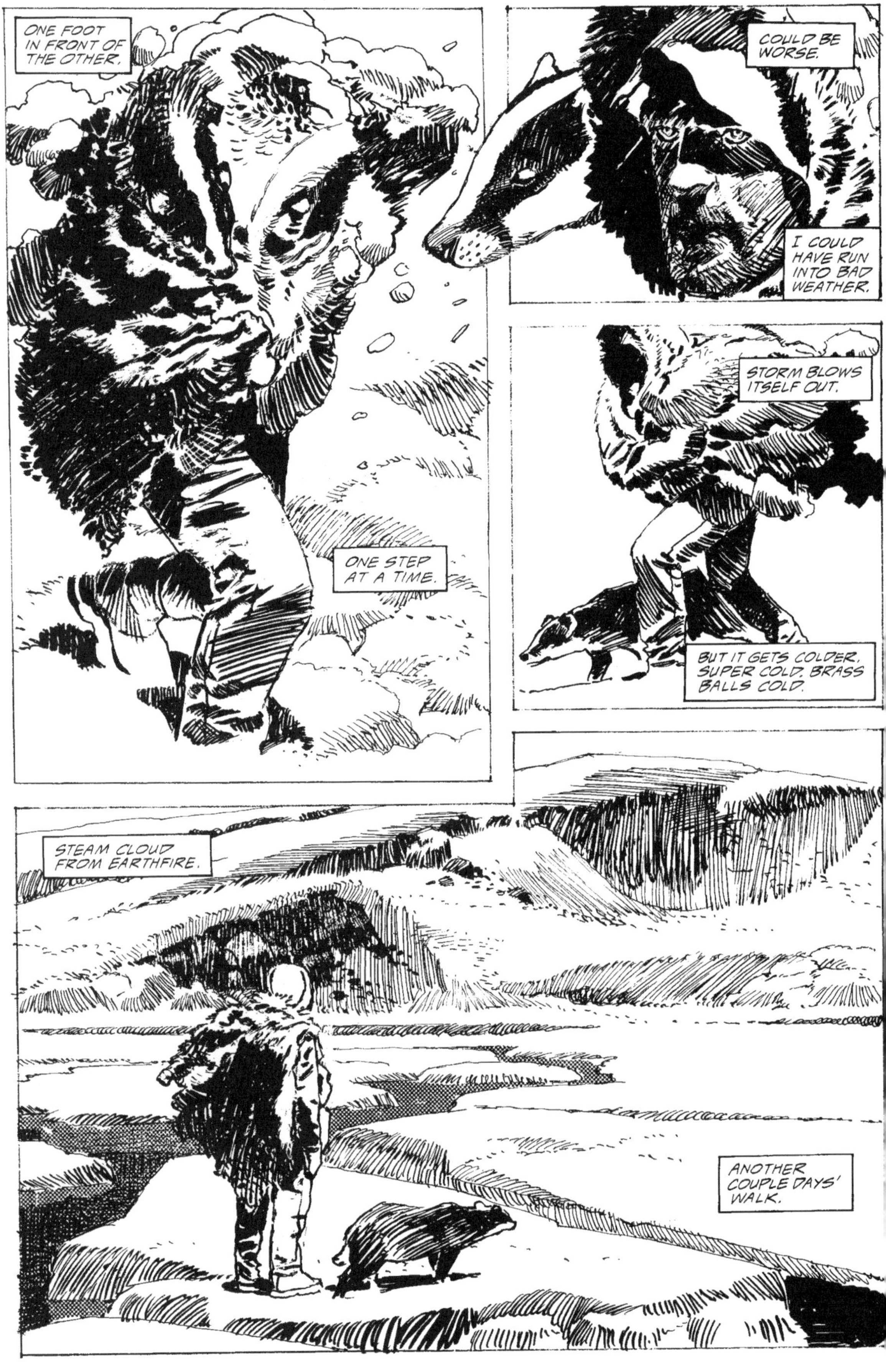
ONE FOOT
IN FRONT OF
THE OTHER.
COULD BE
WORSE.
I COULD
HAVE RUN
INTO BAD
WEATHER.
ONE STEP
AT A TIME.
STORM BLOWS
ITSELF OUT.
BUT IT GETS COLDER.
SUPER COLD. BRASS
BALLS COLD.
STEAM CLOUD
FROM EARTHFIRE.
ANOTHER
COUPLE DAYS'
WALK.

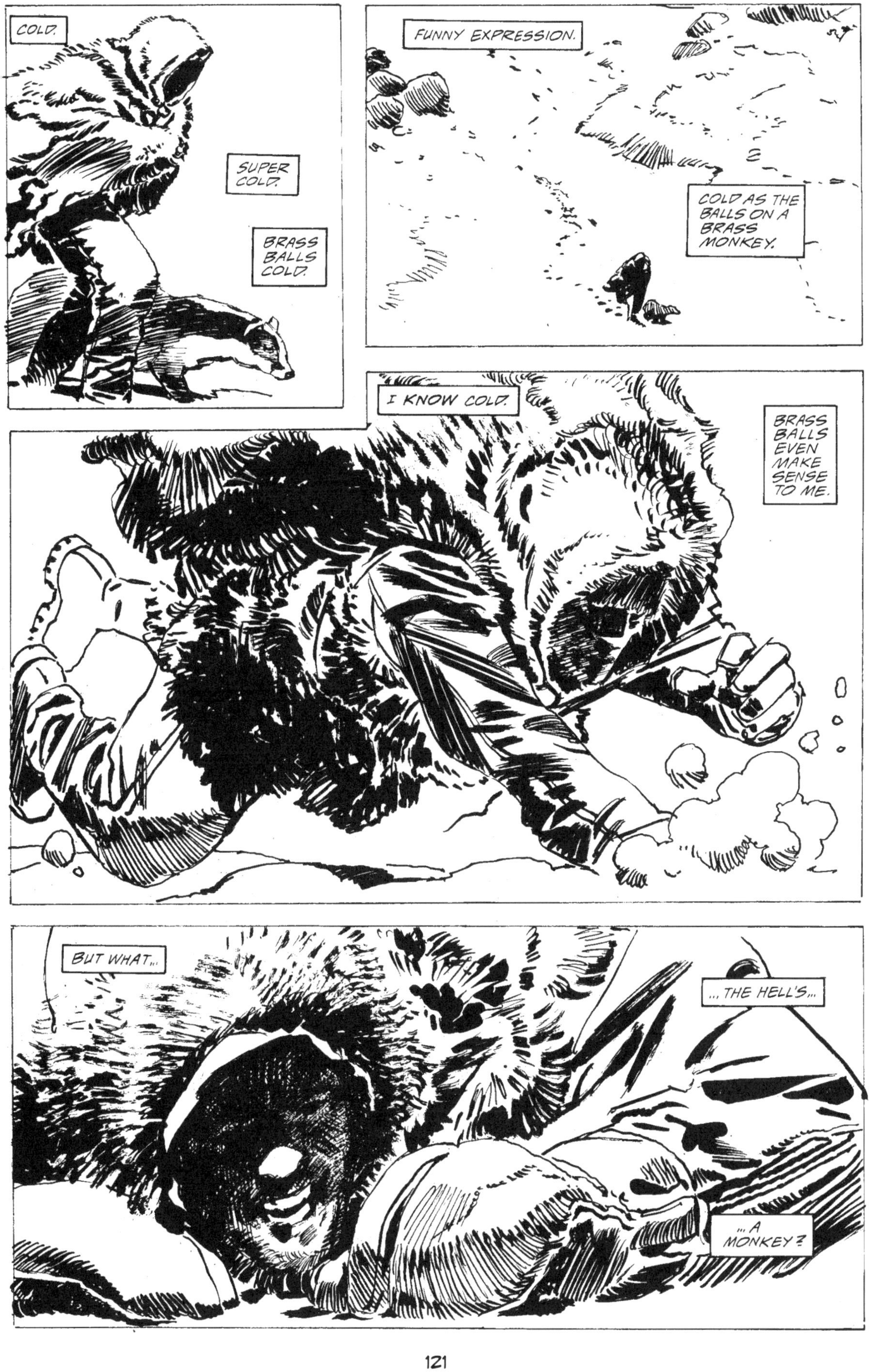
COLD.
SUPER COLD.
BRASS BALLS COLD.
FUNNY EXPRESSION.
COLD AS THE BALLS ON A BRASS MONKEY.
I KNOW COLD.
BRASS BALLS EVEN MAKE SENSE TO ME.
BUT WHAT...
...THE HELL'S...
...A MONKEY?

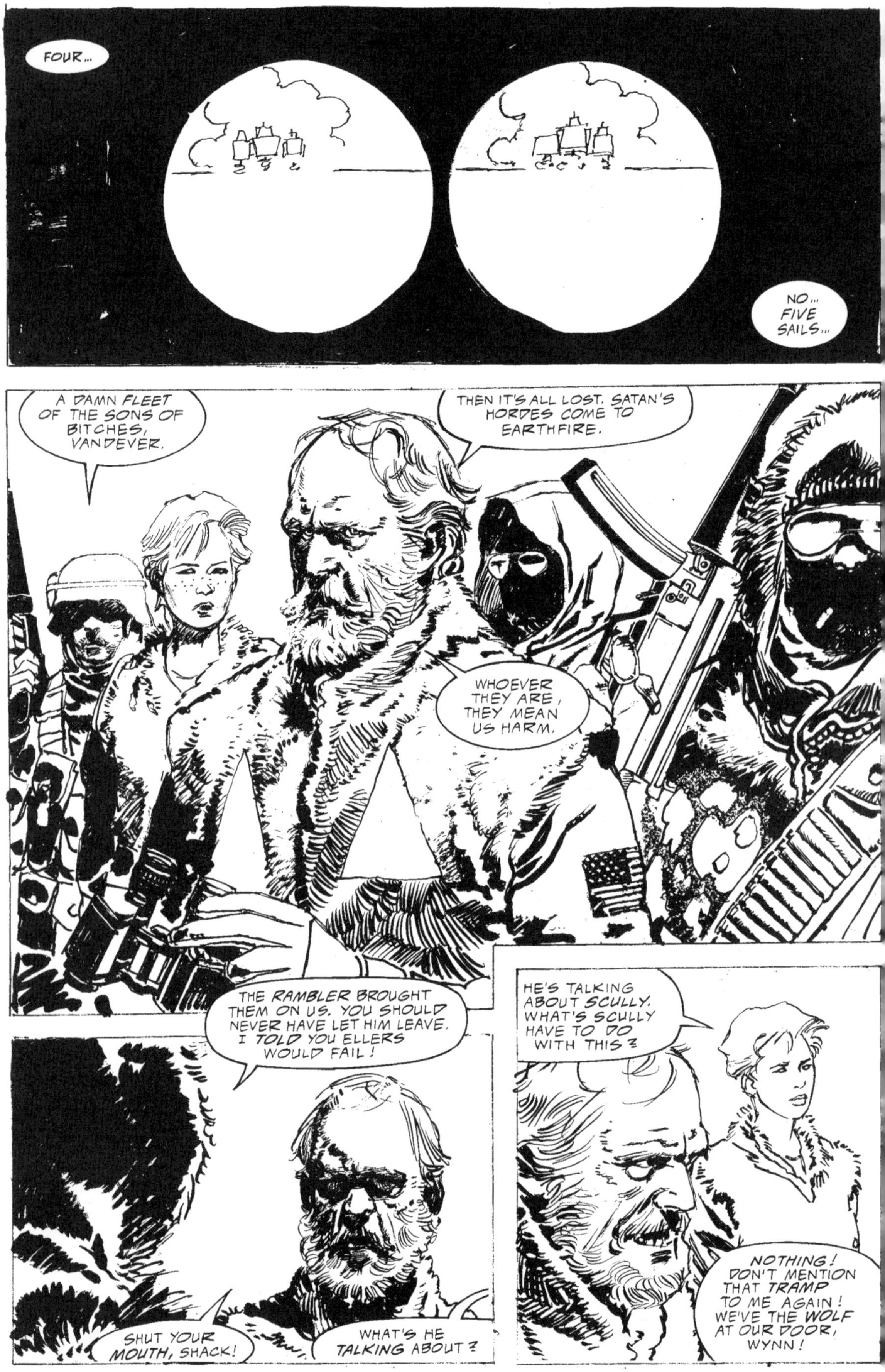
FOUR...
NO... FIVE SAILS...
A DAMN FLEET OF THE SONS OF BITCHES, VANDEVER.
THEN IT'S ALL LOST. SATAN'S HORDES COME TO EARTHFIRE.
WHOEVER THEY ARE, THEY MEAN US HARM.
THE RAMBLER BROUGHT THEM ON US. YOU SHOULD NEVER HAVE LET HIM LEAVE. I TOLD YOU ELLERS WOULD FAIL!
SHUT YOUR MOUTH, SHACK!
WHAT'S HE TALKING ABOUT?
HE'S TALKING ABOUT SCULLY. WHAT'S SCULLY HAVE TO DO WITH THIS?
NOTHING! DON'T MENTION THAT TRAMP TO ME AGAIN! WE'VE THE WOLF AT OUR DOOR, WYNN!

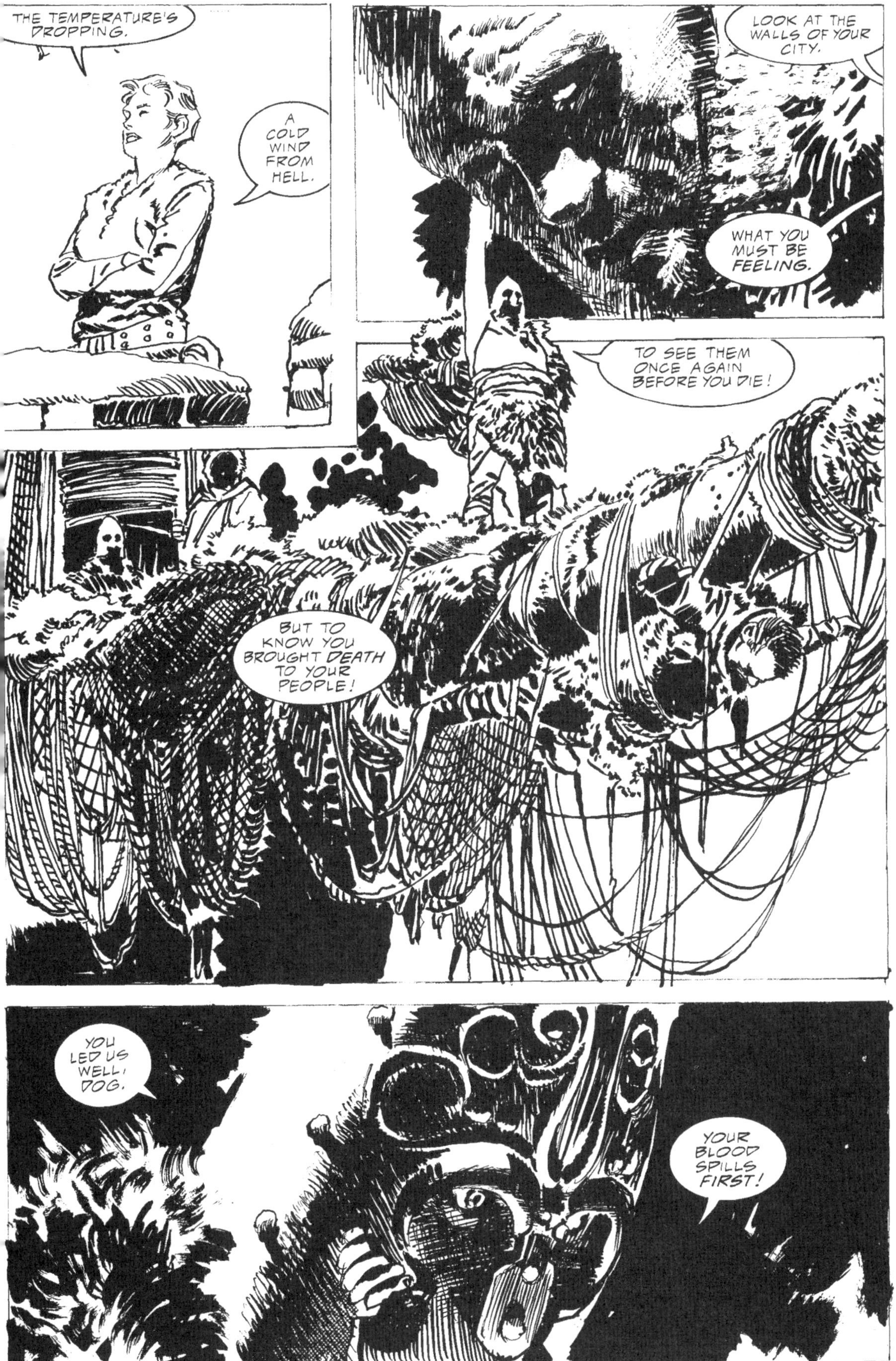
THE TEMPERATURE'S DROPPING.
A COLD WIND FROM HELL.
LOOK AT THE WALLS OF YOUR CITY.
WHAT YOU MUST BE FEELING.
TO SEE THEM ONCE AGAIN BEFORE YOU DIE!
BUT TO KNOW YOU BROUGHT DEATH TO YOUR PEOPLE!
YOU LED US WELL, DOG.
YOUR BLOOD SPILLS FIRST!

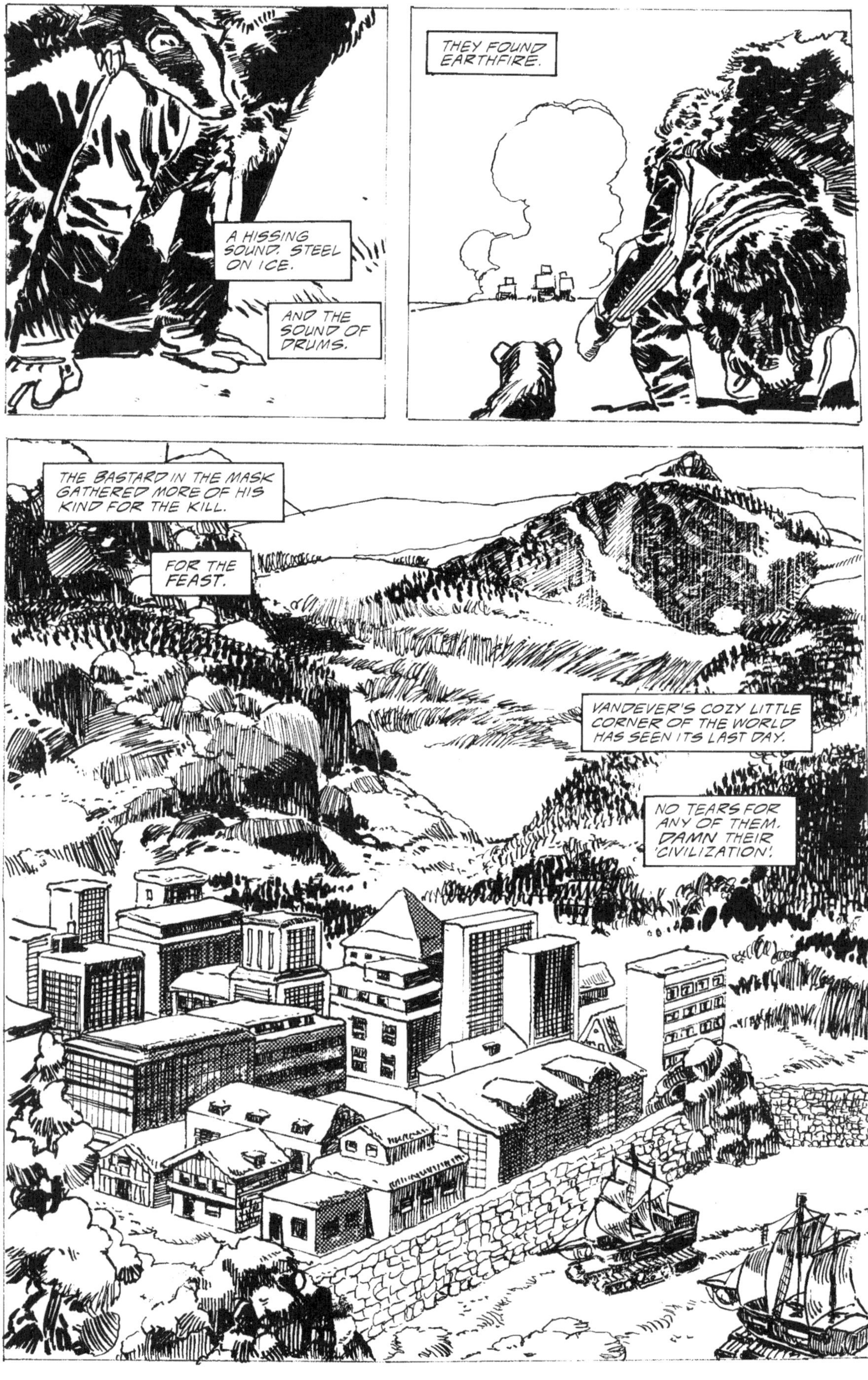
A HISSING SOUND. STEEL ON ICE.
AND THE SOUND OF DRUMS.
THEY FOUND EARTHFIRE.
THE BASTARD IN THE MASK GATHERED MORE OF HIS KIND FOR THE KILL.
FOR THE FEAST.
VANDEVER'S COZY LITTLE CORNER OF THE WORLD HAS SEEN ITS LAST DAY.
NO TEARS FOR ANY OF THEM. DAMN THEIR 'CIVILIZATION'.

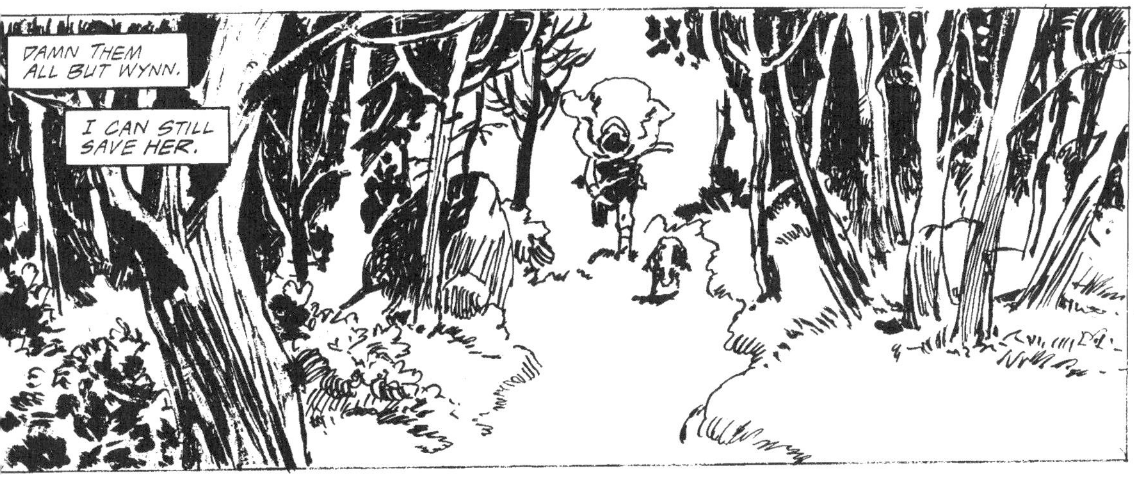
DAMN THEM ALL BUT WYNN.
I CAN STILL SAVE HER.

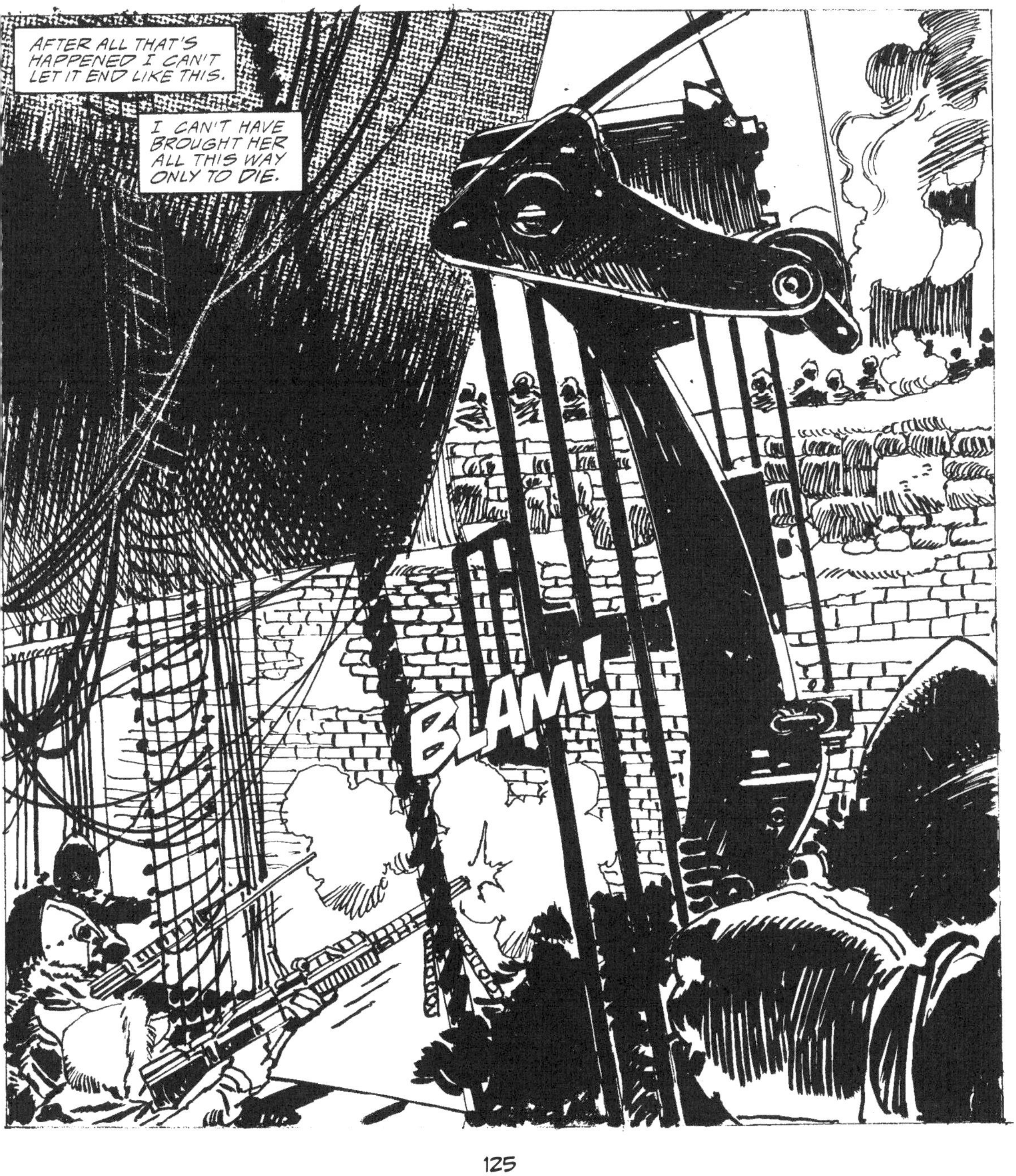
AFTER ALL THAT'S HAPPENED I CAN'T LET IT END LIKE THIS.
I CAN'T HAVE BROUGHT HER ALL THIS WAY ONLY TO DIE.
BLAM!

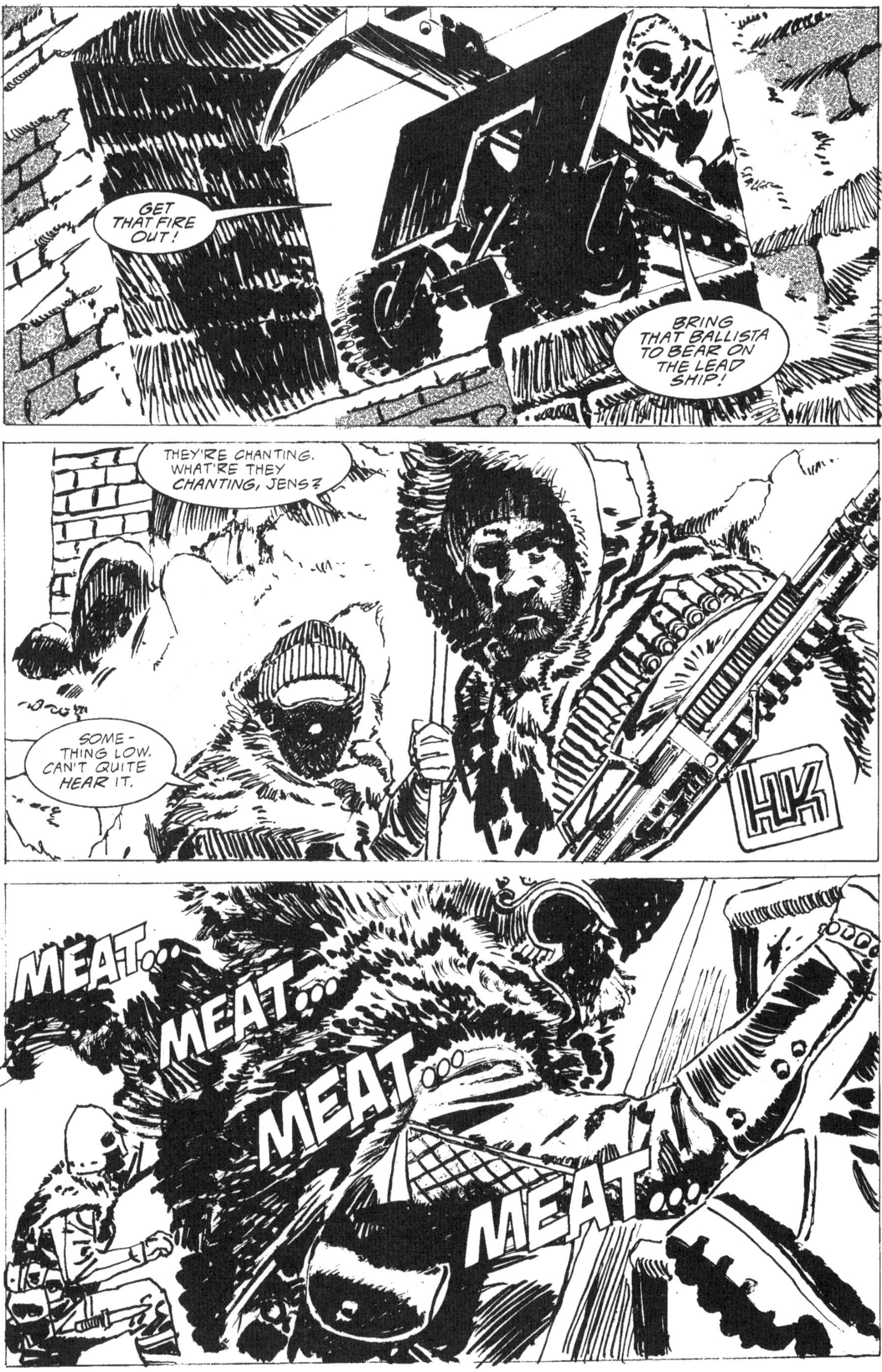
GET THAT FIRE OUT!
BRING THAT BALLISTA TO BEAR ON THE LEAD SHIP!
THEY'RE CHANTING. WHAT'RE THEY CHANTING, JENS?
SOME-THING LOW. CAN'T QUITE HEAR IT.
HK
MEAT...
MEAT...
MEAT...
MEAT...

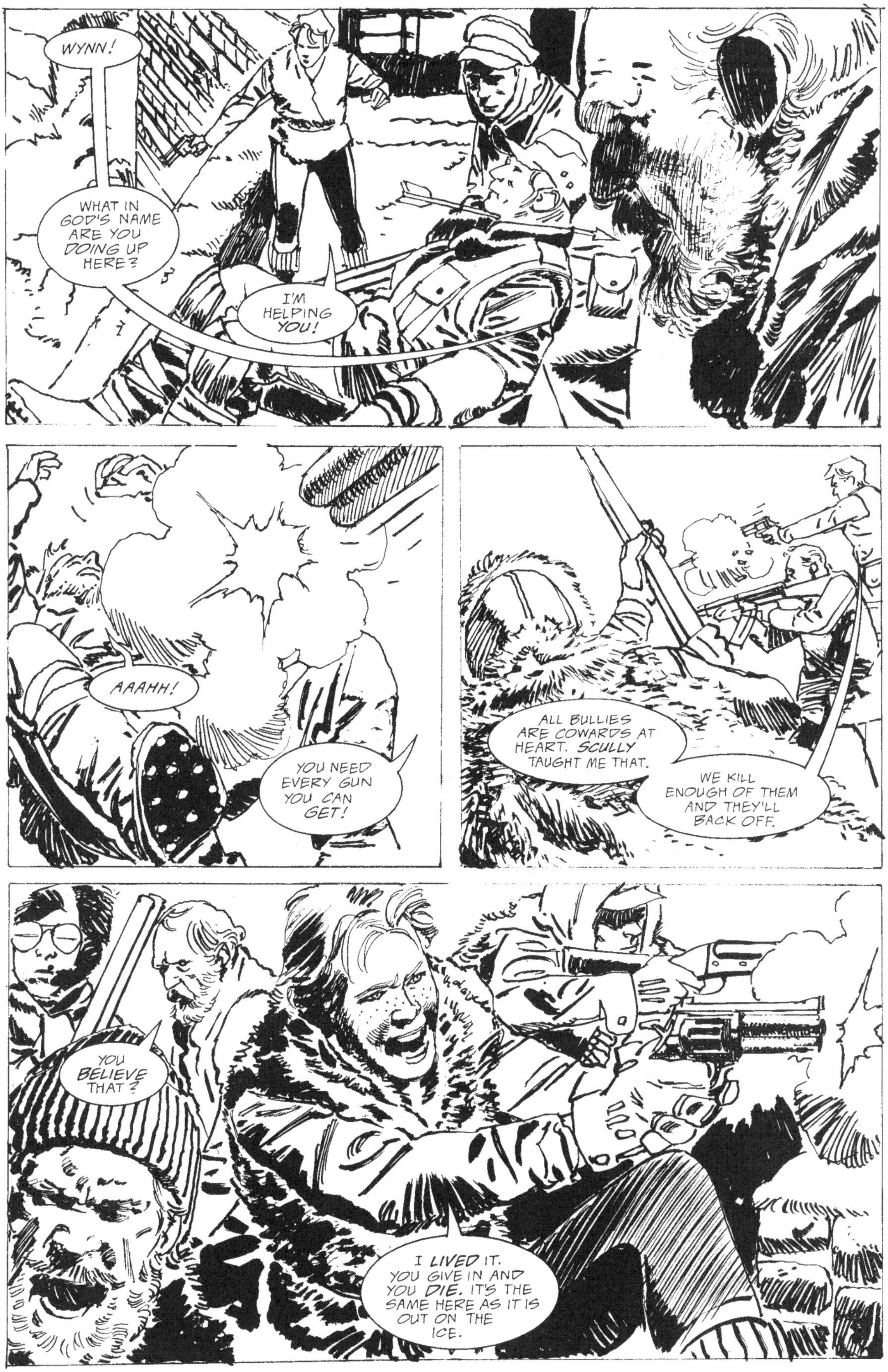
WYNN!
WHAT IN GOD'S NAME ARE YOU DOING UP HERE?
I'M HELPING YOU!
AAAHH!
YOU NEED EVERY GUN YOU CAN GET!
ALL BULLIES ARE COWARDS AT HEART. SCULLY TAUGHT ME THAT.
WE KILL ENOUGH OF THEM AND THEY'LL BACK OFF.
YOU BELIEVE THAT?
I LIVED IT. YOU GIVE IN AND YOU DIE. IT'S THE SAME HERE AS IT IS OUT ON THE ICE.

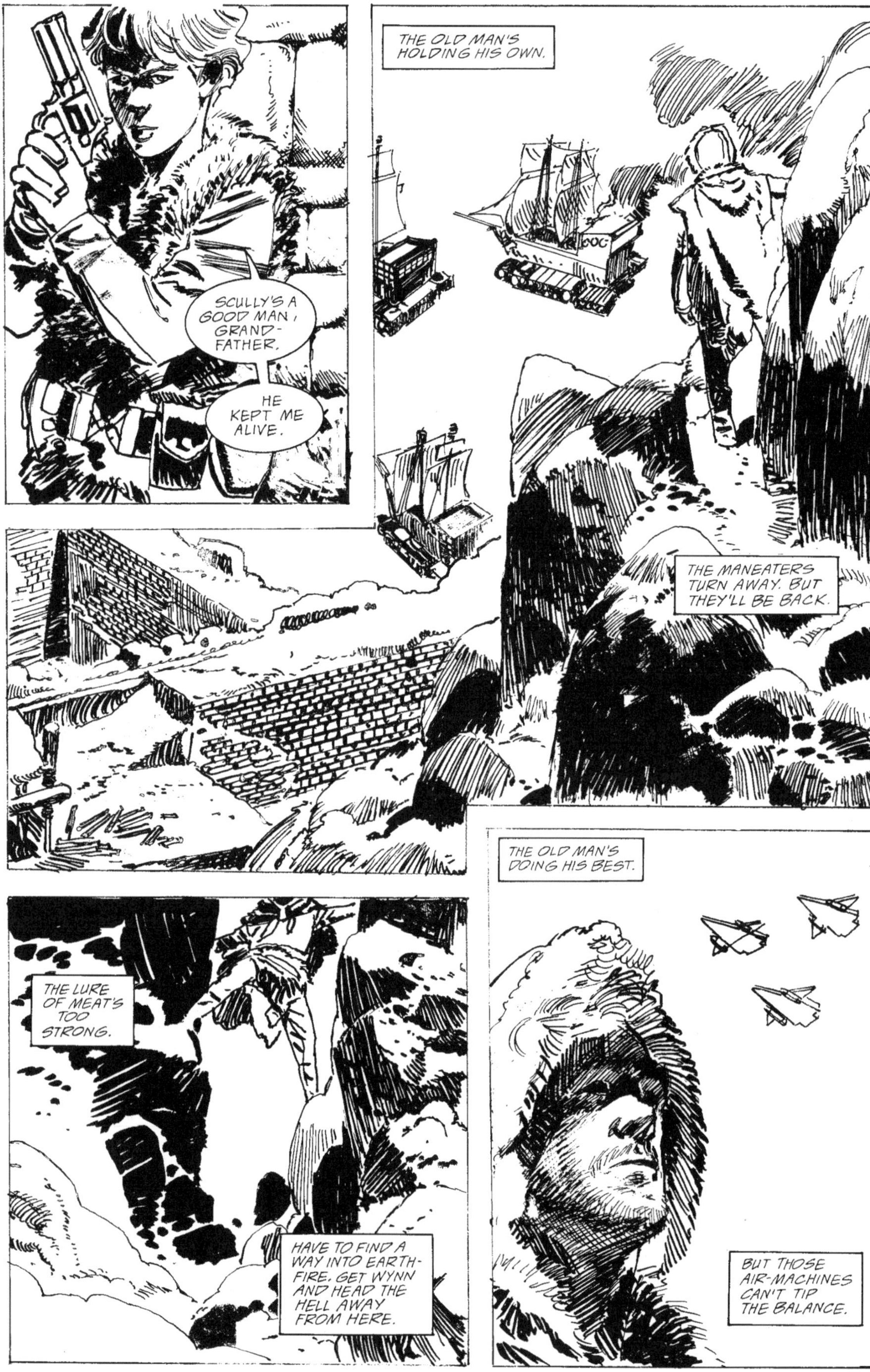
SCULLY'S A GOOD MAN, GRAND-FATHER.
HE KEPT ME ALIVE.
THE OLD MAN'S HOLDING HIS OWN.
THE MANEATERS TURN AWAY. BUT THEY'LL BE BACK.
THE LURE OF MEAT'S TOO STRONG.
HAVE TO FIND A WAY INTO EARTH-FIRE. GET WYNN AND HEAD THE HELL AWAY FROM HERE.
THE OLD MAN'S DOING HIS BEST.
BUT THOSE AIR-MACHINES CAN'T TIP THE BALANCE.

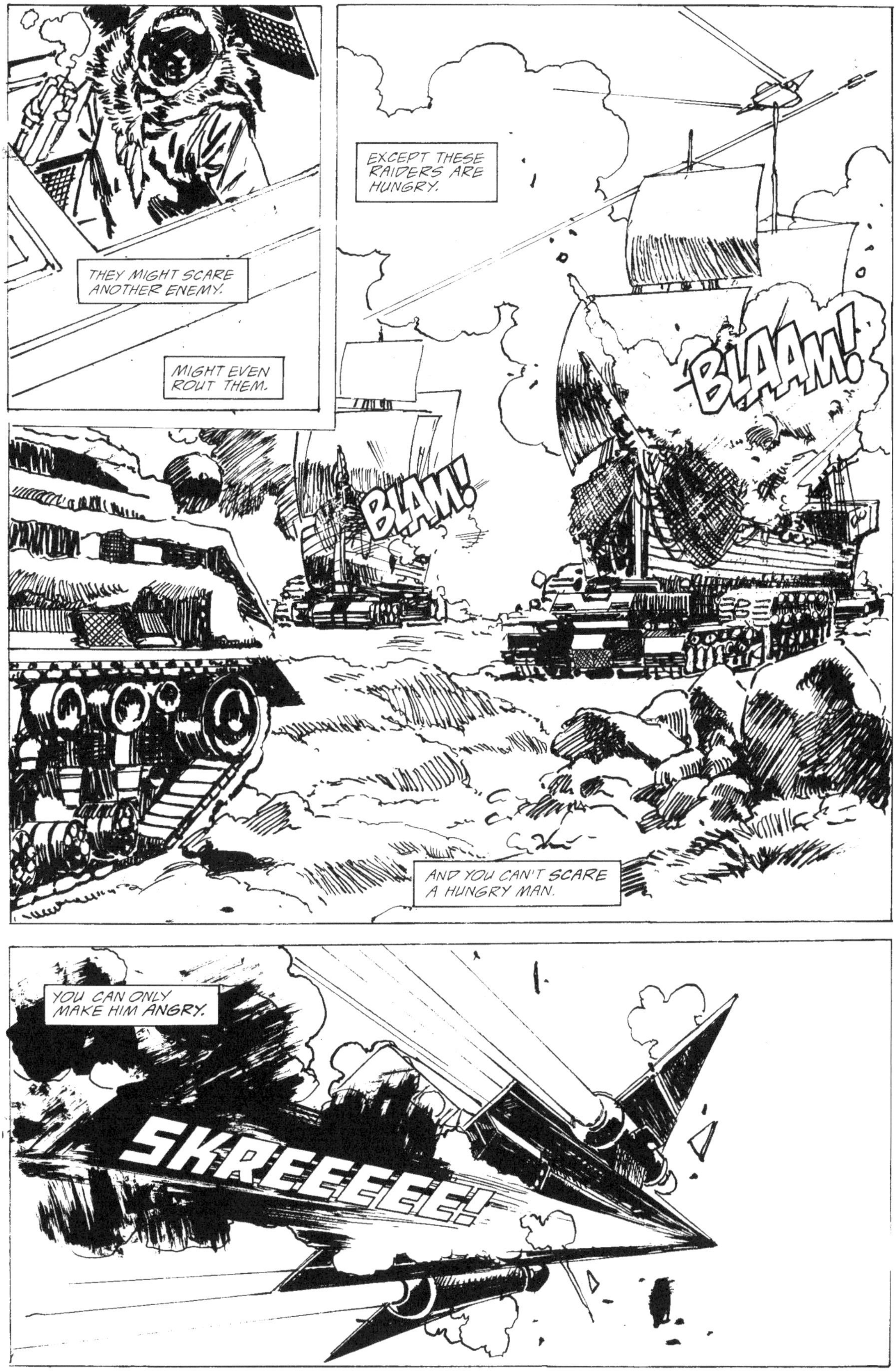
THEY MIGHT SCARE ANOTHER ENEMY.
MIGHT EVEN ROUT THEM.
EXCEPT THESE RAIDERS ARE HUNGRY.
BLAM!
BLAAM!
AND YOU CAN'T SCARE A HUNGRY MAN.
YOU CAN ONLY MAKE HIM ANGRY.
SKREEEEEE!

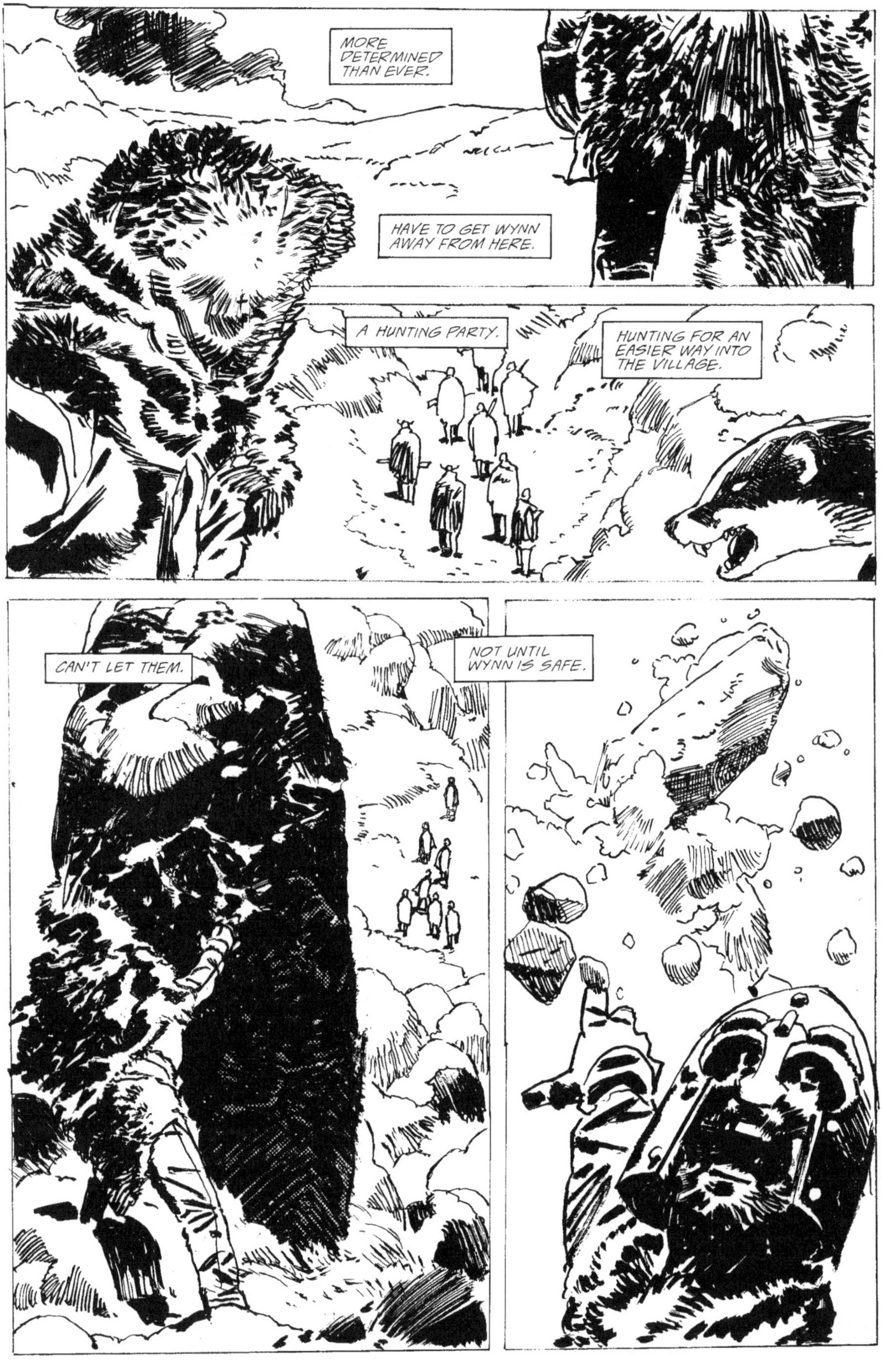
MORE DETERMINED THAN EVER.
HAVE TO GET WYNN AWAY FROM HERE.
A HUNTING PARTY.
HUNTING FOR AN EASIER WAY INTO THE VILLAGE.
CAN'T LET THEM.
NOT UNTIL WYNN IS SAFE.

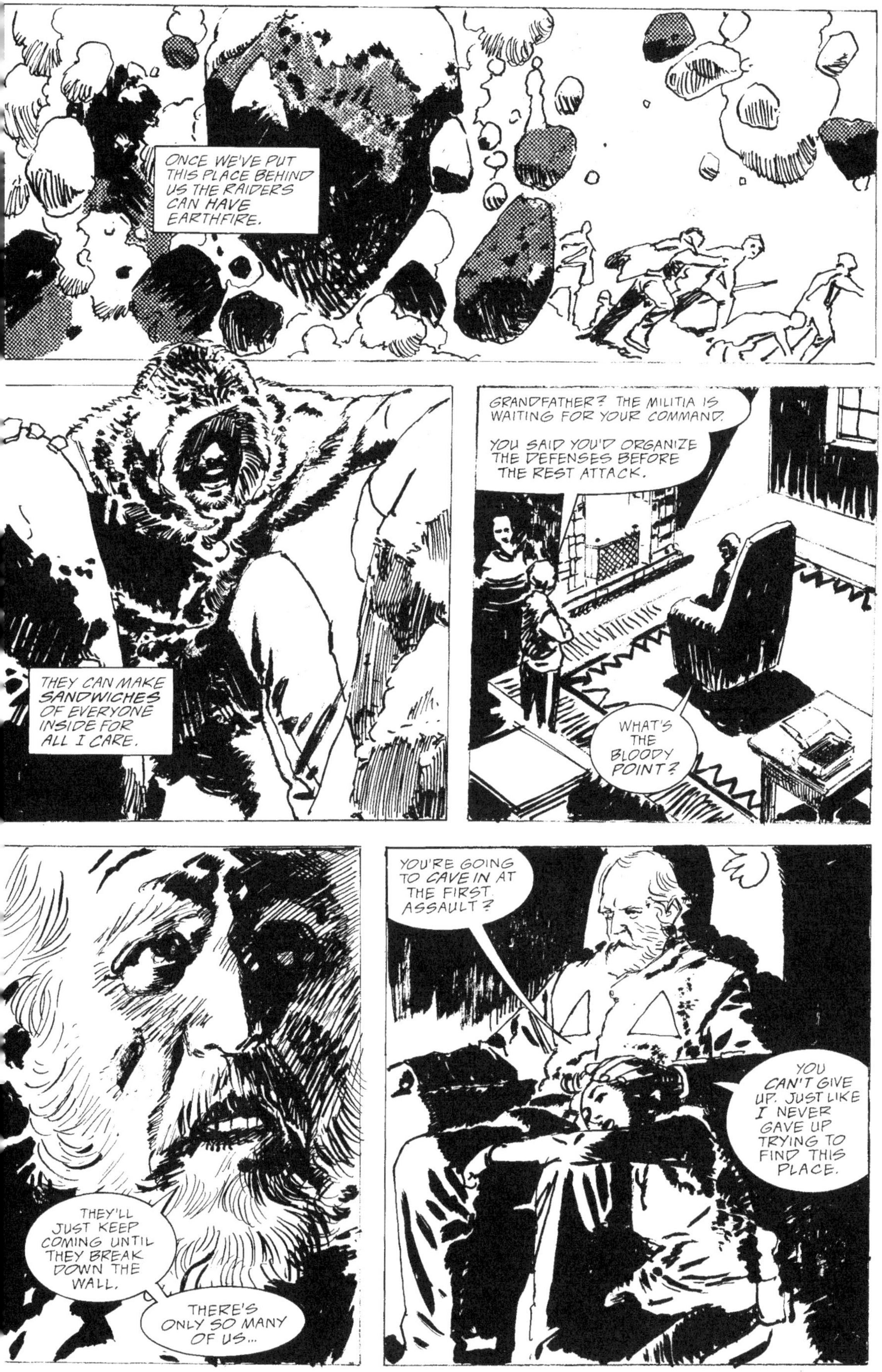
ONCE WE'VE PUT THIS PLACE BEHIND US THE RAIDERS CAN HAVE EARTHFIRE.
THEY CAN MAKE SANDWICHES OF EVERYONE INSIDE FOR ALL I CARE.
GRANDFATHER? THE MILITIA IS WAITING FOR YOUR COMMAND.
YOU SAID YOU'D ORGANIZE THE DEFENSES BEFORE THE REST ATTACK.
WHAT'S THE BLOODY POINT?
THEY'LL JUST KEEP COMING UNTIL THEY BREAK DOWN THE WALL.
THERE'S ONLY SO MANY OF US...
YOU'RE GOING TO CAVE IN AT THE FIRST ASSAULT?
YOU CAN'T GIVE UP. JUST LIKE I NEVER GAVE UP TRYING TO FIND THIS PLACE.

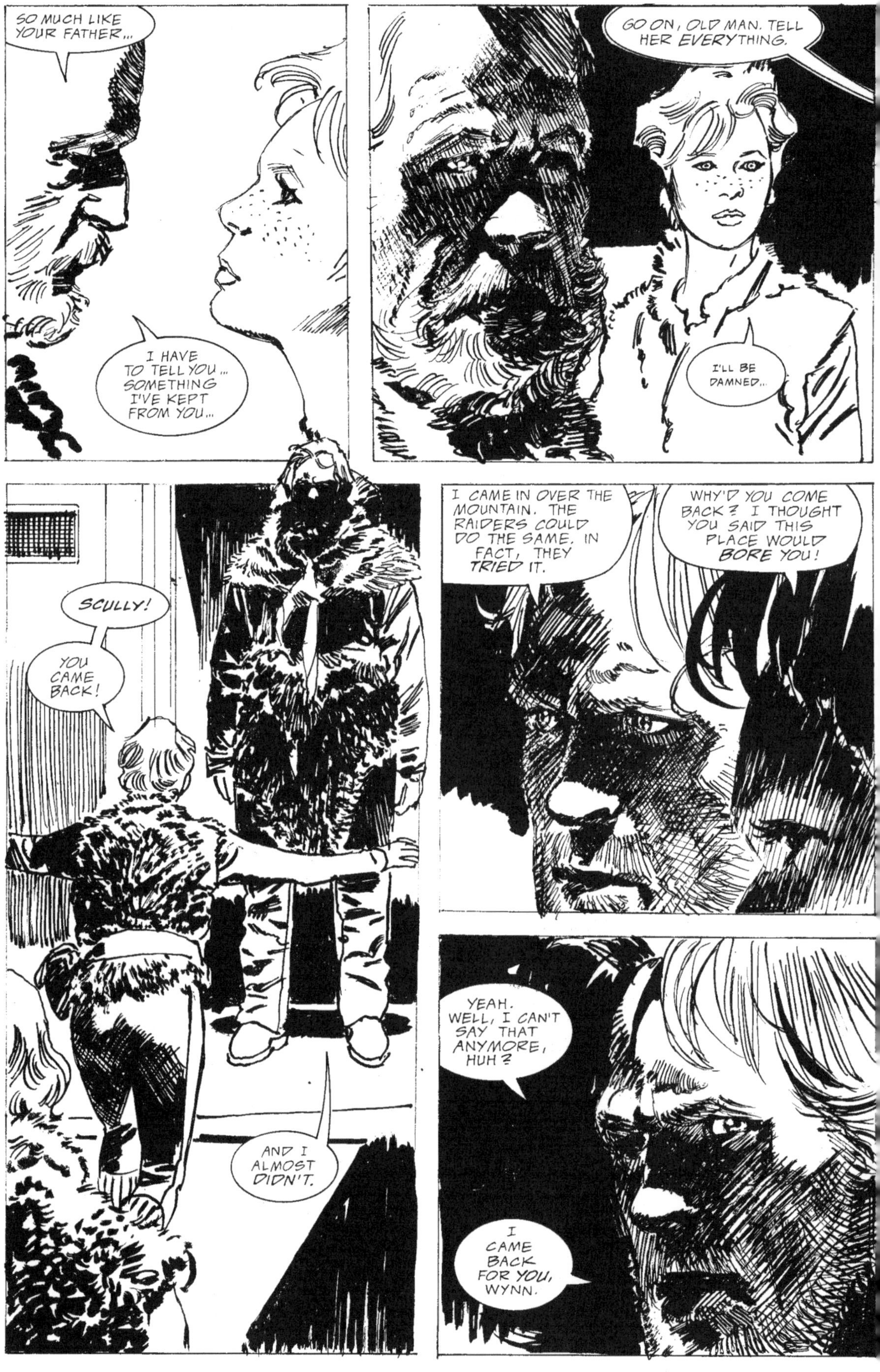

SO MUCH LIKE YOUR FATHER...
I HAVE TO TELL YOU... SOMETHING I'VE KEPT FROM YOU...
GO ON, OLD MAN. TELL HER EVERYTHING.
I'LL BE DAMNED...
SCULLY!
YOU CAME BACK!
AND I ALMOST DIDN'T.
WHY'D YOU COME BACK? I THOUGHT YOU SAID THIS PLACE WOULD BORE YOU!
I CAME IN OVER THE MOUNTAIN. THE RAIDERS COULD DO THE SAME. IN FACT, THEY TRIED IT.
YEAH. WELL, I CAN'T SAY THAT ANYMORE, HUH?
I CAME BACK FOR YOU, WYNN.

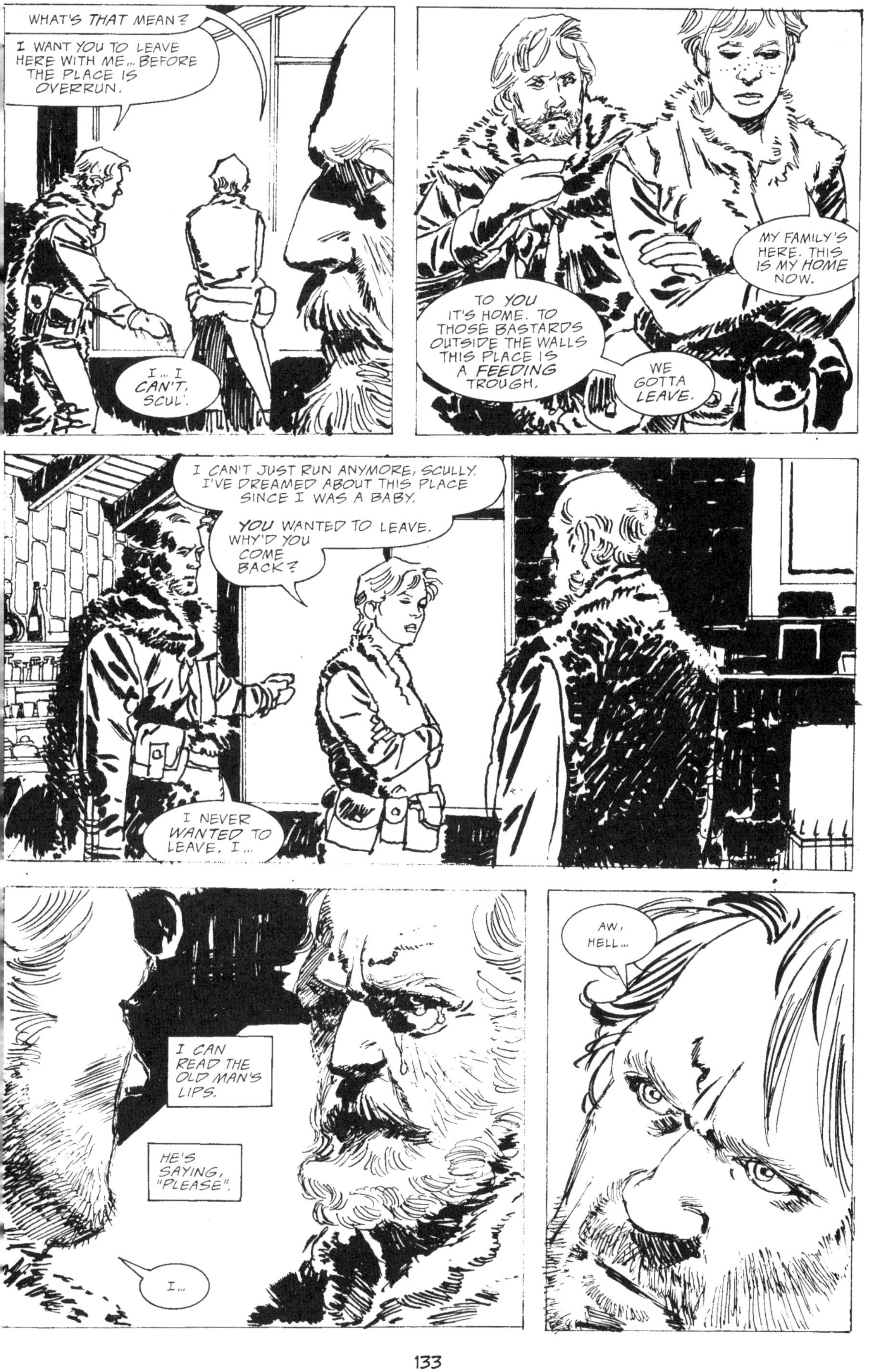
WHAT'S THAT MEAN?
I WANT YOU TO LEAVE HERE WITH ME... BEFORE THE PLACE IS OVERRUN.
I... I CAN'T, SCUL'.
MY FAMILY'S HERE. THIS IS MY HOME NOW.
TO YOU IT'S HOME. TO THOSE BASTARDS OUTSIDE THE WALLS THIS PLACE IS A FEEDING TROUGH.
WE GOTTA LEAVE.
I CAN'T JUST RUN ANYMORE, SCULLY. I'VE DREAMED ABOUT THIS PLACE SINCE I WAS A BABY.
YOU WANTED TO LEAVE. WHY'D YOU COME BACK?
I NEVER WANTED TO LEAVE. I...
I CAN READ THE OLD MAN'S LIPS.
HE'S SAYING, "PLEASE".
I...
AW, HELL...

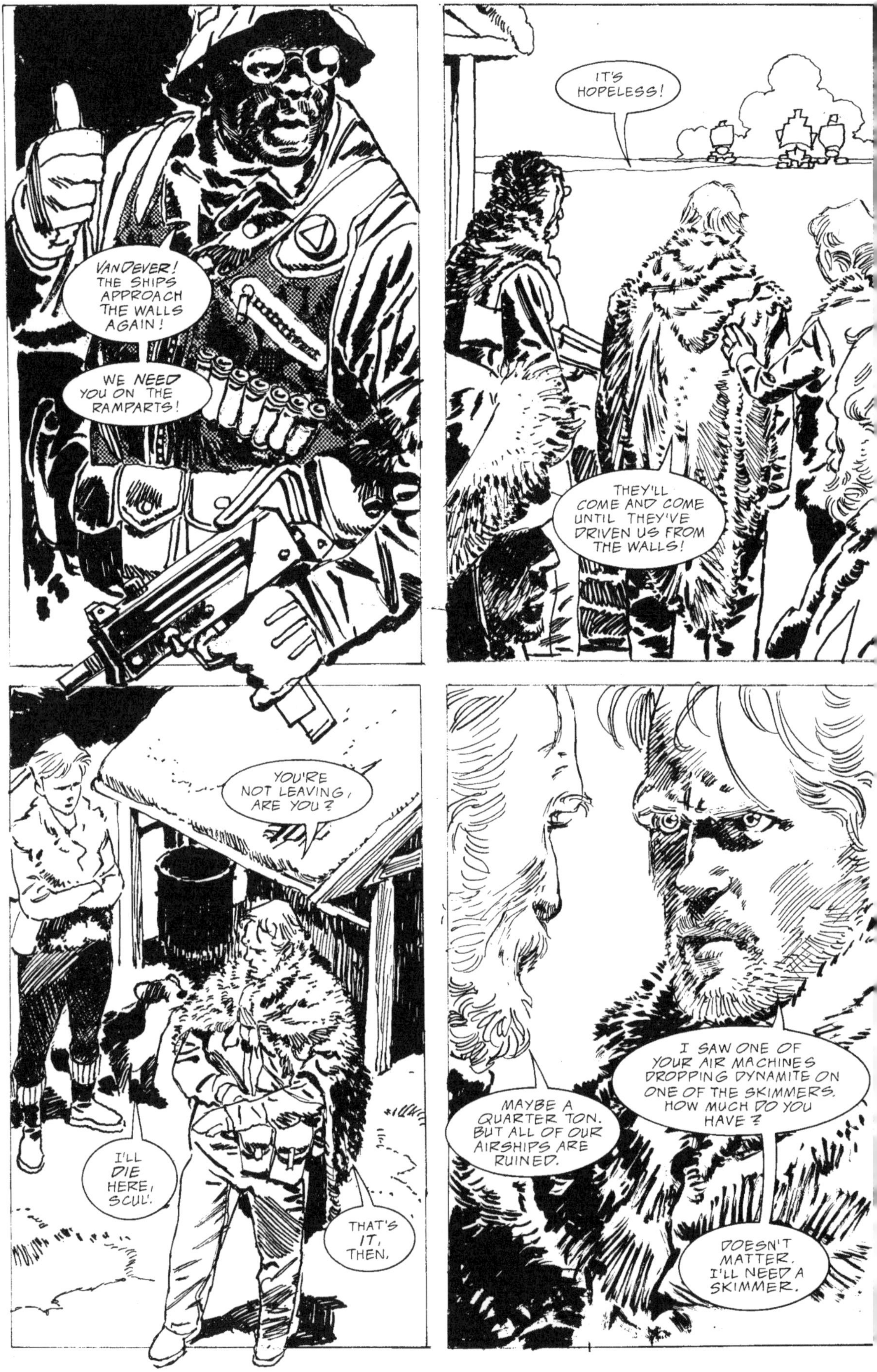
VANDEVER! THE SHIPS APPROACH THE WALLS AGAIN!
WE NEED YOU ON THE RAMPARTS!
IT'S HOPELESS!
THEY'LL COME AND COME UNTIL THEY'VE DRIVEN US FROM THE WALLS!
YOU'RE NOT LEAVING, ARE YOU?
I'LL DIE HERE, SCUL.
THAT'S IT, THEN.
I SAW ONE OF YOUR AIR MACHINES DROPPING DYNAMITE ON ONE OF THE SKIMMERS. HOW MUCH DO YOU HAVE?
MAYBE A QUARTER TON. BUT ALL OF OUR AIRSHIPS ARE RUINED.
DOESN'T MATTER. I'LL NEED A SKIMMER.

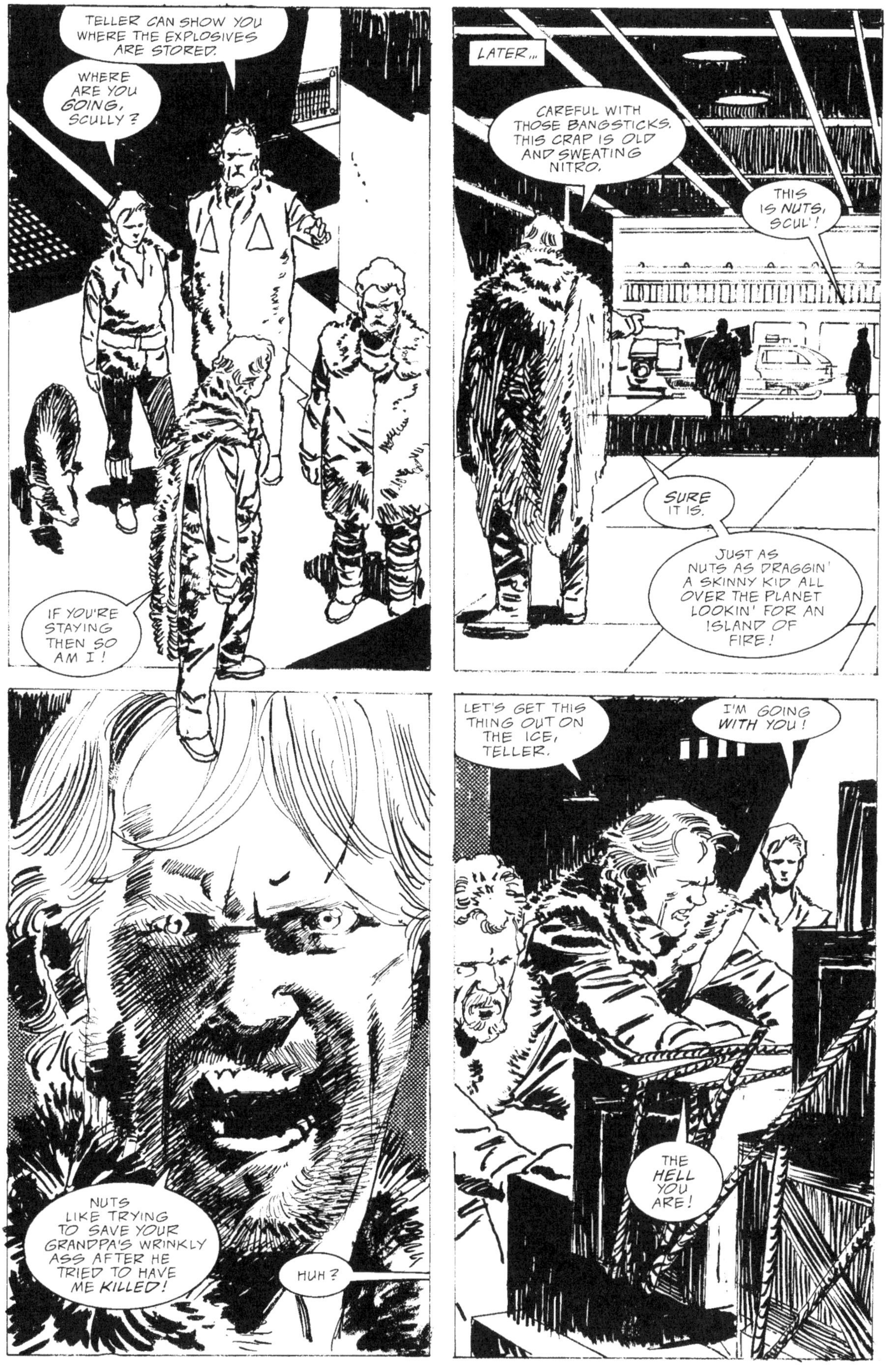
TELLER CAN SHOW YOU WHERE THE EXPLOSIVES ARE STORED.
WHERE ARE YOU GOING, SCULLY?
IF YOU'RE STAYING THEN SO AM I!
LATER...
CAREFUL WITH THOSE BANGSTICKS. THIS CRAP IS OLD AND SWEATING NITRO.
THIS IS NUTS, SCUL'!
SURE IT IS.
JUST AS NUTS AS DRAGGIN' A SKINNY KID ALL OVER THE PLANET LOOKIN' FOR AN ISLAND OF FIRE!
NUTS LIKE TRYING TO SAVE YOUR GRANDPA'S WRINKLY ASS AFTER HE TRIED TO HAVE ME KILLED!
HUH?
LET'S GET THIS THING OUT ON THE ICE, TELLER.
I'M GOING WITH YOU!
THE HELL YOU ARE!

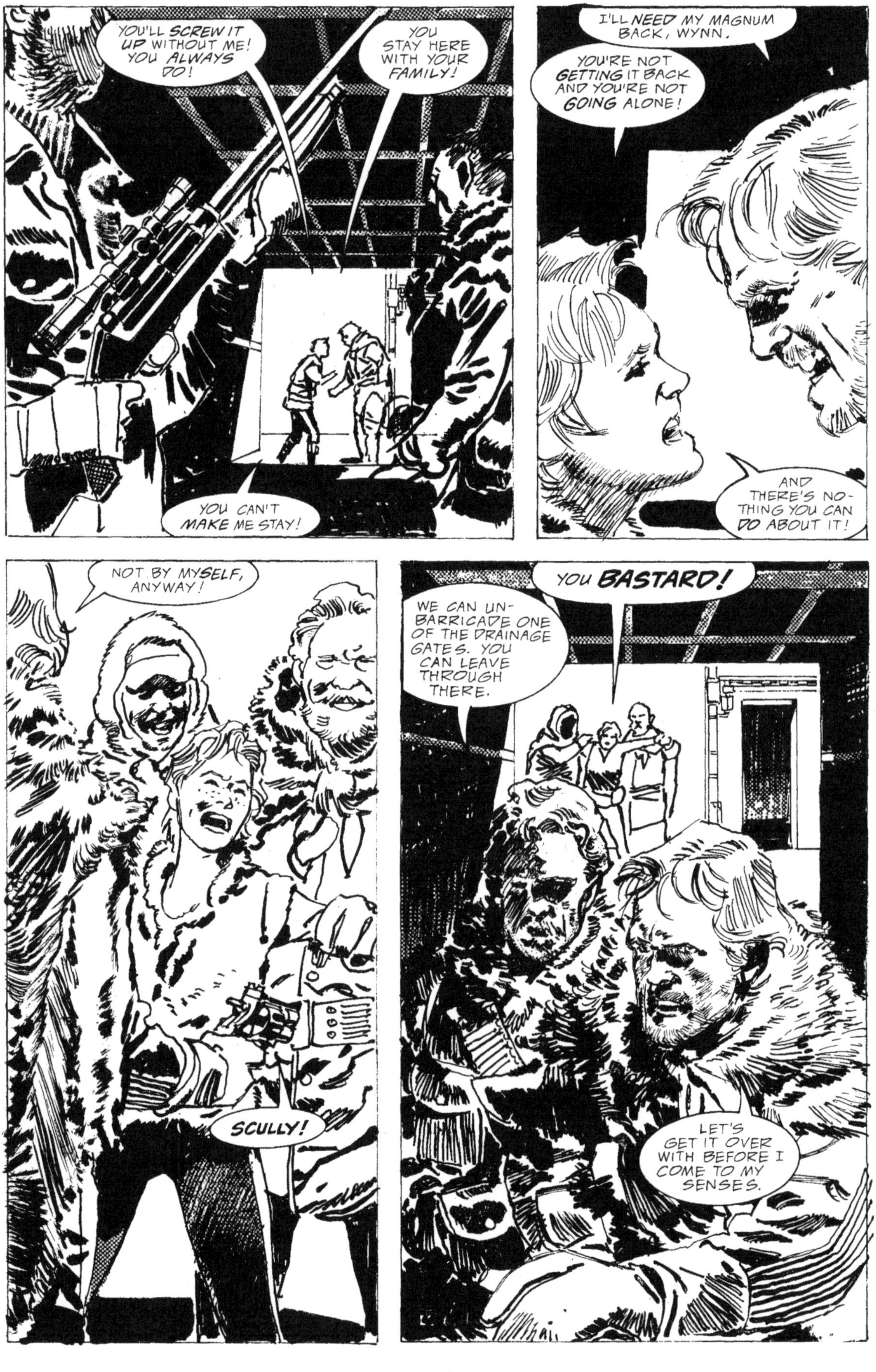
YOU'LL SCREW IT UP WITHOUT ME! YOU ALWAYS DO!
YOU STAY HERE WITH YOUR FAMILY!
YOU CAN'T MAKE ME STAY!
I'LL NEED MY MAGNUM BACK, WYNN.
YOU'RE NOT GETTING IT BACK AND YOU'RE NOT GOING ALONE!
AND THERE'S NO-THING YOU CAN DO ABOUT IT!
NOT BY MYSELF, ANYWAY!
SCULLY!
YOU BASTARD!
WE CAN UN-BARRICADE ONE OF THE DRAINAGE GATES. YOU CAN LEAVE THROUGH THERE.
LET'S GET IT OVER WITH BEFORE I COME TO MY SENSES.

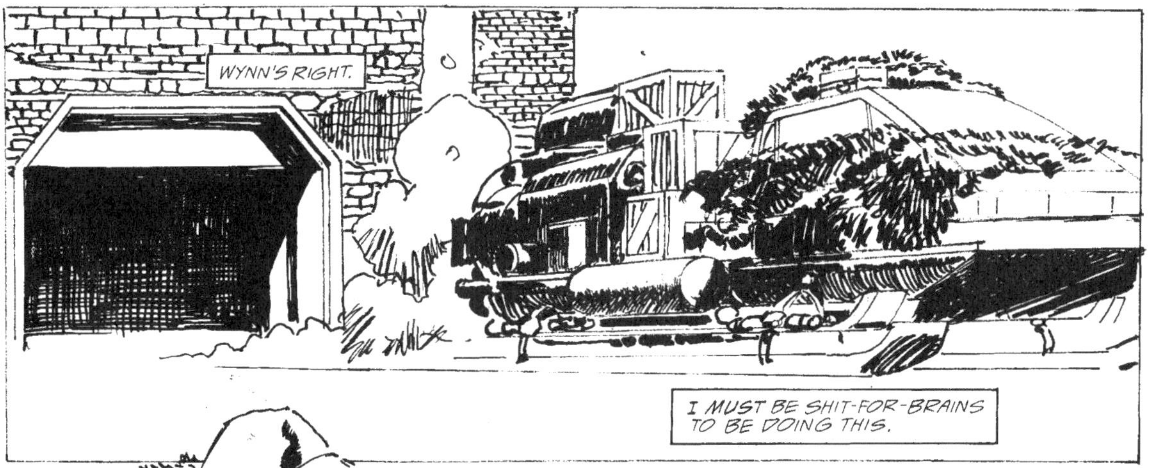
WYNN'S RIGHT.
I MUST BE SHIT-FOR-BRAINS TO BE DOING THIS.

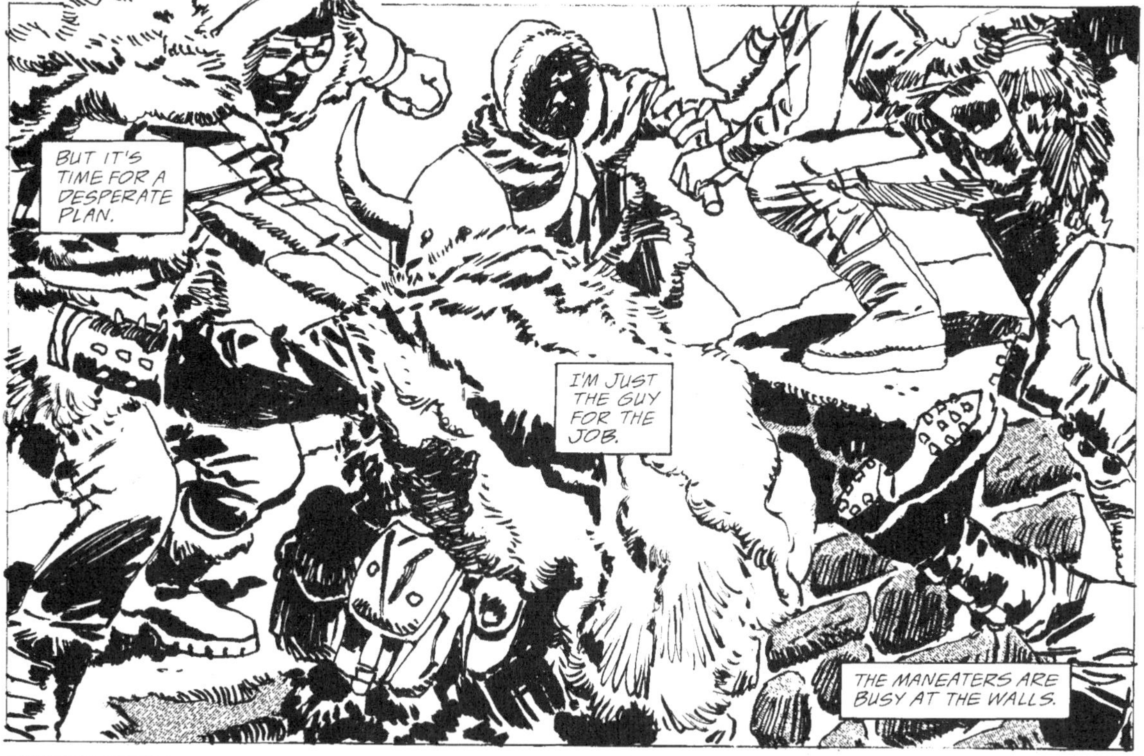
BUT IT'S TIME FOR A DESPERATE PLAN.
I'M JUST THE GUY FOR THE JOB.
THE MANEATERS ARE BUSY AT THE WALLS.

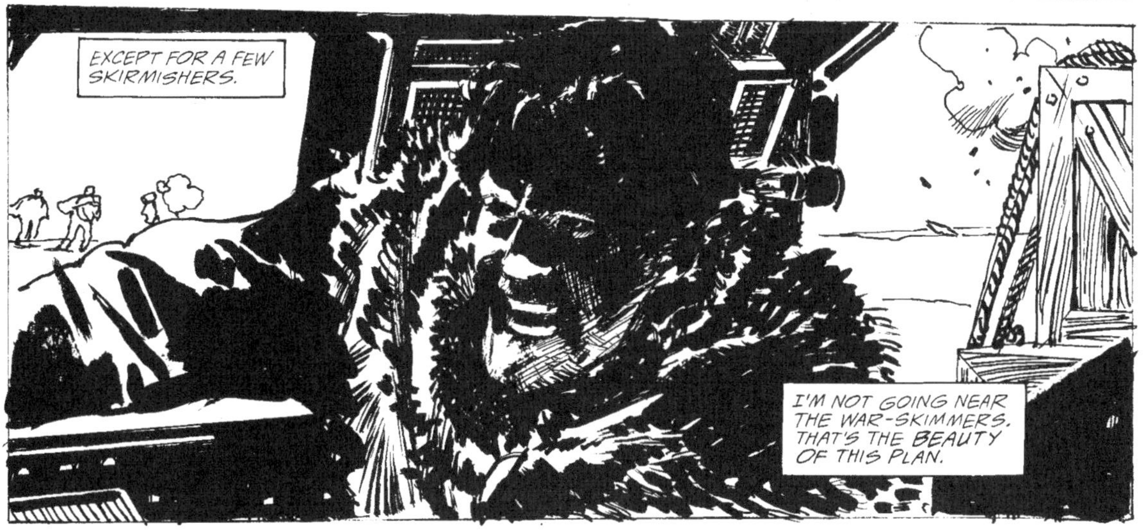
EXCEPT FOR A FEW SKIRMISHERS.
I'M NOT GOING NEAR THE WAR-SKIMMERS. THAT'S THE BEAUTY OF THIS PLAN.

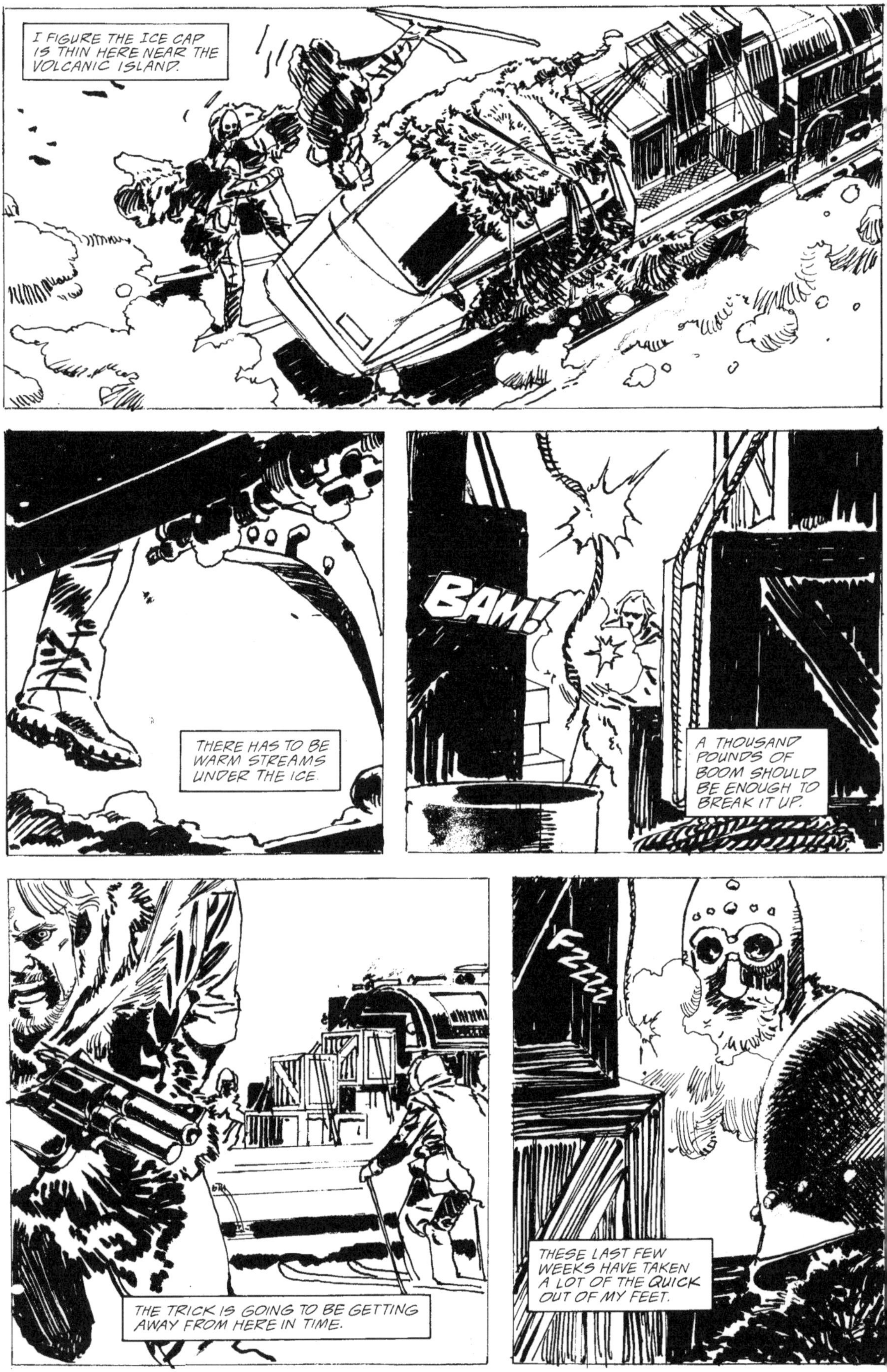
I FIGURE THE ICE CAP IS THIN HERE NEAR THE VOLCANIC ISLAND.
THERE HAS TO BE WARM STREAMS UNDER THE ICE.
BAM!
A THOUSAND POUNDS OF BOOM SHOULD BE ENOUGH TO BREAK IT UP.
THE TRICK IS GOING TO BE GETTING AWAY FROM HERE IN TIME.
FZZZZ
THESE LAST FEW WEEKS HAVE TAKEN A LOT OF THE QUICK OUT OF MY FEET.

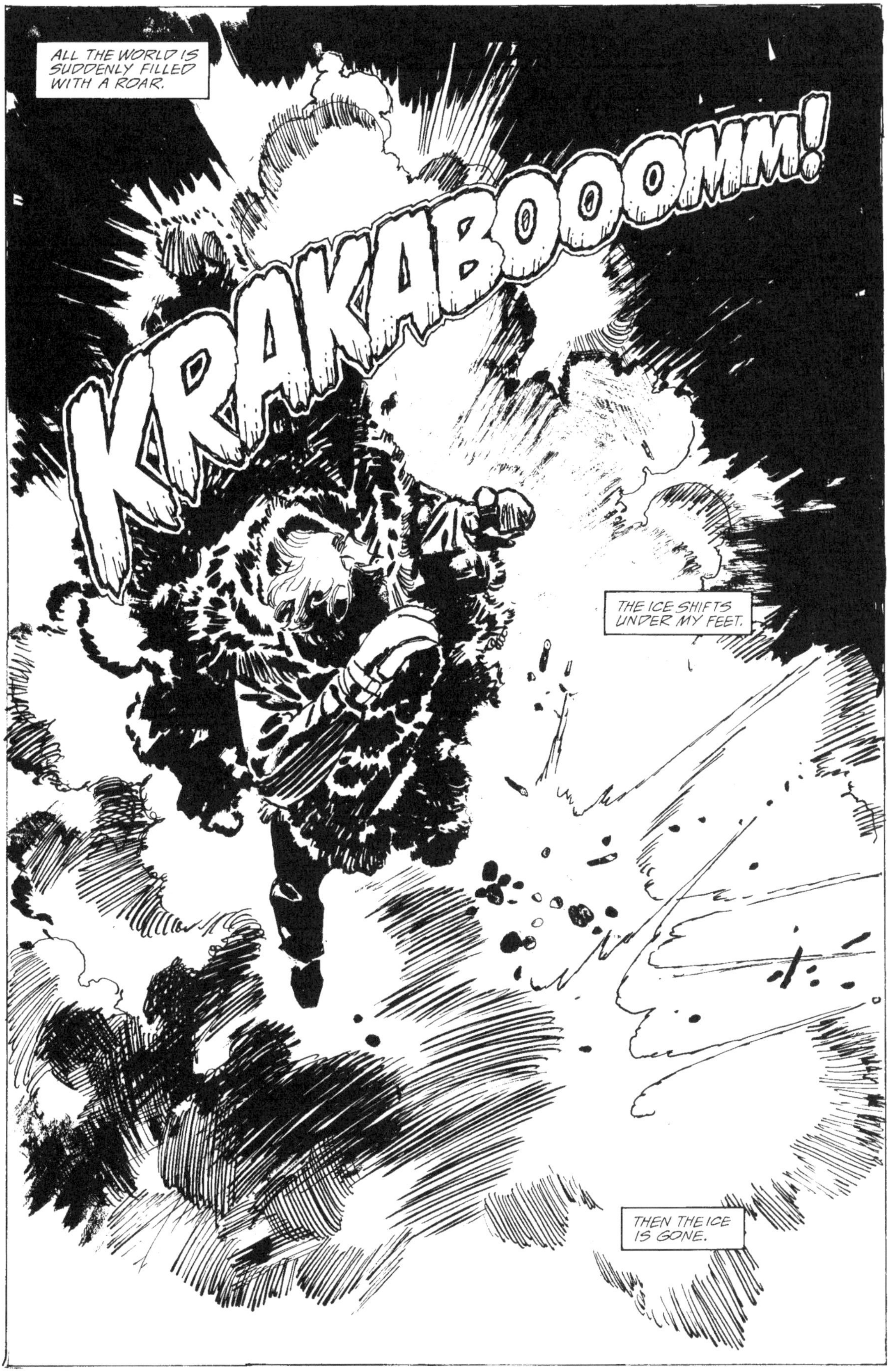
ALL THE WORLD IS SUDDENLY FILLED WITH A ROAR.
KRAKABOOOOMM!
THE ICE SHIFTS UNDER MY FEET.
THEN THE ICE IS GONE.

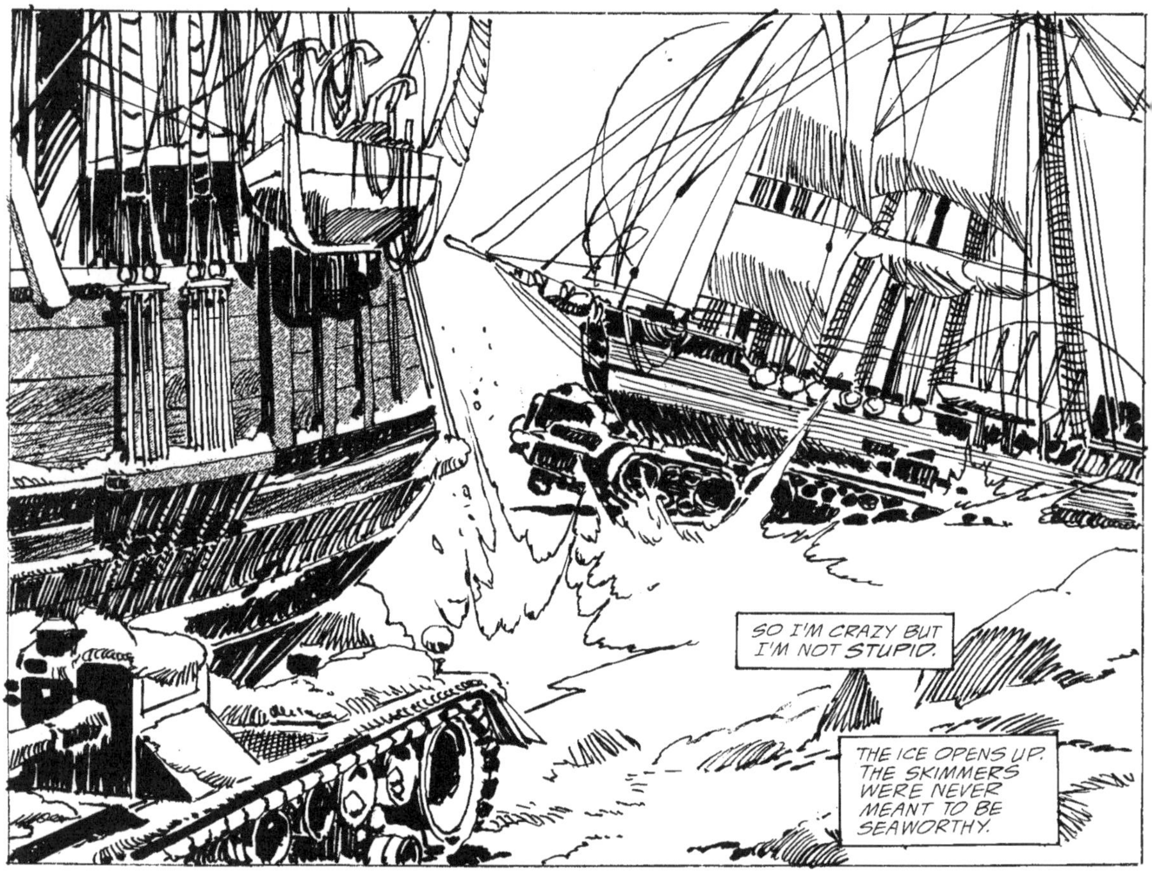
SO I'M CRAZY BUT I'M NOT STUPID.
THE ICE OPENS UP. THE SKIMMERS WERE NEVER MEANT TO BE SEAWORTHY.

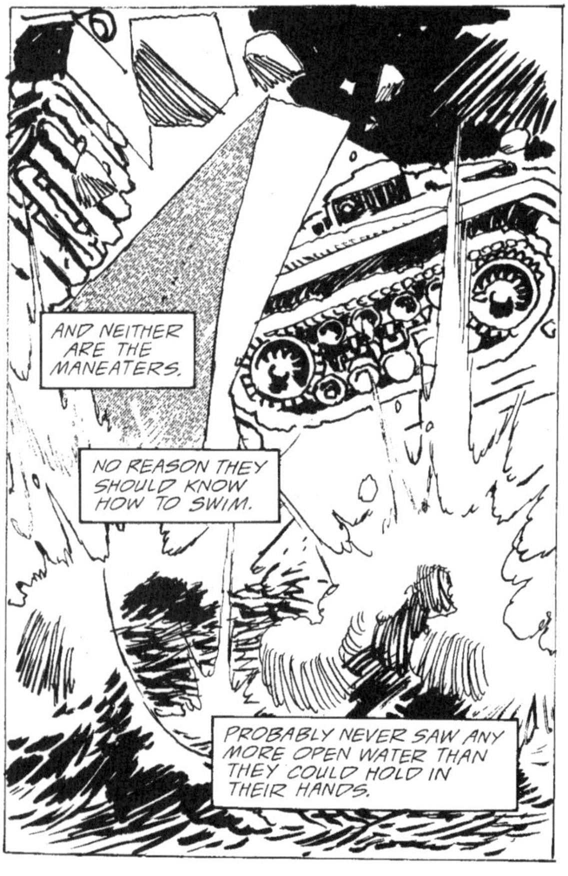
AND NEITHER ARE THE MANEATERS.
NO REASON THEY SHOULD KNOW HOW TO SWIM.
PROBABLY NEVER SAW ANY MORE OPEN WATER THAN THEY COULD HOLD IN THEIR HANDS.

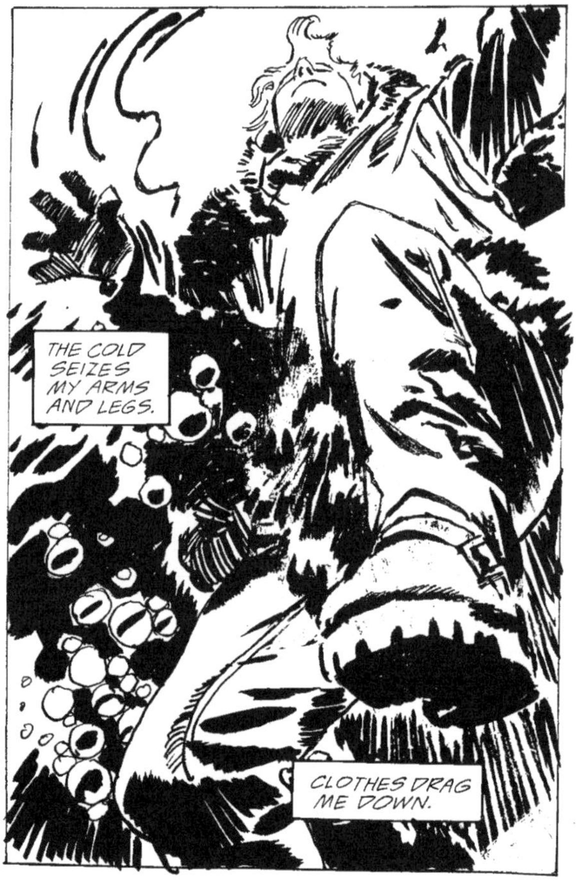
THE COLD SEIZES MY ARMS AND LEGS.
CLOTHES DRAG ME DOWN.

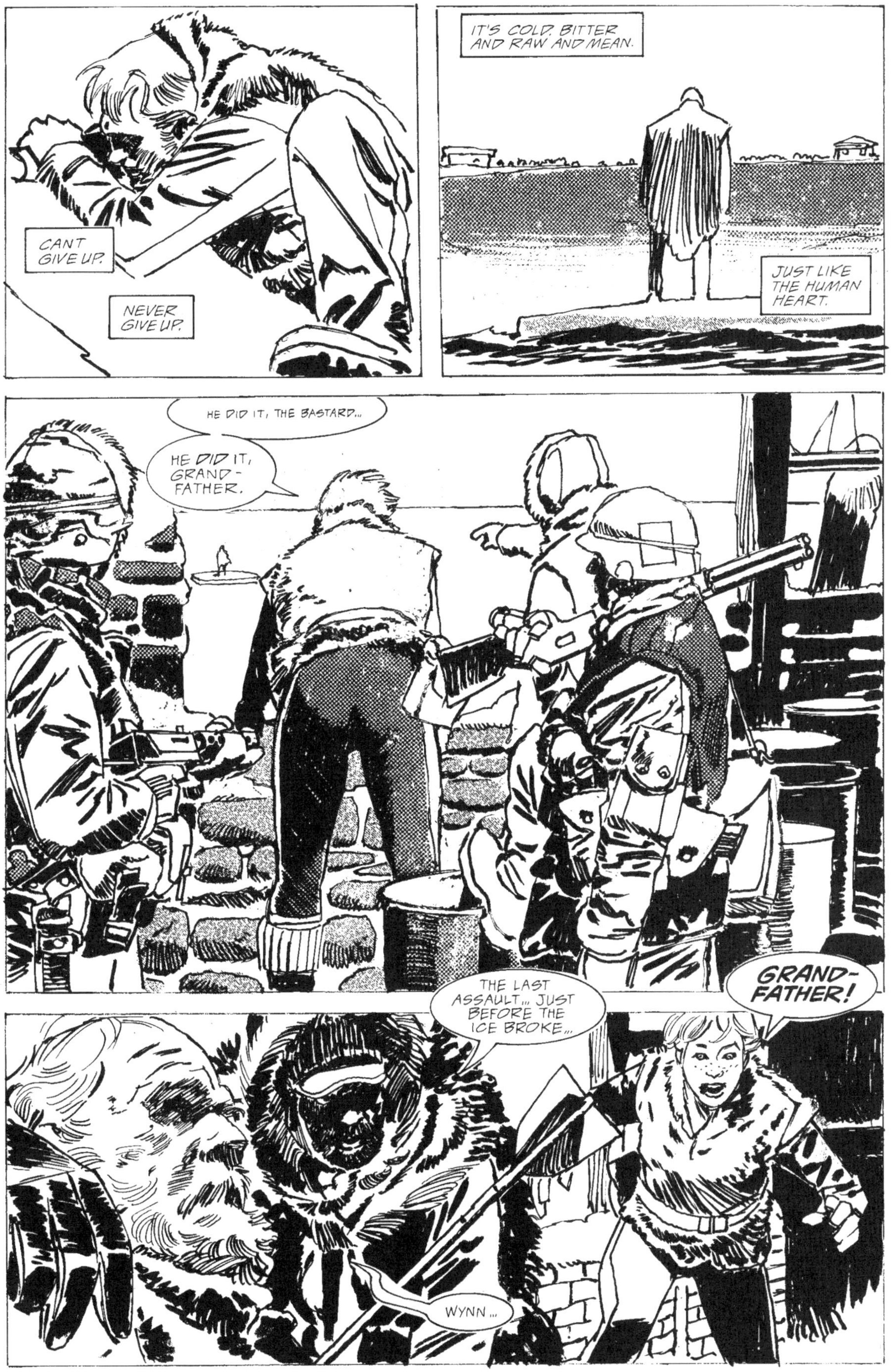
CANT
GIVE UP.
NEVER
GIVE UP.
IT'S COLD. BITTER AND RAW AND MEAN.
JUST LIKE THE HUMAN HEART.
HE DID IT, THE BASTARD...
HE DID IT, GRAND-FATHER.
THE LAST ASSAULT... JUST BEFORE THE ICE BROKE...
GRAND-FATHER!
WYNN...

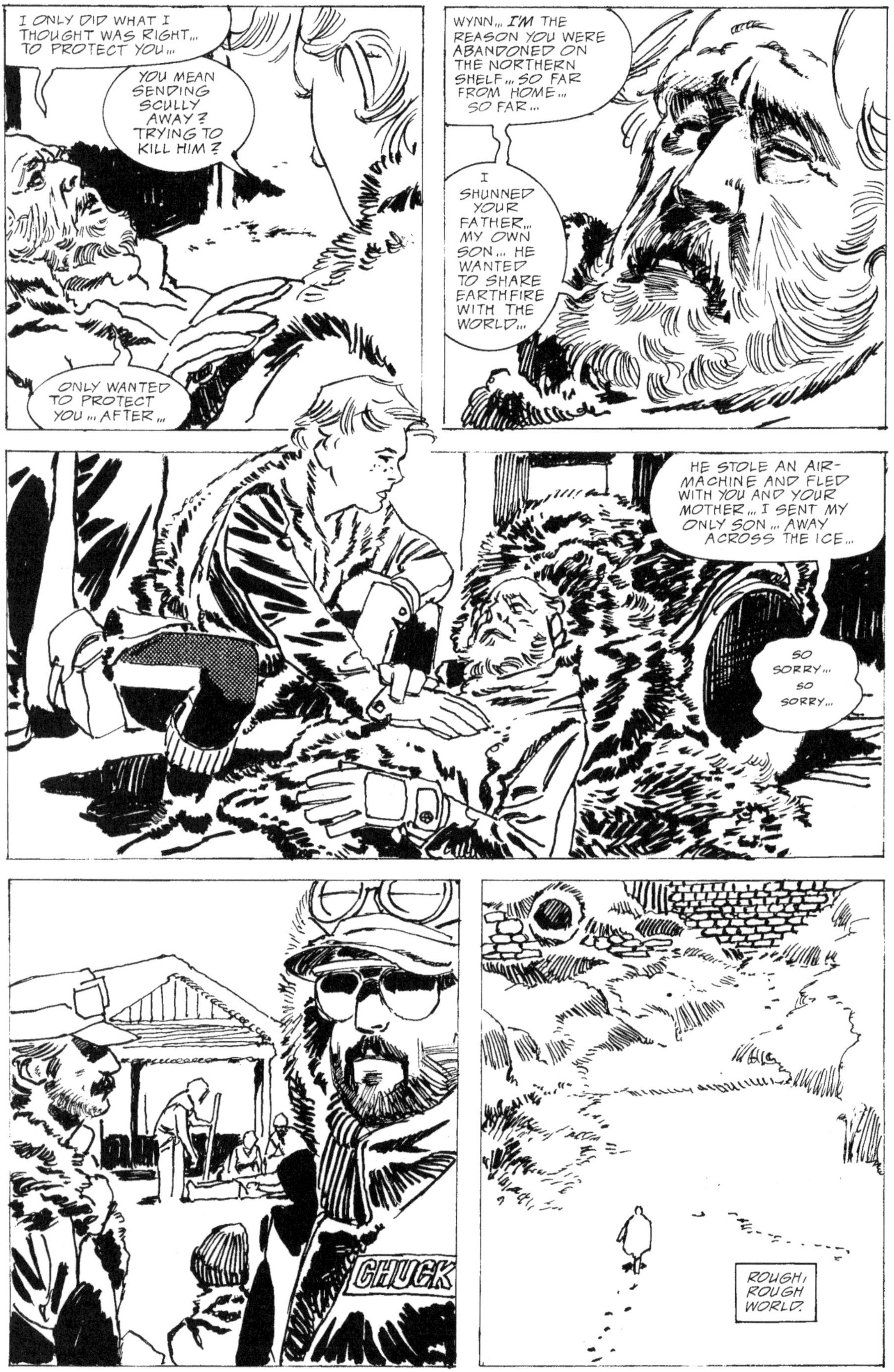
I ONLY DID WHAT I THOUGHT WAS RIGHT... TO PROTECT YOU...
YOU MEAN SENDING SCULLY AWAY? TRYING TO KILL HIM?
ONLY WANTED TO PROTECT YOU... AFTER...
WYNN... I'M THE REASON YOU WERE ABANDONED ON THE NORTHERN SHELF... SO FAR FROM HOME... SO FAR...
I SHUNNED YOUR FATHER... MY OWN SON... HE WANTED TO SHARE EARTHFIRE WITH THE WORLD...
HE STOLE AN AIR-MACHINE AND FLED WITH YOU AND YOUR MOTHER... I SENT MY ONLY SON... AWAY ACROSS THE ICE...
SO SORRY... SO SORRY...
CHUCK
ROUGH, ROUGH WORLD.

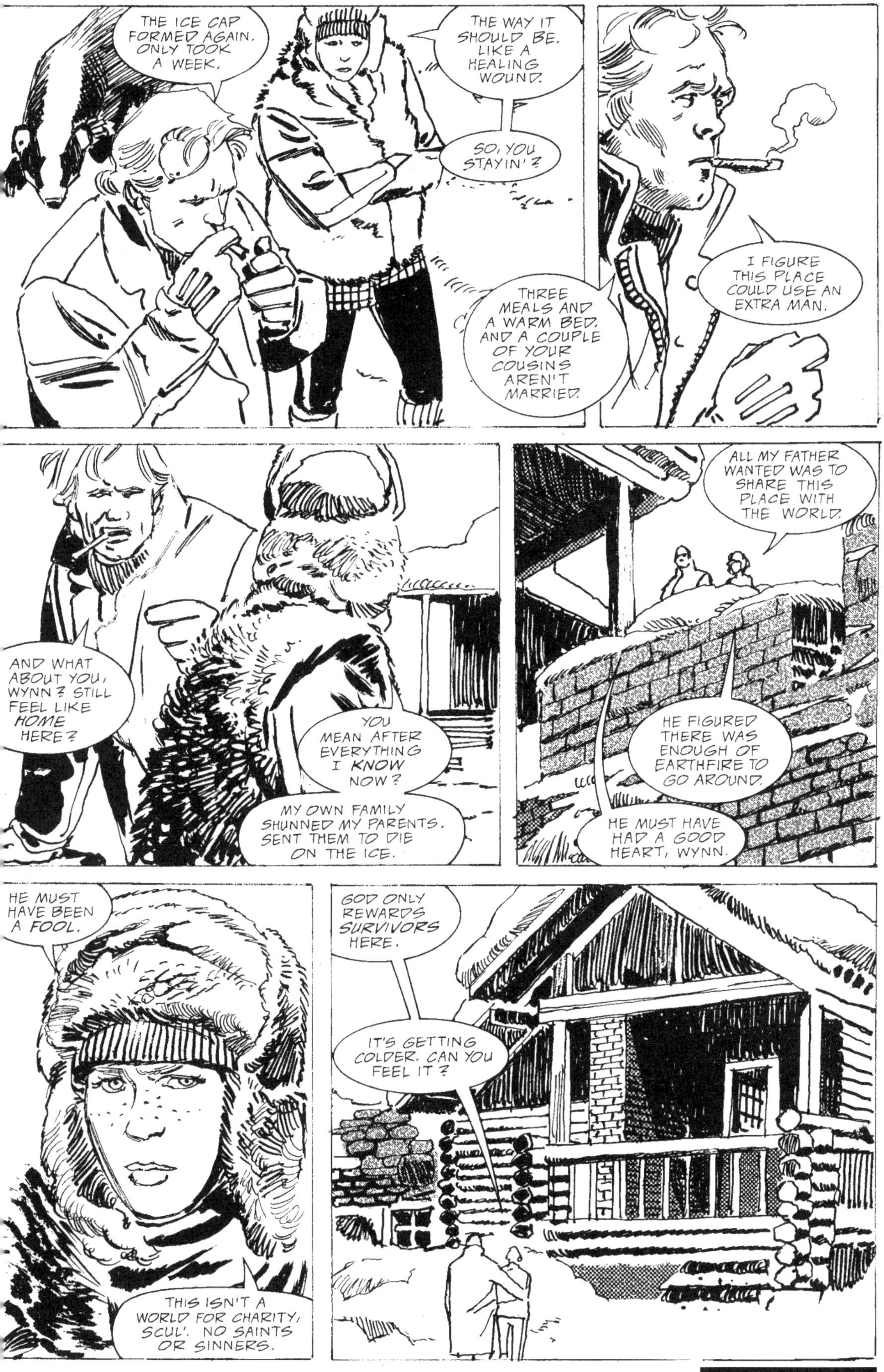
THE ICE CAP FORMED AGAIN. ONLY TOOK A WEEK.
THE WAY IT SHOULD BE. LIKE A HEALING WOUND.
SO, YOU STAYIN'?
THREE MEALS AND A WARM BED. AND A COUPLE OF YOUR COUSINS AREN'T MARRIED.
I FIGURE THIS PLACE COULD USE AN EXTRA MAN.
AND WHAT ABOUT YOU, WYNN? STILL FEEL LIKE HOME HERE?
YOU MEAN AFTER EVERYTHING I KNOW NOW?
MY OWN FAMILY SHUNNED MY PARENTS. SENT THEM TO DIE ON THE ICE.
ALL MY FATHER WANTED WAS TO SHARE THIS PLACE WITH THE WORLD.
HE FIGURED THERE WAS ENOUGH OF EARTHFIRE TO GO AROUND.
HE MUST HAVE HAD A GOOD HEART, WYNN.
HE MUST HAVE BEEN A FOOL.
THIS ISN'T A WORLD FOR CHARITY, SCUL'. NO SAINTS OR SINNERS.
GOD ONLY REWARDS SURVIVORS HERE.
IT'S GETTING COLDER. CAN YOU FEEL IT?

END OF WINTERSEA

ART GALLERY

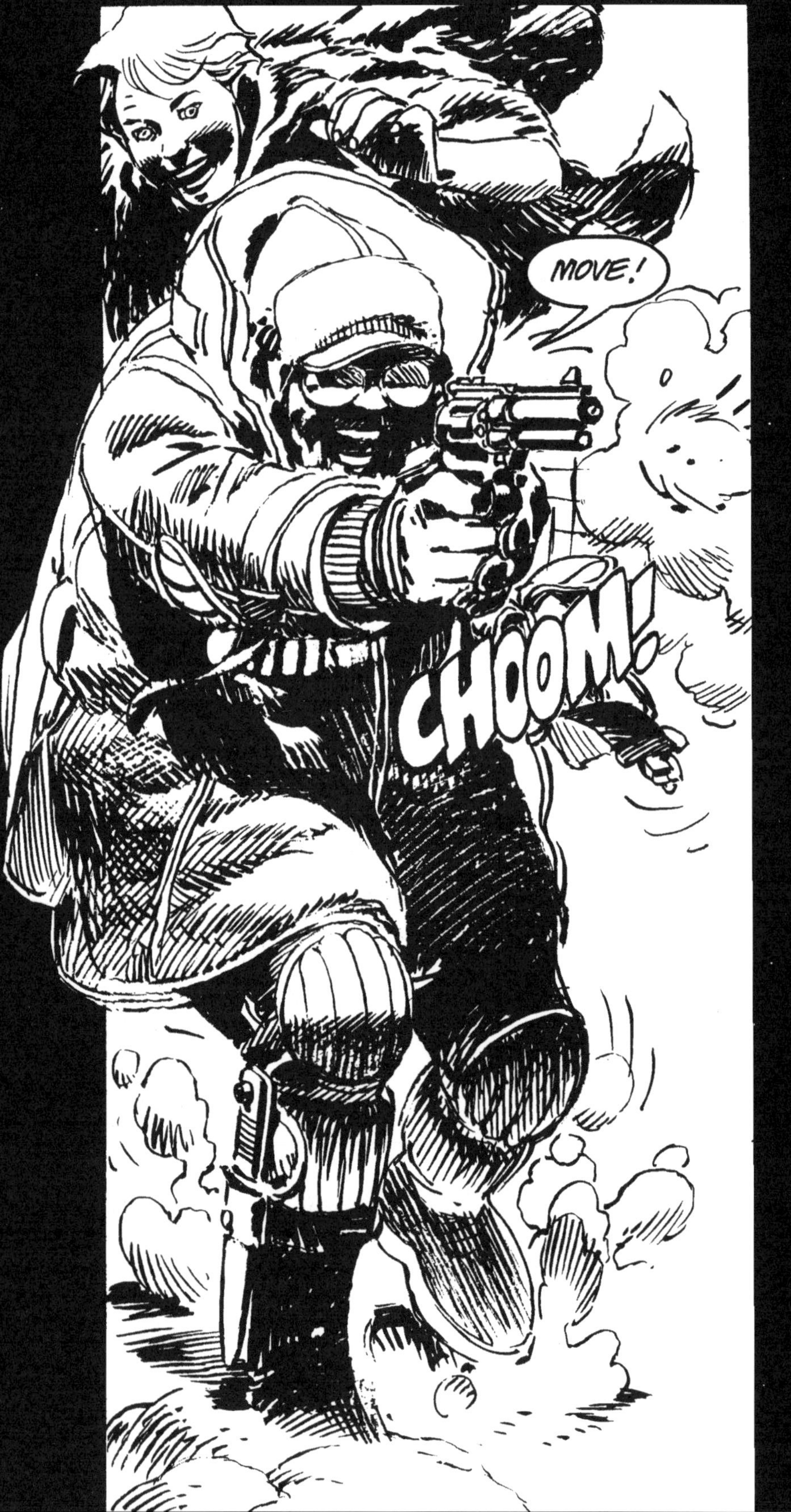
MOVE!
CHOOM!

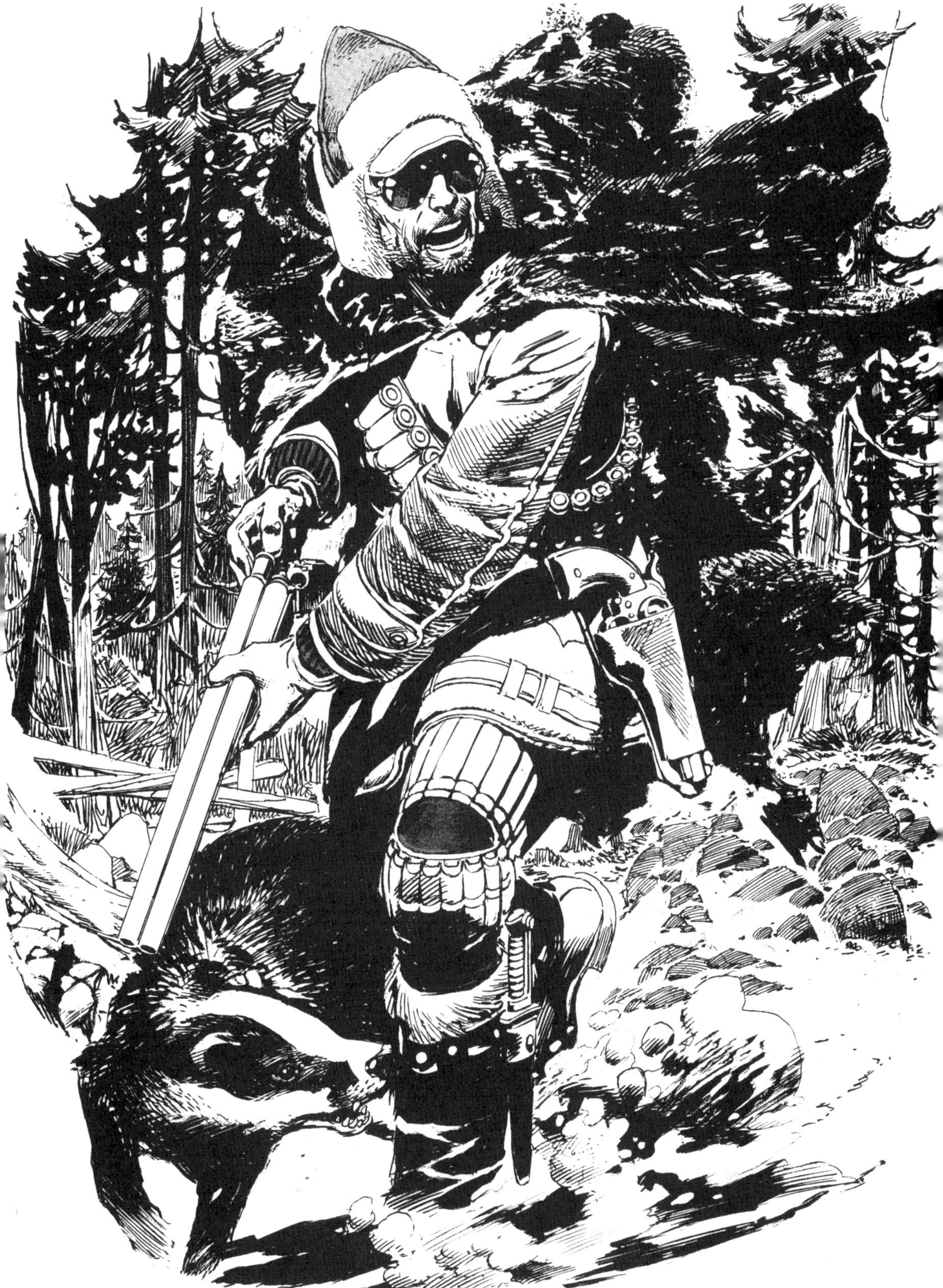
ZAFFINO

¡¡FELIZ 1988!!

TE DESEO A TI Y A TU FAMILIA.

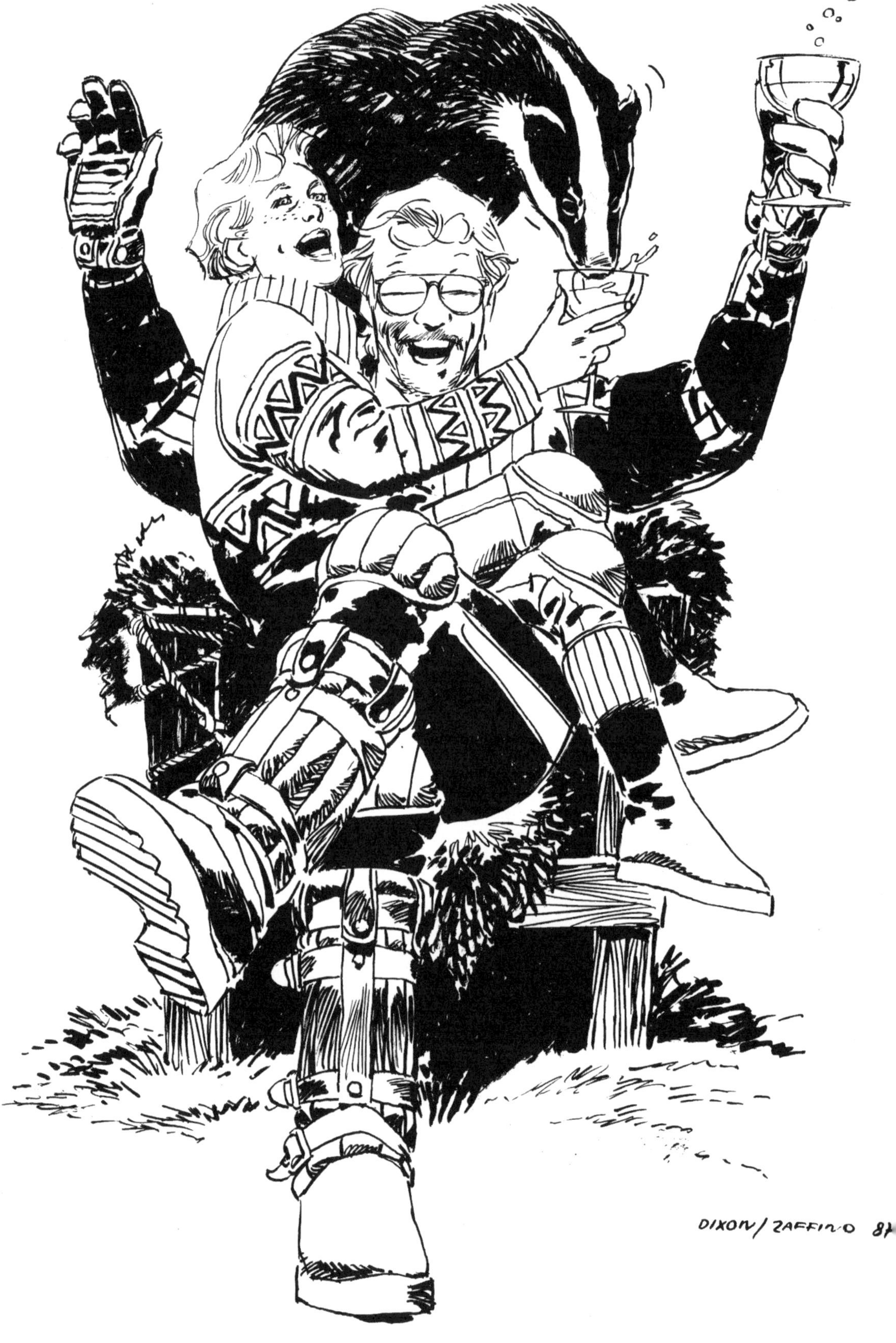
DIXON/ZAFFINO 87

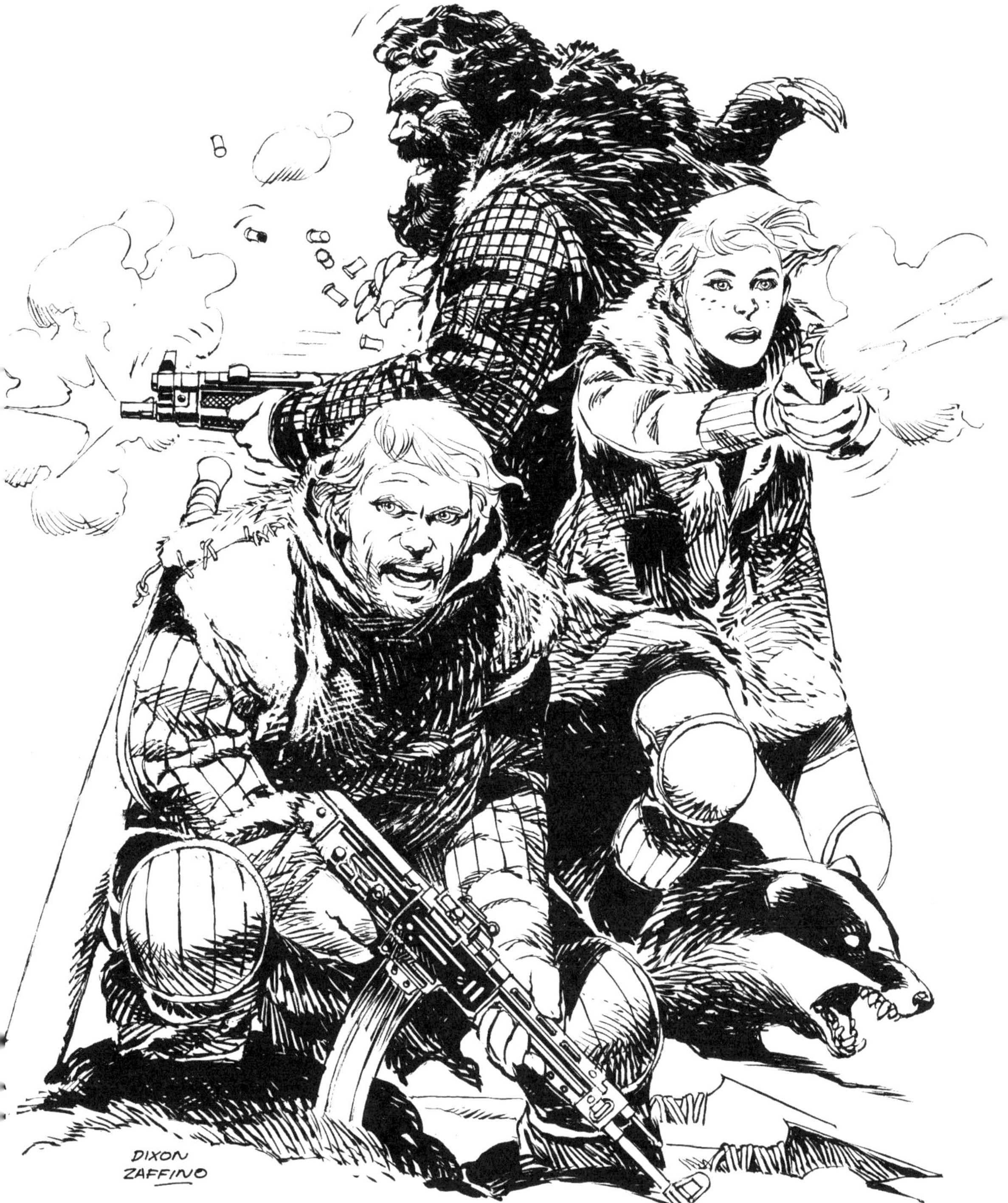
DIXON
ZAFFINO

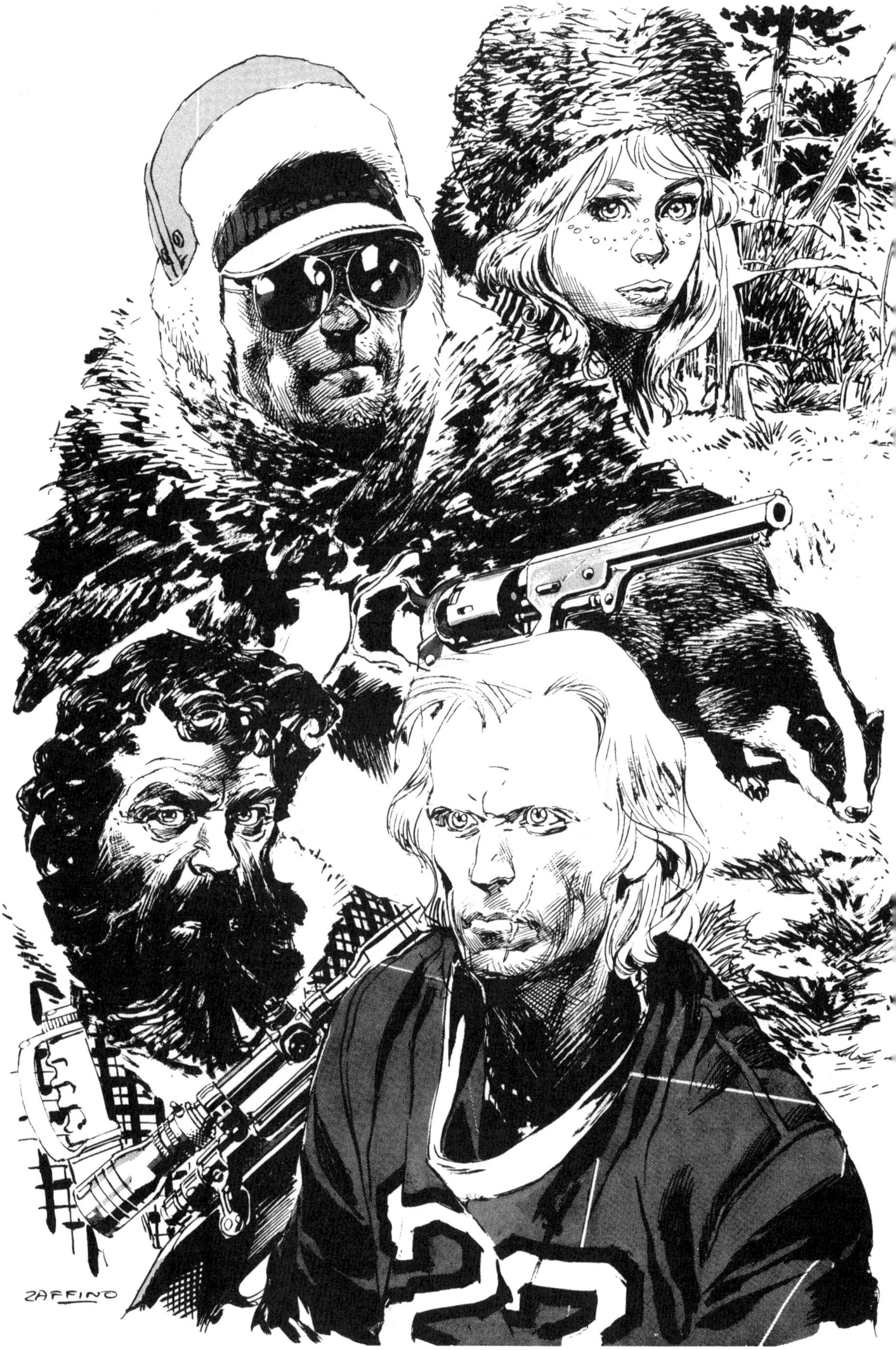
ZAFFINO

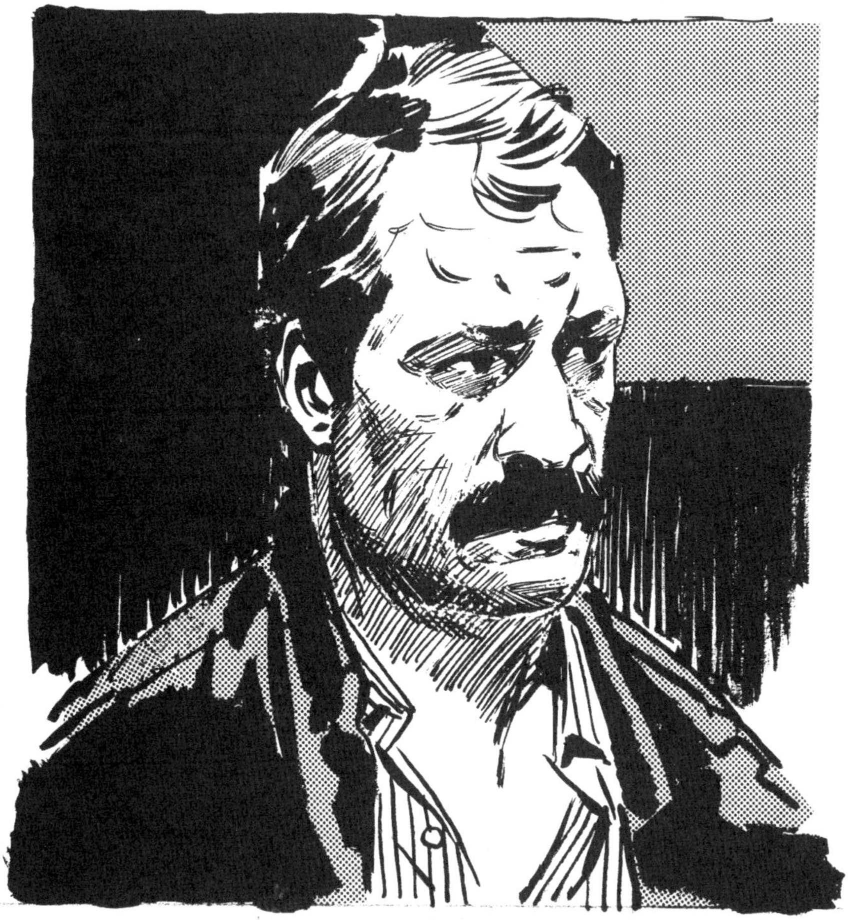

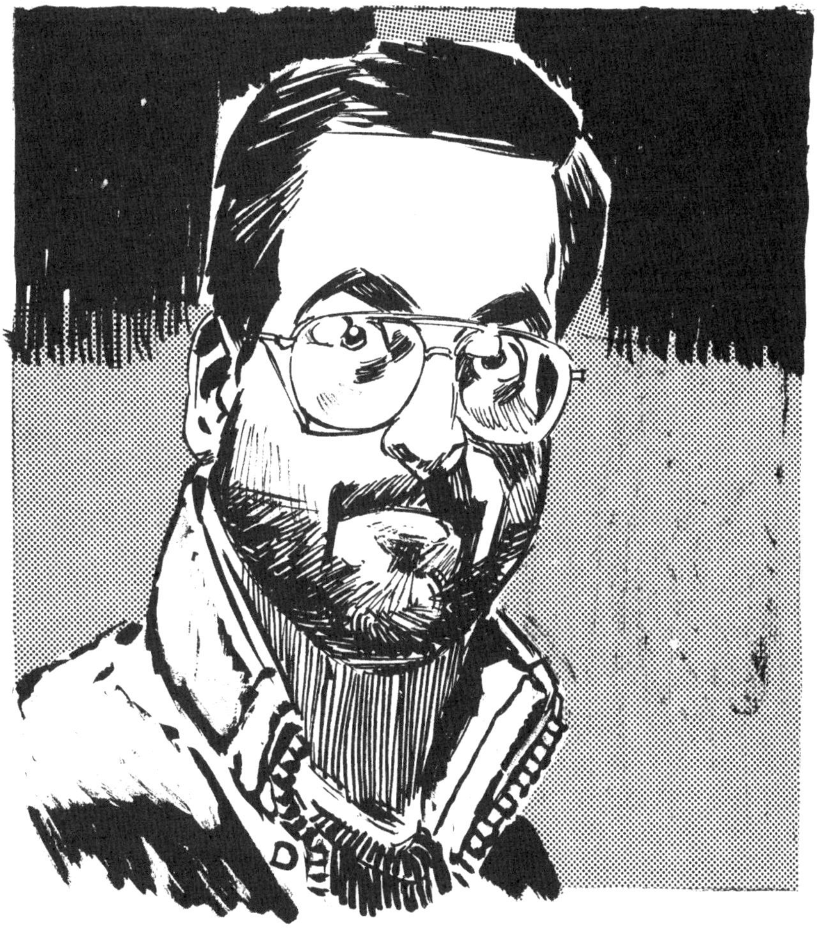

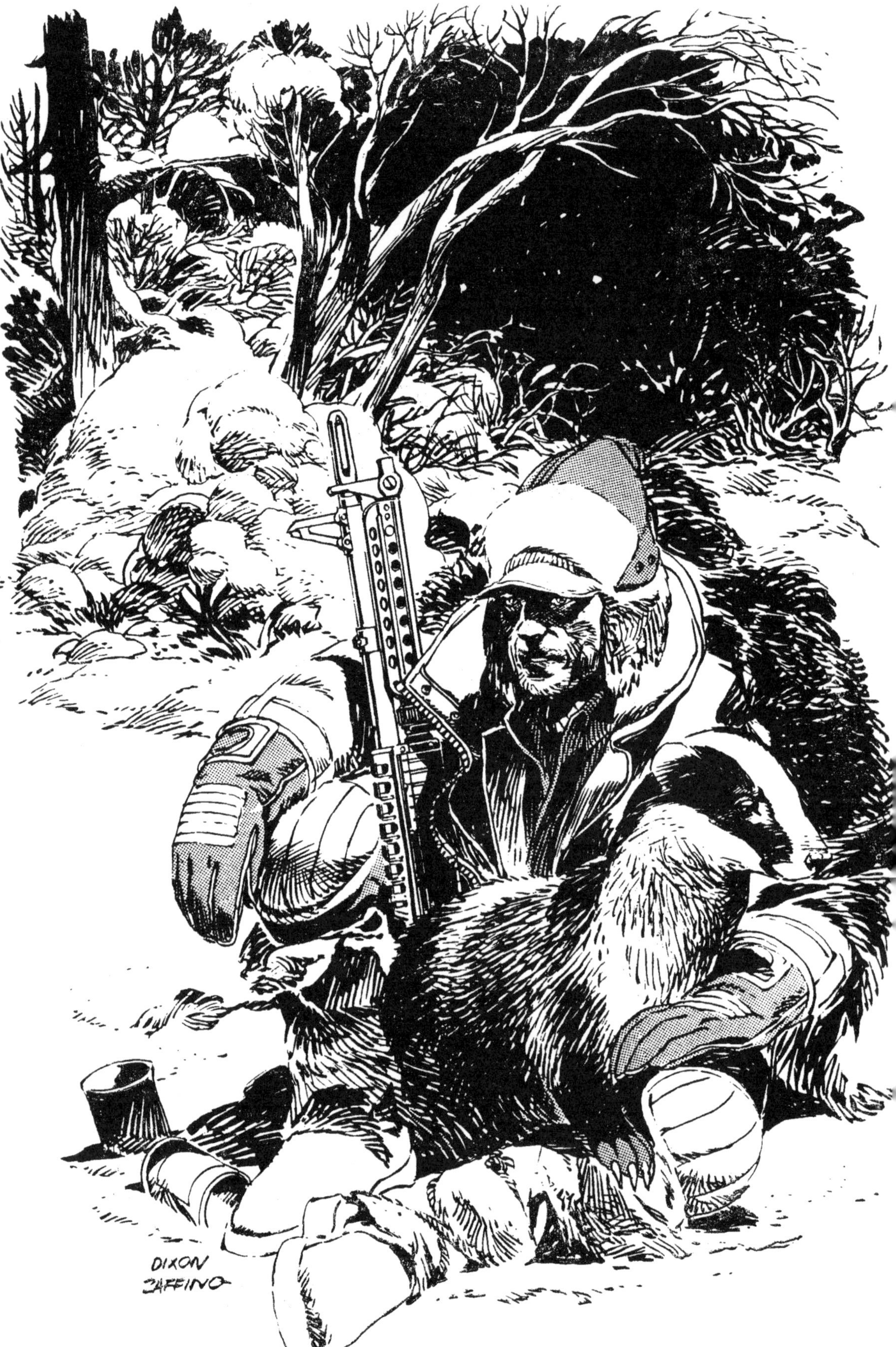
DIXON
ZAFFINO

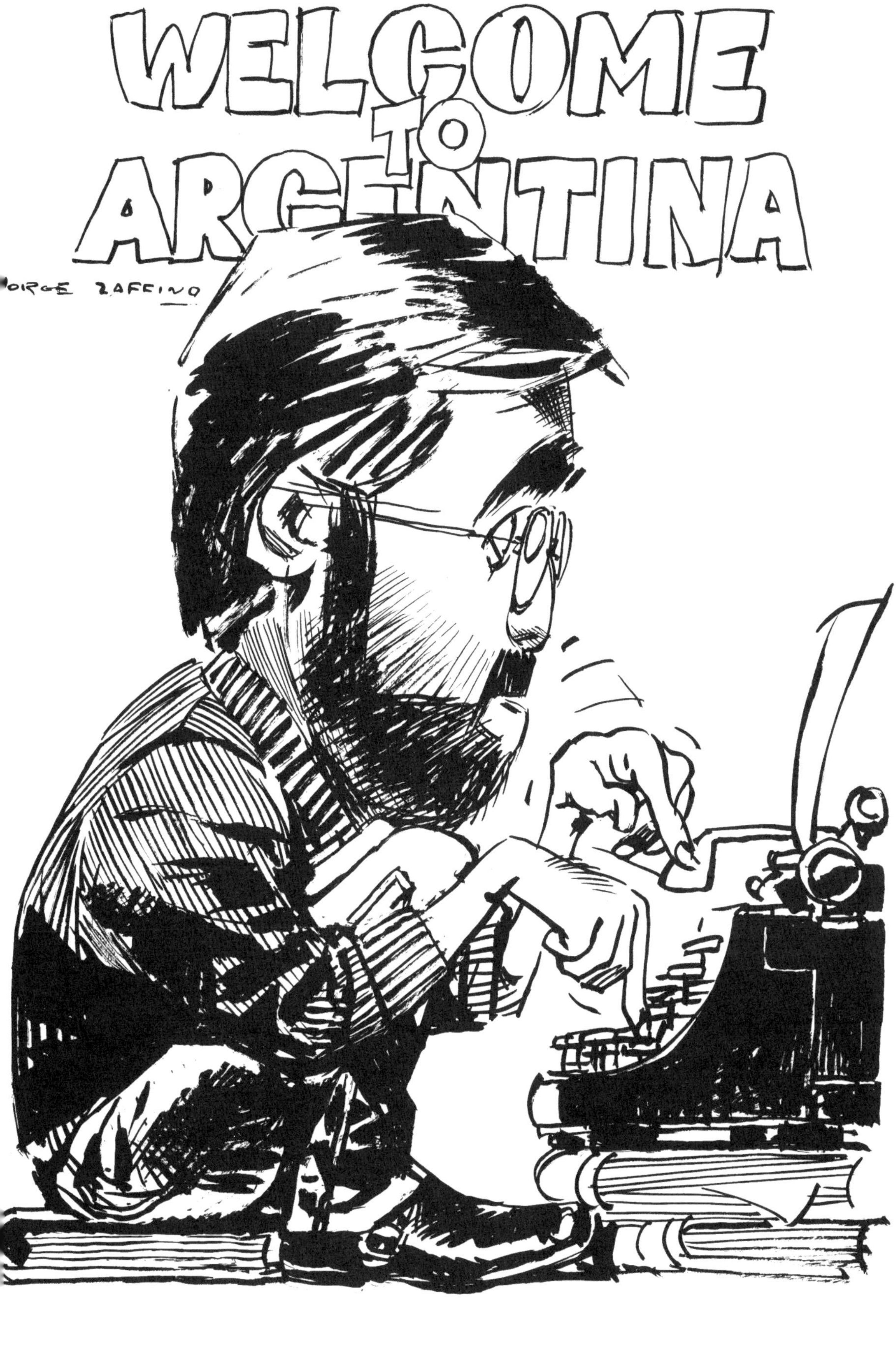
WELCOME
TO
ARGENTINA

WINTER WORLD

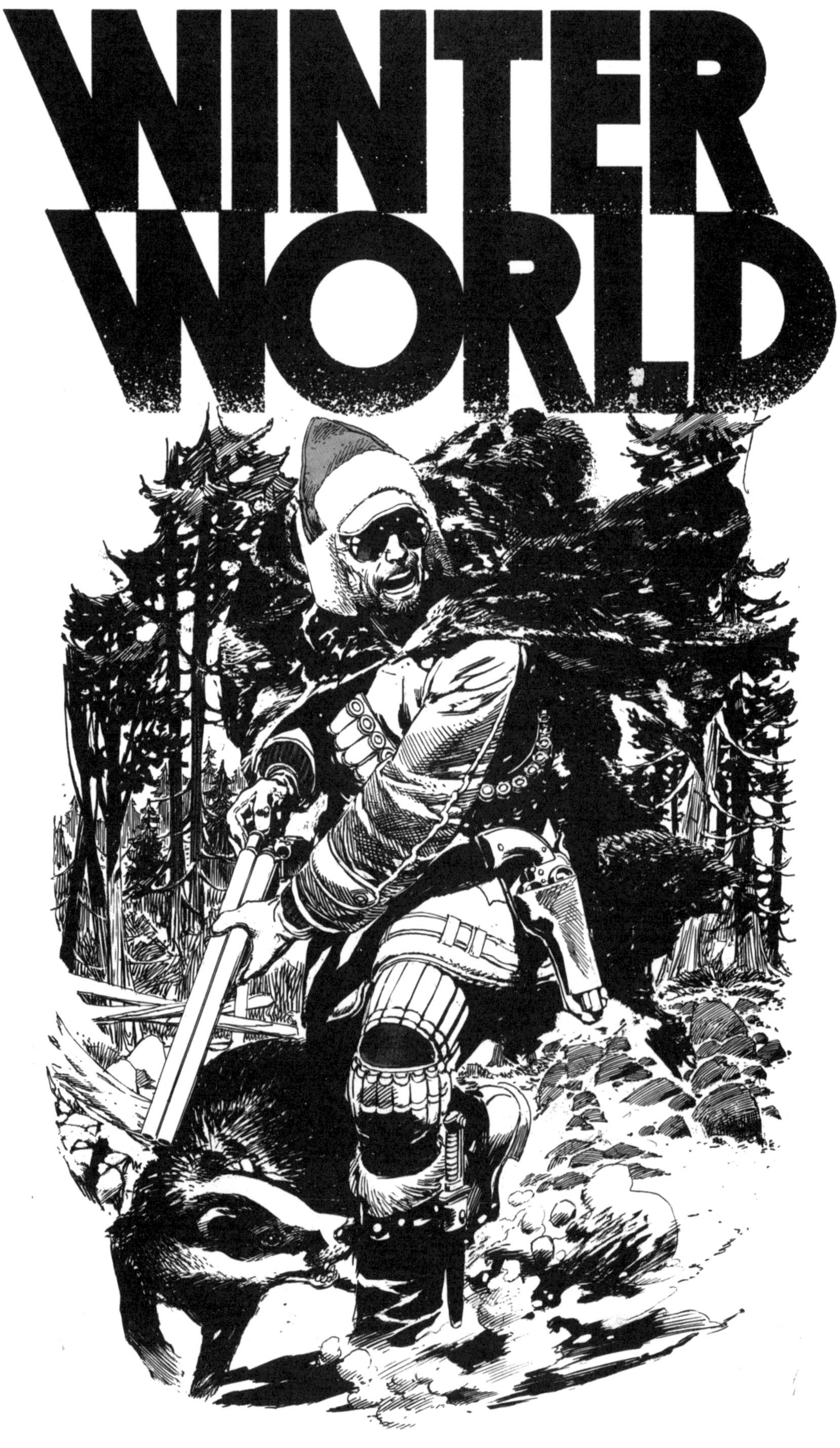